Troy, Gil.
 Leading from the
center

OCT 0 8 2008

LEADING FROM THE CENTER

LEADING FROM THE CENTER

Why Moderates
Make the Best Presidents

GIL TROY

A Member of the Perseus Books Group
New York

Designed by Linda Harper

Library of Congress Cataloging-in-Publication Data

Troy, Gil.
 Leading from the center : why moderates make the best presidents / Gil Troy.
      p. cm.
 Includes bibliographical references and index.
 ISBN 978-0-465-00293-1
 1. Presidents—United States—History. 2. Presidents—United States—Biography.
 3. Political leadership—United States—History. 4. Moderation—Political aspects—
 United States—History. 5. United States—Politics and government. 6. United States—
 Politics and government—Philosophy. I. Title.

E176.1.T785 2008
973.09'9—dc22

                                                                    2008002782

10 9 8 7 6 5 4 3 2 1

To my wife Linda and our four children,
For, with the joy of the dove celebrating spring,
moderating my path by helping me follow this golden law:

". . . preserve sound judgment and discretion,
keep them in mind. These qualities will enliven your soul
and be an ornament gracing your neck. Then you will go
on your way in safety, and your foot will not stumble."

Proverbs 3: 21–23

CONTENTS

Introduction

Presidents as Muscular Moderates

A "Middle Course" for Our "Common Cause"

IT MAY HAVE BEEN THE MOST important dinner party in American history. In June 1790, three titans of the new republic—Secretary of State Thomas Jefferson, Secretary of the Treasury Alexander Hamilton, and Congressman James Madison—broke bread, drank port, and talked late into the night. Dining together, these patriotic statesmen brokered a deal to keep America united. They may be remembered as equally bewigged, staid Founding Fathers, but each was a headstrong individual, and their visions of how America's new Constitution should work clashed. Their political and philosophical disagreements became so intense they would roil George Washington's administration and threaten the states' still fragile, national alliance.

Despite the elegant candlelight at 57 Maiden Lane in New York, the dinner must have been awkward. The host, Thomas Jefferson, an aristocratic polymath but no genius at human relations, was an unlikely mediator who was more partisan than his reputation as the philosopher of freedom would suggest. He had known his fellow Virginian, the shy, cerebral constitutionalist James Madison, for years. Having met the glib, cosmopolitan secretary of the treasury upon returning from France only weeks earlier in March, Jefferson did not yet know Hamilton well enough to loathe him. Within months, the two

1

would become the most famous rivals in early American history, representing opposing camps, ideologies, and sensibilities.

Jefferson had joined Washington's cabinet vowing to avoid petty intrigues; Hamilton and Madison had collaborated on a classic warning against partisanship in writing the *Federalist Papers*. Yet, having fought together to ratify the Constitution, Madison and Hamilton now fought each other over how to implement it. Favoring strong centralized government, Hamilton proposed that the new federal government pay off the states' Revolutionary War debts. More virtuous farmer than sophisticated financier, Madison feared the scheme would penalize responsible states like his native Virginia, which had already settled its debts, and would unfairly reward profligate northern states that had ignored their debts, banking on an eventual federal windfall. Virginia's Revolutionary War hero, Lighthorse Harry Lee, captured the southern sentiment, preferring to dissolve the union rather than succumb to a "fixed insolent northern majority."

"In general I think it necessary to give as well as take in a government like ours," Jefferson magnanimously declared that June. An enlightened rationalist, Jefferson hosted the dinner with Hamilton and Madison because he believed that "men of sound heads and honest views needed nothing more than explanation and mutual understanding to enable them to unite in some measures which might enable us to get along." This repast resulted in the Compromise of 1790.

In this great American accord, the two Virginians, Jefferson and Madison, delivered enough southerners' votes in Congress to pass Hamilton's ambitious, counterintuitive plan to prove America's fiscal responsibility by assuming, then paying off the war debts. In return, Hamilton supported situating the nation's capital farther south along the Potomac River, carving out a city from two slave states, Maryland and Virginia. By August, Jefferson reported that a spirit of compromise had restored the congressional harmony disrupted by the two thorny questions of the debt and the capital's location.

This harmonious tale slights a critical player, President George Washington. Its spirit of moderation testifies to Washington's leadership. George Washington championed the middle course as the best path. As president, he fostered what he called "a spirit of accommodation." Washington embodied Americans' commitment to a "common cause," and he repeatedly urged his squabbling subordinates to find those "mutual concessions which are requisite to the general prosperity," even by sacrificing "individual advantages to the interest of the Community."

George Washington's first inauguration, at Federal Hall in New York City, on April 30, 1789, launched the new nation in a spirit of harmony and compromise. (National Archives)

Unlike Jefferson, Washington was too discreet to leave a diary entry or write a letter detailing his contribution to what must have been many dinners, exchanges, calculations, and clashes before the legendary meal. Even as the president fought pneumonia during the spring, he warned that discretion remained essential. When Washington went sailing with his secretaries of state and treasury that June, he recorded in his diary the fish caught and the warm sentiments exchanged, not the political give and take that undoubtedly occurred among the men.

As the story of the peacemaking banquet took on legendary proportions, it validated Washington's mission to preserve the union's serenity by finding "sensible men" who could resist democratic politics' tide of vitriol. The two volatile questions, of the debt and the capital city's location, terrified Washington. He realized they could upend the states' still uneasy alliance. After Hamilton and Madison had compromised, the president, invoking one of his favorite phrases, invited all Americans to look forward to "enjoying peace abroad, with tranquility at home."

WASHINGTON'S WAY, this often subtle search for the center, has been the secret to American political success. This spirit of compromise is one of America's signature contributions to the noble story of democratic leadership since the 1700s. It is tragic that the capital city named after George Washington, so carefully, sensitively, poised between north and south, would come to represent partisanship, polarization, extremism, and intrigue. By 2007, Connecticut's Senator Joseph Lieberman was complaining, "There is something profoundly wrong when opposition to the war in Iraq seems to inspire greater passion than opposition to Islamist extremism." Defying his party's most passionate partisans, the 2000 Democratic vice presidential nominee denounced this "political climate where, for many people, when George Bush says 'yes,' their reflex reaction is to say 'no.'" In that spirit, New York's legendary Mayor Ed Koch once challenged his constituents, "If you agree with me on nine out of twelve issues, vote for me. If you agree with me on twelve out of twelve issues, see a psychiatrist."

Today's world is too dangerous for Americans to be so deeply, angrily, and unreasonably divided. Enlightened self-interest, wherein the right thing to do is the smart thing to do, calls for reason and unity, not emotion and demagogy. America needs passionate centrists ready to elect presidents leading from the center. And those presidents should be muscular moderates, visionary enough to preserve core values but nationalistic enough and popular enough to root their actions in a broad consensus, which they must often build.

Americans expect their leaders to seek the center. They have long rewarded leaders who built big, broad political tents driven deep into America's rich soil, rather than those who put up partisan lean-tos tilting left or right. Abraham Lincoln's famous Emancipation Proclamation was actually a cautious state document with all the passion of an accountant's ledger. Franklin Roosevelt's New Deal was an incremental zigzag that frustrated communists and plutocrats alike. But rather than representing a failure of leadership, these moments of moderation, like Washington's persistent push for compromise in the 1790s, showcase Americans and their presidents at their best.

In the past, presidents often led from the center boldly. When Abraham Lincoln defined the American nation at Gettysburg, when Franklin Roosevelt restored national confidence during his First Hundred Days, when John F. Kennedy affirmed America's moral commitment to civil rights—they all were leading the country to a new center. But center seeking often required great patience. There were no immediate results when George Washington mediated between warring cabinet secretaries or Abraham Lincoln deliberated and dithered as he wondered how to end slavery without losing the strategic border states. It took tremendous self-control for Theodore Roosevelt to settle 1902's anthracite coal strike by arbitration not fiat and for Franklin D. Roosevelt to inch America step by step toward involvement in World War II. Americans displayed great fortitude as Harry Truman crafted a long-term, bipartisan Cold War containment policy that only truly bore fruit during Ronald Reagan's presidency four decades later. Thinking creatively and cultivating broad alliances, presidents should push voters just enough so they move forward without losing their balance.

George Washington's comportment was contagious. Alexander Hamilton and Thomas Jefferson remained civil toward each other long after they learned to despise one another, as each competed for the great man's blessing. Hamilton in particular became dramatically more vitriolic after he left the cabinet in 1795 and no longer interacted regularly with Washington, his mentor for two decades. Individually and collectively, in his lifetime and after his death, George Washington spread a gospel of civility and centrism that elevated Americans and the presidency.

ALTHOUGH PARTISAN MUDSLINGING is as American as apple pie, there is an equally long and vibrant tradition of cultivating civility and seeking the center. The Founders expected conflict, but they hoped to manage, subdue, and dissipate it. During the fight over ratifying the Constitution in 1787 and 1788, the man who would be remembered as the father of the Constitution, James Madison, wrote the classic American text on the subject. Writing under the pen name Publius with his friends Alexander Hamilton and John Jay, Madison asserted that an effective government could manage "the violence of faction." Madison sought "enlightened statesmen" who could balance clashing agendas, forging compromises that would serve the public good. But relying on leadership was not enough. The genius of the republican system of government was to filter popular opinion, trusting elites to shape popular impulses into constructive patriotic actions.

This vision of a political system balancing factions and refining the "public voice" culminated a twenty-year effort to master the science of politics, American style. Unlike the subsequent French and Russian Revolutions, the American Revolution was a most moderate rebellion. With gentlemen leaders like George Washington and James Madison rising up to preserve the status quo afterward, there was little social dislocation and no mass bloodletting. Fortunately lacking a Robespierre or a Lenin, free of mass seizures and deadly purges, the revolutionary era culminated with the Founders' bundle of constitutional compromises to moderate conflict.

This notion of minimizing clashes, seeking the "public good," is a major theme in American history. The United States was never an all-or-nothing country in which fanaticism reigned. Americans have tempered extreme views with pragmatic concerns. At heart, most Americans are incrementalists, who value change but base it on tradition. We need to reacquaint ourselves with George Washington's open-tent rationalism, Abraham Lincoln's level-headed pragmatism, Theodore Roosevelt's red-white-and-blue romanticism, and Franklin Roosevelt's problem-solving nationalism.

Most modern intellectuals dislike the idea of "nationalism," the "particularly rotten apple," as the leading German philosopher Ulrich Beck has written. Conveniently forgetting that nationalism remains the world's central organizing principle, with 192 nation-states in the United Nations, cosmopolitan critics link nationalism with parochialism, xenophobia, prejudice, extremism, militarism, and mass murder. Associating nationalism with Bosnia's brutality and Nazism's horrors, academics celebrate the European Union and other centers of enlightenment as "postnational." Yet Europeans forget how Germanic Germans remain and how French the French still are, even when they all earn euros.

Nationalism, especially during the twentieth century, has unleashed great cruelty. But nationalism has also fueled many modern miracles, with America's liberal democratic experiment perhaps the greatest success story. Without appeals to the national conscience, without a strong sense of a national purpose, Americans might not have healed the sectional divide, settled the West, won world wars, explored space, formed successful businesses, or created the Internet. The American nation has generated mass prosperity, educated hundreds of millions, absorbed tens of millions of immigrants, encouraged scientific and technological breakthroughs, and spread essential rights along with liberating freedoms. Most important, because of their widespread faith in America's founding tenets, Americans have accomplished all of this without radical revolutions, bloodshed, dictators, or class violence.

American nationalism is not just xenophobia or imperialism; American patriotism is not simply McCarthyism. When Abraham Lincoln invoked "the mystic chords of memory," he was reminding Americans of what united them as one nation—and evoking their highest national ideals. When Ronald Reagan saluted John Winthrop's "shining city upon a hill," he, too, summoned a mythic national past to push the country toward a better future. At its best, nationalism is an essential force in shaping an American center. Appeals to national hopes and virtues can moderate polarizing passions; the American way is to use the collective national identity to raise individuals to higher standards of belief, behavior, values, and accomplishments.

Alas, America's historic commitment to centrism is menaced by the shrill invective resonating in Washington, in the media, on campus, and on the Internet, particularly the "blogosphere." Our culture and politics are well matched. It is difficult to expect a politics of moderation in an age of excess; temperance cannot flourish in a culture of extravagance.

The middle has long been a very appealing, and very American, place to be—and must remain so. The "great American center" has a long, proud history of offering a muscular moderation, not a mushy middle. It is the moderation of the American revolutionaries, who refused to descend into anarchy or replace one monarchy with another. It is the centrism of George Washington, who governed by eloquently appealing to reason, a "middle course," and our "common cause," while balancing off his dueling disciples. It is the cautious, compassionate pragmatism of Abraham Lincoln, who preserved the union while leading it toward abolishing slavery. It is the nationalism of Theodore Roosevelt, who carved out "the plain people" coast to coast as the presidential constituency. It is the visionary, experimental incrementalism of Franklin D. Roosevelt, who led a reluctant America in the late 1930s into the welfare state era, and then in the early 1940s led Americans away from isolation toward a heroic democratic intervention that saved the Western world. It is the bipartisan consensus forged by Harry Truman and maintained by the postwar presidents, culminating in the implosion of the Soviet Union and the crumbling of the communist bloc in the late 1980s and early 1990s. And it is the unity felt on September 11, 2001, as Americans grieved together, worked together, and committed to fighting together against the Islamist scourge.

Chapter by chapter, this book examines some of America's greatest presidents. Emphasizing these great leaders' tactical fluidity and nation-building vision yields fresh explanations for their successes. Other chapters show how too much stubbornness or weakness have caused presidents to fail. In assessing presidencies these days, most journalists tend to be Freudian, emphasizing character, while many historians remain Rooseveltian, judging chief executives by the standards of the ultimate presidential superhero, Franklin Roosevelt. Even the most successful conservative president of the twentieth century, Ronald Reagan, was often defined—and frequently defined himself—vis-à-vis Roosevelt.

Appreciating this tradition of leading muscular moderates challenges the conventional portraits of some of America's most familiar presidents. George Washington, long underestimated as a figurehead, emerges as an effective, statesmanlike force for moderation and reason. By contrast, Abraham Lincoln, frequently hailed as bold and visionary, appears more cautious and consensus building. Theodore Roosevelt, perhaps the most unlikely model moderate given his flamboyance and excitability, was a surprisingly soothing centrist anchored by his romantic American nationalism. And contrary to the continuing portraits of Franklin Roosevelt as either a crusading liberal or status quo sellout, his extraordinary ability to balance and reconcile the powerful forces buffeting America during the Great Depression and building up to World War II comes through clearly.

Looking at Roosevelt's successors, the joint achievement of Harry Truman and Dwight Eisenhower in improvising a bipartisan Cold War strategy and establishing the protocols of the mutually reinforcing cultural consensus looms large. The first two years of John Kennedy's presidency showcase the limits of moderation when pressing moral issues emerge, much like the situation facing the pre–Civil War presidents. But toward the end of his presidency, Kennedy rose to the civil rights challenge, demonstrating how presidents can channel radical impulses functioning as chief executives, not crusaders.

The presidencies of Lyndon Johnson, Richard Nixon, and Jimmy Carter teach different lessons about moderate leadership. Each was surprisingly centrist in policy matters, especially domestically. But Johnson failed because he was too rigid regarding Vietnam. Nixon self-destructed because his tactical aggressiveness belied his policy centrism. Carter floundered because his lack of faith in America's future contradicted Americans' optimistic nationalism.

The three two-term presidents since 1980 offer interesting case studies in presidential statesmanship and center seeking. Ronald Reagan was more centrist than his conservative ideology and rhetoric suggested. Reagan repeatedly compromised, showing far more concern for national unity, relative political calm, and his own personal popularity than for conservative purity. Bill Clinton was even more accommodating than

Reagan. But whereas Reagan remained anchored in his ideology and frequently demonstrated a muscular moderation, Clinton's need to be loved made for a spineless centrism. Finally, if Bill Clinton was too concerned with public approval, George W. Bush has demonstrated the perils of not being sufficiently sensitive to popular opinion. Bush's characteristic go-it-alone stance sullied the "goodly fabric" George Washington wove so carefully, illustrating the broad dangers to the body politic when a president is imprisoned by his convictions.

The Bill Clinton–George W. Bush obsession with winning at any price resulted in two, two-term presidencies, but at great cost. Both Clinton and Bush maneuvered masterfully to maintain power, but they further divided the American people. Just as Americans are starting to measure their "carbon footprints," assessing how many noxious emissions each individual generates, we need to start measuring our leaders' toxic footprints, measuring the poisonous fallout of particular actions, even if they were successful in the short term. During the Monica Lewinsky scandal, Bill Clinton kept his office and maintained his popularity, but at what cost to the nation's soul? George W. Bush in 2004 won his reelection campaign, but at what cost to the nation's psyche? Important presidential duties include strengthening democracy, uniting Americans, and reaffirming ideals; a president who leaves office with a nation further divided, demoralized, and doubting its own virtue is a failure, no matter how popular he or she may have been.

Great leaders are born *and* made. Each successful president brought particular talents and innate personality traits to the table, be it Washington's reserve, Lincoln's humility, Theodore Roosevelt's bluster, Franklin Roosevelt's agility, Truman's directness, John Kennedy's panache, or Ronald Reagan's wit. Presidential success traditionally has married substantive achievement with stylistic popularity. Great presidents also succeeded by rooting their leadership projects in common aspirations their fellow citizens shared, which resonated with broader visions and conceptions of America during their respective eras. George Washington spoke the language of enlightened republicanism in the Age of Reason. Abraham Lincoln's kindhearted, nationalistic, "my policy is to have no policy" approach offered an elastic centrism that enabled a racist America to free the slaves for the sake of union, not egalitarianism. Lincoln's leadership went beyond both the "split-the-difference" compromising of party men like Henry Clay and the zealotry of the abolitionists. He followed a "middle measure" pragmatism, two decades before Charles Peirce formally defined the concept of "pragmatism" in American thought.

After the Civil War, most Northerners feared leaders who were too extremist and disdained those who were too compliant. Abolitionists such as William Lloyd Garrison were as despised as Millard Fillmore and Franklin Pierce, the ineffectual accommodators who could not keep America united. Half a century later, Theodore Roosevelt pioneered a populist nationalism that mobilized a country unified by an increasingly popular and nationalized press. Franklin Roosevelt then perfected it, further weaving the country together in radio's magic web. Finally, the bipartisan consensus leaders of the Cold War spoke authoritatively to a confident country with a strong sense of purpose. Alas, today the ugly political climate reflects a broader cynicism and loss of faith, especially among elites and political players.

Whereas being flexible and moderate helped the greatest American presidents succeed, some of the least successful presidents failed by being too rigid. Ideologues rarely make it to the White House. With the party system of the nineteenth and twentieth centuries emphasizing party loyalty and electability and the modern primary system emphasizing popularity and electability, most successful nominees have been conventional, compromising coalition builders, not flamethrowers. But once in office, some presidents dug their heels in so deeply on certain issues that they failed as presidents. James Buchanan's unyielding support for the illegitimate, proslavery Lecompton constitution; Woodrow Wilson's stubborn championship of the League of Nations treaty; and Lyndon Johnson's commitment to South Vietnam even as the war there escalated, are examples of self-destructive presidential inflexibility. Although the outcome of the Iraq war is as yet unknown, it is clear that George W. Bush's rigidity has proved highly, dysfunctionally divisive. Democratic leadership is a high-wire balancing act. Leaning too far in any direction or holding on too tight to heavy baggage risks a steep fall, often with no safety net.

THE PRESIDENT'S JOB is to preside. And presidents preside most effectively over this diverse country by pursuing centrism rather than riling partisans. Using slim majorities to impose radical changes on the country violates the implicit democratic contract between the leader and the people. Great presidents aim for the center, hitting the popular bull's-eye as close as possible, albeit sometimes after repositioning it.

Today, with America threatened by Islamist terrorism and nuclear roguery, presidents must strive to overcome divisive politics and temper extreme positions. America prospers when it has a president who leads by consensus building. "Soldiering is 99% boredom and 1% sheer terror," one Civil War soldier wrote to his wife. Similarly, effective American democratic leadership requires long bouts of compromising, slogging through, and coalition building, punctuated by bursts of boldness and occasional flights of eloquence.

Admittedly, moderation is an odd thing to get passionate about. It is a posture, a tactic, a strategy, that by definition is not intended to make the blood boil. Moreover, it is a relative, ever-changing position. As public opinion fluctuates, conditions change, issues come and go, the elusive center shifts, too. In most Americans' search for heroes, in modern academics' search for radicals, in the media's mania for headlines, moderation often seems to be a synonym for capitulation or indecision.

Mocking moderates is a great American tradition. No politician in the 1970s or 1980s wanted to be called a "wimp." In mid-twentieth-century America, the dismissive term was "Caspar Milquetoast," the name of the reedy, bespectacled, sniveling cartoon character who insisted on wearing a belt *and* suspenders. Prior to that, the pejorative label was "mugwump," early American slang for an Indian chief, which evolved into a nickname for elite political reformers in the late 1800s. By the 1930s, the *Blue Earth Post* in Minnesota was defining mugwump as "a sort of bird that sits on a fence with his mug on one side, and his wump on the other." In 1992 Vice President Dan Quayle dismissed the Democratic centrist Bill Clinton as a "waffler" whose favorite color was "plaid."

By definition, the very willingness to seek the center and consider various opinions from thoughtful critics makes moderates particularly open to deliberation. But that introspection also encourages the flexibility, civility, creativity, and rationality that are the moderate's hallmarks. The great British philosopher of liberty, John Stuart Mill, taught that polemics suppress dialogue, stigmatizing opponents as "bad and immoral men." The only way to evaluate bold contrary opinions is "by studied moderation of language."

The moderate who listens, who retains self-control, who squelches the temptation to lurch to the left or right, is also proudly rooted in Western thought and the American political tradition. Even though they triggered wide-ranging, even radical, changes, the American revolutionaries created a *moderate* revolution and republic because individual and collective temperance had been imprinted upon them from birth. The major inspirations for American political thought, including the Bible, both Jewish and Christian; the classics, both Greek and Roman;

Puritanism; and the Enlightenment, celebrated modesty, balance, self-denial, and rationality.

The Bible is filled with stories of heroes conquering their passions, their controlling impulses—and suffering the consequences when they indulge their emotions. Leaders, in particular, succeed when they are "discerning and wise," as Joseph is described in Genesis 41:33. When Moses succumbs to anger and hits the rock in his frustrated quest for water, he ends up being banned from entering the Promised Land. His successor, Joshua, is blessed with the chance to lead his people, because as a spy in Canaan he was one of only two out of twelve who could see an optimistic, golden, middle path to success, rather than the ten extremists' nightmarish vision of a terrifying land that the children of Israel could never conquer. Biblical aphorisms emphasized self-control and self-possession. Proverbs 17:27 teaches, "A man of knowledge uses words with restraint, and a man of understanding is even-tempered." In Phillipians 4:5, Paul preaches, "Let your moderation be known unto all men, The Lord is at hand."

In their quest for harmony, balance, and beauty, the Greek philosophers echoed this notion of self-control, temperance, and reason, transforming the Bible's warnings into positive models of moderation. Socrates taught that people "must know how to choose the mean and avoid the extremes on either side, as far as possible." The classic tale of Icarus endorses moderation. Cautioning that his wax wings would not function if they were made wet by the sea or melted by the sun, Daedalus urged his son to "fly the middle course." Icarus's refusal to heed his father's call for moderation had fatal results, as did the Roman descent into decadence. American revolutionaries were steeped in the classics and terrified of replicating the Roman Republic's failures.

The great medieval philosopher Moses Ben Maimon, also known as Maimonides, synthesized the biblical warnings and Greek models to chart "the Golden Mean" or the "Golden Path." Writing in the 1100s, Maimonides calculated his moderation geometrically, urging individuals to calibrate their behavior by placing themselves equidistant from their warring impulses. Defining wisdom as moderation, Maimonides said individuals needed to seek those intermediate midpoints in their emotions, appetites, personal relations, and business lives.

These concepts guided America's early settlers, especially the Puritans of New England. The Puritans were quite zealous about their modesty, although they were not as dour and repressed as they are often depicted. The Puritans were America's most ardent champions of the Protestant work ethic. They cleverly synthesized Calvinist discipline with American ambition by balancing the spiritual and the material, seeking worldly success without profligate excess.

The Enlightenment of the 1600s and 1700s built on this moderate tradition and shaped the environment in which the remarkably reasonable and balanced American Revolution took place. Philosophers in the Age of Reason traced the steady development of Western reason, ignoring the bursts of passion and unreason among the Jews and the Christians, the Greeks and the Romans. From a modern viewpoint, British America's elite colonial society looks tightly wound, elaborately choreographed, and exhaustingly formalistic. But like the moderate imperative itself, the affectations and formality were weapons to civilize what remained a wild, uncontrollable environment.

Balancing out all the "Give me Liberty or give me Death" rhetoric, America's founders were surprisingly deliberative, cautious, and moderate. George Washington linked his faith in reason with his urge to seek the center, to find what he called the nation's unifying "goodly fabric." He recognized that if his reason could lead him to one conclusion, others could reason their way to conflicting, but equally reasonable, conclusions. Preventing a French Revolution–style Reign of Terror was among the American Revolution's great gifts to humanity.

Although often marked by highly partisan debates and occasionally wracked by intense conflict, the United States of America also developed an enlightened democratic reasonableness that has served it well. At critical moments in American history, leaders emerged who could hew a middle path, who could rally a majority of Americans on common ground. The United States was blessed again and again by leaders who created a common language to face challenges. Sometimes Americans were mobilized by the resounding crash of weaponry, as during the two world wars. Sometimes they were inspired by the rhetoric of visionary statesmen such as Franklin D. Roosevelt or John F. Kennedy. And sometimes Americans were united by the staccato beat of factory machines as they pursued prosperity.

Healthy communities need crosscutting loyalties and shifting alliances. In the 1890s, ethnic and religious allegiances undermined class solidarity, saving Gilded Age America from becoming radicalized as Europe was in that era. In New York, Irish Catholic immigrants identified with the Irish Catholic gentry praying with them at St. Patrick's Cathedral. They all voted for Tammany Hall Democrats, unlike the Protestants who, rich or poor, voted Republican. Similarly, Ronald Reagan's coalition in the

1980s made for a less polarized society, uniting hardheaded businessmen, hedonistic yuppies, disappointed blue-collar Roosevelt Democrats, and Bible-toting fundamentalists.

In the spirit of multidimensional identities and crosscutting ties, Rodney King's cry during the 1992 Los Angeles riots after a jury acquitted four white policemen of beating him with nightsticks—"Why can't we get along?"—should resonate widely. Our elites should act more intelligently, reasonably, and constructively. Instead, we get "What's the matter with Kansas?"–type polemics, with experts asking the "little guys" and their wives what is wrong with them, how come they are not voting correctly?

APPRECIATING MODERATION contradicts pop culture and the latest academic fashions. In Walt Disney's Hall of the Presidents and other popular venues, presidential superheroes save America, often with a rhetorical flourish. On the opposite extreme, academic debunkers ranging from the Afrocentrists to Howard Zinn portraying America as a conflict-ridden, rudderless colossus, burdened by impotent leaders or unduly aggressive presidents compensating for individual and national insecurities. Professors honor the antislavery zealotry of John Brown and William Lloyd Garrison over Abraham Lincoln's deliberation. Popularizing the academic trend, History Channel's recent *Ten Days That Unexpectedly Changed America* highlighted Indian massacres, violent clashes between citizens, and radical bombings. These extreme portraits are inaccurate. Balanced analytical history elevates, not just denigrates. We can learn from the coalition builders, not just the partisans; the statesmen, not just the demagogues; and the magnanimous uniters, not just the cranky dividers.

All societies—and especially democracies—need natural mechanisms to resolve conflicts. America's balance seems more difficult to find in a seemingly balkanized world of racial division, ethnic estrangement, religious conflict, geographical tension, and political zeal. Yet American society also functions far more smoothly, effectively, and kindly than the naysayers of the media would ever suggest.

True, many people fear that moderation simply perpetuates the status quo. Compelling moral movements to eliminate slavery and advance civil rights required extremists' radical passion. A democratic society needs its innovative thinkers and activists, what Martin Luther King Jr. called its "creative extremists." Sometimes wrongs must be righted by revolutionaries rather than by committees. But there is no precise formula for determining just how confrontational and controversial public actors should be. Malcolm X, for one, mocked Martin Luther King's approach, snarling that revolutions cannot succeed with victims and oppressors swaying together, singing "We Shall Overcome . . . Suum Day."

PRESIDENTS ARE NOT ELECTED to be revolutionaries. A successful president needs to unite the American people around a cause, as Abraham Lincoln did with the antislavery movement, as Theodore Roosevelt and Franklin Roosevelt did with the push for more economic equity, and as John F. Kennedy and Lyndon B. Johnson did with the civil rights movement. This type of visionary president can help mainstream bold changes for the American people by domesticating them and thus popularizing them. That kind of statesmanship requires an ability to triangulate, finding a position by averaging among extreme viewpoints. A great leader can help forge a consensus and build bridges between different factions.

Muscular moderation should be neither weak nor conformist. The greatest failures in American presidential history were the ciphers, not the hotheads. What distinguishes Franklin Pierce, Ulysses S. Grant, and Warren G. Harding as the most undistinguished of presidents is their passivity. The call for moderation is a delicate balancing act. It requires visionary leaders who can be activist without being extremist, who can galvanize but not polarize. These muscular moderates can calm the waters and shift public opinion while refusing to play up to the demands of partisan extremists.

Some anger is healthy in a democracy. Especially in modern America's consumer-addled, increasingly selfish society, anger motivates. Narcotized by the leisure culture, we need passion to pull ourselves away from our iPods and plunge into politics. Moreover, anger can be logical. The humanitarian philosopher Elie Wiesel notes that anger is the rational response to terrorism. The mass murder of innocents and genocidal calls to destroy America or the West should not be treated lightly. Moderation in no way implies paralysis. But vigorous responses have to be rationally based. Shrill debates obscure real dangers and risk hysterical overreactions.

We need to rediscover the centrality of centrism in American history— and in American life today. Americans get along better than many think, historians claim, and journalists report. American nationalism remains remarkably strong and surprisingly constructive, launching three hundred million people in an ever-improving quest for liberty and equality along with a miraculously successful pursuit of happiness. If we want to prosper and remain safe, we need to cooperate on our common destiny, remember our common ground, and find our common voice. We cannot just vent spleen and play to the extremes. As the American Revolution began, Benjamin Franklin insisted, "We must hang together, gentlemen . . . else, we shall most assuredly hang separately." This quip used to be one of American history's defining clichés. It remains true today.

HISTORY IS NOT A RECIPE; leadership is not formulaic. But we should learn from our past and from our greatest presidents. Center seeking is not pandering; it is community building. Compromising can be courageous, not cowardly. We need leaders who understand, as George Washington did, that reasonable people will disagree; who seek Abraham Lincoln's "middle measures"; who share Theodore Roosevelt's faith in the American nation; and who are willing to experiment, as Franklin Roosevelt did, in the quest for the "greatest good." In an age of terrorism, don't we need Harry Truman's bipartisan foreign policy stopping harsh disagreements at the "water's edge?" After two decades of culture wars, don't we yearn for a president like Dwight Eisenhower, who refused to "go to the gutter," either on the right or the left? And don't we wish that, although debating passionately but respectfully, we could all rally around the original founding vision of this country as an idyllic "city upon a hill"?

When Ronald Reagan invoked the "shining city upon a hill," the controversial conservative president cleverly used Massachusetts Bay Governor John Winthrop's Puritan vision to unite Americans in the 1980s around a traditional American dream. The desire to be more sane, reasonable, constructive, and moderate in politics shaped the discussion in the eighteenth century about the "New World," Lincoln's nineteenth-century rhetoric about "the last best hope on earth," and the twentieth-century vision of "an American century." Americans have traditionally thought of their country as a model for the world, especially in politics; it behooves us to live up to that image.

This search for the center, for a majoritarian stance, may be the quintessential democratic quest. Democracy represents a leap of faith that a diverse group of people can find common ground, be they the 30 students in an elementary school who elect a class president or the 120 million people or so who elect the president to represent 300 million Americans. Making that happen, seeking to make as many people as possible in a given society winners without alienating or marginalizing the losers, is a noble endeavor. Developing the common vocabulary—Madison's "public voice"—and finding that broad social consensus is indeed democracy's "Holy Grail."

Today, more and more people, turned off by the shrill partisanship of public debate, are joining a disengaged majority. They avoid the hardscrabble fights, seeking comfort in what Thomas Jefferson, quoting the Renaissance thinker Michel de Montaigne, called the "softest pillow" of political ignorance. But rather than being forced between the fluffy pillow of political ignorance and the hard rocks of partisan warfare, Americans once again need to seek the Madisonian golden mean. America needs a president willing to embroider a glorious new pattern on Washington's "goodly fabric," exercising a muscular moderation that tackles problems practically, from the center.

Moderate presidents who remain both principled and accommodating can overcome the hyper-partisan rift dividing this country. Even with George Washington's tolerance, Abraham Lincoln's pragmatism, Theodore Roosevelt's nationalism, Franklin D. Roosevelt's greatest good experimentalism, Harry Truman's bipartisanship, Dwight Eisenhower's consensus building, and Ronald Reagan's patriotic inspiration as building blocks, modern America may not find all the answers. But the political process could inspire, not alienate. Politics could become more like high-class theater and less like burlesque, or, even worse, a cockfight.

Of course, American politics has long been brutal, more a contact sport than a civil debate. But attitudes change; leadership counts. Today's sour, cynical climate is a historical construct. It can be fixed. In the twentieth century, Theodore Roosevelt, Franklin Roosevelt, and Ronald Reagan presided over periods of patriotic renewal and increased idealism. In the twenty-first century, that kind of leadership, those kinds of results, are still possible. We eagerly await such a leader.

Civility is mass produced by millions of small but big-hearted gestures but all too easily destroyed by a few loud, small-minded people. All of us, regardless of our political colors, should make amends for the hysteria of these last two decades; reflect on today's continuing tensions; and approach tomorrow with more openness, mutuality, acceptance, respect, humility, and love—even for those who will still dare to disagree with us.

1

WASHINGTON'S WAY

"Liberal Allowances, Mutual Forbearances, and Temporizing Yieldings on All Sides"

AMERICA'S FIRST ACTION HERO, the full-page color advertisement in the *New York Times* proclaimed. The History Channel was promoting its May 2006 extravaganza, *Washington the Warrior*. There was the father of our country, George Washington, looking very buff and manly. In portraits Washington usually appears as elegant and meticulously dressed, flashing his enigmatic smile. This Washington was grimacing, shouting, running, and clutching a musket. A rip in his sleeve exposed a cut on his bicep, offering a macho contrast to his powder-blue frock coat's gold trim and frilly collar.

Yet even though they were promoting this hip, muscular General George Washington on television, the History Channel producers reinforced an older stereotype of President Washington as wooden on their Web site, posting an article describing Washington's "reticence and lack of intellectual flair" and claiming that his "stiff dignity and sense of propriety postponed the emergence of the fierce partisanship that would characterize" succeeding administrations. The image of the buff Washington at war seemed to be overcompensating for the stiff, historical Washington at peace. American mythology consistently casts Washington as the dim bulb among the Founders, the silent, even tongued-tied figurehead who became legendary even though he was not as smart as Thomas Jefferson, James Madison, or Alexander Hamilton.

Despite this image, Washington was a muscular moderate, far shrewder than many acknowledged. Emotionally disciplined, philosophically faithful to an enlightened, democratic "empire" of reason, Washington passionately advocated political moderation. Acknowledging his own shortcomings as a human being, he tolerated and welcomed others' views. He realized that others might reasonably reach different conclusions about important issues. Washington's idea of democratic politics was to seek common ground and blaze a centrist trail.

American historians traditionally hail Washington as a simple republican who spurned monarchical ambitions. But his moderating influence in the clash between Alexander Hamilton and Thomas Jefferson is his most relevant legacy. Washington's approach to the presidency was consensus driven. He unraveled problems deftly, finding the common thread to reconcile opponents. A fresh look reveals Washington as a maestro of moderation, eloquently establishing the search for a "common cause" as an essential prerequisite for presidential leadership, and for American citizenship.

WASHINGTON'S CALL FOR CENTRISM seems to have been a plaintive cry against what most historians consider his administration's defining story. Washington's young country was divided. North opposed south. Agrarian debtors battled urban creditors. Alexander Hamilton's northern nationalists fought the James Madison–Thomas Jefferson, states rights–oriented Virginia alliance, eventually coalescing into the Federalist Party versus the Democratic-Republicans. Their conflicts spawned one of America's gifts to politics—and unexpected keys to centrism: the two-party system.

The Founders despised factionalism even as they spread it. "If I could not go to heaven but with a party, I would not go at all," insisted Thomas Jefferson, who nevertheless subsequently established what became the Democratic Party, today the world's oldest political party. Linking national character with personal character, Washington believed that a noble nation needed virtuous, self-sacrificing, disinterested leaders—altruistic brokers, not zealous crusaders.

The retired General Washington was fifty-five years old when the Constitutional Convention assembled. A Virginia aristocrat made rich through land speculation, a Seven Years' War veteran and Revolutionary War hero, Washington knew just when to retreat yet still appear successful. Tall, statuesque, reserved, George Washington played his role brilliantly. Surrounded by short, foppish blabbermouths like John Adams, Washington looked like a leader and acted like a demigod. His peers—and successors—perceived moral authority in his physical strength and wisdom in his silence.

George Washington's aloofness was legendary. Even to his peers, he was a marble statue brought to life. A brilliant politician, Washington tempered his reticent dignity with a charming affability, earning love and respect from friends and strangers. Still, Washington was no glad-hander. The general advised a young Continental Army colonel, "Be easy and condescending [with] your officers, but not too familiar." Otherwise one risked losing "that respect which is necessary to support a proper command."

During the 1787 Constitutional Convention, the Revolution's financial genius, Gouverneur Morris, scoffed at some Revolutionary War comrades who still found Washington intimidating. Morris boasted of his intimacy with Washington. Alexander Hamilton mischievously offered to bankroll dinner for a dozen if Morris would publicly embrace Washington while saying, "My dear General, how happy I am to see you look so well." At the next official reception, Morris bowed to Washington, shook hands, rested his left hand on Washington's shoulder, and uttered Hamilton's suggested greeting. Washington glared and recoiled from Morris, who quickly retreated into the crowd.

Washington—who loved the theater—consciously played his role as eminent leader. His detachment demonstrated his morality and his stature. The revolutionary generation considered character one's public reputation, living up to the grand persona each gentleman chose. Remembering Rome's fall, eighteenth-century American leaders concluded that republics needed virtuous individuals to preserve national virtue. Worthy, self-sacrificing, disinterested leaders would place the nation's needs before their own and attempt to behave nobly regardless of circumstances.

Having mastered the part of decent youth in the 1730s and 1740s, Washington achieved greater success in many later roles: country squire, general, reluctant head of the Constitutional Convention, and, finally, reluctant president. During the Revolution, following crushing defeats by the well-trained British troops and amid the misery of the Valley Forge winter, George Washington inspired his troops to fight, or flee, another day. The Americans won the Revolution by outlasting the British.

As the war ended, Washington cemented his reputation for virtue by demanding that his subordinates demonstrate their fair-mindedness, even as he demonstrated his legendary magnanimity. Officers who had endured the long struggle expected generous pensions. But America's government under the Articles of Confederation did not enjoy enough power to raise sufficient revenue to reward them. By March 1783, disgruntled officers demanding better pensions were threatening to topple Congress. An anonymous, inflammatory letter urged officers to "mark for Suspicion, the Man who should recommend moderation and longer forbearance."

Washington could have used this issue to seize power or score political points with his men at Congress's expense. But although he empathized with his soldiers, he understood the politicians' limits. The general asserted his authority by postponing a meeting the officers had planned, then addressing them at a time of his choosing. He threw his weight behind the Congress and the young nation's emerging democracy. Demonstrating his showman's flair, Washington calmly approached the podium as he prepared to address five hundred angry officers assembled in Newburgh, New York, on March 16, 1783. Before beginning to speak, he begged the officers' permission to put on his new spectacles, explaining, "I have not only grown gray, but almost blind in the service of my country." With that flourish, Washington won over his audience.

Washington blasted the ungentlemanly "anonymous summons," exclaiming, "how inconsistent with the rules of propriety! how unmilitary! and how subversive of all order and discipline." By repudiating moderation, the authors of the letter had infuriated Washington. He quoted the offending sentence twice in his short, eloquent address. Washington disliked hotheads. Squelching negotiation and discussion would do great damage, he warned, by undermining reason and free speech. Then, "dumb & silent we may be led, like sheep, to the Slaughter." Identifying what would become his central concern for the next decade and a half, Washington urged his comrades "in the name of our common Country" to oppose those who threatened American liberties by rabble-rousing.

Weeks later, in June 1783, with the coup having been aborted, Washington retired from the army. The defeated British monarch George III had noted in 1782 that if Washington could resist making himself king, he would be "the greatest man in the world." By voluntarily relinquishing power, in this case as general and later after two presidential terms, Washington modeled how to be moderate without being weak. Washington the cool pragmatist made a singular contribution to American political philosophy and good governance: Democracies need strong leaders who respect regular rotations of power.

As he would do again when leaving the presidency, when he left the army Washington issued a farewell address, issued as his last Circular Letter to the States. Still fuming, he urged his fellow citizens to take on a "pacific and friendly Disposition" and think nationally. Making "mutual concessions" would foster "general prosperity." Good citizens had "to sacrifice their individual advantages to the interest of the Community."

WASHINGTON GENUINELY FEARED becoming president in 1789. The Constitution was unformed; his fellow citizens were cantankerous, unsure just how united their union of states should be. Many of this young country's fiscal, organizational, and diplomatic problems appeared intractable. Entering politics endangered Washington's greatest personal achievement, his heroic reputation. However, standing on the sidelines and spurning his country's call also risked losing the people's esteem. Ambivalent, Washington passively stood for election rather than actively running. Trying to embody the contemporary sense of national virtue, he did not campaign, but stayed on his Mount Vernon farm, awaiting the people's call. This stately inaction pleased Americans who viewed Washington as an Olympian leader untempted by power. Throughout his presidency Washington, in seeking the high road, often did what he most wanted to do, which gave the American people what they wanted in a leader.

Americans often forget the new republic's fragility. The delegates who created the Constitution at the Philadelphia convention in 1787 had established a governing framework for the new nation, but many questions remained about the government's form and viability. The new country was dangerously ungovernable. Nearly four million people lived on 864,764 square miles, mostly scattered along the Eastern seaboard. From Maine's craggy coast to Georgia's rich red soil, from the urban hurly burly of Boston, New York, and Philadelphia to the lush silence of the Ohio and Kentucky wilderness, Americans lived in dramatically different settings. America's Brits, Germans, Scots, Irish, Catholics, Protestants, Huguenots, and Jews came from dozens of different countries, spoke a Babel of languages, and worshiped in a dizzying variety of ways.

The New England merchants, southern planters, western frontiersman, and mid-Atlantic yeoman farmers had clashing personalities and agendas.

The new states united temporarily to squabble with their neighbors, but most were deeply divided internally. The second-string cities that became state capitals, including Albany, New York, and Harrisburg, Pennsylvania, benefited from the city versus country tensions.

The new nation had to solve pressing practical crises while answering complicated, existential questions. It was unclear if the federal government should assume the states' staggering war debts or how the government could pay annual interest payments totaling $4.5 million, three times its projected revenue. On the western frontier, British troops remained in forts England had promised to vacate, and Native American tribes threatened many settlements. Across the Atlantic, France, having supported the thirteen colonies during the Revolution, expected war-weary America's backing against England in its ongoing conflicts.

Americans wondered how to face these challenges without losing their liberties. The revolutionaries' suspicion of strong executive government persisted. As Washington's presidency began, Rhode Island and North Carolina still refused to ratify the Constitution. Fear of dictators like King George haunted them as they hoped for salvation from a president named George.

Even the act of traveling north from Mount Vernon to assume the presidency in the nation's first capital, New York, affirmed Washington's unique role in America's emerging national identity. So many horsemen escorted Washington's carriage that he spent much of the voyage clouded in dust. The numerous parades and speeches and toasts confirmed his iconic status. Always assessing his audience, Washington worried that such great expectations could deteriorate into equally unrealistic disenchantment. His birthday became a national holiday as his presidency began; how could he top that? Determined to push for unity, the new president vowed to visit all the states. Quietly but patiently, he boycotted Rhode Island until this last holdout joined the constitutional fold.

The first presidential inauguration, on April 30, 1789, was grand. Hundreds shouted "huzzah" after each of the thirteen-gun salutes. Washington's inaugural speech articulated his enlightened nationalism. He pledged that "no local prejudices or attachments—no separate views, nor party animosities" would cloud "the comprehensive and equal eye which ought to watch over this great assemblage of communities and interests." With the national trumping the parochial, he rooted the nation's future success in individual virtue. Just as he had disarmed the officers by sporting spectacles in Newburgh, Washington's nervous excitement moved many observers, who appreciated that he treasured the historic moment.

Devoted to the Enlightenment and revolutionary ideals, Washington hoped his center-seeking presidency would prove to European skeptics that democratic republics could be stable. Writing to a friend in 1790, he envisioned "a government of accommodation as well as a government of Laws." Much was to be done "by *prudence*, much by *conciliation*, and much by *firmness*," Washington added, giving his recipe for governance. Moderation also shaped Washington's signature foreign policy stance, advocating American neutrality amid European scheming.

Above all else, throughout his tenure Washington hoped to keep his fellow Americans cooperating. "Gentlemen," he told Boston selectmen in July 1795, "in every act of my administration, I have sought the happiness of my fellow-citizens." Prizing disinterested nobility, Washington dismissed selfish, local concerns, viewing the United States "as one great whole."

The president first had to convince his own countrymen they could work together. Americans took their Declaration of Independence literally. President Washington sought to embody a unifying national spirit that transcended partisan, regional, ethnic, linguistic, class, and social differences. He selected four appointees for what would be called a "cabinet" who embodied a characteristic balance. New York's Alexander Hamilton as secretary of the treasury and Massachusetts's Henry Knox as secretary of war represented the two leading northern states. Two Virginians rounded out Washington's official family: Thomas Jefferson as secretary of state and Edmund Randolph as attorney general. Knox, a former general, represented the revolutionary soldiers and heroes. Ideologically, Hamilton had distinguished himself as a leading constitutionalist, coauthoring the *Federalist Papers*. Representing the other end of the spectrum, Jefferson zealously guarded liberty and feared centralized power. Randolph initially refused to sign the Constitution, but ultimately supported ratification. Randolph's position reassured antifederalists that national leaders understood their hesitations, while transmitting the strong Washingtonian message demanding loyalty to the new Constitution.

Seeking to rise above particular clashes, Washington championed the mutual over the selfish, the majority over the minority, the nation over the party. He feared factionalism as the democratic disease, rooted in common dreams, nourished by popular passions, yet stoked and easily hijacked by power-hungry schemers. Despising conflict, Washington hoped to preserve

WASHINGTON AND HIS CABINET.

Washington's cabinet, made up, after Washington, of (left to right) Henry Knox, Alexander Hamilton, Thomas Jefferson, and Edmund Randolph, balanced opposing regions and philosophies, but eventually became divided and contentious. (National Archives)

his iconic status and transfer his popularity to the new government. He wanted cabinet members to send him written opinions rather than argue at meetings. He happily delegated small matters to cabinet members and congressional leaders rather than risk his reputation on petty disputes.

During this first term, Washington succeeded. With his encouragement, Congress added the Bill of Rights to the Constitution; the federal judiciary took shape; and the last antifederalist bastions, North Carolina and Rhode Island, finally joined the union. Washington's steadying presence encouraged legislators and citizens to believe in the noble experiment.

Washington's presidential passivity reassured antifederalists that he was no dictator. Respecting congressional and state legislative prerogatives, the new executive positioned himself above the fray. On April 5, 1792, when Washington vetoed Congress's plan for apportioning representatives, he justified the first presidential veto in American history on clear, constitutional grounds, implying that his policy preferences were irrelevant. Washington refused to propose legislation or shepherd bills through Congress. And, unlike the colonial governors, who had interfered in the election of governing bodies, this president avoided involvement in congressional elections. When Congressman John Francis Mercer claimed Washington's endorsement, the president publicly denied commenting on any candidate. Ever the modest national hero, he said that exercising "an influence (if I really possessed any) however remote, would be highly improper."

Ultimately, this presidential modesty enhanced executive power. Exploiting some of the Constitution's ambiguities, some congressmen contemplated expanding the Senate's role of advising and consenting. They wanted to require the president to seek senatorial approval to fire cabinet members as well as hire them. Many congressmen admitted that only their confidence in the incumbent stopped them from endorsing this assault on presidential prerogative.

Almost everything President Washington did became memorable, setting precedents. On August 22, 1789, following the constitutional requirement that he seek Senate approval regarding international treaties, the first president of the United States visited the Senate chamber. The issue, four months into Washington's presidency, concerned relations with Native American tribes. Washington could have set the precedent of periodic parliamentary exchanges between the president and the senators. However, senators who opposed Washington delayed the matter. Washington returned a few days later, and the Senate ratified the treaty. But the president was furious. He vowed "he would be damned if he ever went there again," establishing the tradition of presidential remoteness from Congress. Such self-imposed limits allowed what Vice President John Adams later called Washington's "gift of silence" to amplify the president's voice on those occasions when it was used. Pennsylvania's acerbic Senator William Maclay criticized the former general for acting too kingly in this instance. Washington's decision to distance himself from Congress reflected his obsession with his new office's dignity, as well as his own vain, self-protective streak.

The president was the nation's nonpartisan conscience. In a country always risking division between north and south, Washington's executive compass naturally pointed toward the center. A year into the Washington administration, a surprised Thomas Jefferson noted that the "opposition to our new constitution has almost totally disappeared," thanks to Washington.

When Washington became ill in May 1790, Jefferson shared the general population's anxiety: "It proves how much depends on his life," he observed. Washington showed how great presidents could use reason, restraint, and patriotic appeals to temper the cult of personality that this powerful office inevitably encouraged.

GEORGE WASHINGTON was not a perfect president. As tensions mounted within his administration, his most precious asset—his sterling reputation—was tarnished as partisans from both sides targeted him. When his cabinet erupted in fury, Washington tried to remain on friendly terms with all the combatants. As his administration foundered on the shoals of repeated policy disputes between urbane, pro-British, northern merchants and provincial, pro-French, southern farmers, Washington's broad tastes helped hew a middle path for America's economic development. Although he yearned for his Mount Vernon estate, he also delighted in New York's and Philadelphia's cosmopolitan elegance. He tried to keep America's rural character while modernizing its cities. As both England and France tried to ensnare his nation and administration in their ongoing conflicts, Washington's military credibility and commitment to neutrality helped the young nation avoid European wars.

By 1790, a great battle between Secretary of the Treasury Alexander Hamilton and Congressman James Madison had erupted. The nationalist, cosmopolitan Hamilton wanted the federal government to pay the states' lingering war debts, so that a financially solid America could develop economically. Madison, a provincial Virginian, sympathized with the many strapped southern farmers and other debtors who had sold their securities cheaply to speculators. He and Thomas Jefferson wanted to preserve America's rural character and feared the corruption that elaborate credit schemes and economic development would bring. Still, Washington preserved enough goodwill so that Hamilton could pull off his great moderating coup and stabilize the new nation economically.

The three-way compromise that Hamilton and Madison eventually reached at Thomas Jefferson's dinner table epitomized the spirit of patriotism, moderation, and accommodation that Washington fostered. The federal government assumed the states' debts, asserting federal power and stabilizing American credit abroad. The nation then paid enough of Virginia's and North Carolina's debts to satisfy Madison's allies. And the national capital would be located by the Potomac River, midway between north and south.

In the months before that compromise, the worsening partisanship dismayed Washington. Writing on March 28, 1790, to his confidant, Dr. David Stuart, Washington accepted conflict as natural but wanted to manage it with what he called "mutual forbearance." Washington noted that the states had united against common dangers. Now they needed a "spirit of accommodation" to succeed. The legislature should "assimilate" all these "different interests" and "reconcile them to the general welfare" through "long, warm and animated debates."

In June Washington complained to Stuart that too many government critics pounced easily, dishonestly. This one-sidedness offended Washington's enlightened nature. By assessing "both sides" of an argument, reasonable men, thinking on a "Continental Scale," could reach nonpartisan conclusions. Washington's awareness of America's breadth and diversity evoked James Madison's great moderating vision in Federalist 10. Madison, like Washington, viewed "the mischiefs of faction" as the unhappy but inevitable result of liberty. Rather than suppressing freedom and mandating uniformity, effective governments—and leaders—had to control the effects of factionalism.

It was also in June 1790 that Alexander Hamilton, Thomas Jefferson, and James Madison broke bread and made peace, albeit temporarily. Washington's continuing worry and visionary peacemaking suggest that he may have played a more active role in brokering the compromise than we know, although he was ill at the time. It would have been far more characteristic for him to have engaged in bridge-building efforts, however discreet, than to sit paralyzed without trying to help.

In December 1790, Hamilton's proposal for a partially private national bank triggered another factional showdown. Modeled on the Bank of England, Hamilton's Bank of the United States was intended to expand America's money supply and solidify the country's credit. All three leading Virginians—Attorney General Edmund Randolph, Secretary of State Thomas Jefferson, and Congressman James Madison—demanded a presidential veto of the proposed bank legislation. In addition to fearing such a bank's corrupting influence, they insisted that the Constitution did not grant the Congress such broad powers. Hamilton quickly produced a brilliant pamphlet that saved this initiative. Hamilton rejected Jefferson's strict construction of the Constitution, saying that only acts specifically prohibited could be deemed unconstitutional.

Washington played a judicial role in this controversy, hearing out both sides. Even as the goodwill from the summertime compromise faded, the battling insiders felt that their leader had given them a fair hearing. Nevertheless, the bank battle alienated Jefferson and propelled him toward leading the opposition. Washington increasingly felt compelled to warn Americans "against the baneful effects of the Spirit of Party, generally." More specifically, he noted that "the line between the southern and the eastern interests appeared more strongly marked than could have been wished."

During the following two years, political tensions wracked Washington's official family. Jefferson began plotting with Madison against Hamilton. Jefferson would report that he and Hamilton were "daily pitted in the cabinet like two cocks." Both Hamilton and Jefferson sought out a father figure, and Washington, who had no natural children, obliged. Initially, this competition for Washington's affection, and Washington's genius for generating an atmosphere of decorum, restrained both Hamilton and Jefferson. But increasingly the warring representatives of the Revolution's younger generation demanded total loyalty from the old man of the Revolution, who sought the ever-more-elusive middle ground.

Jefferson taunted Washington, warning him about aggressive presidential statements "calculated to make the President assume the station of the head of a party instead of the head of the nation." In fact, Washington was cautious and disciplined. He ignored the attacks publicly, even as they became more personal. But with the Jefferson–Madison axis becoming a consistent opposition, Washington's silence did not save him from criticism. And whenever the president distanced himself from the Hamiltonian line, he risked incurring the wrath of the newspapers that usually supported him.

Politics and polemics exacerbated personal and ideological animosities between the Hamiltonians and the Jefferson-Madison critics. As the opposition coalesced in the Democratic-Republican political party, and as the propagandist Philip Freneau made the *National Gazette* that party's shrill voice, compromise became elusive; goodwill evaporated. A year after his victory with the national bank, Alexander Hamilton issued his "Report on Manufacturers," advocating tariffs for industry and federally funded internal improvements to America's roads and bridges. These initiatives eventually became the guiding tenets of nineteenth-century American industrial development. Swayed by Jefferson this time, Washington rejected the proposals in the report as beyond "the powers of the general government" and "the temper of the times."

Washington occasionally chose not to hear, or acknowledge, various grumblings around him. Recognition often required responsibility, even action, and Washington felt his power was best applied strategically. The president preferred grumbling about the "infamous Papers" disturbing "the peace of the community" to acknowledging his aides' roles in feeding the press wars.

As Washington's first term ended, Secretary of State Jefferson, planning to resign, met with Washington in May 1792 to condemn Hamilton. Jefferson detailed twenty-one objections to Hamilton and his industrial program, denouncing the secretary of the treasury as a corrupt monarchist. The shocked president found the discussions "painful."

Washington scrambled to preserve the social harmony he craved. He interrupted his summer rest at Mount Vernon in 1792 to try making peace. He warned Jefferson that such bickering threatened America's future. Reminding Jefferson that all human opinions were "speculative" and fallible, Washington begged for "more charity for the opinions and acts of one another in Governmental matters." Otherwise, governing would be impossible. Speaking as one farmer to another, the president warned Jefferson that "if, instead of laying our shoulders to the machine after measures are decided on, one pulls this way and another that, before the utility of the thing is fairly tried, it must, inevitably, be torn asunder." Washington hoped "that instead of wounding suspicions, and irritable charges, there may be liberal allowances, mutual forbearances, and temporizing yieldings on *all sides*." The alternative was apocalypse: "Without them . . . the Wheels of Government will clog; our enemies will triumph, and by throwing their weight into the disaffected Scale, may accomplish the ruin of the goodly fabric we have been erecting."

Three days later, Washington lectured Hamilton by mail. The president pointed out that although political differences were inevitable, discussions should not become extremely personal. Washington chided his protégé: "[T]his regret borders on chagrin" when "zealous patriots" with the same general goal treat each other so uncharitably.

Washington was reminding his squabbling subordinates that they shared a similar vision for the country. That bond should lead them to find "a middle course" when, as reasonable but fallible individuals, they disagreed. Sickened by the thought of America's "Providential" union foundering due to bullheaded idiocy, Washington hoped "that balsam may be poured into *all* the wounds," to "prevent them from gangrening" with the resulting "fatal consequences."

Demoralized by the infighting, ever protective of his reputation, feeling weary, and wary of holding too much power for too long, Washington considered retiring after his first term. However, "North & South will hang together" only "if they have you to hang on," Jefferson warned the exhausted president. Washington's unifying role now imprisoned him.

When he contemplated retiring, Washington asked Madison, not Hamilton, to draft a farewell address reminding Americans that "we are *all* children of the same country." Eventually, Washington relented. Once again, it was both personally convenient and politically expedient to stand for reelection but not actively run. Washington's posture of humbly awaiting the people's call did not preclude the occasional public tour. Triumphal presidential visits in 1792, before state legislators chose their state electors, replenished the reservoir of goodwill Americans had for their president and the country. These stylized interactions with the people also boosted the president's morale. Washington's reelection was never in doubt. Doubts, however, were growing about Washington's mastery of the political scene and his administration.

AFTER HIS REELECTION, Washington unwillingly set an unhappy precedent: the nightmarish second term. Subsequently, Woodrow Wilson, Franklin Roosevelt, Richard Nixon, Ronald Reagan, Bill Clinton, and George W. Bush would stumble and lose effectiveness shortly after winning reelection. Washington's curt, 133-word inaugural speech reflected his bleak mood. What he dreaded occurred, as partisan hysterics repudiated him. Washington remained a muscular moderate, but his tenure would prove that the middle path is not always popular or easy.

Foreign policy intrigues exacerbated domestic tensions. On February 1, 1793, France declared war against Great Britain, Spain, and Holland. The Jeffersonian Republicans wanted the United States to fulfill its historic duty and treaty obligations by supporting France. The Hamiltonian Federalists feared the French revolutionaries as crazed anarchists and preferred banking on England's stability, prosperity, and cultural affinities. Hamilton mocked Jefferson's "womanish attachment to France and . . . womanish resentment against Great Britain."

Remaining neutral would require bold leadership. Washington favored the French, swayed by his Revolutionary War experiences and his good friend, the Marquis de Lafayette. But Washington believed that entering the military conflict would be ruinous for America. He also resented the many rogue French agents, most notably the French Minister "Citizen Genet," who tried to recruit Americans to fight the British and Spanish forces. The president therefore sided with Hamilton, keeping the country nonaligned. Reconciling his "public character" with his private character, Washington refrained from "those intemperate expressions in favor of one Nation, or to the prejudice of another." Still, Washington placated Jefferson by avoiding the term "neutrality" in public statements.

By 1793, the Jefferson–Hamilton clash had spread. What began as an ideological and regional clash was now reinforced by rival parties and vicious, battling newspapers. Not a "party man," Washington warned his own supporters against building the Federalist Party around "*Men, not Principles*," which would only invite chaos. He sought "sensible men" who could resist popular whims, statesmen whose courage and moderation could be "a rallying point for the timid, and an attraction of the wavering." Although disappointed by the partisan warfare, Washington trusted that Americans' more compromising and pragmatic national character would result in a tranquil union, unlike "the restless, ambitious, and Intriguing spirit" of the French.

Washington deployed Hamilton as a conciliator, hoping his subordinates would live up to the roles he cast for them. As the debate over supporting England or France flared up yet again in 1793, Washington instructed Hamilton to write a response to a series of resolutions drafted at a public meeting and presented to the president that would "in your opinion, make it palatable to all sides, or unexceptional."

These appeals to men's better natures sometimes showed Washington to be surprisingly naïve. When Jefferson finally left the cabinet at the end of 1793, Washington did not purge Jefferson's party comrades, despite their persistent attacks on the administration. The president sought to replace Jefferson with Jefferson's friend, and Hamilton's now-bitter rival, James Madison. Jefferson claimed he wanted to return to farming and writing. Washington believed him. Hamilton doubted Jefferson's motives, blaming the wily Jefferson for "all the abuse" heaped on Washington and his administration. Hamilton also predicted that the ambitious Jefferson would plunge further into politics and eventually run for president. Years later, according to Alexander Hamilton's son, John Hamilton, Washington bitterly acknowledged Hamilton's accurate "prophecy," saying that "not a day has elapsed since my retirement from public life in which I have not thought of that conversation."

Although unsuccessful in managing his restive subordinates, Washington squelched a genuine insurrection by firmly following the middle path. Frontiersmen in western Pennsylvania and elsewhere resented the high liquor taxes imposed by the federal government to repay the Revolutionary

War debt. During the Whiskey Rebellion in 1794, five hundred people attacked a federal tax collector. A mob of six thousand threatened to torch
Pittsburgh. Hamilton demanded that the president react strongly and crush
the rebels. Washington carefully gave the rebels a reasonable deadline. He
convened a three-man commission to mediate and offered fair solutions.
Meanwhile, he prepared for armed conflict as a last resort, calling for volunteer soldiers.

Washington was resolute but generous in quashing the rebellion. Five
times as many men as he needed answered his call. He headed a 13,000-man
army in a show of national force, but kept them tightly leashed, preventing
gratuitous violence. When the rebels failed to fight, Washington offered a
generous amnesty program. The result was a resounding victory for the
young democracy, the rule of law, and Washington's administration.

UNFORTUNATELY FOR WASHINGTON, his moderate approach in foreign policy frustrated Federalists and infuriated Republicans. Washington
knew that Hamilton was too controversial to manage America's delicate relations with England. But the Jeffersonians were too hostile. Therefore, in the
spring of 1794 Washington dispatched Chief Justice John Jay as special envoy
to Great Britain. Washington balanced Jay's federalism by changing America's representation in Paris, sending the Republican Madison–Jefferson ally,
James Monroe, to replace the Federalist Gouverneur Morris. The British foreign minister, Lord Grenville, noticed Washington's mixed message and
feared a growing French bias among the former colonists, which may have
encouraged him to help Jay return home with a treaty.

Half a year of secret negotiations resulted in Jay's Treaty, signed on November 19, 1794. The British agreed to withdraw from their garrisons in
America's Northwest. In return, Britain received generous trade concessions; a process for collecting pre–Revolutionary War debts; and America's
acquiescence on other critical issues, including the British Navy's nasty
habit of impressing (forcibly drafting) American sailors. Perhaps the most
controversial provision allowed American ships into the West Indies but
imposed an unrealistic seventy-ton weight limit on freight and banned a
broader trade in cotton, sugar, molasses, and other staples.

Washington wrote in 1795 to Hamilton, who was now back in private
life, that he had no interest in hearing partisans' predictable grievances.
Washington wanted "to learn from dispassionate men" weighing each treaty

provision, delineating pros and cons. This way, the president and the nation could determine "ultimately, on which side the balance is to be found."

Unfortunately, by the end of July 1795, Jay said he could traverse the Eastern seaboard navigating by the light of his own burning effigies. As protestors also denounced Washington in the streets, members of the House of Representatives tried muscling into foreign policy, demanding to see all the correspondence connected to Jay's mission. Aware of the diplomatic and political minuet he had to dance, Washington offered "a just and temperate communication of my idea to the community at large [. . .] guarded so as not to add fuel to passions prepared to blaze," and crafted to avoid riling the European powers. But he refused to undermine his presidential authority or the constitutional process, which gave the Senate, not the House, the power to approve treaties. Washington defied the House and barely secured the Senate's approval.

The treaty eventually benefited the United States, as did Washington's decision to avoid war. But the Jay Treaty controversy unleashed a flood of invective against Washington. This time, seeking the golden mean amid the chaos of British contempt, French persistence, and American passion earned Washington few friends and many enemies.

Writing to Jefferson in July 1796, as his bitter second term ended, Washington uncharacteristically vented his feelings. He resented how parties were undermining his attempt to establish America's "national character." The attacks were on such "exaggerated and indecent terms as could scarcely be applied to a Nero; a notorious defaulter; or even to a common pickpocket." Filled with self-pity but ashamed of his candor—or perhaps trying to make the partisan Jefferson feel guilty—Washington ended by apologizing for indulging his feelings.

Washington's position was difficult to sell because it was difficult to maintain. The French and English were constantly manipulating American citizens and provoking the president. Washington's caution in foreign affairs stemmed from his characteristic moderation and his sense that America lacked the commercial strength and military might for sustained conflict. However, then as now, Americans did not like hearing about the limits of their power. This frustration was compounded by the historic fears of executive dictatorship that had triggered the Revolution. With clever partisans and what Washington called "infamous scribblers" in that "dark age" of partisan journalism fanning the flames, it is not surprising that Washington's moderation was targeted.

BY RETIRING AFTER TWO TERMS, Washington gave the great gift of
sensible centrism to the American people. Washington also taught presidents how to exercise power vigorously but within limits, as he did during
the Whiskey Rebellion and throughout his tenure. His retirement contradicted the accusations that he was a dictator, allowing Americans to sing
his praises once again. His vice president and successor, John Adams, both
jealous and critical, called Washington "the best actor of presidency we
have ever had."

John Adams, inheriting the administration's mess in 1796, lacked Washington's resumé and panache. Jay's Treaty inflamed the French, making
them more aggressive in disrupting American shipping and manipulating
American politics. The result was a quasi-war with France and a veritable
civil war at home, as pro-English Federalists demanded full-scale war with
France. Jefferson, playing the Jacobin cheerleader despite being vice president under Adams, endorsed the French Revolution's bloody Reign of Terror. "Rather than it should have failed," he had written in 1793 of the
French Revolution, "I would have seen half the earth desolated. Were
there but an Adam & an Eve left in every country, & left free, it would be
better than as it is now."

Others, writing in the press and holding forth in the streets, were equally
intemperate, resulting in American history's first backlash against civil liberties, the Alien and Sedition Acts of 1798. In what would become a recur-
ring historical pattern, these attempts to criminalize dissent and ban
foreign radicals triggered their own counterattack. Jefferson and Madison
arranged for resolutions in Kentucky and Virginia to oppose the acts while
affirming both civil rights and states' rights, foreshadowing the great issues
of the nineteenth and twentieth centuries.

Trying to preside amid this bedlam, Adams zigzagged. Sometimes he governed with a heavy hand, infuriating Republicans by signing the Alien and
Sedition Acts, and raising taxes to support a strengthened army. The resulting controversies cemented his historic reputation as a rigid autocrat.

Yet ultimately, Adams followed Washington's path of taking the considered
action if not always the most popular one. When he negotiated an end to the
quasi-war with France, Adams split his own Federalist Party between moderates, who supported him, and Hamiltonian High Federalists, who feared that
making peace with the French meant abandoning the British. It was left for
Adams—quite alone—to praise his own initiative as "the most disinterested,
most determined and most successful of my whole life." Apparently few voters

agreed with him about the "success"; Adams lost his bid for reelection. Historians generally consider him a presidential failure.

Washington's example continued to both enlighten and constrain his successors, who learned from him how to preside over the entire nation. After John Adams's tumultuous term, Thomas Jefferson's inauguration as the third president in 1801 marked the first time under the Constitution that the opposition party took power. In the spirit of Washington, Jefferson's administration began with everyone rejoicing about what did not happen; there was no chaos, no bloodshed. The transition was smooth, peaceful, and democratic.

Hoping to return to first principles, Jefferson took an important, Washingtonian step back toward the center. Now that he was president, the partisan feared partisanship. Every "difference of opinion is not a difference of principle," the new president preached in his first inaugural address. Despite our different labels, we are all brothers, he insisted: "We are all republicans—we are all federalists." Jefferson said that those rejecting union or American republicanism would stand as proof of the folly that freedom tolerates so that reason can triumph.

Jefferson ended his address by echoing Washington's enlightened understanding that human imperfection leads to conflict, and invoking the revered first president as a model. Ignoring his own role in sullying the great man's reputation, Jefferson recalled Washington's disappointment at being attacked so mercilessly. Now praising Washington, Jefferson vowed to do "all the good in my power, and to be instrumental to the happiness & freedom of all."

Washington's vision held. The general welfare, the common cause, the greater good, the search for Washington's holy trinity of "liberal allowances, mutual forbearances, and temporizing yieldings on *all sides*," would continue to pull America's most effective leaders toward the center. And as the lapsed partisan Thomas Jefferson demonstrated in 1801, George Washington would remain the leadership gold standard, an example of principled moderation, nonpartisan patriotism, and even the occasional strategic deafness that his successors would frequently invoke and seek to follow.

Although Washington failed to eliminate parties, America's first president nevertheless set an important standard of effective leadership. No future presidents would have his stature. Only in the twentieth century would presidents again dominate the nation's political culture to such an extent. Still, Washington's way continues to resonate, showing that Americans need to work together and how a leader can be center seeking rather than conflict generating.

2

COMPROMISERS, ZEALOTS, AND CIPHERS

The Blessing of Parties, the Challenge of Slavery, and the Failure of Presidents

TWO CONTRASTING IMAGES illustrate the new republic's political history. The first is from April 30, 1789, when a visibly humbled George Washington delivered the country's first inaugural address in lower Manhattan's Federal Hall. The tall Virginian's appearance in New York symbolized the hopes that a cooperative spirit would unite the two largest states, and the people of these newly united states. The great man's humility moved the crowd. Many rejoiced that they had witnessed virtue personified, with individual and national greatness reinforcing one another.

Thirty years later, in February 1819, America's symphony of states was more frequently discordant than harmonious. Congressman James Tallmadge proposed two conditions for accepting the Missouri territory into the union. The New Yorker suggested banning new slaves and freeing all slaves born into the new state once they turned twenty-five. Furious Southerners threatened to secede from the union. Tallmadge snapped, "if a dissolution of the Union must take place, let it be so!" One traumatized New Hampshire lawmaker prayed "that a similar discussion will never again take place in our walls." Months later, after the combatants had compromised, this "fire bell in the night" still upset Thomas Jefferson. He feared his "generation of 1776" had made "a useless sacrifice." The succeeding generation's "unwise and unworthy passions" threatened Americans' self-government.

Three decades into the American constitutional experiment, the Founders could take great pride in many accomplishments, some expected, others surprising. The Revolution's spirit continued, with a powerful Congress restraining the presidency. Despite the Framers' initial opposition to parties, they had emerged as essential ballasts, channeling conflict and frequently facilitating compromise. And despite the Founders' elitism, they had constructed the world's first mass-based popular democracy.

Yet Thomas Jefferson's fears in 1819 were reasonable. Conflict over slavery already threatened the American union. America's widespread injustice against millions of kidnapped Africans and their descendants mocked the country's defining ideals. The broad coalition parties, so effective in building America in so many ways, failed to meet their largest challenge: They could not solve the slavery puzzle, wherein Southerners used their right to liberty to deprive blacks of their right to equality. The passive presidents that these parties produced were equally ineffectual.

More than any other issue in American history, the question of slavery seemed to pose a simple, up or down choice between moral reform and an immoral system. Today, in hindsight, fanatical abolitionists appear to be the heroes against the fanatical Southern "fire-eaters" and their more moderate, or apathetic fellow citizens, both North and South. A closer examination reveals, however, that ignoring Washington's way nearly destroyed America. Lackadaisical presidential leadership fueled the sectional tensions and eventually ignited a civil war.

History teaches that the world we know had to be invented. No matter how natural today's realities or yesterday's events appear, specific historical forces produced them. While nature's laws are constant, historical conditions are constantly changing, often yielding surprises. One of American politics' defining institutions, the two-party system, is doubly strange. Enduring political parties defied the Founders' fears of perpetual factionalism, while the big-tent parties that developed were more inclusive and pragmatic than their European equivalents. That even these parties failed to manage the slavery debate shows just how volatile politics had become by the mid-1800s.

Nineteenth-century Americans believed the two-party system had grown naturally, spawned by freedom of speech. Historians subsequently added elaborate ideological, economic, cultural, and political explanations for the system's

development. Yet the two-party system reflected the unintended consequences of the Founders' designs. Winner-take-all elections resulted in one
party in power and an opposition party, both seeking broad coalitions with
popular messages. Minority parties, attracting votes but not victories, gained
no political power; no proportional pieces of the pie were fed to these more
peripheral groups. By getting 100 percent of the power even with less than 50
percent of the vote, the permanent factions that George Washington
abhorred actually stabilized and moderated American politics. The winner-
take-all system created broad, nonideological parties that regularly tempered
passions, mediated differences, and maintained civility.

Fortunately, George Washington's disapproval did not stop parties from
developing. The regional alliances that emerged during his administration
channeled conflict. The Federalist Party of Alexander Hamilton and John
Adams gradually dissolved after 1802, leading to a two-decade "Era of Good
Feelings," with one Jeffersonian Democratic-Republican party dominating.
This initial system accustomed Americans to the idea of parties and the reality of two stable factions, always competing. "I consider the party division of
whig & tory the most wholesome which can exist in any government, and
well worthy of being nourished, to keep out those of a more dangerous character," former president Thomas Jefferson wrote in 1822, showing an American tendency to read intelligent design into improvised realities.

America's two-party system truly emerged with the 1820s' democratic
revolution, often called the Jacksonian revolution. Andrew Jackson symbolized the changes but did not cause or embody them all. The Industrial
Revolution that was transforming America's economy and society resonated with the political revolution transforming America's politics and
society. These changes made the parties more democratic, mobilizing millions of voters. Barely 350,000 people voted in 1824, out of a population of
10 million. Nearly 1.2 million voted four years later, and that number doubled by 1840, out of a population by then of 17 million. Organized and mobilized, white American men felt invested in the society and engaged in
politics, minimizing the alienation Europeans were experiencing as deafen-
ing, dirty, dehumanizing, factories spread.

America's leaders already understood by the 1820s that the growing regional polarization regarding slavery threatened the nation's future. The
North–South alliance within Jackson's Democratic Party rested on a fragile
interregional peace. The democratic nationalism that Jackson forged was
an attempt to squelch the sectionalism he feared.

Andrew Jackson harnessed the growing force of public opinion to expand the presidency. A craggy-faced former general with a distinguished,
untamed mane of white hair, Jackson parlayed his 1814 Battle of New Orleans triumph into a presidential victory fourteen years later. Bringing his
national fame to the White House, Jackson unleashed the presidency's popular power. He appreciated how the president's dual roles as king and prime
minister reinforced each other. His classic proclamation during the fight
over maintaining the Second Bank of the United States in 1832, "The
bank . . . is trying to kill me but I will kill it," shows how Jackson took presidential power personally. For Jackson, that power resided in his ability to
command people's attention, earn popular affection, and enact his policies.

Jackson's revolution revived revolutionary-era fears of popular dictators.
Traditionalists vainly fought the spread of white male suffrage. Critics of
"King Andrew's" expansion of presidential prerogative established the
Whig Party, hoping to restore America's political equilibrium.

Democracies were more volatile than the Founders' gentlemanly pow-
dered-wig and white-breeches politics. American politicians increasingly
favored florid oratory, shrill editorial rhetoric, and killer campaign mudslinging, all reflecting the young country's robust, unfiltered, democratic vitality. During the 1828 presidential campaign, even as Jackson's supporters
had hailed the "ardor of thousands" redeeming the nation, Jackson's opponents claimed his wife was a bigamist and accused him of murdering six
young soldiers who had deserted. Jackson was strong enough and popular
enough to dismiss these extreme attacks when campaigning and governing;
his successors would miss having such might.

Unlike Washington, Jackson loved a good fight. Like Washington, Jackson knew how to make strategic concessions to maintain national unity
while proclaiming victory. As Jackson's first term ended, Southern farmers'
opposition to higher tariff rates triggered South Carolina's "Ordinance of
Nullification," rejecting the national tariffs of 1828 and 1832. Governor
James Hamilton Jr. sought 12,000 volunteer soldiers to reinforce the state's
threat. Jackson responded nimbly. In his annual message to Congress on
December 4, 1832, Jackson appeased the rebels. Encouraging "moderation
and good sense," he offered to lower the tariff.

Six days later, Jackson counterpunched. He claimed that the organic nation once known as "the *United Colonies of America*" predated the individual
states or the Constitution. The Constitution "forms a *government,* not a
league," Jackson insisted, repudiating Southerners' states' rights claims.

Jackson's cautious Northern ally, Martin Van Buren, wanted to avoid the constitutional argument. Jackson characteristically replied, "No my friend, the crisis must be now met with firmness, our citizens protected and the modern doctrine of nullification and secession put down forever." A month later, Jackson backed up his theorizing with brute force. He proposed congressional legislation authorizing military intervention to enforce revenue laws; at the same time the talented legislator Henry Clay crafted a compromise tariff bill. Both bills snaked through Congress. South Carolina rescinded its tariff nullification, but then nullified the "Force Bill" as the federal military threat vanished. With the tariff lowered, Southerners claimed victory, even as Jackson proclaimed, "I have had a laborious task here, but nullification is dead."

Andrew Jackson set crucial precedents for presidential leadership that his immediate successors ignored. He helped the parties appreciate and tap into democracy's people power. Yet most party leaders preferred their presidents to be seen and not heard. Parties sought pliable candidates who would defer to the party establishment and avoid any controversy. Chosen for only one ability—"electability"—Jackson's successors deferred to Congress and accepted the job description as "chief magistrate."

After Jackson retired in 1837, the party system became ever more popular, judging by the number of voters, the intensity of campaigning, and the stridency of the rhetoric. Politicking became the national pastime, engaging the masses with entertainment and statesmanship. By 1860, nearly 5 million people voted in a country of 31 million, with 387 daily newspapers and an average daily circulation approaching 1.5 million. But democracy was dyspeptic. Then as now, the press and the politicians played to the extremes, amplifying the angry voices and silencing the complacent majority in the middle. But then, unlike now, the president lacked the stature to transcend the polarizing politics. A march of mediocre presidents from 1837 to 1861 resulted. None of the eight presidents up until the Civil War would approach Jackson's popularity or impact. They occupied an office with limited power, leaving the nation vulnerable as secessionist tensions increased.

SLAVERY WAS AMERICA'S BIRTH DEFECT, always present; sometimes debated intensely, sometimes politely ignored. White Americans felt united by the Revolution, the Constitution, liberty, democracy, English, and a belief in America's Manifest Destiny to spread from the Atlantic to the Pacific Ocean. Although a growing network of roads, canals, railways, and telegraph wires bound Americans closer together, whenever a slavery-related controversy flared, the country seemed cobbled together by a handful of hasty compromises.

The Constitution symbolized America's compromising spirit; Washington D.C., represented the Washington administration's accommodation. Even during the "Era of Good Feelings," with President James Monroe burying the Federalist Party, claiming Americans constituted "one great family with a common interest," the cycle of conflict and compromise intensified. Speaker of the House Henry Clay worked his magic as America's Great Compromiser. His 1820 Missouri Compromise banned slavery north of the 36'30 line, except for Missouri, which entered as a slave state, balanced by Maine's entry as a free state.

Over the next thirty years, Henry Clay helped hold the Union together. He designed the 1833 tariff reduction, helping Jackson end the nullification crisis. After Jackson, Clay partially filled the leadership vacuum left by the succeeding low-profile presidents. An American nationalist, the tall, thin, sensitive Kentuckian was also an exuberant gambler with an outsized ego, happy to save the republic frequently and flamboyantly. The need for all these great compromises and compromisers proved the system's great strengths and weaknesses. The slavery issue became the wedge prying apart America's central institutions and nationalizing spirit.

An unspoken deal infused America's compromising spirit. Enough Northerners accepted slavery without moral judgments, and enough Southerners felt ashamed of their "peculiar institution," for the system to function. Enslaving fellow human beings embarrassed George Washington, who freed his slaves in his will. Thomas Jefferson attempted to free all the slaves when he drafted the Declaration of Independence. Northern opponents expected that the constitutional ban on the slave trade after 1807 would doom slavery eventually. However, slavery actually gained force in the Deep South.

By the 1830s, apologists were rising in the South as abolitionists arose in the North. In the lower South, the plantation economy boomed. "Cotton capitalism" boosted Southern confidence and self-righteousness. Rather than viewing slavery as only a necessary evil, the leading Southern legislator, John C. Calhoun, had declared slavery "a positive good" in 1829, "the most safe and stable basis for free institutions in the world." Some Southern thinkers abandoned America's fundamental belief in natural rights inhering in all, defining rights narrowly as "what society acknowledges and sanctions . . . nothing else."

Meanwhile, in the North economic progress and the spread of liberty made slavery first impractical, then unacceptable. By 1849, only five of the original thirteen colonies remained slaveholding—Virginia, Maryland, South Carolina, North Carolina, and Georgia. With more railroads, roads, telegraph wires, newspapers, magazines, and novels connecting the North and South, Northerners became more conscious of Southern slavery. A greater national feeling made Northerners feel complicit in the moral crime. The upper class's reforming spirit and the spread of democracy compelled more people to act.

William Lloyd Garrison epitomized the enraged abolitionist. "On this subject, I do not wish to think, or to speak, or write, with moderation," Garrison thundered on January 1, 1831, launching his paper, *The Liberator*. "No! no! Tell a man whose house is on fire to give a moderate alarm; tell him to moderately rescue his wife from the hands of the ravisher." Most Southerners feared that Garrison's minority views represented the North as a whole.

Abolitionism's Northern critics worried that Newton's third law applied to politics: for every action there was an equal and opposite reaction. A young Whig politician from Illinois, Abraham Lincoln, agreed that slavery was "an unqualified evil to the negro, the white man, and the state." But he warned that spreading "abolition doctrines tends rather to increase than to abate its evils" by galvanizing Southerners to defend slavery. After the Nat Turner slave rebellion in 1831, terrified Southerners defended slavery more aggressively. Regional pride came into play. "Death is preferable to acknowledged inferiority," said one Southern zealot. The rhetoric on both sides sizzled as the issue continued unresolved.

Then, in a good news, bad news scenario, America expanded. After the Mexican–American War ended in 1848, the United States acquired much of today's Southwest, including California. Abolitionists and "Free Soilers" vowed to keep any new states formed from the new territory free. "Everything has taken a Southern shape and been controlled by Southern caprice for years," Connecticut's Gideon Welles complained, demanding that Congress contain the further spread of slavery. Southerners feared losing political power and moral standing if Northerners welcomed non-slaveholding Western states to the Union.

Reflecting the growing schism, in 1848, the Free Soil party nominated former President Martin Van Buren for president. In Jackson's day, the slippery Van Buren epitomized the Jacksonian Democrats' North–South alliance, sustained by mutually beneficial compromises. Now Van Buren emerged as an antislavery crusader. Atoning for years of rationalizing Southern villainy, the former president proclaimed slavery contrary to "the principles of the Revolution" and subject to congressional limitation. The Free Soilers won no electoral votes but attracted 14 percent of the popular vote, reflecting abolitionism's increasing popularity in the North. Straining to maintain their fragile coalitions, the major parties sought candidates who could calm both sides. Denouncing Van Buren as "the Judas Iscariot of the nineteenth century," the Democrats nominated Lewis Cass. This Jacksonian former general from Michigan was a "Doughface," a flexible Northerner with Southern principles. The Whig nominee, and ultimate winner, the Mexican–American War hero General Zachary Taylor, was a pro-Union Southern slaveholder. National parties were splintering, especially the Whigs. Zachary Taylor would be the last Whig elected president. By 1856 the party had vanished.

As Taylor entered the White House, the country drifted into crisis. California and New Mexico demanded statehood as free states. The divided House of Representatives voted in sixty-two rounds before choosing a Speaker of the House. Meanwhile, nine Southern legislatures sent delegates to a Nashville convention that considered revolutionary defenses of Southern rights.

President Taylor carefully followed the party script. He invoked George Washington's name when pleading for unity but defined his job as enforcement and implementation. Taylor deferred to Congress for policy making. Dodging conflict, appalled by congressional firebrands, he encouraged the citizens in the previously Mexican territories to organize themselves for statehood and decide themselves about slavery. Southerners cursed Taylor as a traitor for accepting the possibility that two free states would join the union.

Henry Clay tried crafting one more compromise. With the range of a Hudson River School artist painting a landscape, with the precision of George Washington surveying property, Clay introduced a series of compromise bills. A legendary flurry of arm-twisting, bribing, speechifying, and shouting ensued. Friendships crumbled. Mississippi's Senator Henry Foote supported Clay and lambasted Missouri's Senator Thomas Hart Benton for refusing to back the legislation. After Foote abused him for weeks, Benton started shouting. Foote drew a pistol. "Let the assassin fire!" Benton yelled, tearing open his vest.

A straight-shooting general uncomfortable with politicians' wiles, President Taylor proved stubborn and naïve. Holding out for his own approach, he rejected Clay's compromise, angering both Southerners and Northerners. Meanwhile, the Texas militia threatened to invade neighboring New Mexico over a boundary dispute. Taylor sought to reinforce the federal troops. Southerners threatened to join the Texans and impeach Taylor if fighting began. Amid all this tension, in July 1850, Taylor suddenly died of a stomach ailment.

Taylor had marginalized Vice President Millard Fillmore, along with many Whig regulars. Inheriting the presidency, Fillmore fired the entire cabinet and backed Clay's compromise. A Whig loyalist, the stolid new president from Buffalo, New York, naturally deferred to Clay, the more established Whig.

The Compromise of 1850 admitted California as a free state. Two other bills passed the same day organized the rest of the territory into New Mexico and Utah, without restrictions on slavery. One of the bills also settled the Texas–New Mexico boundary dispute. A fourth bill enacted a strict Fugitive Slave Law, requiring federal officers to capture escaped slaves up North. And a fifth bill prohibited the slave trade but not slavery in Washington, D.C.

Crowds hailed the heroes of compromise. Fillmore saluted this "final settlement" of all sectional disputes. Senator Lewis Cass of Michigan proclaimed the regional issue dead: "I do not believe any party could now be built up in relation to this question of slavery. I think the question is settled in the public mind."

The euphoria and apparent peace vanished quickly. This compromise was not much of a compromise—or too much of one. No one was satisfied. Henry Clay's nationalist attempt to craft one omnibus package had failed, rejected in the summer of 1850 shortly after Taylor died. The legislation eventually passed because the young Democratic senator from Illinois, Stephen A. Douglas, organized shifting congressional coalitions that reflected sectional differences, not national concerns. Southerners supported the individual planks that pleased them, just as Northern representatives endorsed the pro-Northern legislation. The misnamed Compromise of 1850 failed to find common ground, the essential element of compromise. This was no Washingtonian vision; it was a prelude to disaster.

A *Harper's Weekly* caricature depicting the events of April 17, 1850, when, during the heated debate over admitting California as a free state, Mississippi senator Henry S. Foote drew a pistol on Thomas Hart Benton of Missouri. (Library of Congress)

The compromisers had bowed to sectional differences to pass the legislation. The compromise package granted federal approval to actions that both sides abhorred. Southerners fumed that they risked losing their God-given and revolution-sanctioned property rights if they traveled with slaves to California. Similarly, the legislation compelled Northern cooperation in arresting runaways, making Northerners feel that rather than just tolerating an evil in a neighboring region, they now were forced to help commit the crime at home. After federal troops returned one escaped slave from Boston to his master in Virginia, the textile tycoon Amos A. Lawrence recalled, "we went to bed one night old fashioned conservative, Compromise Union Whigs & waked up stark mad Abolitionists." President Fillmore saw the slavery issue as a political challenge to national unity. He ignored the growing moral outrage. By 1852 Fillmore had lost the Whig nomination, as his party fragmented over the compromise fallout and soon disbanded.

With the abrupt transition from the hapless Zachary Taylor to the colorless Millard Fillmore, the presidency seemed rudderless. Legislators can only do so much. At their best, lawmakers excel at balancing competing interests, distributing goodies, and mollifying each side. But when America

Engraving celebrating the Washingtonian statesmen at the helm after the Compromise of 1850. Henry Clay is seated at center. (Library of Congress)

needed leadership, when Americans needed to move together in one direction, the large shoes of George Washington and Andrew Jackson remained unfilled.

WITHOUT A VIGOROUS, forward-looking center seeker leading the country, it seemed more difficult to imagine a middle path. Demagogues on both sides inflamed popular passions. Northerners talked of the Slave Power, the Slaveocracy, the slave oligarchy. Southerners complained about Northern political control, economic domination, and condescension. In defending their slave-based civilization ever more aggressively, Southerners caricatured Northern society ever more cruelly. "Free society! We sicken at the name," a Georgia newspaper snarled in 1856. "What is it but a conglomeration of greasy mechanics, filthy operatives, small-fisted farmers, and moon-struck theorists," with no "gentlemen" to be found among them.

In the 1850s Americans began to view the struggle as an "irrepressible conflict," in the antislavery activist William Seward's phrase, "them" or us.

One proslavery Kansas editor daydreamed about killing an abolitionist: "If I can't kill a man, I'll kill a woman; and if I can't kill a woman, I'll kill a child!" Southerners began envisioning a Confederacy that would be the world's greatest republic, fulfilling revolutionary ideals while civilizing slaves along Christian principles. Abolitionists rejoiced that "every five minutes gave birth to a black baby," its infant wail heralding the voice that would "yet shout the war cry of insurrection; its baby hand would one day hold the dagger which should reach the master's heart." Other abolitionists blasted their sniveling, compromising Northern neighbors who refused to join their crusade.

The slavery issue proved toxic. National institutions that once unified the country became consumed by the issue and collapsed. The Methodists and the Baptists split in the 1840s. The Whig Party dissolved, and the Democrats lost their national majority, with an anti-Democratic majority emerging in the North. As the Whig Party disappeared, an antislavery Republican party emerged. The backlash against the Supreme Court's decision in the *Dred Scott* case in 1857, denying slaves freedom and blacks citizenship even in the North, was so intense, it diminished the court's courage and impact for decades. By the 1850s the Southern fire-eaters' prophecies that the Free Soilers wished to abolish slavery everywhere, not just in new territories, had become self-fulfilling. Absolutist abolitionism converged with the more pragmatic strain of political antislavery sentiment, motivated by fear of the Slave Power.

LIKE A TEENAGER whose physical growth outpaces his moral development and impulse control, American democracy generated great passion without good judgment. Moderates became silent and commonsense could not prevail. The Kansas–Nebraska struggle reflected the issue's explosive and increasingly irrational nature. Few slaves would till the rocky, arid soil of Kansas and Nebraska profitably, minimizing the threat to the North or the benefit to the South. But by the mid-1850s, practical realities were largely ignored. Southerners demanded free access to the territories, with their slaves. This breached the Missouri Compromise line, a political improvisation Northerners now elevated into a "sacred compact."

Early in 1854, anxious to organize the Kansas–Nebraska territory, Senator Stephen Douglas proposed repealing the Missouri Compromise and allowing slavery north of the line consecrated in 1820. Elected as an undistinguished compromise candidate from New Hampshire, far too partial to alcohol, President Franklin Pierce characteristically first tried dodging the issue by forwarding it to the Supreme Court. But Douglas, Secretary of War Jefferson Davis, and four leading Southern senators who lived together at the "F Street Mess" burst into the White House on Sunday, January 22. The president was startled. He did not conduct business on the sabbath. Douglas and the others insisted that if Pierce did not endorse the repeal, the Democratic Party would lose the South. Pierce allowed his Democratic allies to intimidate him. The resulting legislation infuriated Northern Democrats and Whigs. Maine's Whig Senator William Pitt Fessenden spoke for many when he said, "The more I look at it the more enraged I become. It needs but little to make me an out & out abolitionist."

The rhetorical and legislative battle turned violent, with guerrilla warfare erupting in Kansas and Nebraska. The shock of "Bleeding Kansas" was compounded in 1856 by the caning of Senator Charles Sumner in the Senate chamber by Southern Congressman Preston Brooks. The fury of Brooks' assault snapped his gutta-percha cane on Sumner's head. It took Brooks about one minute to flog Sumner; it took Sumner four years to recover, and the Union even longer.

Brooks became a hero to Southerners, outraging Northerners. "Hit him again," Southerners yelled, sending Brooks hundreds of new canes, some of sturdier hickory. Northerners muttered about how "low" a civilization the South had become. Motivated, finally, to get involved, America's great advocate of the "middle measure," Ralph Waldo Emerson, could not "see how a barbarous community and a civilized community can constitute one state. I think we must get rid of slavery, or we must get rid of freedom."

As Northerners denounced Southern barbarism, on May 24, 1856, two days after the caning, John Brown led a band of zealots into an area near Pottawatomie Creek, Kansas. Brown split open the skulls of five proslavery settlers with razor-sharp broadswords. Now the South could denounce Northern barbarism. Three years later, the fiery Brown, whose wild hair, long beard, and religious piety gave him the aura of a biblical prophet—or madman—raided the federal armory at Harper's Ferry, Virginia. Brown was caught and hanged. He became a martyr to the North, the true face of abolitionism to the South, and an embarrassment to moderate antislavery Republicans. John Brown confirmed Southern moderates' longstanding lament that "the fanatics at the North have taken the most effective means not to leave a single friend of emancipation in the Southern states."

Terrified, Southerners suppressed any dissent even more rigorously. Southern attempts to ban Northern newspapers intensified. Southern denunciations of Yankee capitalism and self-righteousness became even more hysterical. By 1860, J. D. B. De Bow's pamphlet, *The Interest in Slavery of the Southern Non-Slaveholder,* explained the aristocratic slaveowners' broad regional support. The nonslaveholding Southerners feared social and economic competition from freed blacks. In a twisted salute to the American dream, the poor aspired to own their own slaves.

John Brown's violence overshadowed the 1856 presidential election, which featured the new antislavery Republican Party's first serious presidential campaign. The winner in 1856, Democrat James Buchanan of Pennsylvania, beautifully suited the mid-nineteenth-century party system. This meant that he was most unsuited to the task facing him and his country.

A former congressman, senator, ambassador, and secretary of state under James Knox Polk, Buchanan was the Democratic Party's ideal candidate, a Northerner sympathetic to Southern slaveholders and hostile to abolitionists. Like Pierce, he lacked convictions. Buchanan caved in to the Southern demand to support the nonrepresentative Lecompton state constitution guaranteeing slavery in Kansas. Unlike Pierce, Buchanan was a hot-tempered mediocrity. Senator Stephen Douglas warned the president that devious proslavery legislators had manipulated the convention in Lecompton, Kansas. Buchanan foolishly threatened his fellow Democrat, and essential ally. "Mr. Douglas, I desire you to remember that no Democrat ever differed from an administration of his own choice without being crushed," Buchanan snapped. Buchanan reminded Douglas that Andrew Jackson as president had humbled two dissident Democratic senators. Douglas replied, "Mr. President, I wish you to remember that Gen. Jackson is dead, sir."

Ultimately, the senator defeated the president. After fierce partisan and sectional combat, Buchanan failed to push through the Lecompton constitution. The loss humiliated the president and divided the Democratic Party, dooming the Democrats in the next election and for much of the next half-century. During the excruciating four-month interregnum after Abraham Lincoln's election in November 1860, as Southerners agitated for secession, the incumbent president languished. Despised by Northerners for his antagonistic stances, scorned by Southerners for his impotence, Buchanan symbolized the massive presidential failure building up to Civil War. "If you are as happy in entering the White

House as I shall feel on returning [home] to Wheatland," Buchanan told his successor on inauguration day, "you are a happy man indeed."

"LIBERTY AND SLAVERY—Civilization and barbarism are *absolute* antagonisms. One or the other must perish on this Continent," Abraham Lincoln's law partner, William Herndon, wrote to Senator Charles Sumner shortly after Lincoln's election in 1860. "Compromise—Compromise! Why I am sick at the very idea. Fools may compromise and reason that all *is* peace; but those who have read human history—those that know human nature . . . know that Compromises aggravate *in the end* all our difficulties." Herndon captured both Northerners' and Southerners' emerging frustration with compromise as futile. By the time the fighting began only a few months later, decades of tension gave it an air of inevitability.

The upcoming bloodbath between the North and South appeared unavoidable and justifiable. And compromising over slavery seemed not only unwise but unnatural. "The gigantic crime of human slavery in America may, in the providence of a righteous God, be waiting for a bloody baptism, that shall wash it out forever," the Concord, New Hampshire *Independent Democrat* editorialized in January 1861, just before the conflict began. Eighty-eight years later, in 1949, applying the lessons of the fight against Nazism, the great American historian Arthur M. Schlesinger Jr. wrote, "The unhappy fact is that man occasionally works himself into a log-jam; and that the log-jam must be burst by violence. We know that well enough from the experience of the last decade." Today, historical fashions treat John Brown's fanaticism as holy and humane rather than criminal and counterproductive.

Just because the Civil War was justifiable does not mean it was inevitable. Just because John Brown was on the right side of the argument does not justify his slaughtering innocent civilians. Many other countries' regional tensions did not degenerate into bloodshed, just as other countries eliminated slavery legally and gradually, rather than abruptly and violently. It is possible to appreciate how many things had to go wrong without questioning whether Lincoln and the abolitionists ultimately were right.

Moral outrage against slavery should not blind us to the costly violence that resulted and might have been avoided: 620,000 Americans died by the end of the Civil War. Southern extremists did their best to silence Southern moderates, inflame Northern radicals, and defer what might have been slavery's inevitable decline. In turn, extreme abolitionism substantiated

Southern fears, undermining any chance of compromise or of a peaceful resolution to the sectional conflict. Thanks to the agitators' constant pressure, the slavery issue intensified, infusing all the sectional tensions in America, until the nation exploded. By 1861, the inter-American struggle had grown far beyond the dreams or nightmares of all but the harshest extremists.

America's no-holds-barred and immature democracy, led by second-raters who were tactically and politically handcuffed, inflamed the situation. Zachary Taylor, Millard Fillmore, Franklin Pierce, and James Buchanan dominate lists of the worst American presidents because they failed to lead at a critical time in national life. Their inability to master the growing factionalism endangered the entire "happy" American experiment, as George Washington had feared would happen. They helped give compromise and centrism a bad name. Their impotence meant that the silent majority, which celebrated the Compromise of 1850, was drowned out by the angry minority. Incapable of meeting the moral challenge of Southern slavery, these presidents left the field to extremists such as the abolitionist William Lloyd Garrison and the proslavery advocate John C. Calhoun. No one could channel the zealotry until Abraham Lincoln came along.

The four passive presidents' resumés were no less distinguished than those of some of America's greatest leaders. Taylor had been a victorious general, Fillmore a vice president, Buchanan secretary of state. Taylor, Fillmore, Pierce, and Buchanan possessed the character traits often prized today at civic celebrations and presidential funerals: the "dignity" of a George Washington, the "decency" of a Gerald Ford, the "optimism" of a Ronald Reagan. These mid-nineteenth-century presidents, however, were products and prisoners of a political system that prized "electability" over real ability and deference to party over independence of spirit. They perpetuated the status quo. Congressmen dominated and party prerogatives triumphed because the "Second American Party System" was designed that way. As a result, Fillmore deferred to Clay, Pierce surrendered to Douglas and the "F Street Mess"; Buchanan, keeping his own counsel, became ornery and made empty threats.

None of these presidents reframed the major question facing the nation. Instead, their incompetence helped push Southerners and Northerners into a zero-sum game in which one region's gain was the other region's loss. The Civil War could only have been prevented had national needs, feelings, and visions trumped sectional ones. Only with Abraham Lincoln did a revolution in presidential leadership begin that could deliver a national consensus. But Lincoln's changes to the presidency only gained traction in the twentieth century, after Franklin Roosevelt institutionalized Theodore Roosevelt's affirmative, nationalistic leadership.

Historians are justifiably uncomfortable with the "if" of history. No one knows *if* slavery would have disappeared by the 1860s or 1890s, or 1900s naturally, without a civil war, as it did in Great Britain, Mexico, and elsewhere. And no one knows *if* more effective presidential leadership could have staved off the sectional fight. We do know that no strong vision came from the White House at that time. We also know that "compromises," such as the 1850 deal, did not temper the extremes, but simply piled up policies Southerners found unpalatable with other policies Northerners hated equally vehemently. That kind of legislative horse-trading was the leadership model of the party-oriented American system, which established some of the basic parameters of America's functional democracy. But when it came to the moral challenge slavery posed and the political challenge the North–South gulf presented, the system failed. America needed a different leadership model, but would get one only in the twentieth century.

Various actors have a variety of roles to play on the historical stage. John Brown, William Lloyd Garrison, and John C. Calhoun would have made disastrous presidents. Significantly, when the antislavery forces gathered sufficient strength, they established a political party, the Republican Party. The abolitionist politicians who led the party, the Salmon Chases and the William Sewards, were more moderate than the zealots who first shaped the abolitionist movement. When the party sought to win a national election, it chose an even more moderate antislavery politician, Abraham Lincoln.

This point does not negate the radicals' importance. It casts them in their proper roles. There should be a constructive dynamic: Radicals articulate ideas and uphold ideals, whereas leaders translate moral abstractions into more realistic, popular, and palatable policies. Presidents should not be rabble-rousers; they must be leaders. That lesson would become clear during the crucible of Civil War, with Abraham Lincoln at the helm.

3

ABRAHAM LINCOLN'S
MIDDLE MEASURE

A Cautious Politician's "My Policy Is to Have No Policy" Pragmatism

AMERICAN MYTHOLOGY TREATS it as one of the nation's shining moments. Amid a bloody civil war, the saintly president freed the slaves with one pen stroke, signing the Emancipation Proclamation. But in fact, Abraham Lincoln's melodiously titled statement on September 22, 1862, was more practical policy than soaring poetry. The historian Richard Hofstadter scoffed that it had "all the moral grandeur of a bill of lading."

This limited executive order only freed slaves in the rebel states. Thus, Lincoln helped nudge the war toward becoming a fight against slavery while still placating the marginally loyal but passionately slave-holding border states. Such caution was the key to Abraham Lincoln's greatness. Thanks to Lincoln's leadership, by 1865 the remaining slaves in the Union became free. Nevertheless, even during the nation's terrible Civil War, Abraham Lincoln always sought the great American center, preferring incremental pragmatism to zealous extremism.

Steeped in America's founding ideals and the Founders' restraint, Lincoln became a calm leader at a time of great turbulence, a man of measure tempering a politics of passion. He balanced many competing impulses: his aw-shucks Western populism with wannabe Eastern ambition, his frontier sensibility

with statesmanlike eloquence, his provincial background with a national vision. As a lawyer he loved the Constitution, but as a humanist he sought
change. He outmaneuvered the Northern extremists while trouncing the
Southern fanatics. Even as he fought for total victory, he sought to heal his divided nation. Lincoln functioned as America's gyroscope, steadying a reeling
nation. He understood that the revolutionary changes the nation needed were
best implemented as deliberately as possible.

LINCOLN NOT ONLY SAVED the nation, he also redeemed the emerging American approach to leadership. "Father Abraham" rescued the two-
party system from its failure to solve the slavery question while proving that
democracies could survive with resolute yet reasonable leaders. Amid the
Civil War's fury, Abraham Lincoln revived George Washington's moderating vision. Delivering the Gettysburg Address to "the nation" in November
1863, Lincoln tapped into the power of American patriotism. "Government of the people, by the people, for the people" thrived only when the
people united. From his cautious Emancipation Proclamation to his subtle
Reconstruction policy, Abraham Lincoln was a pragmatic nationalist, willing to assert power if necessary, but preferring to find a golden middle path.

Lincoln's disingenuous statement to a Kentucky newspaper editor in 1864
captured his approach: "I claim not to have controlled events but confess
plainly that events have controlled me." If Lincoln had been as humble as
he liked to sound, he would have avoided politics—and been far less effective. But like Washington, Lincoln understood the power of indirection and
statesmanlike restraint or deniability. Happy to appear ignorant when that
was convenient, Lincoln often mentioned the Irishman who forswore liquor,
then told his bartender he was not averse to having a spot added to his
lemonade, as long as he did not know about it. Lincoln mastered the tides
buffeting his country with the kinds of skills he once used piloting a flatboat
down the Mississippi River: sailing forward toward his destination; tacking
left or right as necessary; sometimes steering hard, sometimes floating passively; and blaming setbacks on natural forces beyond his control.

Abraham Lincoln's story further suggests that there may have been less
bloody ways to end slavery. Lincoln, the leader who freed the slaves and
saved the Union, often clashed with abolitionists and radical Republicans.
Both groups denounced him so fiercely at times that he dismissed them as
"fiends." Lincoln's presidency reaffirms the importance of presidential center seeking, while illustrating the constructive tension that can result from

radical outsiders demanding change, especially when fighting a monstrous injustice like slavery. For democracy to progress, the leader must channel the fanatics' intense energies, transforming their high-voltage vision into lower wattage, commonsense policies suitable for domestic consumption.

ON JANUARY 27, 1838, a gawky but charismatic twenty-nine-year-old state legislator addressed the Young Men's Lyceum of Springfield, Illinois. His subject was America's political future, what he called "the perpetuation of our political institutions." Distressed by recent violence, including the hangings of gamblers and blacks in Mississippi and the burning of a black freedman accused of murder in St. Louis, Abraham Lincoln defended the rule of law. Prophetically, he warned his fellow Americans against violently sliding toward "national suicide." Critical of slavery's supporters but uncomfortable with abolitionists, he ignored the mob killing of the antislavery journalist Elijah Lovejoy only months before and ninety miles away. The lanky legislator echoed George Washington, tying America's future to "[r]eason, cold, calculating, unimpassioned reason." With *general intelligence, sound morality,* and in particular, *a reverence for the constitution and laws*," Americans could weave "the proud fabric of freedom," guaranteeing a glorious, democratic future.

As America stumbled toward the brink of "national suicide," as party hacks like Millard Fillmore, Franklin Pierce, and James Buchanan occupied Washington's chair, Abraham Lincoln ambled toward the White House. Lincoln believed the Declaration of Independence and the Constitution embodied America's enlightened nationalism. Though later remembered as a martyr to the antislavery crusade, Lincoln was a conciliator who wanted to build the nation by resolving conflicts rationally.

Like all politicians, Lincoln was his own myth's first and most effective purveyor. But his log cabin origins were real. Born in 1809, in Hardin, Kentucky, he had minimal formal schooling. Lincoln settled in southern Illinois in 1830 and volunteered for the Black Hawk War in 1832, although it ended before he and his fellow soldiers reached the battlegrounds. Lincoln served as a surveyor, postmaster, and rail splitter, in New Salem, Illinois, from 1833 to 1836, when he was admitted to the Illinois Bar. The heights he eventually reached made him living proof of the American dream.

Lincoln fell into politics naturally, propelled by his zest for storytelling, his prominence as the town postmaster, and the dividends from Andrew Jackson's democratizing revolution, even while championing Jackson's rival,

Henry Clay. Despite his apparent simplicity and hulking gawkiness, Lincoln was ambitious and sophisticated. With an outsized personality matching his tall frame, he towered over his peers. Lincoln moved to Springfield, Illinois, in 1837, and began carving out a reputation as an outstanding jury lawyer. From 1834 to 1842, Lincoln was a Whig state legislator. Most men from his modest background, in his region, were Democrats. His Whig affiliation reflected his grand aspirations to pull himself up by his bootstraps, as did his marriage in 1842 to a Southern belle, Mary Todd. A committed Whig, Lincoln celebrated middle-class frugality, temperance, and hard work. As a self-made man, his faith in the dignity of labor and America's freedom of opportunity intensified his disgust for slavery.

Living the American dream, Lincoln championed the American system. He embraced the Declaration of Independence's revolutionary implications, promising liberty and equality for all. On the other hand, with his lawyerlike respect for process, he wanted transformational change through constitutional means. Lincoln believed that the national glue the Declaration provided stemmed from its gift of liberty, which he hoped to spread throughout America—and the world.

A Henry Clay nationalist, Lincoln revered Clay's enlightened Washingtonian rationalism and passionate nationalism. Committed to Clay's policy of building national infrastructure, Lincoln trusted government to fulfill communal visions individuals never could achieve alone. When his hero died in 1852, Lincoln praised the Great Compromiser's genius for calming popular passion with creative resolutions that "duly weighed every conflicting interest." Lincoln dreamed of governing with "all appetites controlled, all passions subdued, all matters subjected . . . . Hail fall of Fury! Reign of Reason, all hail!"

LINCOLN WORSHIPED the Constitution's wisdom. He doubted anyone could improve it and feared where changes, once begun, would end. Reflecting the mix of discipline and denial effective moderation requires, he advised, "Better . . . habituate ourselves to think of it as unalterable."

Lincoln's nuanced, constitutional nationalism distinguished him from the abolitionists and the Southern apologists. Lincoln dismissed the antislavery agitators, who would "tear to tatters" America's "now venerated constitution; and even burn the last copy of the Bible, rather than slavery should continue a single hour." Like most people living in an imperfect society, he hoped for change without too much inconvenience; he wanted slavery to vanish but he would not sacrifice constitutional principles to speed reform. Lincoln also rejected proslavery advocates like John C. Calhoun, who undermined Jefferson's holy writ, the declaration that all men are created equal. In eulogizing Clay, an antislavery slaveholder, Lincoln acknowledged the fear of change. Working through Clay's contradictions, and presumably his own, Lincoln revealed his own status quo conservatism, every moderate's great vice.

Despite his nationalism, Lincoln lived a provincial life. He first visited Washington, D.C., after winning election to Congress in 1846. In his most controversial move, Congressman Lincoln charged that President James Knox Polk had lied to justify the Mexican War and overstepped the president's constitutional bounds. Lincoln was not a pacifist. He was a Whig constitutionalist resisting presidential overreach. Despite warnings of a growing backlash back home in Illinois during that popular war, Lincoln persevered. He explained to his worried law partner, William Herndon, that he had no choice but to speak out and be honest.

Lincoln enjoyed Washington enough to regret that he had promised his Whig backers to serve only one term. He could not break his word and run again unless a popular groundswell drafted him. In fact, his opposition to Polk made him so unpopular that even his Whig successor lost to the Democrats.

Lincoln's political career stalled. Despite campaigning eloquently for Zachary Taylor's presidential bid in 1848, Lincoln failed to get an attractive job offer for himself or any important Illinois Whigs. He returned to Springfield in 1849, dispirited by his impotence, sobered by his imprudence. He learned to stay more attuned to popular opinion.

The antislavery passions stirred by the Southern fight to impose slavery in the Kansas and Nebraska territories moved Lincoln, along with many others in the 1850s. But unlike many others, he kept his cool. A Christian love for his Southern neighbors and patriotic reverence for the Constitution tempered his hatred for slavery.

In 1854 the Kansas–Nebraska Bill, introduced by Senator Stephen Douglas, called for settlers in each territory to decide the slavery question for their future states, without congressional input. On October 4, 1854, Lincoln emerged as a national leader with a powerful three-hour speech repudiating Douglas's "popular sovereignty" doctrine—in the Senator's presence. Typically nuanced, Lincoln neither affirmed racial equality nor endorsed eliminating slavery. He opposed extending slavery into the new territories, even with popular approval. Lincoln rejected Americans' hypocrisy in encouraging slavery while purporting to champion freedom. Still, Lincoln hoped, as Henry Clay had, that slavery would gradually disappear and the freed former slaves would "return" to Africa.

Despite his impassioned speechifying, Lincoln choreographed an excruciating dance for himself as the temporizing Whig Party dissolved and the crusading antislavery Republican Party emerged. He left Springfield when the new state Republican Party met there to organize; some thought intentionally, to avoid being publicly identified as an ardent abolitionist, others said coincidentally. The Republicans nevertheless appointed him to their central committee. Lincoln did not consent, did not approve, did not resign. Hedging, he tried to appear unworthy, not uninterested.

Lincoln was in a bind. His eloquence, moral outrage, and delight in contradicting Stephen Douglas made him famous for being antislavery, but he opposed slavery's extension, not its existence. Lincoln tried remaining loyal to the dying Whig Party as it divided over slavery without alienating Republican leaders mobilizing to fight the evil. In 1855, he still called himself a Whig, but admitted his confusion as the party splintered. By 1856, he was helping the new Republican Party in Illinois mount its first presidential campaign.

Lincoln feared the "Republican" label as too radical because leading abolitionists had founded the party around one central issue: opposing slavery. He sought a broad coalition to stop Nebraska's entry into the union as a slave state. Lincoln chaired an anti-Nebraska state convention in Bloomington in May 1856. Coincidentally, it met days after Charles Sumner's beating on the Senate floor by his Southern rival inflamed passions on both sides. Watching convention delegates arrive at the train station, Lincoln was delighted to see Norm B. Judd, a wishy-washy, anti-Nebraska Democrat. "That is the best sign yet," he told his friend. "Judd is a trimmer."

In his speech at the convention, Lincoln mesmerized the delegates, demanding a reasonable, united front against extending slavery. Observers were so moved they failed to transcribe the speech. This "lost speech" later enhanced Lincoln's legend. Meanwhile, as he campaigned, opponents mocked Lincoln's cowardice.

In shaping the Republican Party's identity in Illinois and becoming its most prominent state leader, Lincoln served Northern racism while appearing to advance abolitionism. He wanted the new territories for "white people" only. This clever if amoral posture reassured Northern voters. Seeking popularity, not building consensus, Lincoln emphasized full equality when addressing abolitionist groups and celebrated white purity the farther south in the state he went. This was typical for Illinois; settled by both Northerners and Southerners, it mirrored the nation's divisions.

Lincoln's ambition to advance himself and his cause led to his famous debates with Senator Stephen A. Douglas during the 1858 campaign for the U.S. Senate. At that time candidates for the Senate did not face the electorate; they had to shape the makeup of the state legislatures, which chose them. During those debates, Lincoln balanced his personal feelings—insisting that "I have always hated slavery"—against his more tentative proposals, simply to keep slavery Southern.

Although he did not win the Senate seat, Lincoln attracted statewide support from Republicans and moderates moved by his eloquence. His most powerful argument, which revealed his core values, was quoting the elitist Southern philosopher George Fitzhugh to warn Northern laborers that Southerners wanted to enslave them all. This assertion made the antislavery struggle a fight for white, not black, freedom.

Still, Lincoln's pussyfooting infuriated both abolitionists and Southerners. "I do not believe in the anti-slavery of Abraham Lincoln," one black abolitionist shuddered as Lincoln rose to power, remembering Lincoln's refusal to sign a petition permitting free blacks to testify in Illinois. "If we sent our children to school, Abraham Lincoln would kick them out, in the name of Republicanism and anti-slavery!"

Throughout the 1850s, Abraham Lincoln's fence sitting made it clear he was a politician, not a crusader. Coming of age during the Jacksonian revolution, Lincoln was a party man. He exhibited the loyalist's pragmatism. "I am for the regular nominee in all cases," he once said. In his 1852 eulogy for Henry Clay, Lincoln explained: "The man who is of neither party is not, and cannot be, of any consequence." Sometimes it seemed that Lincoln built his national reputation despite himself. He delighted in rhetorical combat and enjoyed the accolades. But he remained calm during a time of great turmoil, sometimes sounding more radical than he was, but usually seeking the center.

AS THE 1860 PRESIDENTIAL CAMPAIGN approached, Abraham Lincoln's growing reputation triggered rumblings of support for a presidential run. The pillars of the Republican Party, William Henry Seward and Salmon P. Chase, each expected to be the nominee. Lincoln played it cool. "My name is new in the field; and I suppose I am not the first choice of a very great many," he told a friend. "Our policy, then, is to give no offense to others—leave them in a mood to come to us, if they shall be compelled to give up their first love." Many Republicans feared Seward and Chase were too radical, while others worried about trusting the nation to a one-term Whig congressman.

Lincoln's strategy exploited his rivals' weaknesses. Hoopla about "Honest Abe's" rail-splitting in the past created popular excitement that softened his image, emphasizing that he was no extremist. One Currier and Ives cartoon showed Lincoln straddling a rail held up on one end by a slave and on the other by the Republican editor Horace Greeley, with Lincoln complaining that the rail was "the hardest stick I ever straddled." Greeley endorsed the strategy of running on popular non sequiturs, proclaiming, "We can prove that you have split rails & that will ensure your election to the Presidency."

In the rollicking 1860 general election, Lincoln faced three other major candidates, proof that the country was fragmenting. John Bell, a former Whig leader from Tennessee, represented the Constitution Union party. Seeking harmony by sidestepping the slavery question, the party's only platform was the Constitution. Ominously, the Democratic Party split. Buchanan's Vice President John C. Breckinridge appealed to Southerners defending slavery, while Stephen A. Douglas tried to save the union by leaving the decision about slavery to each state. One cartoon showed Breckinridge, Douglas, and Lincoln each tearing off a section of the American map, with Bell feebly gluing fragments back together.

As Lincoln followed nineteenth-century political tradition and remained silent at home, the campaign erupted. With Lincoln appealing to Northerners, Breckinridge appealing to Southerners, and Douglas and Bell increasingly marginalized, American voters understood that their country's future was threatened. One angry editorial from Georgia cried, "[W]hether the Potomac is crimsoned in human gore, and Pennsylvania Avenue is paved ten fathoms deep with mangled bodies . . . the South will never submit to such humiliation and degradation as the inauguration of Abraham Lincoln." Revealing his own prudent mindset, Lincoln did not anticipate "any formidable effort to break up the Union. The people of the South have too much sense."

On election day, Lincoln squeaked through with barely 40 percent of the popular vote. In ten slave states he received no votes. Still, he received almost 60 percent of the electoral votes because he swept the populous Northern states. Springfield's cautious, astute strategist had triumphed. Lincoln vowed to maintain his "conservative" position. He reassured Southerners that he did not want to abolish slavery. He reassured Northerners that he would block slavery's extension by popular sovereignty or constitutional fiat. And he reassured all Americans that he would tolerate no attempts at secession. Lincoln believed he had a mandate for moderation, continuing his careful navigation between the twin poles of abolishing and expanding slavery.

MANY SOUTHERN FIREBRANDS rejected Lincoln's victory, branding him the abolitionists' stalking horse. On December 20, 1860, three months before his inauguration, South Carolina seceded from the Union. Mississippi, Alabama, Florida, Georgia, Louisiana, and Texas quickly followed. By mid-February 1861, as Lincoln left Springfield to take office in Washington, civil war loomed. Lincoln proposed reconciliation. He bore "no malice toward any section." But, he said in a speech in New Jersey on February 21, prompting spontaneous applause, "it may be necessary to put the foot down firmly." The next day Lincoln vowed that "there will be no bloodshed unless it be forced upon the Government."

Eventually, Lincoln defeated the Confederacy, kept the restive Union together, and paved the way for a more humane and robust vision of American nationalism and government. His emergence as a political genius surprised most contemporaries. With the Constitution his guide and national unity his goal, Lincoln's philosophy, strategy, and personality proved mutually reinforcing. He proved to be more levelheaded than many more experienced politicians. Genuinely humble and greeted with low expectations, he disarmed critics and rivals. He would apologize when necessary but never let anyone forget who was boss. Like his twentieth-century successor Ronald Reagan, Lincoln used his humor, folksiness, and modesty to expand his political power and enhance his personal stature.

Reviewing Lincoln's now legendary leadership, the mist of myth often obscures the man and the moment. Delivering his first inaugural address on March 4, 1861, the man who would become the "Great Emancipator" played the humble conciliator. He repeatedly reassured Southerners that he would not "interfere" with slavery. He vowed to respect American laws, including the odious Fugitive Slave Law. Adding that a minority cannot dominate, the new president trusted majority rule, even as its positions changed. He requested patience and brotherly love. Offering his formula for conjuring a compromising spirit, Lincoln counseled "[i]ntelligence, patriotism, Christianity, and a firm reliance on Him, who has never yet forsaken this favored land."

Lincoln's majoritarian moderation often attracted attacks from all sides. Francis P. Blair, a Jacksonian who helped found the Republican Party, and the father of Lincoln's postmaster general, reminded the president of Andrew Jackson's motto: "[I]f you temporize you are lost." William Seward, Lincoln's secretary of state, entered office mistaking Lincoln's prudence for weakness. Seward expected to function as prime minister, reducing the president to a figurehead. However, Seward quickly learned who was the leader, and never to underestimate him. If something "must be done, I must do it," Lincoln bristled.

The secessionists continued to clamor. Lincoln never forgot that he had won only 40 percent of the popular vote, partially because Seward, Southerners, and other critics never let him forget. Lincoln's Republican Party was an improvised, contentious coalition. Northern Democrats, smarting from their party's implosion, mistrusted the new president. Perhaps most daunting, Lincoln needed to keep as many states loyal as possible, especially the border slaveholding states between the North and South, which were of questionable loyalty yet critical strategically. With the nation's capital sandwiched between two slave states, Maryland and Virginia, the Union's defense hinged on keeping Maryland in the Union.

Characteristically playing off competing factions, Lincoln cobbled together a cabinet he considered "balanced and ballasted." Ideologically, counting Lincoln there were four former Whigs, and four Free Soil Democrats, two of whom were hard-liners, and two appeasers. Geographically, the cabinet represented all regions, including the slave states. Seward, choking on having to assist Lincoln as well as serve with his bitter rival, Salmon Chase, hesitated to join Lincoln's "compound Cabinet." Ultimately, Seward grandly refused "to leave the country to chance."

Lincoln's contentious staff of brilliant egotists contrasted with the pallid cabinet of yes-men in James Buchanan's preceding administration. "We needed the strongest men of the party in the Cabinet," Lincoln later told a reporter. "I had no right to deprive the country of their services." Lincoln was right. It takes greater strength—and earns more respect—to dominate piranhas than goldfish. Although the cabinet would clash on individual issues, it provided Lincoln with a variety of viewpoints from which to craft his own way.

When Lincoln became president in March 1861, Southerners had been besieging Fort Sumter, the federal outpost in Charleston, South Carolina's harbor, since late December 1860. Secretary of State Seward advised abandoning Sumter to make peace. Postmaster General Montgomery Blair and others advocated an aggressive attempt to deliver provisions, assert American sovereignty, and restore national pride.

Lincoln sought a middle path. His reading of the Constitution reinforced his political instincts that responsibility for starting any violence had to fall on the rebels. The Southerners should fire the first shot. Impatient Republicans muttered that Lincoln had "no fixed policy except to keep mum and see what end those seceding states will come to." All attempts at compromise failed.

The Confederates attacked before Lincoln could reinforce the fort. Major Robert Anderson and his hungry soldiers eventually surrendered, but with a flourish, a fifty-gun salute to the tattered American flag. Four more states, including Virginia, seceded after Fort Sumter fell. Fortunately, the crucial border states of Maryland, Delaware, Kentucky, and Missouri remained loyal. Lincoln could fight on solid ground. Lincoln told Congress that the rebels "have forced upon the country, the distinct issue: 'Immediate dissolution, or blood.'"

Suddenly, a novice president weaned on the Whig doctrine of limiting executive power had to extend presidential power dramatically. Lincoln raised an army, suspended basic rights such as habeas corpus, and started navigating the constitutional complexities of fighting the Confederacy like a hostile foreign power without recognizing each state's secession as legitimate. After four months of unilateral, unprecedented moves, Lincoln convened Congress for a special session. Lincoln invoked the "plain people's" power in what he called "essentially a People's Contest." Expanding government's goal to "afford all, an unfettered start, and a fair chance in the race of life," Lincoln said that the rebels' extraordinary challenge justified exceptional steps to save this unique democratic experiment, the United States of America.

EARLY, CRUDE INDICATORS that Lincoln's approach was balanced came from the criticism heaped on him from all sides. "If both factions, or neither, shall abuse you, you will probably be about right," Lincoln advised subordinates mediating disputes. "Beware of being assailed by one, and praised by the other." Radical Republicans blasted Lincoln for appeasing the South and fighting halfheartedly. Disgruntled Democrats and some ex-Whigs accused Lincoln of being a despot. Folksy and foxy, Lincoln camouflaged his sophisticated understanding of constitutional prerogatives in one of his homey aphorisms: "A limb must be amputated to save a life but a life is never wisely given to save a limb." Even while expanding presidential power, Lincoln acknowledged his Whig roots—and preserved American democracy—by refusing to initiate legislation in Congress and refusing to postpone or suspend elections.

For two years, while struggling for military victory, Lincoln also struggled with the slavery question. His priorities were clear. He fought to save the Union at any cost. Reflecting Northern public opinion, mollifying border state sensibilities, acknowledging the Constitution's approval, and remembering his many promises, Lincoln was willing to keep slavery to save the Union. Abolitionists mocked the president's moderation, denouncing him as weak, cowardly, clumsy, unprincipled, and unintelligent, tone deaf to slavery's moral issues and blind to the great threat Southerners posed. "A more ridiculous farce was never played," they muttered, as they watched the president trying to fight the slaveholders without freeing the slaves.

Lincoln inched toward emancipation. He encouraged Congress to consider reimbursing slaveholders. He signed a bill banning slavery in Washington, D.C. But he refused to overstep his powers or outrun the fighting majority's consensus. When generals John C. Frémont and David Hunter freed slaves in conquered territories in Missouri in 1861 and Georgia, Florida, and South Carolina in 1862, the president rescinded their orders.

In a typically mature, disciplined statement, Lincoln distinguished between his "*official* duty" and his "oft-expressed *personal* wish that all men everywhere could be free." He feared adopting "radical and extreme measures, which may reach the loyal as the disloyal." In 1863, as political pressure grew, Lincoln challenged his abolitionist Secretary of the Treasury, Salmon P. Chase, to find constitutional justification for freeing the slaves. Lincoln admitted that emancipation would be the right thing to do and the popular move. But "would I not give up all footing upon constitution or law?" the president asked. "Would I not thus be in the boundless field of absolutism?"

Lincoln tried to protect the Constitution without exceeding its constraints, to preserve the people's power. But the unprecedented threat to the Constitution required unprecedented responses. This political and personal quandary intensified the president's natural melancholy. Doing his duty was difficult. But in true nineteenth-century style, the anguish made the task feel more virtuous. Individuals, especially politicians, were not supposed to indulge their consciences.

Always thinking ahead, Lincoln trusted the abolitionists and radical Republicans to clear the path toward emancipation. He once told two abolitionist clergymen that most Northerners cared about military success; they did not care about blacks. But the president calculated that eventually,

"We shall need all the anti-slavery feeling in the country." Lincoln told the clerics that in convincing their congregations to accept abolition, "you may say anything you like about me, if that will help. Don't spare me."

The war proved much harder to win than Lincoln expected. In spring 1862, General George B. McClellan's Union army failed to reach the Confederate capital of Richmond via the Virginia peninsula. The defeat demoralized the Union. The economy was suffering. Young Northerners stopped volunteering for the army. Lincoln's frustration with his army and his generals increased.

Ironically, the failed peninsular campaign gave Lincoln what he needed. The Confederate Army was using slaves on the battlefield to cook food, dig trenches, build fortifications, and staff hospitals. This freed more Confederate soldiers to fight. Many slaves were also running farms, maintaining the rebel home front. By defining the issue of freeing slaves as a "military necessity," Lincoln could use presidential war powers to emancipate slaves in the rebellious territories. On July 13, 1862, Lincoln told trusted cabinet members that emancipation was "essential for the salvation of the nation, that we must free the slaves or be ourselves subdued." On July 17, Congress passed the Second Confiscation Act, freeing the slaves belonging to disloyal citizens.

Lincoln's cabinet members disagreed so strongly about how and when to emancipate the slaves that friendships had ruptured. Lincoln demonstrated how he dominated his headstrong advisers. The president knew what he wanted to do. He had learned to lead, not consult endlessly. Further debate would only intensify the rancor and confusion. On July 22, 1862, Lincoln read the draft of his Emancipation Proclamation to the cabinet. He was informing his advisers, not soliciting their opinions. Lincoln wanted to read the announcement a few months before the New Year, to give Confederates until January 1 to end the rebellion or watch the slaves go free. Postmaster General Montgomery Blair of Missouri warned Lincoln that the border states might bolt. Secretary of War Edwin M. Stanton rejoiced, however, hoping to mobilize three and a half million freed slaves for the Northern effort, or at least to neutralize their contributions to the South.

Secretary of State William Seward feared such a declaration following a defeat might make Lincoln look desperate. He advised waiting "until the eagle of victory takes his flight," then hanging the "proclamation about his neck." Lincoln decided to tweak his plan, not reformulate it. Following Seward's advice, he waited until the Union repulsed the Confederate invasion

Although many critics recognized—and mocked—Abraham Lincoln's disorderly, deliberate decision-making style (above), especially concerning freeing the slaves, many supporters preferred to see President Lincoln as a composed, authoritative statesman, issuing the Emancipation Proclamation in 1863 (next page) calmly yet boldly. (Library of Congress)

at Antietam on September 17. That bloodiest one-day battle in American history, with its 23,000 casualties, was nevertheless a major Northern victory.

Thanks to Seward, the proclamation, published on September 23, was well-timed. The conversation about slavery in the North had progressed so far, the pressure had grown enough, that Lincoln did not appear to be an extremist. The abolitionist governors in Massachusetts and elsewhere had grown restive, hesitating to send more troops into battle. With the war now being fought for liberty and union, and with Confederate General Robert E. Lee's forces stopped in Maryland, Northern idealism and confidence surged.

Lincoln's plodding path to emancipation helped nudge Northerners toward an antislavery position. Yet even this partial freeing of the slaves infuriated many Democrats, especially those in the still-slaveholding border states. Democratic legal experts condemned the president's "radical departure" from

American respect for property and more than seventy-five years of proslavery jurisprudence. The Democratic *Chicago Times* charged that the Proclamation made the war "a contest of subjugation"—exactly what "abolitionism has designed from the outset." This opposition justified Lincoln's prudence in limiting the emancipation. The Union was not strong enough, and Washington, D.C., remained too vulnerable militarily to risk losing any more states. (Only the ratification of the Thirteenth Amendment in December 1865 would abolish slavery completely.)

In a nation torn between the politically untenable poles of perpetuating an evil institution and abolishing it immediately, Lincoln had done the seemingly impossible: forged a middle path. Step by excruciating step, earning credibility along the way even while frustrating some, Lincoln led the skeptical North from fighting a war just for union to fighting against slavery as well. The president pragmatically focused on day-to-day realities rather than daunting abstractions. Lincoln understood that radical surgery would have shocked the body politic and would not have held. "If he does not drive as fast as I would," the abolitionist Owen Lovejoy observed in 1862, "he is on the right road, and it is only a question of time." By improvising a path to emancipation, Lincoln assured slavery's eventual abolition, even among the loyal border states.

Midway through his first term, with the Union still threatened, Lincoln nevertheless felt vindicated. His lifelong commitment to building consensus tempered with moral vision was bearing fruit. Lincoln learned to pick his battles and marshal his forces, politically and militarily. He advised Attorney General Edward Bates that when "a practical question arises . . . decide that question directly, and not indirectly." Addressing "a general abstraction" risked "including a great deal more." Facing an intractable issue, he remembered the farm boy who, stymied by stumps that were too tough to uproot, too wet after rains to burn, "plowed round them."

Traumatized Americans needed a strong chief executive, grounded in righteousness but not self-righteous, able to lead but also able to listen. As he grew confident in office, Lincoln became more candid about his tactics. When ideologues clashed in Missouri in 1863, Lincoln refused to take sides in an ongoing "pestilent factional quarrel." "I could wish both to agree with me in all things; for then they would agree with each other, and would be too strong for any foe from any quarter," he said wistfully. Failing that, he pronounced, "I hold whoever commands in Missouri, or elsewhere, responsible to me, and not to either Radicals or Conservatives. It is my duty to hear all; but at last I must . . . judge what to do and what to forbear." The "conservative Republicans think him too much in the hands of the radicals," one *Harper's* columnist wrote admiringly in the summer of 1863, "while the radical Republicans think him too slow, yielding, and half-hearted." In liberating the slaves, even though only in the rebel territory, Lincoln had freed himself to become a bolder, more effective leader.

STEP BY STEP, Abraham Lincoln led the Union to victory. Eventually he found a general, Ulysses S. Grant, with the qualities Lincoln most admired in himself. "The great thing about Grant is his perfect coolness and persistency of purpose," Lincoln explained. He "is not easily excited . . . and he has the *grit* of a bull-dog! Once let him get his 'teeth' *in*, and nothing can shake him off."

Still, in 1864 Lincoln feared he might lose reelection and the war. He prepared a memorandum during the summer of 1864 planning a smooth transition during the long stretch between the election and the next inauguration if he lost. In any case, Atlanta's fall on September 1 secured Lincoln's victory, as bullets swayed the ballots.

For his second term, Lincoln continued what the *New York Times* had called his "masterly inactivity," seeking the middle path for postwar reconstruction. Lincoln articulated his governing template in his grand, humane, second inaugural speech, seeking "to bind up the nation's wounds" with "malice toward none, with charity for all." As the war was drawing to a close, his postwar reconstruction planning revealed a Washingtonian tendency to define reasonable positions and forge common ground, avoiding Henry Clay's one-for-you and one-for-me compromises. Lincoln wanted to integrate the freed black slaves and reintegrate the Southern rebels while keeping Republicans politically dominant. He preferred rebuilding to revenge, positive incentives for loyalty to mass punishment for treason.

Predictably, Lincoln's tempered policy outraged the radical Republicans, who had long despised Lincoln's "criminal vacillation." Some Republicans advocated what Wendell Phillips called a "baptism of blood" to purge the republic's sins in general and the South's in particular. Senator William Fessenden mocked Lincoln's initial reconstruction scheme as "silly. . . . Think of telling the rebels they may fight as long as they can, and take a pardon when they have had enough of it." The Republican radicals' anger was so harsh that when Lincoln was assassinated by John Wilkes Booth in April 1865, some greeted Andrew Johnson's rise as "a godsend to the country."

The radicals soon soured on Johnson, too. President Johnson lacked Lincoln's political instincts and the credibility earned by winning the war. Booth's bullet deprived the nation of a chance to see what Lincoln's moderate reconstruction could have accomplished. Instead, there was a destructive dynamic between the hapless Johnson, whom many considered too forgiving of his fellow Southerners, and the radical Republicans. The result was the first impeachment of a president and a haphazard reconstruction policy. Rather than maximizing blacks' rights and minimizing Southern pain, the resulting mishmash often minimized blacks' rights and maximized Southern pain. Reconstruction freed the slaves and established the legalized infrastructure for blacks to become citizens, but a century later they would still be waiting for equal rights.

Lincoln's assassination made him a martyr. As Americans rushed to deify him, saying, as did one Connecticut parson, "Jesus Christ died for the world, Abraham Lincoln died for his country," Lincoln's virtues reflected all the virtues Americans wished to see in themselves. Thirty years after the assassination, even many Southerners honored their old adversary. Alabama's Senator John T. Morgan claimed that Lincoln's "most conspicuous virtue . . . was the absence of a spirit of resentment or oppression, toward the enemy—and the self imposed restraint under which he exercised the really absolute powers within his grasp."

Lincoln's restraint stemmed from his democratic faith and his humble roots. Exercising both his faith in the people's power and his lawyerly reliance on the Constitution's structures, Lincoln saw the legitimacy popular government granted to a leader as a limiting force, not an avenue for aggrandizement. He trusted the people's wisdom, respecting the periodic elections that kept leaders accountable and replaceable. In addition to the temperamental inclinations, strategic calculations, and philosophical considerations that kept him grounded as a leader, Lincoln respected constitutional and democratic constraints. He would do what was necessary to keep the country alive, but wanted to stay within limits and in sync with popular opinion.

Balanced, prudent, and moderate, Abraham Lincoln was a great and good man whose genius, like George Washington's, lay in that ineffable quality called judgment. In 1864 Harvard's romantic poet, James Russell Lowell, praised Lincoln as ideal for leading a democracy, in which "a profound common-sense is the best genius for statesmanship." Lincoln's good judgment, common sense, democratic humility, pragmatism, and humanity not only saved the Union; he forged a new center. After Abraham Lincoln's liberal nationalistic leadership, "these United States" became known as *The* United States. Moreover, this united nation began wiping away the moral stain of having enslaved millions. To this day, Lincoln's example and accomplishments inspire his successors as that effort continues.

4

THEODORE ROOSEVELT'S
DEMOCRATIC TWO-STEP

The Rise of the Romantic,
Nationalist Presidency

THE ASSASSINATION OF PRESIDENT WILLIAM MCKINLEY in Buffalo, New York, on September 6, 1901, wrenched Americans back to the
trauma of Abraham Lincoln's murder. "We are too old to heal of such a
wound," sixty-four-year-old Secretary of State John Hay mourned. Hay, who
had been with Lincoln at Ford's Theatre the night he was assassinated, sym-
bolically transferred the martyred sixteenth president's halo to McKinley's successor, Theodore Roosevelt. After Roosevelt won election in his own right in
1904, Hay gave the president a "mourning ring" with a strand of Lincoln's hair
mounted behind glass. Hay asked Roosevelt to wear the ring on inauguration
day, saying, "you are one of the men who most thoroughly understand and appreciate Lincoln."

Theodore Roosevelt loved the gift—and of course the Lincolnian seal of
approval. This Republican Roosevelt modeled himself on the first Republican
president. Amid crises he drew strength from Lincoln's determination during
the Civil War. Roosevelt justified expanding executive power, as Lincoln had,
because the president represented what Lincoln had called "the plain people."
Roosevelt invoked Lincoln so frequently that he seemed to forget that eight

presidents, including seven fellow Republicans, had served during the thirty-six years separating the Roosevelt and Lincoln administrations.

Roosevelt rejected the passive precedents of Rutherford B. Hayes, Chester Arthur, Benjamin Harrison, and Grover Cleveland. He championed the "national government" not the federal government. And he praised "statesmen of the national type": George Washington, Abraham Lincoln, and Supreme Court Justice John Marshall. By advocating a national government, Roosevelt combined nationalism and moderation into his vision of leadership and his presidential mission. A great American president needed to find the center, recruiting as many citizens as possible to support a grand, national enterprise, Roosevelt believed. Without an expansive vision and popular support, there was no ballast, no greatness.

By temperament, Theodore Roosevelt was an unlikely candidate to join a pantheon of moderate heroes. Lacking George Washington's disciplined reserve or Abraham Lincoln's melancholy self-criticism, Theodore Roosevelt was impulsive, verbose, and flamboyant. "Whew, after an hour with him, you just have to wring his personality out of your clothes," a stunned visitor exclaimed. When Roosevelt tried to justify his outrageous behavior in abetting the 1903 Panamanian coup against Colombia, which secured the Panama Canal treaty, his attorney general advised him not to try putting "any taint of legality about it." More pointedly, Secretary of War Elihu Root told him, "you were accused of seduction and you have conclusively proved that you were guilty of rape."

Roosevelt dramatically expanded the presidency, the only office filled by a nationwide electorate. As the "plain people's" man in Washington, Roosevelt pursued policies that resonated broadly and united an increasingly diverse nation, now a coast-to-coast empire. Domestically, Roosevelt took unprecedented initiatives for a chief executive, advancing the Progressive movement's agenda while remaining conservative. His rhetoric about trust busting was more impressive than his record in dismantling monopolies; his barbs against plutocrats more sweeping than any measures he proposed. He sought to navigate between the extremes of antibusiness radicalism and predatory capitalism.

Still, Roosevelt understood that power in a democracy was on loan. Despite accusations of megalomania, Roosevelt honored George Washington's two-term tradition by retiring after seven and a half years in office. This move distinguished between expanding presidential power and seizing it. It became clear how much Roosevelt had sacrificed when he ran again for president in 1912 on the Progressive Party ticket. He justified this return to presidential politics by blasting both the Democrats and the Republicans for failing to protect the American people's interests from the corporations. But he also admitted, in office and in retirement, that he loved being president.

The Roosevelt administration's two defining phrases revealed the creative tension that characterized his record. The "square deal" spoke of his substantive, Progressive commitment to protect workers and corporations thanks to an empowered government. The "bully pulpit" showed that Roosevelt understood that the White House provided a unique pipeline for communicating with the American people.

At the beginning of the twentieth century, Theodore Roosevelt demonstrated how a president could shape national consciousness, even without the context of a major crisis. His great gift to the American people was an invigorated sense of nation with the president at the nation's emotional and political epicenter. His great gift to his successors was an invigorated office, more suited to mastering modern challenges.

THE MODERN AMERICAN PRESIDENCY was not invented overnight. The Founders had opposed a powerful executive, who might resemble a monarch. Abraham Lincoln enhanced executive power, but on the sly and during wartime. His humility, and the Republican radicals' impatience with his sometimes calculated, sometimes improvised middle measures, obscured his unprecedented expansion of presidential powers.

After Lincoln, the radical Republicans in Congress restored congressional power. They impeached Andrew Johnson for overstepping his bounds, nearly removing him from office. Subsequently, from the 1870s through the 1890s, the Gilded Age Congress dominated. One stolid, jowly, ineffectual chief executive after another led the country, with a sluggishness reflecting these presidents' small town origins. The one chief executive who entered office (in 1869) already knighted as a great man, Ulysses S. Grant, promised to defer to Congress, and he did. Rutherford B. Hayes, James A. Garfield, Chester A. Arthur, and Benjamin Harrison were all cautious, plodding leaders. The one Democratic president between James Buchanan and Woodrow Wilson, Grover Cleveland, elected in 1884 and again in 1892, was equally unimaginative. By 1888, Americans, along with British observer Lord Bryce, wondered, "Why Great Men Are Not Chosen Presidents?"

After the Civil War, as before it, Americans sought the comfort of cautious presidents. Presidential mediocrity, Bryce explained, began with the selection process. Emphasizing party loyalty and electability favored "the safe man" over "the brilliant man." Americans wanted presidents who were good, not great. A president's "main duties are to be prompt and firm in securing the due execution of the laws and maintaining the public peace," skills better suited to railway management, not statesmanship. Bryce mourned that presidents were not selected for "eloquence," "imagination," or "profundity of thought or extent of knowledge." Actually, these qualities risked unnerving Americans, who associated them with dictatorship.

Nevertheless, astute observers—and those fearing powerful executives—sensed a shift by the turn of the century. In 1901, the reporter Henry Litchfield West decried the president's "growing powers." With the chief executive "elbow deep" in money from tariffs and custom duties, the White House, "where one man sits in almost supreme power," had muscled out the Capitol, "where the people's representatives assemble." Foreshadowing present-day complaints, West blamed the people for neglecting democracy in a mad dash to make money. Distracted Americans believed the "king can do no harm." He can, West warned.

Surprisingly, West's article targeted William McKinley. Although today he is remembered as another unimpressive, mediocre president, McKinley led America into war against Spain in 1898, launching America's imperial adventures. Still, within six months of West's article, Theodore Roosevelt truly would unnerve critics of presidential power. Roosevelt extended the president's symbolic and substantive roles beyond Lincoln's wildest dreams and West's worst nightmares.

If Abraham Lincoln was the emerging presidency's zen master, demonstrating the potential of the office while minimizing his own power, Theodore Roosevelt was the whirling dervish, enlarging the office through frenzied activity. A belching locomotive of a man, with a barrel chest seemingly made of iron, endless energy, and a surprisingly high-pitched voice when he speechified, Roosevelt was energetic, not fanatical. Like Lincoln, Roosevelt respected the Constitution and the people's will. Such sensitivities frustrated other Progressives, who were demanding revolutionary changes. Roosevelt raised expectations about what the president and government could do, setting the stage so his distant cousin Franklin Roosevelt could secure America's entry in the 1930s into the club of liberal, industrialized, welfare state democracies.

Theodore Roosevelt believed that the president, as the "steward of the people," worked for the people and could not "content himself with the negative merit of keeping his talents undamaged in a napkin." He reversed the accepted constitutional polarities. Traditionally, presidents only did what the Constitution specifically permitted. This president did "anything that the needs of the Nation demanded," unless the Constitution specifically prohibited it. This approach propelled Roosevelt into unprecedented actions: mediating labor disputes, spearheading prosecutions of corporations, brokering peace agreements between warring countries, and creating vast tracts of federal parkland. "I did not usurp power," he later insisted coyly, "but I did greatly broaden the use of executive power . . . . I acted for the common well-being of all our people."

An award-winning and prolific historian long before becoming president, Roosevelt justified his brashness by noting that America was no longer the Framers' loose confederation of squabbling states. The Civil War had transformed diverse, often competing, states into a united nation. By 1870 America had emerged with a powerful army; a national currency; an expanded federal government; and a new ideological script emphasizing the nation not the regions, including new national holidays such as Thanksgiving and Memorial Day. The emergence of this new idea of the nation made the nineteenth-century passive presidency obsolete.

Through the bully pulpit Roosevelt transformed the president into the national poet, not just the national focal point. When praising his Republican party as "the Nationalist" party, Roosevelt repudiated the Democrats' racist "States-rights fetich [sic]," challenging his constituents to be "Americans first and party men second." Building on Lincoln's eloquence, Roosevelt fused European romanticism with American patriotism. The result was as colorful as the rainbow blur of an Impressionist painting, as resounding as the crashing cymbals in a Beethoven symphony, as sublime as the lyricism of a poem by Walt Whitman. Fortunately, Roosevelt's Americanism lacked the orthodoxy that would make French nationalism so stifling and German nationalism so lethal in the twentieth century. America's saving grace, its grounding element, was the democratic centrism rooted in the Constitution's boundaries, Washington's reason, and Lincoln's humility, which Roosevelt expressed as respect for the American people.

ROOSEVELT'S VISION OF CONSTRAINED reform shifted America's center of gravity without destabilizing the country. He was a nineteenth-century man of character leading in the personality-driven twentieth century. Born just before the Civil War, in 1858, Roosevelt's instincts for

Theodore Roosevelt, shown speaking here at the Battery in New York City, used the White House as a bully pulpit to unite the American people and expand the presidency. (Library of Congress)

centrism were honed as he reconciled his love for his Southern belle mother, who smuggled relief packages to Confederate relatives during the Civil War, with respect for his patriotic father, who befriended President and Mrs. Lincoln.

The sheltered son of a philanthropic banker, from his cushy Gramercy Park townhouse young "Teedie" watched New York City pulsate as the nerve center of a country whose population jumped from 40 million in 1865 to 75 million in 1900. America's Gross National Product doubled as a 35,000-mile-track railroad system grew to 200,000 miles, with a million railroad workers, and as raw steel production ballooned from 300,000 to 11 million tons. The city clicked, buzzed, rang, and whirred as magical machines such as the telegraph, the telephone, the sewing machine, the electric lightbulb, and, eventually, the motor car, transformed daily life.

As part of the old New York aristocracy, the Roosevelts and other blue-bloods felt squeezed in the changing society. They recoiled at the poverty, the crime, and the grime tarnishing their city. They disliked the strange accents, customs, and smells imported by the twenty-five million immigrants who arrived between the Civil War and the first World War. And they bristled as captains of industry flashed their newfound wealth, buying respectability with riches that most established American aristocrats could not match. With the aristocrat's addiction to the easy living money brings, but lacking the go-getter's zeal for actually making it, Roosevelt respected money without worshipping it. Like his father, Roosevelt would be better at spending money than earning it. Like his father, Roosevelt would see his fellow aristocrats' weaknesses and yearn for change without destroying the whole system.

Uninterested in simply pursuing leisure or making money, Roosevelt chose public service after graduating from Harvard College in 1880. Beginning as a New York State assemblyman, he forged a middle path, championing workers' rights while acknowledging owners' rights to profit. In the 1880s Roosevelt also wrote sweeping works about American history, publishing inspiring narratives about the War of 1812 at sea and the settling of the West. The towering heroes, significant battles, and frontier dramas he portrayed reflected his romantic view of America's national enterprise.

Roosevelt found both the writer's life and what he called "the strenuous life" appealing. After his first wife and his mother died, coincidentally on the same day in February 1884, Roosevelt purchased a ranch in the Dakota Badlands. There he recovered from his heartache, proved his toughness, and became the living embodiment of the romantic cowboy ideals he had already started immortalizing in his writing.

Returning to New York City in 1886, Roosevelt remarried, continued writing history, and eventually resumed his political career. He headed New York's Board of Police Commissioners from 1895 to 1897. While reforming the police force, Roosevelt prowled New York's slums nightly with his friend, the urban chronicler Jacob Riis. This confrontation with New York's poverty pricked Roosevelt's conscience while his hands-on oversight of New York's often unruly "coppers" confirmed his status as a "good government" crusader against corruption.

Roosevelt was a Republican Party loyalist. But his agenda aligned him with America's Progressives, the mostly urban, middle-class activists whose reforming impulses championed order and honesty in society and government. Seeking to temper the Industrial Revolution's most devastating effects,

Progressives worked to help government counter growing corporate power. They objected when financial trusts spread their tentacles into so many industries, crushing the little people. And Progressives demanded more dignity, education, and money for the laborers generating the riches so many bosses hoarded.

In 1897 President McKinley appointed Roosevelt assistant secretary of the navy. When the Spanish–American War erupted, Roosevelt volunteered, returning from Cuba a war hero. In 1898 he was elected New York's governor. By 1900 he was President William McKinley's running mate. Then, abruptly, in September 1901, following William McKinley's assassination, Theodore Roosevelt became the youngest president ever, just shy of his forty-third birthday. His patriotism and martial spirit had propelled him into the limelight, but his romantic nationalism and Progressive commitment to political efficiency and social justice shaped his agenda.

CONSCIOUS OF HIS YOUTH and the tragic circumstances of his promotion, Roosevelt promised to continue McKinley's policies. As a patrician turned president of the people, Roosevelt built his moderating leadership mission on an unstable core. While converting public attention into an effective governing tool, he wavered between demonstrating his sterling character and exhibiting his outsized personality, between achieving and showboating, between defending workers and mollifying bosses.

Roosevelt entered office with a sophisticated understanding of American history. He embraced the "Lincoln School of American thought," reconciling big government Hamiltonianism with Jeffersonian populism. Roosevelt traced his identity as a Republican and a nationalist to Alexander Hamilton's commitment to governing effectively by stretching the Constitution as far as possible. Roosevelt justified this constitutional aggressiveness by invoking Jefferson's faith in the people. Jeffersonians were no longer allergic to big government; Hamiltonians would learn by the end of the century to dislike the government they had worked so hard to expand. During this time of ideological transition, Roosevelt's Jeffersonian populism provided a liberal wrapping on conservatives' traditional doctrine, reorienting government. Expanding government to serve the people without undermining them would pose as great a challenge as limiting businesses without choking the bosses. At critical moments, whether confronting striking coal miners or arrogant bankers, Roosevelt would gingerly balance between influencing and intruding, directing and dominating.

America needed a strong government and an active president because big businesses were careening out of control. Roosevelt criticized America's "riot of individualistic materialism," which allowed "the strong to wrong the weak." Corporations such as Standard Oil and Union Pacific were making huge profits. The rich lived grandly. Yet the poor folk who produced the wealth shared little of it. Excess threatened moderation; greed undermined idealism.

In the age of America's first billion-dollar corporation, United States Steel, amid a frenzy of corporate mergers, the government risked becoming irrelevant. Against this modern power, government power "remained archaic and therefore practically impotent," Roosevelt mourned. The central question of the era was "whether the Government had power to control them at all." Roosevelt believed that big business justified big government.

President Roosevelt chose to function as an arbitrator, saving corporations and workers from themselves. A turning point occurred in the fall of 1902, early in his presidency, when a long, bitter anthracite coal strike in Pennsylvania threatened millions heading into winter with a shortage of fuel. More than 140,000 coal miners stopped working. Roosevelt avoided interfering "as long as I could." Eventually, he compared the threat of a significant number of Americans having no coal for heat during a harsh winter to being "threatened by the invasion of a hostile army of overwhelming force." With no constitutional mandate to act, previous presidents would have been paralyzed. But Roosevelt's "Jackson-Lincoln" theory of executive power plunged him into the fray, because the Constitution did not directly ban his taking action.

Roosevelt offered to mediate, not dictate. He summoned the coal mine owners and the United Mine Workers union leaders to Washington on October 3, 1902. The owners berated the president for even agreeing to meet with the anarchistic labor radicals. Some corporate chieftains said Roosevelt's administration would fail if it could not even handle these union outlaws. Stung by one critic in particular, Roosevelt would recall, "If it wasn't for the high office I held I would have taken him by the seat of the breeches and nape of the neck and chucked him out of that window." This most unpresidential tenor, always bubbling under the surface, made Roosevelt seem an unlikely mediator. But this potential explosiveness also made Roosevelt effective. People feared his unpredictability and his willingness to use his power, epitomized in his slogan, "speak softly but carry a big stick."

Negotiations stalled over who would serve on a commission to resolve the issues. The owners vetoed having any labor representatives. Roosevelt cleverly placed a labor leader in the slot reserved for an "eminent sociologist." Roosevelt was bemused and dismayed that these "captains of industry" would risk so much—and cave so quickly—when all he had "to do was to commit a technical and nominal absurdity with a solemn face."

The strategy worked because Roosevelt had established credibility with the disputants. He especially earned labor leader John Mitchell's trust by appointing a Catholic bishop to the panel, knowing that most of the strikers were Catholics. Roosevelt believed that he had averted a "[n]ational calamity," saving "the great coal operators and all of the class of big propertied men . . . from the dreadful punishment which their own folly would have brought on them if I had not acted." He also protected the workers from the backlash their more radical leaders could have triggered. Roosevelt saw himself not only as a mediator but as a middle man, representing the nation. "I am President of all the people of the United States, without regard to creed, color, birthplace, occupation or social condition," he announced. "My aim is to do equal and exact justice as among them all."

Roosevelt's moderation was muscular militarily, politically, and morally. The president's authority and willingness to deploy troops colored every meeting with the owners and the strikers, as did his growing popularity. When violence erupted in the coal fields during the strike, Roosevelt secretly ordered a general to develop a plan for seizing the minefields. Congressman James E. Watson, the House Republican whip, confronted the president when briefed about the contingency plans: "What about the Constitution of the United States? What about seizing private property without due process of law?" Grabbing the congressman's shoulder, Roosevelt barked, "The Constitution was made for the people and not the people for the Constitution."

Roosevelt asserted presidential power to demonstrate government's centrality in solving national problems. During this crisis he reread the biography of Abraham Lincoln by John Hay and John Nicolay, identifying with Lincoln's attempts to navigate between abolitionism and appeasement. Roosevelt would demonstrate that center seeking was not for the passive or faint of heart. His involvement was proactive, courageous, and aggressive. Eventually, Roosevelt's commission awarded a 10 percent pay increase to the miners and reduced their working hours. Americans cheered their president's unprecedented involvement in a domestic dispute.

A pragmatist, Roosevelt judged government agencies by asking whether they practically improved the lives of "the mass of the people." He saw the president as the chief designer and sculptor of policies protecting Americans. Roosevelt offered a square deal to all—business, labor, and consumers. He did not inherently oppose bigness; behavior, not size, was the problem.

Like Lincoln, Roosevelt took some satisfaction in being lambasted by both political extremes. Radicals abhorred the president's establishment ties and policies, and big business advocates such as the corporate lawyer Henry W. Taft charged that Roosevelt stood for "a pretty pronounced type of socialism." Roosevelt laughed off the "epithet," knowing it was the usual reward for efforts "on behalf of justice to the workingman." Roosevelt rejected the socialist assumption of an inherent conflict between wage earners and employers. As a nationalist and a centrist, he acknowledged different groups' "different economic interests" but subsumed "group interests" to "the common, overlying interests of all."

Roosevelt attributed socialism's failure to the primacy of private property, the ease of securing a small stake in American society. His nationalist vision invited compromises based on common "interests." But he overlooked America's many crosscutting alliances and tensions. If regional, religious, racial, and ethnic ties all had reinforced class divisions, centrist appeals would have been less effective. But because the different economic interests cut across North–South, Catholic–Protestant, black–white, and immigrant–native divisions, among others, socialism never gained much traction, whereas Roosevelt's "plain people" nationalism and commonsense centrism did. The identity that most effectively swallowed other allegiances was the grand old label of American.

Roosevelt's neutrality infuriated his social peers. He puffed himself up while sounding humble, at their expense. "I am genuinely independent of the big monied men in all matters where I think the interests of the public are concerned."

Roosevelt's assault on America's fundamental leadership model worked. He explained that "the Presidential office tends to put a premium upon a man's keeping out of trouble rather than upon his accomplishing results." Someone with "a very decided character" polarizes, making "ardent friends and bitter enemies." Roosevelt feared the friendships would be fleeting, while the enemies would be dedicated and vengeful. Human nature favored "the dark horse, the neutral-tinted individual" rather than "the man of pronounced views and active life."

Roosevelt fancied himself such a definitive man, but he had a cautious streak. By striving to satisfy both corporations and workers, he frustrated more uncompromising Progressives. Often Roosevelt chose to tackle one or two extreme situations with maximum fanfare rather than implementing systematic change. For example, the president preferred using a targeted approach to growing corporate trusts, rather than breaking up too many corporate combinations. Roosevelt complained that financier J. P. Morgan arrogantly treated America's president like "a big rival operator who . . . intended to ruin all his interests." Roosevelt took the popular step of instructing the Department of Justice to prosecute the Northern Securities Company, Morgan's monopolistic railroad combine. In 1904 the Supreme Court found that the company had illegally restrained trade under the Sherman Anti-Trust Act.

Roosevelt explained that the "Northern Securities case definitely established the power of the Government to deal with all great corporations." He rejoiced in securing the precedent, even though mergers continued concentrating corporate power. Roosevelt's emboldened but still cautious Justice Department would file forty-five more cases against monopolies using the 1890 Sherman Antitrust Act, earning him the popular nickname "Trustbuster."

Roosevelt's commitment to trailblazing led him to more compromises than his reputation—and rhetoric—suggested. In 1906, after reading Upton Sinclair's exposé of unsanitary industrial butchering in The Jungle, Roosevelt acted on what he had read, but cautiously. First he discreetly dispatched two investigators to the meat packing houses, who confirmed the worst of Sinclair's descriptions. Then he pressured Congress to pass the Meat Inspection Act of 1906, which implemented new sanitation standards in plants and federal inspection of meat. In the legislative horse-trading that resulted, Roosevelt secured more inspections but offered more lenient enforcement. The biggest meatpacking firms cynically welcomed expensive requirements that would burden their small competitors. Only insiders noticed the burdensome compromise, while public opinion hailed Roosevelt for vanquishing corporate evil and protecting American consumers and workers. Roosevelt had secured his victory, and, again, a precedent.

Radicals worried that the limited successes and painful compromises were sapping progressivism. The haggling over the Hepburn Act in 1906 infuriated progressives, particularly Wisconsin's crusading reformer, Senator Robert M. La Follette. The bill authorized the Interstate Commerce Commission to set maximum freight rates in the railroad industry. Republicans, funded by railroad companies, limited the ICC's powers, especially by allowing the conservative, pro-business courts to review and thus restrict the ICC's actions.

Roosevelt hailed the Hepburn Bill as a breakthrough, finally allowing the Interstate Commerce Commission to control the rapacious railroads. Roosevelt laughed at the Republicans' childish tactics when they had Democratic Senator Ben Tillman of South Carolina sponsor the legislation. Tillman and Roosevelt were feuding. Republicans assumed Roosevelt would refuse to work with the senator. Instead, Roosevelt worked with Tillman through intermediaries and marveled at his opponents' inability to appreciate his broader vision. Roosevelt would go with Tillman "or with any one else just so long as he was traveling in my way—and no longer."

Roosevelt expanded federal prerogatives and demanded corporate responsibility in numerous ways. He made the federal government responsible for conserving more than 230 million acres, designating national parks, forests, game reserves, and bird preserves. He made employers responsible for workers' injuries with the 1908 Federal Employers' Liability Act. Roosevelt also mediated between the "ultra-radicals" and the "conservatives." He found both sides obsessed with trivialities. Roosevelt believed that he secured "justice" for the corporations and the workers. The railroads' profitability had to be protected, too. Once again hewing a middle path, he said, "The public, the shippers, the stock and bondholders, and the employees, all have their rights, and none should be allowed unfair privileges at the expense of the others."

WITH CAREFUL BUT TRAILBLAZING REFORMS affecting basic transportation, sanitation, compensation, and conservation, Roosevelt modernized the longstanding democratic impulse favoring muscular moderation. Reflecting the new century's obsession with the psyche, one reporter, Henry Herzberg, called Roosevelt's search for the middle a "psychology of inconsistency." Roosevelt wrestled between his "aristocratic will" and a "democratic desire to please." These conflicting impulses made Roosevelt daring yet cautious. Herzberg recognized America's developing national character reflected in Roosevelt's "nervous energy, the irrepressible ambition."

As president, Roosevelt proved particularly effective in harnessing newspapers' nationalizing and moderating potential. Newspapers in Roosevelt's day were centripetal forces binding Americans in a common narrative, with joint concerns, a familiar language, and a national agenda. Roosevelt's genius for compromise and publicity often blurred. "When do I get the ear of the people?" Roosevelt asked Edward Bok of *Ladies' Home Journal*. This typically Rooseveltian question enlisted the magazine publisher in the president's perennial search for attention. Reporters deemed Roosevelt "the greatest publicity promoter among the sons of man to-day." They claimed his motto was, "Let me have free access to the channels of publicity and I care not who makes my country's laws—or what the other fellow does."

Theodore Roosevelt was his own greatest press agent. "My father wants to be the corpse at every funeral, the bride at every wedding and the baby at every christening," his acerbic daughter Alice Longworth once said. Wherever Roosevelt went, publicity followed.

America's industrial and demographic revolutions also revolutionized journalism. From 1890 to 1900, with the population increasing from 63 to 76 million, the number of daily newspapers jumped from 1,610 to 2,226. Average daily circulation almost doubled, from 8.4 to 15.1 million. Perpetually hunting for readers, publishers such as Joseph Pulitzer and William Randolph Hearst demanded dramatic stories. Mass newspapers mass-produced sensationalism. Readers became wrapped up in regular national melodramas, starring the heroes and villains of the moment.

Commanding center stage as a national hero, Theodore Roosevelt wooed, entertained, and bullied the press. He postured for reporters— speaking, gesticulating, even governing with an eye toward how it would play in the papers. Roosevelt was capable of planting a story, then disclaiming it—a technique later immortalized as the trial balloon. "Platitudes and iteration are necessary in order to hammer the truths and principles I advocate into people's heads," he said. Roosevelt's charm reduced reporters, some complained, to cuckoos, roosting in the White House, delighting their editors and the public by chirping the president's song.

Roosevelt protected his image fiercely. Any cuckoos who crossed the president risked exile—both from Roosevelt's good graces and a good shot at the front page. With his self-dramatizing flair, Roosevelt reduced everyone around him to bit players in his own life story. Reporters who displeased him ended up in the "Ananias Club," named after the early Christian who dropped dead when the Apostle Peter chided him for lying. Roosevelt "corrupt[ed] the press," the crusading liberal journalist Oscar Villard recalled, remembering watching in fascination and disgust as the president "warped and twisted, consciously or unconsciously, by his fascinating personality the judgments of the best of reporters."

However, Roosevelt could not appear too self-aggrandizing. America's sober, puritan farmers still set the national tone. They mistrusted anyone who appeared too "big for his britches" or eager for the spotlight. During the 1904 presidential campaign, Republican National Chairman George B. Cortelyou ordered the president's secretary, William Loeb, to photograph the president in his office. Loeb reported to Cortelyou, "I had to bullyrag the President into it . . . . If it gets out that the President has sat for a photographer, however, I am in for all sorts of trouble."

Roosevelt's legend took on a life of its own. On a hunting trip in Mississippi in 1902, the president's guides cornered a small bear. Roosevelt refused to shoot the poor animal. The *Washington Post*'s Clifford Berryman sketched a cartoon of the noble president and his bear. Berryman then began using a cuter, cuddlier version of his original bear as a symbol in many of his Roosevelt cartoons. This mixed with two separate toy manufacturers' efforts to market bear dolls. Reflecting how the new president dominated American consciousness, all these efforts were ground up in the maw of American popular culture. The result was the "Teddy bear," which immortalized Roosevelt and helped expand his power, but used a nickname he detested.

TO FRIENDS AND FOES, Roosevelt's precedent-making behavior upstaged his center seeking; like a crow, the singular noise he made belied his surprisingly collaborative approach to group nest building. The 1904 presidential campaign became a referendum on Roosevelt and his conception of an expanded presidency. The main campaign issue was "YOU yourself— Theodore Roosevelt," the *New York World* editorialized in July 1904. "The issue is forced upon the country by your . . . strong, able, ambitious, resourceful, militant, passionate personality." Frustrated by their Republican rival's popularity, editors who favored the Democrats feared Roosevelt. Caricaturing him as heavy-handed and power-hungry, they said Americans had to choose "a Personal or a Constitutional government—the sovereignty of a party dictator or the sovereignty of the people." A few weeks later, the *World* wondered whether the president was a megalomaniac or merely a demagogue.

As Democrats denounced Roosevelt's imperialistic, impetuous "Executive Usurpation," Republicans defended him as a democratic hero. At the Republican convention, Senator Albert J. Beveridge of Indiana praised Roosevelt because "he does things the people want done; does things, not merely discusses them." California's George A. Knight linked Roosevelt's presidency with his romantic version of American nationalism: "Our country is big and broad and grand; we want a President typical of the country, one who will preserve her history, enforce her law, teach Americanism and fight the wrong. Theodore Roosevelt, 'thou art the man!'"

Roosevelt interpreted his landslide victory in 1904, garnering 56.4 percent of the popular vote and 336 of 476 electoral votes, as a popular seal of approval on his new, nationalist, center-seeking presidency. Roosevelt's reputation as a peacemaker received an international seal of approval when he won the Nobel Peace Prize in 1906 for mediating an end to the Russo–Japanese War of 1905. His foreign policy, like his domestic policy, was frequently more cautious, more averse to conflict, and more constructive than his rhetoric suggested. His efforts in mediating an end to the Russo–Japanese War reflected a characteristic Roosevelt mix of secret negotiations, public postures, and pacific results. As with his mediation during the miners strike, Roosevelt proved more willing to threaten than to act. He often declared victory without any shots being fired or serious consequences being suffered on either side. When Germany menaced Venezuela in 1902, Roosevelt's threat to Germany was enough to force the European power to retreat.

With new appreciation for presidential power, Americans rallied around their larger-than-life president. Thanks to Roosevelt, they felt better about their country and themselves. The journalist H. L. West, who had condemned William McKinley's power grab in 1901, buried his constitutional concerns. Celebrating Roosevelt as a bold "flesh-and-blood President" with a grand leadership style, West rejoiced, "He shatters precedent without a tremor . . . If he is convinced that a thing must be done, action follows conviction without delay."

The power of the presidency obligated Roosevelt to serve only for "a limited time," he explained as he voluntarily retired in 1909. The move also defused charges of self-interest. As the "President of the plain people," Roosevelt refused "to destroy their ideal of me." American politics remained tied to the republican conception of self-abnegation as virtuous and power as dangerous. Roosevelt walked away still popular, powerful, and enthralled with the job.

Abraham Lincoln had appeared vacillating but was steely enough to propel the nation forward amid great crisis. By contrast, Theodore Roosevelt always appeared tougher and more definitive than he actually was. His blustery style suited a time when the challenges were frequently more abstract and less incendiary. Nearly a century later, Bill Clinton would admire Roosevelt's ability to mold America even without the kind of trauma that Lincoln—or Roosevelt's eventual successor, Franklin Roosevelt—would face.

AS THE FIRST PRESIDENT who was born in the second half of the nineteenth century, only six-and-a-half years old when he witnessed Abraham Lincoln's funeral procession, Theodore Roosevelt truly was a child of post–Civil War America. Roosevelt grew up in a country that was no longer merely a collection of disparate states. As a citizen, a politician, and a historian, he delighted in his grand American heritage. He saw a strong, effective government led by a powerful, assertive, unifying president as the extension and guarantor of that national greatness. Lacking George Washington's enlightened reticence and Abraham Lincoln's melancholy patience, Theodore Roosevelt plunged into what he called "the arena" of public life and wanted his fellow citizens to join him.

Roosevelt's vitality fed off America's energy. He personified the American go-getter. With factories expanding at a dizzying pace, immigrants mobbing ports of entry, and inventors devising magical products to make America stronger, richer, better, it was difficult not to be swept up in the magnificent American epic.

Nevertheless, to his credit, Roosevelt's nationalism involved more than cheerleading. He recognized the problems of bullying big businesses, rapacious robber barons, underpaid laborers, and dispossessed immigrants. He understood that improving America involved problem solving not just boosterism, and that America's greatness required social justice and equality, not just sweeping expansion and prosperity.

Theodore Roosevelt empowered future presidents by using his bully pulpit to tap into America's romantic nationalism. Becoming the nation's patriot-in-chief made the president both a better kinglike symbol and a more effective prime minister. As the president loomed larger in America's national psyche, the presidency's substantive and constructive power grew. That was Roosevelt's great legacy—a power and impact not surpassed until another Roosevelt entered office during a greater national crisis and set to work.

5

FRANKLIN D. ROOSEVELT AND THE NEW DEAL

The Radical as Moderate

DESPITE A TWENTY-FOUR-YEAR AGE GAP between them, Theodore Roosevelt genuinely liked Franklin D. Roosevelt. With typical TR bluster, he once told Franklin's mother, "I'm so fond of the boy, I'd be shot for him." In turn, Franklin idolized his presidential cousin. After graduating from Theodore's alma mater, Harvard College, and marrying Theodore's niece, Eleanor, in 1905, Franklin followed in TR's footsteps as a New York state legislator, assistant secretary of the navy, a young vice presidential nominee, and New York's governor. When FDR was assistant secretary and occupying TR's old offices, colleagues mocked FDR's affected echoing of TR's favorite exclamation, "Bully!"

As president, Franklin Roosevelt expanded Theodore Roosevelt's patriotic, and surprisingly centrist, bully pulpit. Both presidential Roosevelts demonstrated how inclusive appeals to the nation could galvanize Americans toward constructive actions. A vigorous, romantic nationalism informed both Roosevelts' centrism. They defined the president's job in a democracy as taking strong policy positions that would unite as many Americans as possible. When Theodore Roosevelt talked about the "national" government rather than the "federal" government, he challenged his constituents to be

"Americans first" and state men, or "party men," second. When Franklin Roosevelt addressed "my friends" in his nationally broadcast radio fireside chats in the 1930s, he welcomed Americans across the country into one neighborly community.

Whereas some European forms of romantic nationalism degenerated into extreme ideologies, such as fascism and state communism, that fed demagogic dictators, the Roosevelts' democratic centrism tempered American nationalism. Their brand of nationalism invited all Americans to uphold and enjoy the country's most noble ideals. Both Roosevelts had autocratic streaks and tremendous destructive potential. But each controlled those impulses. Their populist, nationalist presidencies were improvisational, not ideological. Admirers praised Theodore Roosevelt, then Franklin Roosevelt, for being shrewd enough to dodge imprisonment by consistency; detractors abhorred their hit-and-miss fickleness.

The two Roosevelts emerged as the titans of early twentieth-century America's moderate, enlightened, democratic nationalism. To an extent, Theodore Roosevelt's personality and bluster outshone his actual accomplishments. Perhaps TR's greatest achievement was the aura of presidential authority he created for himself. Facing more defining crises, Franklin Roosevelt's accomplishments were written in exclamation points: He solved the Great Depression! He won World War II! Yet TR's personality balanced a presidency that was more moderate than revolutionary, and FDR secured his two great achievements incrementally. Had Theodore Roosevelt been the imprudent leader he first appeared to be, or had Franklin Roosevelt been the revolutionary that the Right feared and the Left craved, neither would have been a successful president, and the nation would have suffered. Creating a national unity that was dynamic yet reasonable, vigorous yet judicious, was the key to their respective accomplishments—and America's twentieth-century rise to power, wealth, and stability.

Both Franklin Roosevelt and Theodore Roosevelt balanced the needs of workers, corporations, and consumers. Both revolutionized Americans' expectations of the government and presidency. And both endured the enmity of many from their own elite class, who branded them traitors for "indulging" the masses. Franklin Roosevelt was blessed to be working in a post-TR world, with an already invigorated presidency. Facing greater challenges than his cousin had, he left a greater historical legacy.

FDR developed TR's improvements on the Washington-Lincoln model of muscular moderation in ways TR never imagined. Theodore Roosevelt's bully pulpit was limited by the range of his voice and the spells he could cast on reporters. Revolutionary changes in modern media helped Franklin Roosevelt address millions directly via the radio and appear larger than life in newsreels. Mass producing an intimate bond amid national crises and governmental expansion created the modern, imperial presidency.

Franklin Roosevelt saved the American system by tempering a massive expansion of presidential power with a humble, agile search for the center. On occasion he stumbled, sometimes overreaching, sometimes retreating before the status quo. Nevertheless, he mastered alarming challenges. Many feared America might not survive first, the Great Depression, then the terrible world war. America was deeply divided, and many European political systems at the time cracked under similar strains. Through both his policies and rhetoric, Roosevelt became modern America's economic savior, social conscience, protector, and peacemaker. He restored confidence to a doubting people. Roosevelt redefined America's government and presidency, simultaneously reviving American nationalism. He transformed the American social covenant, making it a communal responsibility to care for America's once-forgotten men and women. And Roosevelt led the country cleverly and effectively against the German and Japanese fascist threat.

Franklin Roosevelt's triumphs expanded the president's ability to respond during emergencies and calmer times. He created a template for presidential action and activism tempered by flexibility and statesmanship. With radicalism threatening from within and without, Roosevelt not only preserved the American center, he repositioned and strengthened it. And he did it all with élan, great charm, and a steady smile.

THE LIFELONG "TUTORIAL" of TR's example proved particularly useful to Franklin Roosevelt in responding to the country's economic devastation when he became president in 1933. Triggered by foreign debt, wild speculation, structural deficiencies, and limited economic intelligence, the Great Depression, which caused mass misery and deep despair, radically challenged American capitalism. The Gross National Product dropped 25 percent between 1929 and 1932. One out of four American workers lacked a job in 1932. The front-page stories were heartbreaking. Thousands of families lost their homes. Children across the country dined on boiled dandelions. The

American Federation of Labor found Americans' "state of mind bordering on hysteria," as radicals advocated centralized planning and collectivism to replace the chaos of individualism and private property they blamed for causing the disaster. Fearing revolution, General Douglas MacArthur led troops against 25,000 unemployed army veterans marching for their military bonuses in Washington, D.C., in July 1932. In 1937, Franklin D. Roosevelt would still find "one-third of a nation ill-housed, ill-clad, ill-nourished."

Roosevelt's centrism can only be appreciated by understanding the depth of America's social, economic, and ideological crises. America in the 1930s appeared ripe for revolution, with anger in the streets, destitution on the farms, and labor violence in the factories. Mass poverty was a social cancer unraveling America's moral and communal fabric. Rates of burglary, prostitution, and suicide soared while rates of home ownership and marriage plummeted. The rhetoric and threats from the Left and Right became more desperate and extreme.

The growing popularity of Marxist ideas in America radicalized the political and social climate. Russia's 1917 Bolshevik Revolution fed a utopian longing among American intellectuals that blinded many to communism's pathologies. America's Great Depression confirmed their faith in Soviet communism. In 1932, many of America's leading writers, professors, and journalists, including Theodore Dreiser, Sidney Hook, and Lincoln Steffens, demanded "the overthrow of the system which is responsible for all crises." Idealizing the Soviet Union, they deemed capitalism "destructive of all culture," seeing communism as civilization's savior.

With unemployment spreading, corporate assets shrinking, and factory orders drying up, wages plummeted, unions organized, and workers took to the streets. Striking miners and pea pickers, longshoremen and auto workers, often beat up "scabs" for crossing picket lines while risking beatings by corporate thugs or National Guardsmen. In 1931, 40,000 miners in West Pennsylvania went on strike; in the resulting confrontation deputies killed at least two strikers. During that same year 10,000 miners struck in Harlan County, Kentucky, with fierce clashes resulting in the deaths of one miner and three deputies.

With American capitalists flummoxed, European-style communism and socialism confidently explained the downturn and promised salvation. After languishing during the post–World War I Red Scare and the economic boom of the 1920s, the American Communist and Socialist Parties reawakened. In the 1932 presidential election, with approximately 38 million Americans voting, the Communist ticket attracted

102,991 votes. The Socialist candidate for president, Norman Thomas, tripled his 1928 tally, winning 918,000 votes. During the campaign, the *New York Times* ran articles by intellectuals insisting, "We are entering upon the era of plans," predicting that "collectivism may triumph." North Carolina's Governor O. Max Gardner warned Roosevelt about the dangers of "violent social and political revolution."

Yet even as radicalism surged, many Americans mistrusted the big government and powerful bureaucracies that accompanied the Soviet model of communism. The business cycle was expected to right itself. Few trusted the government to solve their personal problems. Most struggling Americans blamed themselves for what had happened. Although the populism and progressivism of the early twentieth century had partially tempered industrialization's excesses by offering some worker protection and some constraints on big business, corporations still enjoyed great political and economic power. In the 1920s, pro-business forces feared the "Bolshevik" scourge while repudiating many of the Progressive ideas of Theodore Roosevelt's day. That decade's succession of passive presidents—Warren G. Harding, Calvin Coolidge, and Herbert Hoover—presided over regulatory rollbacks, tax cuts, union defeats, and a corporate resurgence.

During his two terms in the White House, from 1913 to 1921, the Progressive intellectual Woodrow Wilson had continued Theodore Roosevelt's nationalist revolution. Ideologically, Wilson championed the smaller-is-better "New Freedom" of Supreme Court Justice Louis Brandeis, seeking democratization through decentralization. In practice, Wilson perpetuated Theodore Roosevelt's new nationalism, big government approach, especially once America plunged into the Great War. Presidents Harding, Coolidge, and Hoover rode the backlash against Theodore Roosevelt and Woodrow Wilson, restoring the presidency to its historically modest role.

Depression-era America needed a leader who could alleviate the immediate suffering, preserve private property, reignite the corporate engines, and restore public confidence. The ideal leader would stabilize the political situation by answering the masses' demands for economic relief and social justice while jumpstarting the economy by reassuring the bosses. The need for such a visionary grew as radicals trolled for votes in America and dictators arose in Europe. "Mr. President, if your program succeeds, you'll be the greatest president in American history," an admirer told Franklin Roosevelt when he assumed the presidency. "If it fails, you will be the worst one." Roosevelt responded, "If it fails, I'll be the *last* one."

Remarkably, during the Great Depression the great American center held. Germany succumbed to Nazism and Italy to fascism. The United States remained democratic, moderate, and stable.

FRANKLIN ROOSEVELT WAS BLESSED with an inept predecessor, making it easy for him to assume an initial aura of success. Hoover proved, as James Buchanan had, that great troubles do not always yield great presidents. President Hoover considered the downturn in the nation that began in 1929 a psychological problem more than an economic one. Knowing that the business cycle had always fluctuated, he awaited prosperity's return. In 1932 he was still insisting, "What is needed is the return of confidence." To appear unruffled, he continued dining formally in the White House. The politically tone-deaf president feasted in white tie and tails as American citizens picked through garbage cans for scraps to eat.

Furious Democrats crafted a lasting image of an insensitive, passive Republican president. In fairness, Hoover eventually realized he had to spend government funds to solve the problem and began overcoming America's longstanding, bipartisan aversion to an imbalanced budget. Trying to "prime the pump," he added $423 million to federal public works programs. In December 1931, he encouraged New York financiers to float a $500 million fund for troubled banks. By 1932, desperate, he launched the Reconstruction Finance Corporation (RFC) to prop up railroads, banks, and other financial institutions. While Hoover's use of federal power in the economic realm set a new precedent, he did not fund it adequately. Of the limited funds that were appropriated, none went for social welfare, even though America's voluntary social safety net was in tatters. And what little Hoover did came without reassurance or vision.

The Democrats nominated an unlikely savior in the form of a millionaire playboy crippled by polio. Somehow Franklin Roosevelt charmed the masses while reassuring the bosses. With his pince-nez, cigarette holder, and patrician accent, Roosevelt oozed entitlement. But with a quick smile and a lilt in his voice, his enthusiasm was infectious and all-American.

Although polio had rendered his legs useless when it struck the athletic thirty-nine-year-old in 1921, Roosevelt had a powerful upper body, a sculpted torso, and strong arms. From his sufferings with this disease a warmer, more empathetic, socially minded Roosevelt emerged. Navigating his greatest personal crisis, Roosevelt cultivated a jaunty optimism and devil-may-care élan that would instill confidence in Americans. FDR usually sat with others, even when orating, hiding the fact that he could not stand, so that America's leader would not seem weak.

During the presidential campaign, Roosevelt previewed what would be his centrist policies to revive America's economy and spirits. He boldly promised the American people a "new deal." He was pragmatic, embracing many different approaches simultaneously. Sometimes he satisfied conservatives by demanding a balanced budget. Sometimes he echoed Theodore Roosevelt's big government rationale that if the Constitution did not ban an executive action, it was legitimate if necessary. At other times he pleased small government Brandeisians by endorsing state-level experimentation. Roosevelt was also bipartisan, wooing Republicans as President Hoover's campaign imploded.

To create a popular mandate for the substantial changes he advocated, Roosevelt played to all sides. Hoover alternately blasted him as a "chameleon on plaid" and for endorsing "the same philosophy of government which has poisoned all Europe . . . the fumes of the witch's caldron which boiled in Russia." Even Roosevelt's running mate, the conservative Texan John Nance Garner, warned Roosevelt's people that "if he goes too far with some of these wild-eyed ideas we are going to have the shit kicked out of us." Yet the populist Huey Long complained, "When I talk to him, he says 'Fine! Fine! Fine!' But [the conservative Senate Majority Leader] Joe Robinson goes to see him the next day and again he says 'Fine! Fine! Fine!' Maybe he says 'Fine!' to everybody."

ROOSEVELT CLEVERLY BALANCED bold leadership with agile, even inconsistent, policy making. Roosevelt aide Raymond Moley insisted, "If we can't get a President with a fluid mind, we shall have some bad times ahead." This fluidity became clear during Roosevelt's much-improvised First Hundred Days. From the start he captured the public imagination, giving an impression of progress. The flurry of activity and new policies set a standard for all future presidents, who now chart what they do during their initial three and a third months. The special congressional session Roosevelt convened on March 9, 1933 passed legislation revolutionizing the federal government. But law by law, initiative by initiative, Roosevelt produced a contradictory hodgepodge of philosophies and actions.

Roosevelt wanted to save the nation by leading from the center, creating a shared sense of the common good. He redefined the American covenant, increasing both the citizens' sacrifice and federal power. Roosevelt used military metaphors to galvanize Americans to fight the Depression. During his inauguration, Roosevelt evoked "this great army of our people" twice. He mentioned discipline five times. Roosevelt wanted to balance Americans' traditional individualism with the growing faith in collective action.

Using his grab bag of leadership techniques, Roosevelt tackled many different social and economic problems simultaneously. Surrounded by clashing advisers proposing varied solutions, "Dr. New Deal" prescribed a wide array of medicines. He provided suffering Americans with immediate relief, such as providing 250,000 jobs through the Civilian Conservation Corps. He tried to stimulate a recovery by taking America off the gold standard. And he sought lasting reforms by fixing the banking system and other economic structures. The symbolic and the substantive harmonized in these "3 Rs." When he declared a bank "holiday," which sounded less scary than a "shutdown," Roosevelt reassured bank customers and prevented a wave of bank failures. In his first fireside radio chat, on March 12, 1933, the aristocratic president demonstrated his familiar style as he assured his "friends," the American people, "that it is safer to keep your money in a reopened bank than under the mattress."

The president's dazzling round of activities burst through traditional logjams. Tacking left, his Emergency Banking Act of March 9, 1933 enabled the government to keep weak banks closed and certify strong banks' solvency. A hastily assembled group of officials occasionally consulted with bankers as they rushed to draft the legislation. "We had forgotten to be Republicans or Democrats," Roosevelt's brain-truster Raymond Moley later recalled. "We were just a bunch of men trying to save the banking system." Roosevelt's tinkering with these citadels of capitalism unnerved conservatives. Liberals were also frustrated. The president refused to nationalize the banks, explaining, "I've just had every assurance of cooperation from the bankers."

With his next bill, the Economy Act of March 20, 1933, Roosevelt tacked right. This legislation mandated the prevailing economic orthodoxy, promising governmental and budgetary discipline by reducing federal employees' salaries. Leading progressive Democrats in Congress were so disappointed with this classically conservative move that they refused to vote for the bill. Ever resourceful, and determined to lead, Roosevelt cobbled together a temporary coalition, combining Republican legislators with economically conservative and moderate Democrats.

Roosevelt also understood the power of a goodwill gesture. In May 1933, two months into the New Deal, a second Bonus March, of mostly Communist

Franklin D. Roosevelt, carefully seated with others at a Civilian Conservation Corps camp at Big Meadow, Virginia, in 1933 soothed an unnerved and increasingly radicalized nation, with flamboyant gestures and creative back-to-work programs such as the CCC. (Library of Congress)

veterans, descended on Washington. Rather than deploying troops to confront them. Roosevelt embraced the vets. He ordered the garrison at Fort Hunt to offer the men meals, supplies, and tents. He sent First Lady Eleanor Roosevelt to greet the marchers. He eventually offered them all dollar-a-day jobs in the newly created Civilian Conservation Corps (CCC). The president also met with three marchers individually. Roosevelt immediately rebuffed their requests for mass pension payouts, but gracefully, with a smile. He is "the most likeable fellow I ever met," one of the three men proclaimed. One veteran quipped, "Hoover sent the army, Roosevelt sent his wife."

Roosevelt was a tinkerer, not an ideologue. "Rules are not necessarily sacred, principles are," he preached. Some reformers advocated elaborate government planning. Some trusted industry to create constructive partnerships with government. Others preached a gospel of decentralization.

Linking his experimenting with his liberal optimism, Roosevelt encouraged creative risk taking in policy making.

With his true genius for inclusion, Roosevelt swept up activists from across the spectrum into his whirlwind. Business groups were energized, responding to Roosevelt's challenges with their own proposals for jumpstarting the economy. Radicals were equally galvanized, surprised to be so welcomed. Being able to organize workers, as the United Mine Workers and CIO did, claiming, "The President Wants You to Organize," kept workers, no matter how angry, within the American consensus. However, Roosevelt bristled at the slogan, and some aides proposed suing the unions to stop misrepresenting him. But at the time many people perceived unions as knights of labor fighting for justice. Roosevelt recognized the benefit of appearing to champion millions of long-neglected voters, now streaming to become Democrats.

Roosevelt believed in dialogue and negotiation. When warring factions lobbied the president on May 10, 1933, about the first New Deal centerpiece, the National Industrial Recovery Act (NIRA), he listened to each faction. He then suggested that the combatants lock themselves in a room until they reconciled their differences.

Roosevelt's centrist strategy for saving the NIRA worked. Pro-corporate forces walked away satisfied with the power businesses had kept to negotiate codes of fair competition. Labor radicals obtained Section 7A, which would become known as labor's Magna Carta, legalizing collective bargaining. And the big government supporters walked away with a $3.3 billion public works program. Realizing Roosevelt's vision of a cooperative, mobilized citizenry, the "Blue Eagle" seal of approval on businesses adhering to the National Recovery Administration (NRA) codes invited consumers to support businesses dealing fairly with labor.

The bolder the bill, the more desperately Roosevelt needed competing blocs' endorsements. NIRA proved particularly controversial. Not everyone approved of the compromises reached. Communists and share-the-wealth demagogues like Senator Huey Long condemned the plan as a fascist intrusion of governmental power that co-opted the forces for social justice. Many business leaders also feared government's intrusion into corporate life.

Ultimately, Roosevelt's centerpiece legislation accomplished little. In 1935 the Supreme Court declared the NIRA unconstitutional because it gave the NRA virtually unfettered powers. In a breach of constitutional etiquette, Roosevelt attacked the Court's "horse-and-buggy definition of interstate commerce." He fumed, "Don't call it right or left; that is just first-year high school language." Yet he was privately relieved by the Court's decision. The NRA "has been an awful headache," he confided.

Roosevelt's First Hundred Days modernized the presidency on his terms. Breaking with the past, Roosevelt made the White House a laboratory cooking up, then monitoring, new governmental initiatives. Suddenly, the executive branch was micromanaging the currency through the Emergency Banking Relief Act, electrifying the South via the Tennessee Valley Authority (TVA), eliminating corporate abuses via the Federal Securities Act, and helping individual homeowners with the Home Owners Refinancing Act. Through a new "alphabet soup" of agencies, the CCC (Civilian Conservation Corps), the PWA (Public Works Administration), the AAA (the Agricultural Adjustment Administration), and the NRA (National Recovery Administration) of the NIRA, the government hired millions of unemployed Americans and became ever more intertwined in American life. These jobs put money in citizens' pockets while helping restore Americans' faith in the future.

Roosevelt shifted liberalism from its Jeffersonian insistence on small government to a Hamiltonian appreciation of governmental power. Roosevelt was neither a reactionary nor a radical. The fundamental governing system survived. Private property remained. But the New Deal created a government-sponsored social welfare infrastructure and reoriented Americans' attitudes toward the government, the presidency, and their fellow citizens.

Using the newspapers, radio, and newsreels gave Roosevelt unprecedented power to forge a consensus. As Adolf Hitler used the radio demagogically, cultivating an authoritarian cult of personality, Franklin Roosevelt used the radio democratically, fostering a nationwide sense of responsibility. Roosevelt's signature singsong opening, "My friends," created trust between the man talking into a metal rod and millions sitting in their living rooms. Where Hitler shouted, Roosevelt quipped; where Hitler whipped his followers into a frenzy, Roosevelt soothed his fellow citizens so they could start working together.

Pioneering the fireside chat in 1933 was the most famous example of the way Franklin Roosevelt increased contacts between the president and the American people. He entered their living rooms, dominated their front pages, and starred in their larger-than-life cinematic news digests. Roosevelt revived the White House press conference, meeting reporters 337 times in his first term alone. He invited Americans to sit together at the "common table," to find a "common meeting ground," to give "common consent" by undertaking a "great common effort" to achieve the "great common purpose." He also mastered the traditional weapons in the presidential arsenal, the on-site visit, the executive order, and the formal policy speech, as well as deploying First Lady Eleanor Roosevelt to further extend his reach.

The debut of Roosevelt's informal radio talks inspired over half-a-million letters. The burgeoning White House mailbags measured the president's growth as a popular figure. Herbert Hoover had received an average of 600 letters per day; Roosevelt received 450,000 in his first week. This personalized presidency helped forge a national consensus and keep the country centered. Roosevelt's warmth turned friends into devotees and even had many critics succumbing to his charm.

ROOSEVELT'S CAREFUL CENTRIST legislative blitz created a social welfare state, American style. The new programs respected individualism and preserved private property, even while expanding the government as never before. However, for all his moderation and attempts to mollify various parties, Roosevelt proved extraordinarily controversial.

Critics on both left and right called Roosevelt a dictator, a charlatan, a demagogue. They despised him for co-opting their agendas and their leaders. From the right, the plutocratic publisher William Randolph Hearst began calling FDR SDR: "Stalin Delano Roosevelt." Roosevelt particularly resented the attacks of the businessmen, who felt betrayed by him as a fellow member of America's ruling elite, and threatened to fire any junior executives who voted for him. One business leader harrumphed, "Anybody who is for Roosevelt is just too stupid to be of any good to me." From the left, the Communist leader Earl Browder accused Roosevelt of "carrying out more thoroughly and brutally than even Hoover the capitalist attack against the masses." More subtly, the great American philosopher John Dewey predicted Roosevelt's "piecemeal" approach would doom liberalism, which needed to "socialize the forces of production" to be effective.

The stakes were so high, the demands from both sides so conflicting, that vituperative attacks were inevitable. By being decisive, Roosevelt invariably disappointed some constituencies. He was careful, however, to make sure that both liberals and conservatives occasionally won and occasionally lost. Roosevelt also realized that the masses on the left represented both more votes and more potential disruptions. As long as he conceded enough to business, Roosevelt could bash capitalists when he needed to placate the Left. This strategy worked especially well in 1935, when the stock market rallied thanks to the confidence resulting from the surge of government spending, and some prosperity returned. These apparent economic successes allowed Roosevelt to posture more dramatically for liberals, knowing that conservatives were relatively content with the state of the economy.

By 1935, with opposition growing from all sides, the economy still sputtering, and the Supreme Court invalidating critical legislation, Roosevelt once again offered new proposals. Now designated the Second New Deal, these policies demonstrated new attitudes toward direct relief. What Americans traditionally considered beyond the government's domain was becoming a necessity. Despite growing resistance, Roosevelt attacked big business and championed the poor more aggressively than before.

The Social Security Act of 1935 was the Second New Deal's centerpiece, and arguably the single most dramatic New Deal reform. The Act helped the elderly poor immediately and began a federal pension plan gradually. It eventually offered unemployment insurance, federal aid to dependent mothers and children, and assistance to the blind and handicapped. Half a century of progressive agitation culminated in this legislation. Roosevelt made this great leap seem like a logical next step. His genius for making revolutionary changes appear inevitable built popular support for these audacious steps. The Democratic party became America's party, the party of activist government protecting the middle class and the poor.

Roosevelt wanted to provide "cradle to grave" security, but constructing a workable plan took years. Advisers and activists debated whether there should be cash grants or welfare programs, whether support should be national or state-based, whether social welfare guaranteed dignity or destroyed individual responsibility. Some economists viewed the programs as a just and efficient economic stimulus; others feared the deflationary impact during a recession of all the pension money withdrawn from circulation. Eventually, one of Roosevelt's most progressive advisers, Rexford Tugwell, stopped fighting a payroll tax because it was regressive. He admitted that he and the relief czar, Harry Hopkins, "wanted a social security system much worse than we wanted our own bill. And when the time came we stopped arguing." Roosevelt himself acknowledged that the legislation was but "a cornerstone in a structure which is being built but is no means complete."

Such comprehensive social insurance deviated from American constitutional practice and offended many conservatives, both rich and poor.

The National Association of Manufactures blasted this attempt at "ultimate socialistic control of life and industry." To soften the blow, Roosevelt
injected an all-American centrist twist into this legislative masterstroke.
Workers would pay into the Social Security system for decades before getting their payouts. This innovation reinforced the sanctity of private property, individual dignity, and government centrality. "We put those payroll
contributions there so as to give the contributors a legal, moral, and political right to collect their pensions and their unemployment benefits,"
Roosevelt explained. The individual contributions also guaranteed the
program's future. "With those taxes in there," Roosevelt declared, "no
damn politician can ever scrap my social security program."

After vigorous debate, most members of Congress could not oppose
helping the American community's weakest, sickest, and oldest members.
The House passed the bill 371 to 33. The Senate bill passed two months
later, in June 1935, 76 to 6. Roosevelt's Social Security Act truly was a bipartisan bill enjoying overwhelming support.

In running his administration, as with leading the people, Roosevelt saw
himself as an orchestra conductor. He made beautiful music out of many individual, potentially discordant, sounds. Raymond Moley fumed that when
Roosevelt had received two contrasting tariff policy speeches in 1932, the
candidate told his speechwriter, "weave the two together." To achieve harmony, Roosevelt could be ruthless, undercutting his potential adversaries.
Like Lincoln, Roosevelt was a strong leader, confident enough to hire strong
personalities—and strong enough to dominate them. By constantly picking
different favorites and crafting positions from advisers' various suggestions,
he kept his aides off balance.

One bitter feud pitted the irascible Secretary of the Interior Harold Ickes
against the crusading relief worker Harry Hopkins. Ickes, controlling the Public Works Administration (PWA), preferred carefully planned, centralized
building initiatives. Hopkins, who would control the rival Works Progress Administration (WPA), advocated a multitude of decentralized programs to em-
ploy millions immediately. Roosevelt invited both on a presidential cruise to
bond. However, he also undermined Ickes, implying that Ickes would control
all public works programs but actually shifting significant power to Hopkins.

Roosevelt frequently sidestepped conflict through such deceptions. When a
Washington Star headline announced ICKES IS SHORN OF PWA POWER, Ickes exploded. "I never thought I would talk to a President of the United States the
way I talked to President Roosevelt," Ickes later confessed. Ever charming,

Roosevelt calmed Ickes, promising to issue a press release affirming Ickes's status as PWA's administrator. Still, Roosevelt maintained Hopkins's authority and did not apologize to Ickes.

As a centrist, Roosevelt also wielded executive power cautiously. He was happily cruising from the Caribbean to Oregon via Hawaii when labor violence rocked San Francisco in July 1934. Longshoremen seeking union recognition had been striking since May. On July 5, Bloody Thursday, union members had clashed with police. Two strikers died and sixty-four were hospitalized. Enraged, the radical unionist Harry Bridges called a general strike in San Francisco for July 16, 1934. One hundred thousand striking workers soon paralyzed the California city. Many Americans feared the long-dreaded revolution was arriving. They urged the president to deploy troops to break the strike. "Everybody demanded that I sail into San Francisco Bay, all flags flying and guns double shotted and end the strike," Roosevelt said. "They went completely off the handle."

Roosevelt knew that breaking off his vacation would risk starting the panic he was determined to prevent. He did not mobilize the National Guard, counting on this being taken as a demonstration of respect for labor. His inaction deprived the strikers of a focal point for their anger, a violent clash with citizen-soldiers, and a way to nationalize the issue. The strike whimpered to an end four days later. The Longshoremen's union won recognition and Roosevelt earned labor's respect.

Throughout the 1930s, unions were thriving, fueled by New Deal legislation preserving labor's right to organize, economic anger, and a surge of collectivist idealism. The labor movement, with 3 million workers in 1933, had expanded to 8.5 million workers by 1940 and 10.5 million workers in 1941. Two and a half years after the San Francisco general strike, the CIO, the industrial workers' union, established itself with spontaneous sit-down strikes involving half a million men in Atlanta, Kansas City, Cleveland, South Bend, Detroit, and, most famously, Flint, Michigan.

Talk of revolution and of establishing a worker's party was widespread. Roosevelt feared both. His respect for labor's needs, and his refusal to call in national troops to deal with the sit-down strikes, set an important example. The governors of the relevant states were equally deferential. Other politicians, including Vice President John Garner, condemned the "leftist hooliganism" infecting the country. "Well, it is illegal," Roosevelt admitted of the sit-down strikes, in which workers occupied factories, in some cases for weeks. But he abhorred the idea of "shooting it out and killing a lot of people because they have violated the law of trespass." Assuming that, "There must be another way," he asked, "Why can't those fellows in General Motors meet with the committee of workers?" Thanks to Roosevelt, some of America's corporate giants, including United States Steel, General Motors, and General Electric, grudgingly accepted the new union.

Roosevelt's statesmanship averted serious violence and gave workers a historic victory, unionizing industrial America on a grand scale. He tempered his ideological shift toward labor, the Left, the "forgotten," with a healthy dose of pragmatism and self-discipline. By refusing to insert himself paternalistically into local incidents, he helped the labor movement without alienating middle-class voters, many of whom were unnerved by the strikes.

Dominating the center during such a volatile time, Roosevelt sustained attacks from the left and the right. His union supporters, especially the United Mine Workers' fiery John L. Lewis, resented the president's calculated inaction during the sit-down strikes and other labor disputes. In 1937 Roosevelt condemned violent wildcat steel strikes that triggered corporate reprisals, wishing a "plague on both their houses." Lewis exploded.

Roosevelt knew what he was doing. As Theodore Roosevelt had taught him, knowing when to relinquish power, or when not to exercise it, is an essential skill. Moreover, speaking for all Americans sometimes entails condemning both sides and requires an agility that borders on duplicity. Roosevelt's centrism was a delicate balancing act, piling competing weights on different ends of the scale as needed.

THE 1930s WERE TUMULTUOUS. Change did not come easily. The economy remained sluggish. Radical demands and conservative complaints bombarded the White House. Yet out of this turmoil a new equilibrium emerged, which shaped the 1936 election.

Like many great leaders, Roosevelt was an egotist, supremely pleased with himself and contemptuous of critics. As the business backlash grew, Roosevelt indulged more of his radical streak. He wrapped his radicalism in traditional garb, wanting to restore "ancient truths" whereby "we apply social values more noble than mere monetary profit." Expanding government's role to protect America's "forgotten," he turned the presidency's moral power against the country's elite. Gone were Theodore Roosevelt's niceties about reform for the good of business. Periodically, FDR denounced the greedy "economic royalists" trying to enslave the American people, and by extension, their government.

Surprisingly, Roosevelt used strident language to position himself in the center for his 1936 reelection campaign. His rhetoric reflected the tenor of the times and his strategy in dealing with partisans. Satisfied that he had served the business community by saving capitalism and restarting the economy, Roosevelt happily fed the populist beast. He did, however, criticize capitalists and their excesses without repudiating capitalism itself.

Even while baiting his wealthy peers, Roosevelt resented their criticism. He marveled at their inability to see the big picture, to appreciate that he had saved the whole concept of private property at the cost of a little more regulation and a bit more taxation. To illustrate the point, during the 1936 campaign Roosevelt joked that in the summer of 1933 a gentleman with a silk hat fell off a pier. A friend saved him from drowning, but the hat sank. The old guy originally thanked his friend. Three years later, the gentleman, missing the big picture, was yelling about his lost hat.

Herbert Hoover was still reeling from being demonized, still trying to rehabilitate his reputation. Hoover dismissed Roosevelt as a snake-oil salesman who made himself look important. Hearing Roosevelt chide the rich for worrying about their proverbial silk hats, Hoover speculated that the manipulative Roosevelt had secretly pushed the old guy off the dock to get a job as a lifeguard.

Roosevelt recalibrated Americans' traditional fears. He invoked a potent American image, claiming that the "average man" faced the same challenges from these "new mercenaries" of business that confronted "the Minute Man of seventy-six." He preached at the 1936 Democratic Convention, "Better the occasional faults of a government that lives in a spirit of charity than the consistent omissions of a government frozen in the ice of its own indifference."

The strategy of Roosevelt's opponent in the presidential race, Kansas Governor Alfred M. Landon, reflected how much the Depression and Roosevelt had shifted Americans' political center. The Republican nominee sounded like a Roosevelt Democrat, vowing to provide government relief, fight monopolies, and respect labor's right to organize. Although criticizing the New Deal as chaotic, spasmodic, and despotic, Landon attacked Roosevelt's methods, not his aims. Landon denounced the Social Security Act as "unjust, unworkable, stupidly drafted and wastefully financed." Republican-leaning factories distributed pro-Landon placards warning workers that they would be sentenced to perpetual pay reductions caused by Social Security's automatic payroll deductions, unless they voted out Roosevelt. But it would have been political suicide for anyone to reject the idea of Social Security itself. In only a year, this improvised deviation from constitutional tradition had become politically untouchable.

Landon could not compete with signs dotting the country proclaiming, THANK GOD FOR ROOSEVELT. Assistant Secretary of State Breckinridge Long observed that in 1932 voters chose Roosevelt glumly, to punish Hoover. In 1936, most voters happily rallied around this big picture centrist, emitting rays of hope amid black clouds of despair.

Like Theodore Roosevelt, Franklin Roosevelt emphasized the presidency's uniquely national perspective. As "President of all the people," Roosevelt insisted in 1936, "There should be no bitterness or hate where the sole thought is the welfare of the United States of America." Roosevelt listed all that he had provided for the "whole Nation," including cheaper electricity, better and cheaper transportation, low interest rates, sounder home financing, and better banking. The Republican journalist William Allen White appreciated how modern media and popular culture reinforced the president's national standing, telling Roosevelt, "For box office attraction, you leave Clark Gable gasping for breath."

After the reelection campaign had ended with a Roosevelt landslide of 60.7 percent of the popular vote yielding a lopsided electoral count of 523 to 8, FDR sought to heal any partisan rifts. Addressing reporters at the Gridiron Club before Christmas 1936, Roosevelt praised "our American tradition of tolerance" in a world gripped by "fear, hatred and bitter political rivalries." FDR emphasized that his New Deal revived "the basic idea of society and of the nation itself that people acting in a group can accomplish things which no individual acting alone could even hope to bring about." Two years later, before the midterm elections, Roosevelt proposed "calm argument," not "unfair blows" for the campaign. He told a story about two Chinese people arguing heatedly: "A stranger expressed surprise that no blows were being struck. His Chinese friend replied: 'The man who strikes first admits that his ideas have given out.'" Throughout his lengthy time in office, Franklin Roosevelt kept generating more ideas and more sweeping visions.

THE 1936 ELECTION became a referendum on Roosevelt. Franklin Roosevelt's victory was the greatest since Theodore Roosevelt's win in 1904. This triumph solidified the New Deal's gains, but FDR, now at his peak, would soon stumble.

Within a year, the New Deal had stalled and Roosevelt had over-stepped. Just as he had taught the country—and future successors—how much presidents could accomplish, Roosevelt was about to reveal the office's limits. His victory in the election, the rhetoric praising him as America's savior, and his crusading fury at his greedy opposition reinforced a sense of invincibility and righteousness. Roosevelt had become too used to demonizing his opponents, surmounting obstacles, and dismissing any resistance to his plans as evil and stupid. Anxious to accelerate his agenda, he appeared to forget how important it was to keep reform progressing at a proper pace and avoid running over too many of the critics trying to block the road.

Even though he had been secretly relieved when the Supreme Court invalidated the NIRA, Roosevelt resented the "Nine Old Men" as a last bastion of conservatism that repudiated his other programs. Roosevelt proposed adding to the Court one new justice for each sitting justice older than seventy years of age. The scheme would have yielded six Roosevelt appointees. The president explained that, "The Court has been acting not as a judicial body, but as a policy-making body," risking becoming, as one justice indiscreetly said, a "super-legislature." In March 1937, in a fireside chat begging the nation to help "save our national Constitution from hardening of the judicial arteries," Roosevelt made a personal appeal: "You who know me will accept my solemn assurance that in a world in which democracy is under attack, I seek to make American democracy succeed."

But many feared that Roosevelt's ego and his plan actually threatened democracy. Even liberal icons such as Justice Louis Brandeis and Senator Burton Wheeler objected. A progressive Westerner, Wheeler considered the court "reactionary." Still, he feared Roosevelt's move would destroy "the court itself." From the Republican side, Herbert Hoover warned about subordinating "the court to the personal power of the Executive," fearing it threatened "our form of government." Cries of "usurpation," "despotism," "rubber stamp," and "executive aggrandizement" filled the air. The *New York Times* compared the battle to the struggle over slavery.

Uncharacteristically, Roosevelt remained self-righteous and rigid. He refused to compromise. He decided that after wagering so much personal standing and political capital on the fight, half measures would not do.

Roosevelt's plan failed. A lopsided Senate vote of 70 to 20 in July 1937 sent the legislation back to the judiciary committee, where it was stripped of its most controversial provisions. Until the court-packing scheme, many

Roosevelt initiatives had stretched the Constitution without subverting it. Expanding presidential and congressional power was one thing; undermining the third branch was another. This plan was too radical for the people, for Roosevelt's centrist mandate, and for a president who was personally more popular than his program. Americans remained committed to the Founders' constitutional structure. They still feared dictators.

One element that helped kill the plan was the "switch in time that saved nine." The Court's swing justice, Owen J. Roberts, began approving New Deal initiatives, undermining Roosevelt's rationale for packing the Court. Social Security, which had been challenged as unconstitutional, narrowly passed muster in May 1937, with a vote of five to four. Older justices began retiring. Over the next four years Roosevelt would fill seven vacancies. By June 1938, with a Roosevelt Court emerging, the president rejoiced, "The attitude of the Supreme Court towards constitutional questions is entirely changed."

As Roosevelt regrouped, another recession hit, triggered by a second stock market crash in the fall of 1937. A nine-month downturn began. Four million more jobs disappeared. Roosevelt gambled again, this time on the congressional midterm campaigns. He tried to purge disloyal Democrats from office, recruiting candidates to oppose them in the primaries. Although Roosevelt helped retire one New York Democrat, Congressman John J. O'Connor, overall the effort failed. The targeted Democrats, mostly Southern, returned to Congress, furious at their party leader. In 1938 the divided Democrats lost seventy seats in the House and seven seats in the Senate, marking the first Republican gains since 1928. Even with those dramatic losses, the Democrats still controlled both houses.

Americans seemed to be losing faith in themselves and their president. It was difficult to believe during Christmastime 1938 that the magician had any more tricks up his sleeve. Roosevelt was becoming a lame duck midway through his second term. A failing president, he seemed locked into George Washington's tradition of retiring after two terms. With the economy worsening, Franklin Roosevelt was looking more like Herbert Hoover every day.

Even as criticism mounted, and his day-to-day power seemed to ebb, Roosevelt's stature and legend grew. With his flamboyant gestures, Roosevelt injected hope into the collective American narrative at a time of great despair. With his grab bag of reforms, Roosevelt made the presidency and the federal government the new centers of national problem solving.

For all his self-assurance, Franklin Roosevelt experimented and improvised, as the cartoonist James T. Berryman recognized in this cartoon from the mid-1930s, in which the president is shown fishing around for a new recovery program. (Library of Congress)

Roosevelt changed the way the American government did business and related to business. Critics from the left who dismissed the New Deal as a "reshuffle" or repackaging overlooked how innovative and invigorating it was; critics from the right who called the New Deal revolutionary, rather than a package with some revolutionary changes, ignored how effective Roosevelt was in saving America's capitalist democracy. But the Court-packing fight and his failure to purge the conservative Democratic congressmen sobered Roosevelt. He was more cautious in the following years. As the subsequent struggle over entering World War II showed, despite his second term lapses, Roosevelt had learned how to find that muscular middle, clearly standing for something but compromising when necessary.

IN POPULAR MYTHOLOGY, during World War II the omnipotent Franklin Roosevelt unified the nation with his eloquence and strategic focus. In fact, Roosevelt staggered into the war years. In the 1940 presidential election, Roosevelt's percentage of the popular vote dropped to 54.7 percent; a setback after he had won 60.7 percent four years earlier.

As the American government debated entering World War II, Roosevelt applied the lessons he had learned so painfully in 1937 and 1938. He did not rock the constitutional boat. He did not outrun public opinion. His cautious progress offered a model of democratic leadership. He stayed half a step ahead of his constituents, neither bold enough to lose them nor accommodating enough to lose sight of his goal. Roosevelt was a maestro of moderation during the two years preceding Pearl Harbor. Subtly but boldly, he transformed an isolationist country still reeling from the Great War and the Great Depression into a responsible superpower.

The interventionist debate could not abide a mushy man of the middle. Roosevelt emerged as a muscular moderate. He was temperate, reasonable, bipartisan, but visionary. Persuading—not commanding—Americans to enter the war sharpened his communication skills. He delivered some of his best speeches during 1939 and 1940, defining the "Four Freedoms" that all citizens of the world deserved.

Roosevelt balanced his public eloquence with private wiles. Staying just far enough ahead of public opinion to shape it required him to endorse each baby step as if it were the final destination. For example, even while repeatedly proclaiming America's neutrality, Roosevelt frequently nudged Americans toward supporting England and the Allies. "This nation will remain a neutral nation," Roosevelt said when Germany invaded Poland in 1939, "but I cannot ask that every American remain neutral in thought as well. Even a neutral has a right to take account of facts." This strategy required some indirection, even misdirection. Still, Roosevelt's approach should inspire all his successors. He tugged public opinion gently forward, neither yanking too hard nor losing his grip.

The fight over entering World War II was vicious. Antisemitism, nativism, and fear fueled the fires. Partisans mounted aggressive campaigns on the streets, in movie theaters, on the airwaves, and in the halls of Congress. Each side sensed a chance at victory. Interventionists noted America's deep identification with England and France, especially after the Great War. Some polls estimated that 80 percent of Americans favored the Allies after Germany invaded Poland in 1939. Isolationists were equally cocky; only 50 to 60 percent of the population polled in other surveys favored assisting England and France, and even most of those in favor wanted America to avoid combat.

Most Americans in the 1930s were isolationists. World War I—the Great War—had violently thrust the United States into European affairs, triggering

great revulsion among the population at large. After the bloody trench warfare in France, after the Treaty of Versailles failed to achieve President
Woodrow Wilson's pie-in-the-sky ideals, many Americans reverted to their
traditional isolationism. Many Americans felt the country's sacrifices had
been fruitless. During the 1920s some wanted to ignore the world, whereas
others embraced the era's legalistic attempts to outlaw war.

During the 1930s, as Adolf Hitler expanded Germany in the West, Japan became more aggressive in the East, fighting China over Manchuria.
Isolationists in Congress passed a series of neutrality acts. Still, Roosevelt
laid the groundwork for America's reengagement with Europe, believing
that another war might be necessary. Despite the obvious growing tensions
in Europe, Germany's invasion of Poland on September 1, 1939, shocked
most Americans. However, it only confirmed many isolationists' instincts.
A three-day national radio campaign triggered one million telegrams, letters, and postcards warning Congress to avoid Europe's conflict.

As Roosevelt danced a political minuet, pretending not to run while
yearning for a third term in 1940, he also danced a diplomatic minuet, pro-
fessing neutrality while starting to favor England and intervention. A public opinion war erupted. Many interventionists feared for the future,
doubting liberal democracies' power to defeat the fascist threat. William
Allen White, a Midwestern Republican journalist, formed the Committee
to Defend America by Aiding the Allies in May, 1940, demanding that
America help England and the Allies with everything short of troops.

An odd mix of right-wing isolationists and left-leaning pacifists established the America First Committee in September, 1940. The most prominent isolationist was the aviation hero of the 1920s, Charles Lindbergh.
"Lucky Lindy" camouflaged his soft spot for the Nazis and his hostility toward Jews with the rational argument that America, which was militarily
unprepared, should avoid war unless it could win. Senator Gerald P. Nye of
North Dakota insisted that the European war was not "worthy of the sacrifice of one American mule, much less one American son."

Even as President Roosevelt signed the various neutrality acts that the
isolationists passed, he hedged: "History is filled with unforeseeable situations that call for some flexibility of action." Roosevelt felt a strong bond
with Europe based on the enlightened West's common past and shared
fate. As early as 1935, Roosevelt confided to his aide, Rexford Tugwell,
that he feared another European conflagration coming. Throughout the
decade Roosevelt laid the groundwork for America's reengagement with

Europe. In his 1936 State of the Union address, Roosevelt warned Americans—and the world—that "the peoples of the Americas must take cognizance of growing ill-will, of marked trends toward aggression, of increasing armaments, of shortening tempers." The next year Japan's occupation of large parts of China prompted him to propose "a quarantine of the lawless, a quarantine of those that threaten world peace."

Roosevelt sympathized with Great Britain. But unlike Woodrow Wilson, he feared outrunning public opinion. Throughout the spring and summer of 1940, Roosevelt tried to sensitize Americans to European suffering, the millions in Belgium and France, "running from their homes to escape bombs and shells and fire and machine gunning, without shelter, and almost wholly without food." Americans were enduring a "rude awakening," the president insisted. He accelerated defense production and detailed the improvements: 215 ships "laid down or commissioned," doubling the Army's size, increasing "useful aircraft" from 1,127 to 2,892. These figures appealed to voters and cautioned America's potential enemies.

Roosevelt tried to undermine the isolationists' platform plank by plank. He wanted to destroy the "illusion that we are remote and isolated" without panicking the "calamity-howlers." The Atlantic and Pacific Oceans no longer insulated Americans from the world. Roosevelt proclaimed, "Our Bunker Hill of tomorrow may be several thousand miles from Boston, Massachusetts." Roosevelt had compared combating the Great Depression to fighting a war; now he prepared Americans for war by invoking the great fight against the Great Depression.

Roosevelt avoided a backlash against his unprecedented run for a third term by emphasizing that he was being drafted due to the diplomatic emergency. He used his expanded presidential powers to advance his candidacy while building the necessary "arsenal of democracy." Inching toward supporting England, Roosevelt developed a clever ruse in September 1940. America offered Great Britain fifty aging destroyers for the rights to construct military bases on British possessions. This masterstroke, known as the "Destroyer-Bases Deal," began the "lend-lease" program, which became official in March 1941 when Congress passed the Lend Lease Act. The president could now lend or lease any equipment to any nation whose defense he considered essential to the defense of the United States. In helping the Allies while sidestepping congressional demands for neutrality, this program helped nudge Americans from isolationism toward interventionism.

In the East, the Japanese looked increasingly threatening. On September 27, 1940, Japan, Germany, and Italy created the "Axis alliance." Roosevelt embargoed scrap iron and steel exports to all countries outside the Western Hemisphere except Great Britain. This move hurt Japan, which needed imported steel. Roosevelt also hardened his rhetoric. Before the Axis pact, during the presidential campaign he often avoided defining the enemy, preferring to speak of the "present emergency." On December 29, 1940, he let loose, claiming, "Never before since Jamestown and Plymouth Rock has our American civilization been in such danger as now." He targeted the "Nazi masters of Germany" seeking to "enslave the whole of Europe" along with their Japanese allies.

Throughout 1941, Roosevelt continued quietly improving America's defenses while edging the country toward war. As a much-needed bonus, America's increased defense production jumpstarted the economy, something the New Deal had not accomplished. Roosevelt developed an overarching ideological framework for the conflict. When articulating the Four Freedoms individuals deserved throughout the world, Roosevelt justified intervention to protect freedom of speech and expression, freedom of worship, freedom from want, and freedom from fear.

Still, Roosevelt could not convince all Americans that the United States needed to enter the war. As the conflict grew more violent, isolationists grew more virulent. Students were almost uniformly isolationist. The Harvard *Crimson* demanded "Peace Now." Even soldiers also failed to recognize the danger. In the summer of 1941, servicemen in Mississippi booed a newsreel showing President Roosevelt meeting General George Marshall. When a clip showed Senator Hiram Johnson advocating isolationism, the soldiers cheered.

Although he clearly favored Great Britain, Roosevelt promised he would not risk American lives unless attacked first. It was an excruciating time. The accumulation of bad news, greater tension, and more warnings ratcheted up the tension with no resolution. Germany and Japan took more territory daily. Roosevelt stewed impatiently, wanting to act "quickly, boldly, decisively." He admitted privately, "I am waiting to be pushed into the situation." He also agreed it was awful "to look over your shoulder when you're trying to lead and find no one there." Interventionist staffers began losing patience. Roosevelt had invited two establishment Republicans to join his third-term cabinet. Frank Knox, the 1936 Republican vice presidential nominee, became secretary of the navy. Henry Stimson, who had served as William Howard Taft's secretary of war and Herbert Hoover's secretary of state, became secretary of war again.

This bipartisan gesture was inspired. Independent-minded and interventionist, Stimson pushed the president. He understood that Americans needed Roosevelt's moral leadership and should not be dragged into war. When Roosevelt told Stimson that patrolling neutral waters to protect British ships against Nazi raids was a step forward, Stimson exclaimed, "Well, I hope you will keep on walking, Mr. President. Keep on walking!"

Roosevelt improvised more steps toward war to give an illusion of momentum. On May 27, 1941, the president proclaimed "that an unlimited national emergency exists and requires the strengthening of our defense to the extreme limit of our national power and authority." Gradually, the rush of events and Roosevelt's deliberate pace combined to produce the result he was seeking. In October 1941, *Time* magazine reported a "switch" in student opinions. At Princeton, the percentage of freshmen willing to fight overseas jumped in one year from 33 to 82 percent.

The government, however, remained immobilized. In mid-October, Britain's ambassador to the United States, Lord Halifax, described Roosevelt's paradoxical predicament to British Prime Minister Winston Churchill. The president was balancing overlapping, contradictory polls showing that 70 percent of Americans wanted to avoid war yet 70 percent also wished to crush Hitler. If Roosevelt "asked for a declaration of war, he wouldn't get it and opinion would swing against him," Halifax reported. "He therefore intended to go on doing whatever he best could to help us, and declarations of war were out of fashion."

Roosevelt painstakingly, sometimes dishonestly, forged the path for Americans toward war. He contained his strong feelings against the Axis, reassuring voters that he would avoid American bloodshed long after he had realized that American military involvement was inevitable.

Despite all the tension, the Japanese sneak attack on Pearl Harbor in December 1941 shocked the country. Roosevelt's reputation for omnipotence and indirection was so well established that many Americans believed he must have known about the Japanese plans. But it is more likely that through American confusion and miscalculation, the Japanese deception worked. Roosevelt and his beloved Navy were genuinely surprised. In the preceding years, Roosevelt had established America's war policy. Thanks to him, America was already preparing for war, with factories humming and soldiers being trained.

Although the Japanese attack and Hitler's subsequent declaration of war against the United States clarified America's status, Roosevelt had already led the American people on a remarkable journey. A nation extremely resistant to war in 1939 was ready to fight by 1941. In a classic example of the alchemy between a great leader and his flock, the American people seemingly ceded the decision-making process to Roosevelt, who led them to the necessary moral conclusion. In the 1940s America was blessed with a president who reframed the debate and repositioned popular opinion. Without Roosevelt's leadership, the question might have remained, "Why shed American blood on foreign soil?" Roosevelt cast the war as an ugly but necessary fight for freedom even before America was attacked. But for all his planning, Roosevelt, in this case, did not overstep. He did not plunge into war once he had made a convincing case; he waited until conditions made war unavoidable.

Roosevelt's strategy and patience helped Americans understand why they were fighting and that the fight would be difficult. Initially, American troops failed to stem the Japanese advance in the Pacific. Only in mid-1942 did America begin winning.

Freed from the purgatory of neutrality, Roosevelt thrived. He was effective diplomatically, meeting with Winston Churchill and Joseph Stalin, his Soviet counterpart, in Teheran in 1943, then at Yalta in 1945. He was smart militarily, allowing his generals to win the war even while making his presence felt. And he was brilliant politically, soothing the nation and uniting the political parties, at least temporarily. Roosevelt played his part well, appearing humble in victory, resolute in defeat. And even while managing the war, Roosevelt planned for peace, laying the groundwork for a United Nations, his improvement on Wilson's League of Nations.

Roosevelt also presided over—and helped define—a period of unprecedented national agreement. The bombing of Pearl Harbor united Americans as never before. Building on a common culture and unifying technologies like radio and the movies, Americans now shared a common goal. The nation became as important as the family, the church, and the school. More than a "war to end all wars" or a fight for democracy, this was a war for the American home, a war for Americans' way of life.

Fittingly, the artist Norman Rockwell depicted President Roosevelt's "four freedoms" in domestic tableaux of a town hall and a Thanksgiving turkey, of churchgoers praying, and a child snugly falling asleep. The American family represented the front line in the fight for freedom. Popular culture promoted patriotism and wartime sacrifice with Rosie the Riveter advertisements, Rita Hayworth pinups, U.S. savings bonds drives and USO dances to the upbeat swing melodies of Benny Goodman and Duke Ellington. As Germany collapsed in 1944 and 1945, confirmation of the Nazis' horrific crimes justified all this patriotic bonding. The war ended with Americans more sure than ever of their war effort's righteousness, their leader's virtue, and their country's greatness.

BY THE TIME ROOSEVELT DIED in April 1945, an Allied victory was imminent and the United Nations was forming. Domestically, "Dr. Win the War" had accomplished what "Dr. New Deal" could not. The American economy began its longest, richest boom ever.

By adhering to the center, Roosevelt struck political gold. Responding boldly to crises, Roosevelt preserved America's governing structure. Radicals complained in the 1930s that Roosevelt did not do enough for labor. Influential business leaders detested him for doing too much. They accused him of subverting American traditions, especially the tradition of small government and individual liberty at home and the isolationist tradition abroad. Still, most Americans considered Roosevelt a great liberal hero. He made the government the protector of the weak and made the Democrats the liberal party by uniting ethnic groups, immigrants, blacks, laborers, and farmers behind it. To his supporters, Roosevelt was a constructive reformer who made America's government more democratic, humane, and effective. To most Americans, especially when compared to Herbert Hoover at home and Adolf Hitler abroad, FDR was a presidential superstar who ended the Depression and saved the world from fascism.

Offering a model for democratic leadership, Roosevelt was always in front by a half-step, with a clear direction, propelling the nation onward. He empowered the people and himself by empowering the presidency, the government's most democratic yet dictatorial institution. Theodore Roosevelt tapped the power of romantic nationalism to make the presidency dominate American consciousness. Franklin Roosevelt molded the modern nationalist presidency into an essential tool shaping American daily life and managing national crises.

In the great American tradition, Roosevelt was a pragmatist, not an ideologue. His greatest achievement was saving American democracy and Americans' faith in democracy. He balanced the era's collectivism with

America's enduring individualism, the command economy with people power.

What, then, makes Roosevelt a centrist? Is a centrist an extremist who peddled his vision to the people and became popular? Here it helps to use the historian's favorite text—context—and examine the president's tactics and policies, not just his rhetoric and vision.

As a centrist, Roosevelt met extremist elements halfway. When judged against the rhetoric of his predecessors, the Harding-Coolidge-Hoover trio, it is understandable why conservatives saw President Roosevelt as a Bolshevik, a dictator. But when judged against the Left's increasing demands and the pro-business Right's despair, Roosevelt's harshest rhetoric seems tame. Roosevelt wore the mantle of pragmatic liberalism proudly. "Mr. Roosevelt did not carry out the Socialist platform," America's leading Socialist, Norman Thomas, complained, "unless he carried it out on a stretcher." "A radical is a man with both feet firmly planted in the air," Roosevelt explained in 1939. "A conservative is a man with two perfectly good legs who, however, has never learned to walk forward. A reactionary is a somnambulist walking backwards. A liberal is a man who uses his legs and his hands at the behest . . . of his head."

Ending his first fireside chat in 1933, amid the great banking crisis, Franklin Roosevelt emphasized the American people's interdependence. He envisioned a continent-wide constituency united by symbols, a rich history, and challenging times, facing a glorious future. He told the American people: "It is your problem no less than it is mine. Together we cannot fail." Thanks to this centrist and nationalist vision, Americans came to believe in Roosevelt and, once again, in themselves.

6

TRUMAN, EISENHOWER, AND AMERICA'S BIPARTISAN CONSENSUS

Building Political Unity
through Cultural Conformity

THANKS TO THE GREAT DEPRESSION and World War II, mid-twentieth-century Americans were all too familiar with catastrophe. Most had seen disasters change lives abruptly. Franklin Roosevelt, Harry Truman, and Dwight Eisenhower helped transform fear of what could go wrong into a nationwide effort to live a normal life. As America lurched from world war to Cold War, Harry Truman crafted a bipartisan policy to contain the Soviet Union. By the end of his term, Americans' fear of communism made the policy more popular than the president himself. Dwight Eisenhower's consensus culture, propped up by his celebrity as a general and by economic prosperity, elevated the bipartisan policy into a defining, unifying ideology. By mobilizing the citizenry through the prose of everyday life, these leaders shaped a poetic and heroic chapter in American history and the annals of democracy.

Forging this consensus was neither easy nor inevitable. As World War II ended, many Americans were tired of fighting and enamored with the Soviets, our supposedly gallant allies. The bold but nuanced policy of containing, not conquering, communism, buttressed by this strategy's own organizational alphabet soup of IMFs and NATOs, had to be invented and sold to Americans and the free world.

Moderate leaders had to nurture a political consensus around containment. Harry Truman overcame his inexperience and occasional petulance to blaze a trail in foreign policy that proved remarkably reasonable, durable, and successful. Truman's Republican successor, Dwight Eisenhower, overcame his distaste for Truman and his own hair-trigger temper to make Truman's Cold War policy not only bipartisan but mostly nonpartisan. This triumph of moderation, with a balanced diplomatic strategy, enjoyed widespread political approval that a broad cultural consensus reinforced.

Presidents Truman, Eisenhower, Kennedy, and Johnson built their political consensus on America's remarkable postwar cultural consensus. These presidents led a generation raised on common ideals; united by dramatic experiences from the Great Depression to World War II; and committed to America as a land of middle-class prosperity, genteel sensibilities, bourgeois morality, and democratic principles. Most Americans shared a view of the world emphasizing devotion to family, church, community, nation, and God, along with precepts such as fidelity, honor, patriotism, self-control, and faith. Individual Americans did not always do the right thing, but they agreed on what the right thing to do was. Mass culture, especially newspapers, radio, movies, advertising, and television, reinforced—some would say imposed—this surprisingly standardized culture.

Unduly romanticizing the fifties' consensus glosses over the common scars the Great Depression and World War II had left on the American population. Those shared traumas fueled Americans' craving for a tranquil, cohesive culture, which the tidal wave of consumerism happily satisfied. New suburbs, shopping malls, and consumer goods helped Americans feel rewarded for decades of sacrifice. As Americans united around these new ways of living, they also rallied around the strategy to fight communism.

Examining the politics of the 1950s, especially the robust foreign policy stances, offers valuable, underutilized ideas and approaches. President Harry Truman's tenure was rocky; he left office extremely unpopular. Nevertheless, he engineered the consensus that prevailed for decades and laid the groundwork for America's Cold War victory in the late 1980s and 1990s.

The Red Army, Soviet atomic tests, Communist rhetoric, Western spies, and China's emergence as a second Marxist power united Americans in fear. And some demagogues, most notoriously Senator Joseph McCarthy, exploited American anxiety to ruin lives. But bold leadership, creative coalition making, and enduring American ideals helped keep the country sane and the foreign policy constructive. Harry Truman and Dwight Eisenhower choreographed the Cold War consensus by applying timeless skills to specific historical challenges. The rise of Cold War consensus politics shows how immoderate individuals can forge a moderate strategy.

OF THE TWO PRESIDENTS who built the postwar consensus, one, Dwight Eisenhower, entered the White House as a celebrity, while the other, Harry Truman, had lived most of his life in obscurity. On April 12, 1945, as Congress adjourned, veteran Speaker of the House Sam Rayburn served a few friends their afternoon round of bourbon and tap water. One of them, a shy, trim Missourian who looked like a Midwestern bank manager, may have wondered what he was doing in such august company. Originally a farmer, after he returned from World War I, his Kansas City clothing store thrived temporarily, then failed. Unthreatening to party bosses, he accepted a series of political appointments in his native Independence. Lucky breaks, including a rivalry between two leading Democrats that unexpectedly catapulted him to victory, made Truman Missouri's senator in 1934, and in 1944, vice president, when Franklin Roosevelt muscled out Henry Wallace. Even as vice president, Harry Truman's legal residence remained his mother-in-law's house in Independence (and she remained convinced he would never amount to anything).

Before Vice President Truman sipped his bourbon, the White House called. There, Eleanor Roosevelt approached him, draped her arm over his shoulder, and told him the president had died. Truman sighed and asked Mrs. Roosevelt "Is there anything I can do for you?" She replied, "Is there anything we can do for you? You are the one in trouble now."

In April 1945, when Franklin Roosevelt died, Harry Truman was in trouble. For twelve years Franklin Roosevelt had so dominated the office that few could conceive of anyone else as president, and many resisted calling the new chief executive by that title. With minimal preparation, Truman faced Herculean tasks. In his first few months in office, Truman completed Roosevelt's mission, managing the surrenders of Germany and Japan and authorizing the world's first nuclear bombing. He launched the reconstruction of Japan, Germany, and the rest of Europe, culminating in the 1947 Marshall Plan, which remains the gold standard for constructive assistance to distressed nations. Truman also navigated the treacherous

Even as he forged a lasting, effective, bipartisan Cold War containment policy, Harry Truman endured constant gibes, like this one
from cartoonist Clarence Daniel Batchelor, that he could not measure up to Franklin Roosevelt, his predecessor, or to the requirements of the newly expanded presidency. (Library of Congress)

transition from a wartime alliance with the Soviet Union to Cold War enmity with the Communist superpower.

Most Americans, from the poorly briefed new president on down, were
simply not prepared to shift from fighting Nazism to fighting communism.
Crafting a restrained, bipartisan, Cold War policy to contain the Soviet
Union became Truman's greatest achievement. Forging a muscular middle was daunting. Congressional Democrats were torn between Southern

conservatives and Northern New Dealers, while Republicans squabbled between interventionists and isolationists.

Truman also faced a formidable challenge in overcoming sympathy for Joseph Stalin's Russia. Making his Cold War strategy all but sacrosanct so quickly was a nearly miraculous achievement. America had spent four years allied with the Soviet Union. Many American writers, professors, and reporters had spent decades enamored of Marxism. Truman's own commerce secretary, former Vice President Henry Wallace, frequently praised Russia's "social economic justice" and "economic democracy."

Truman constructed foreign policy as a bipartisan issue, thanks especially to Michigan's once isolationist Republican Senator Arthur Vandenberg. On Friday, April 13, his first full day in office, Truman lunched with seventeen congressional leaders. Vandenberg hailed this unprecedented move for ending Roosevelt's era of presidential unilateralism. Vandenberg's pronouncement that "politics stops at the water's edge" would build a popular consensus behind America's containment strategy. Vandenberg remained a Republican and occasionally contradicted the president, saying that frank exchanges facilitated true unity. The senator saw himself leading the "loyal opposition" putting "national security ahead of partisan advantage."

Senator Vandenberg's journey from ardent partisan isolationist to leading bipartisan interventionist reflected the massive ideological shift Roosevelt had facilitated, culminating with America's entry into World War II. Vandenberg's rift with the Republican isolationists underlined the continuing American resistance to becoming a world superpower. America did not even have a standing army. Many isolationists, such as "Mr. Republican," Ohio Senator Robert Taft, reluctantly accepted the fight against fascism but hoped that returning to normalcy would include restoring America's characteristic insularity.

Facing a divided country and a treacherous world, Truman crusaded for cooperation. In his first speech to Congress, on April 16, 1945, Truman said only "a united nation deeply devoted to the highest ideals" could provide the "enlightened leadership" the world needed. The disastrous final meeting between Franklin Roosevelt, Winston Churchill, and Joseph Stalin at Yalta in February, 1945, helped the Soviets dominate Eastern Europe. Just before he died, Roosevelt banged his fist on his wheelchair's arm, denouncing Stalin for breaking "every one of the promises he made at Yalta." By March 5, 1946, when Winston Churchill traveled to Westminster College in Fulton, Missouri, the British icon

was mourning the iron curtain descending across Europe as "police governments" spread in "the Soviet sphere." Initially, the American public
condemned Churchill for war-mongering. Only 22 percent of Americans
polled approved an anti-Soviet alliance between the United States and
Great Britain.

Harry Truman's first great accomplishment was conveying a sense of national emergency to his fellow citizens. Americans were tired of fighting for
liberty and primed to pursue happiness. The president wanted Americans
to understand the new geopolitical situation, explaining that, "What happens abroad happens to you." Like waves pounding on the shore, headline
after headline about Soviet troops lingering in Iran, Soviet leaders denouncing America, and Soviet spies afoot soon confirmed Truman's and
Churchill's warnings. By August 1946, 60 percent of Americans feared the
Soviet Union wanted to rule the world, and 78 percent believed Soviet
spies were infiltrating America.

Although more Americans heeded Truman's warnings about the Soviets, many still harbored doubts about him as president. Even isolationist
Republicans began attacking Truman and the Democrats as soft on communism, while Henry Wallace liberals, whom Truman dismissed as crack-
pots, attacked him from within the Democratic Party as too harsh on the
Soviets. In September 1946, Wallace delivered a controversial speech attempting to appease Moscow. Wallace feared that Truman's talk of bipartisanship made the Democrats too deferential to hard-line Republicans.
Wallace claimed that Truman had approved the text of his speech. Embarrassed, Truman eventually fired Wallace but was criticized for delaying his
response.

Meanwhile, Truman's popular approval sank to 32 percent amid para-
lyzing strikes, rising inflation, mounting meat shortages, and the vexing
challenge of reintegrating sixteen million soldiers into society. From the
left, labor leaders condemned the president for betraying them and
Franklin Roosevelt's legacy by confronting striking miners and railroad
workers. From the right, Southern Democrats angered by Truman's stance
in favor of black civil rights stopped donating to the Democratic National
Committee.

Truman was so unpopular that he did not campaign during the 1946
midterm elections. Democrats desperately played recordings of various
Franklin Roosevelt speeches. "To Err is Truman," Republicans proclaimed.
Their winning campaign slogan asked bluntly, "Had enough?"

Republicans won both Houses of Congress for the first time since 1928, forcing Truman to become even more bipartisan. As the forlorn president returned to Washington from Missouri, only Undersecretary of State Dean Acheson greeted him at Union Station. This moving example of Acheson's loyalty offered devastating proof of Truman's political frailty.

IN 1947, TRUMAN'S COURTING of Vandenberg and others bore fruit. Truman really needed Republican cooperation, as Vandenberg now led the Senate Foreign Relations Committee. Echoing George Washington's enlightened civility, the president did not claim that he and his fellow Democrats were more devoted to the nation than "others of another party." His foreign policy, he said, was "a national and not a party program."

This new cooperative spirit quickly faced a major test. In Greece and Turkey, anticommunists were fighting for their freedom against local communists funded by the Soviets. Great Britain was too spent to support them. Britain abandoned its historic role as the global policeman just as the Soviet Union was becoming the international outlaw. Stalin's operatives were agitating all over the world, making particular progress with important but shaky Western allies like Greece and Turkey.

"We are met at Armageddon," Dean Acheson exclaimed when briefing Vandenberg and other influential senators about this crisis. Fearing "Soviet penetration" on three continents, Acheson gave an agricultural spin to what would become the domino theory: "Like apples in a barrel infected by one rotten one, the corruption of Greece would infect Iran and all to the east," then continue. Only America could restrain communism's march.

Vandenberg replied that there was "only one way to get" what Truman needed. "That is to make a personal appearance before Congress and scare the hell out of the American people." Harry Truman understood that he needed to inject idealism into the anxiety to make anticommunism stick. Addressing a joint session of Congress in March 1947, Truman used the word "free" twenty-four times, contrasting American liberty with Soviet oppression. In the congressional address, Truman made the issue black and white, declaring, "It must be the policy of the United States to support free peoples who are resisting attempted subjugation by armed minorities or by outside pressures."

Truman proposed granting $250 million to Greece and $150 million to Turkey. The "free peoples of the world look to us for support in maintaining their freedoms," Truman said. "If we falter in our leadership, we may endanger the peace of the world." This grandiose statement, which would become known as the Truman Doctrine, vowed preemptive American intervention worldwide. The Republican Congress's approval of the requested aid launched an enduring bipartisan Cold War foreign policy. That June, Secretary of State George Marshall unveiled the Marshall Plan, a comprehensive European recovery program.

Aided by exceptional advisers, Harry Truman brilliantly balanced anxiety and idealism, fear mongering and institution building. Tacking between the harsh attacks of the anticommunist Right and the soft-on-communist Left, Truman dominated the center. Responding assertively but not belligerently to the Soviet threat, Harry Truman garnered wide endorsement for American foreign aid programs and international community building. Americans built structures for international cooperation that they would have condemned twenty years earlier for violating national sovereignty. The International Monetary Fund and the International Bank for Reconstruction and Development, which would eventually become the World Bank, were formally established on December 27, 1945. Both integrated Americans into the world economy and the world of foreign aid. The North Atlantic Treaty Organization (NATO), launched on April 4, 1949, confirmed America's diplomatic and military interdependence with Europe. These institutions helped rebuild Europe; eventually undermined Soviet Communism; and became some of the most effective instruments for American influence, assistance, and self-protection abroad.

Isolationism was dead; bipartisan interventionism was surging. Although few could anticipate the initiatives' success and reach, both Democrats and Republicans cheered the moves. Bipartisan majorities ratified these cornerstones of Truman's foreign policy, as well as the UN Charter. In the spring of 1948, Truman signed the generous Foreign Assistance Act, pouring what would eventually be $13.3 billion into Europe under the Marshall Plan. Congress had passed the bill 329 to 74. In July 1949, the Senate ratified the North Atlantic Pact, eventually establishing NATO, 82 to 13. Truman called the European economic assistance "perhaps the greatest venture in constructive statesmanship that any nation has undertaken," proving "that a bipartisan foreign policy can lead to effective action." Most significantly, these bipartisan policies overturned America's traditional policy of remaining neutral in Europeans' peacetime affairs.

IN CREATING the postwar infrastructure, Harry Truman tapped deep re-serves of presidential power. A president allied with senators from the op-posing party to "save the world" discovered unprecedented latitude. Truman introduced laws redefining America as a postwar superpower with a standing army, an elaborate intelligence apparatus, and philanthropic ten-tacles throughout the world. But passing this revolutionary legislation was not an FDR-like adventure of wheedling the best deal possible through elaborate negotiating and posturing. Truman mixed creative statesmanship, effective salesmanship, and power politics, leavened by a no-nonsense pragmatic centrism and a disarming Midwestern simplicity.

Two Harry Trumans emerged as president. Truman could be prickly and decisive, sometimes mulish and verbally violent. He bombed Nagasaki after bombing Hiroshima, confronted rebellious subordinates and Joseph Stalin, cussed colorfully with his poker-playing buddies, and "gave 'em hell." But Truman could also be sweet in private and cautious in public, even excruci-atingly uncertain. This Truman grounded his major foreign policy moves in bipartisan consensus. Publicly, the two personas clashed, confusing ob-servers, although decades later Americans would express great nostalgia for Truman's plain-speaking ways.

The bruising 1948 election battle brought out Truman's scrappy side. The bipartisan visionary who deftly managed foreign crises often functioned as a dyspeptic pit bull on domestic issues. In two sentences Truman could switch from class warfare to a bipartisan Cold War appeal. This frequently excited crowds, but it rankled his allies, endangering future cooperation.

Franklin Roosevelt's domestic legacy remained a flashpoint. Considering the entire New Deal one extended—and mistaken—emergency plan, many Republicans hoped to return to "normal" by undoing it. Labor leaders and Progressives wanted to institutionalize what had been improvised during the war and fulfill Franklin Roosevelt's promise to remember the forgotten.

The shrill Left versus Right conflict allowed Truman to forge a vibrant center. Truman saw himself in the Andrew Jackson, Abraham Lincoln, and Theodore Roosevelt tradition as the plain people's man in Washington. He estimated that the lobbyists infesting postwar Washington represented 15 million Americans, leaving the remaining "150 million" with "only one man, the President."

Convinced that he was running to save America from plutocrats at home and Communists abroad, Truman ran a peppery and polarizing campaign leavened with a mass appeal. Truman's aides, James Rowe and Clark Clifford, explained that the New Deal's programs had splintered the parties into special interest groups, yet Roosevelt's leadership had forged the nation into a mass audience seeking an appealing "vote-getting picture of the president." Choreographing for Truman what Roosevelt had developed naturally, Rowe and Clifford suggested a two-tiered strategy. Truman would make "incidental gestures" appealing to the masses, combined with tailored appeals to Roosevelt's coalition of workers, ethnic groups, immigrants, and blacks.

Rabble-rousing while preaching, Truman targeted "the special interest lobbies," the "isolationists and reactionaries," and "the profiteers and the privileged class." Even while being presidential, Truman often inserted a partisan edge. He vowed as president to operate apolitically, seeking "the welfare of all our people . . . based upon a progressive concept of government." "Progressive" was a code word for Democratic New Dealer. Truman thus risked giving his party too much credit for bipartisanship, a concept that works best when shared.

In 1948, Truman's occasionally prickly, sometimes partisan, and quite vigorously muscular moderation clashed with the milquetoast moderation of the Republican nominee, Thomas E. Dewey. Dewey, rehearsing prematurely for his inauguration, ran a quiet campaign, dispensing vague, don't-rock-the-boat bromides endorsing "unity and efficiency." Truman articulated his vision of muscular moderation, insisting that real unity "required leadership" and vision. Oozing Missouri machismo, Truman said his bipartisan foreign policy was "achieved by men—Republicans as well as Democrats who were willing to fight for principles before these principles became obvious to everyone."

Truman's surprise victory reinforced his myth making. The generally accepted historical story about 1948 attributes his victory to his passionate campaigning. In this interpretation, moderates need not apply for presidential nominations. Dewey's temerity embodies centrism's impotence, and Truman's combativeness sets the standard for campaigning. But Truman ran a shrewd campaign, not just a bombastic one. He shored up all the elements of the New Deal Democratic coalition while excoriating the Republicans for the "do nothing" Congress.

When Truman had shrewdly called Congress into a special "Turnip Day" session on July 26, 1948, he had proposed sweeping progressive legislation. Predictably, the Republicans stonewalled, which propelled labor and other key voting blocs toward the president. In many ways, Truman won Roosevelt's fifth term. Truman's coalition building—and his steadiness against the Soviets—proved equally as important as his whistle-stop campaigning.

TRUMAN WON THE ELECTION, but he was scarred. Republicans resented his on-again, off-again bipartisanship. Truman's second term would end in shambles. In 1949, after the Communist Mao Zedung's triumph in China, Republicans bellowed, "Who lost China?" as if China had been America's to win or lose. The lament reflected the growing fear of communism along with the Western rationalist's presumption—still operative today—that all political effects are attributable to the West. The complaint became a convenient club for flogging the Truman White House.

With political tension mounting at home, the Korean conflict nearly destroyed the Truman presidency. Communist North Korea's invasion of South Korea in June 1950 threatened the postwar order and prompted an American-led United Nations army. Most Americans initially supported the nation's entry into the war. Truman convincingly framed the conflict as a life and death struggle between freedom and communism. But the war soon degenerated into a divisive stalemate and a political albatross, bogging down 5.7 million troops. Americans lost patience after China counterattacked and repelled the United Nations forces in the north. Ultimately, 54,426 Americans died. Increasingly, President Truman's approach seemed amateurish and dangerous, with the world careening toward nuclear war. An ailing Senator Vandenberg retired in 1950 and died in April 1951, depriving Truman of an essential ally as Americans began questioning their president's competence.

Ominously, Republican Senator Joseph McCarthy and his allies hijacked anticommunism. They accused Truman and the Democrats of being soft on the policy the Democrats themselves had pioneered. Even though McCarthy's extremism contrasted with Truman's more balanced anticommunism, the senator's demagoguery would define the movement and the moment. Truman nobly confronted McCarthy and defended subordinates accused of subversion. Truman vetoed the Internal Security Act of 1950, also known as the McCarran Act, compelling Communist organizations to register with the government. Truman denounced the bill as a threat to civil liberties, but the panicky Democratic Congress overrode his veto and enacted the law.

As Truman struggled with Korea and communism, corruption charges involving some of his Missouri cronies rained down on the administration. The massive postwar demobilization fed inflation and triggered a rash of strikes. Truman's popularity rating tanked. Still, he kept calling for "a true bipartisan foreign policy" to ensure the "survival of our country." Truman appealed to "the wiser heads of the Republican party" to contain the "old, unreconstructed, isolationist wing of the Republican Party." Republicans, Truman snapped, "haven't had a single constructive idea about foreign policy" since Senator Vandenberg died.

JUST AS TRUMAN was visionary enough not to let his contempt for McCarthy blind him to the dangers of communism, Truman also was mature enough to distinguish his flagging popularity from the need to strengthen the anti-Soviet consensus. Joseph Stalin's Soviet Union was murdering millions of citizens and oppressing tens of millions of Eastern Europeans. Communism was gaining a foothold in the Third World. Truman's bipartisan foreign policy made containing the Soviets a transcendent, apolitical issue. Even after Nazism fell, many American leaders feared dictatorships were more potent than democracies. This democratic inferiority complex emerged in the 1930s and lasted well into the 1980s.

President Truman launched a campaign to galvanize "Mr. and Mrs. United States" against communism. This constructive, moderate advertising and educational campaign responded to Stalinism's crimes and McCarthy's assaults. Truman's anticommunism entailed embracing the American way of life, not subverting American freedoms.

The 1950s cult of consensus developed around the home, the school, the church, and the government, to counter communism. The shared threat sensitized Americans to their common values. The Cold War became a showdown over competing lifestyles. In his February 1946 "Long Telegram," explaining how to contain communism, the diplomat George Kennan argued that a strong American home made America strong abroad. Every American technological innovation and paycheck cashed, every happy American and satisfied American family, provided "a diplomatic victory over Moscow worth a thousand diplomatic notes and joint communiqués."

Truman's definition of America's national mission galvanized Americans, even if it did not boost his popularity. The government tapped advertising wizards to create compelling radio and television ads. The Truman administration marketed Americanism through vehicles such as "The Free-dom Train." Nearly four million Americans in 326 cities and towns across the country hopped aboard from September 1947 to January 1949, to see a rolling National Archives exhibition containing the Declaration of Inde-pendence, the Constitution, the Truman Doctrine, and other sacred texts. Patriotic speeches and frenzied parades greeted the train. Some people waited six hours in line for a chance to see the show.

TRUMAN BUILT political consensus on a remarkable cultural consensus. The strong, united nation that George Washington had imagined, Abra-ham Lincoln had saved, and the two Roosevelts had defined, was coalesc-ing. Unlike in most European countries, American nationalism became ideological, not ethnic. Although today it is more fashionable to focus on America's divisive problems, America draws its strength from common ideas and ideals. As a continental power with a diverse population, without these common values the country could not function, let alone have de-feated the Nazis, contained the communists, integrated immigrants, and landed men on the moon.

Unity is not uniformity, and consensus is not complete absence of con-flict. Compared to today's chaotic cultural carnival, mid-century Ameri-cans appear to have been eerily homogenous. Yet even in the apparent national consensus, Americans were a diverse lot with a dizzying array of racial, ethnic, class, and religious distinctions. America was still integrat-ing the 22 million immigrants who arrived between 1890 and 1924 and their offspring. Many still spoke different languages, celebrated particular ethnic festivals, populated specific neighborhoods, and even dominated certain jobs.

The Depression, the New Deal, World War II, and the Cold War were nationalizing and anchoring experiences. Similarly, the prosperity-driven consumer culture bewitched Americans with a peculiarly uniform and mass-produced version of individualism. At mid-century, middle-aged Americans' country was more centralized, commercialized, urbanized, and homogenized than their parents' America. Turn-of-the-century America had been dominated by farmers, not city folks, by horses, not horseless car-riages, by state and local governments, not the national government with an international agenda. The America of the 1950s was happier, freer, and more humane. Workers enjoyed more leisure time and education, more po-litical power and individual discretion, more money in their pockets and dignity on the job. The great miracle of modern America offered a widespread middle-class prosperity on a scale unprecedented in world history. A typical, working-class American could own a home, drive a reasonably new car, and enjoy a level of material comfort that was unheard of even a generation before.

Intellectuals were fascinated with the reasonable, liberal, "vital center" that was emerging, as Arthur M. Schlesinger Jr. called it. Struck by the pragmatism that the historian Daniel Boorstin argued was the "genius of American politics," many leading thinkers declared that Americans were witnessing what the sociologist Daniel Bell called "the end of ideology" as materialism and freedom trumped the abstractions that often turned into totalitarianism.

In 1950s America, consumerism undermined communism. The great American buying spree, fed by burgeoning production lines, fueled by rising wages, and celebrated by Madison Avenue advertisements, inoculated millions to the lure of Marxist egalitarianism. The baby boom and building boom, the rush to suburbia and escape from politics, characterized the times. As the suburban developer William Levitt famously observed, "No man who owns his own house and lot can be a Communist. He has too much to do." American politics was characterized by centrism rather than extremism as in Europe, because most Americans were more committed to paying their mortgages than to changing the world.

Truman and his presidential successors built an American patriotism based on consumerism, careerism, and community. A stable "fortress" society developed with a strong sense of community. People remained loyal to their hometowns, their local grocers, their baseball teams, their first jobs, their first loves. The resulting political culture was also materialistic, anti-intellectual, suffocating, and intolerant. The 1950s' defining cultural products were mass-produced, monolithic, and enveloping. From best sellers such as *Betty Crocker's Picture Cookbook*, Norman Vincent Peale's *The Power of Positive Thinking*, and the authorized *F.B.I. Story*, to Levittown, Holiday Inns, McDonalds, Disneyland, and Barbie, Cold War culture was often one-size-fits-all. Some dissenting voices spoke out, but the culture in general remained remarkably uniform, patriotic, and focused.

The miracle of television propagated this consensus, bringing cultural homogeneity into people's living rooms. Popular culture provided a binding audiovisual language essential to nation building. Television, especially initially, was a powerful community builder defining Americans' public conversation.

Dwight Eisenhower sits with his wife, Mamie, at the 1952 Republican National Convention in Chicago, marveling at the magical television, which will extend the president's reach and, at least initially, unite Cold War America. (Library of Congress)

Tapping the power, NBC's founder, David Sarnoff, ordered his executives to "convert" their "products into the necessary weapons of war." In those days television broadcast a defining national vision that by its very need to be broad was instinctively moderating.

THE COLD WAR'S enveloping and vital center proved popular during the 1950s. Harry Truman's successor, Republican Dwight Eisenhower, marched into the White House as a war hero and a balm after Truman's combative tenure. For Eisenhower, bipartisanship in confronting enemies beyond "the water's edge" was not enough. He cultivated a broader cult of consensus in political and popular culture.

The cult of consensus on Main Street, on Capitol Hill, and on campus suited Dwight Eisenhower, the genial son of Kansas turned international war hero. "I like Ike," summed up the bipartisan sentiment. During the

1952 campaign to succeed Harry Truman, the satirist Mort Sahl noted that Eisenhower supported integration gradually, and his Democratic opponent Adlai Stevenson supported integration moderately: "It should be possible to compromise between those extremes." As candidate and as president, Eisenhower would test different labels for his mainstream approach, calling it "dynamic conservatism," "progressive, dynamic conservatism," "progressive moderation," "moderate progressivism," and "positive progressivism." Frustrated by all this center seeking, the conservative Russell Kirk scoffed that Eisenhower was no conservative, "he is a golfer."

Democratic politicians awoke after election day in 1952 terrified. Would the first Republican president since Franklin Roosevelt dismantle the New Deal? Eisenhower had capped his military career by serving in 1951 as Supreme Commander of the Allied Powers in Europe. He was unlikely to dismantle the Cold War foreign policy he helped design. But Eisenhower's domestic inclinations were unknown.

Republicans were torn. The 1952 party platform repudiated the New Deal as a failed attempt to bring "national socialism" to America. The platform denounced the Democrats for producing high taxes, arrogant bureaucrats, diminished state powers, and economic stagnation. Yet the party abandoned the ideological stalwart Senator Robert Taft to nominate Eisenhower, the popular and centrist celebrity. Eisenhower ran an upbeat, vague campaign. His inaugural speech neglected domestic affairs while advancing the Cold War view that the world was pitting the forces of slavery against the power of freedom.

Eisenhower respected the domestic and foreign policy consensus. He rooted his moderate vision in "a rule of reason": respond to conditions as they are, not as ideologues wish they were. Eisenhower explained to his brother Edgar, a doctrinaire conservative, that if any political party "attempted to abolish social security, unemployment insurance, and eliminate labor laws and farm programs, you would not hear of that party again in our political history." Two decades into the Roosevelt revolution, the number of those who rejected fundamental social welfare building blocks was "negligible and they are stupid," Eisenhower proclaimed.

Eisenhower's most dramatic and most centrist action would be passive. By maintaining signature New Deal programs such as Social Security, Eisenhower ratified Roosevelt's vision and guaranteed that America would maintain its welfare state. Eisenhower also averted a bruising partisan battle.

True, he disappointed the Republican Right. But his assessment of conservatives' limited power and limited wisdom, though harsh, was accurate.

Like Truman, Eisenhower had a temper, but Eisenhower worked hard to suppress his emotions. He would often scribble down the name of someone who infuriated him on a piece of paper and put it in a drawer. This ritual acted on his anger without his succumbing to it. The technique was not foolproof, however, and Eisenhower deployed his temper effectively. Subordinates worked hard to avoid eliciting a presidential eruption peppered with what they delicately called "army language."

Eisenhower entered office blessed by a Republican majority in the House and the Senate. The conventional wisdom, recalling the Truman roller coaster, was that, as one *New York Times* headline declared, WHEN FOREIGN POLICY WAS BIPARTISAN, IT SUCCEEDED. Otherwise, it failed.

Eisenhower's operating vision included the citizens cooperating, the government assisting when necessary, and the president mediating when pressed. He began his inaugural address with a prayer he wrote asking for harmony amid diversity "under the concepts of our Constitution." In his first State of the Union address on February 2, 1953, Eisenhower called for cooperation between the executive and legislative branches, luxuriating "in the spirit of true bipartisanship."

John Foster Dulles, Eisenhower's new secretary of state, promised to improve upon Truman's foreign policy bipartisanship. Dulles had negotiated a bipartisan foreign policy agreement during the 1944 campaign with Franklin Roosevelt's administration, and championed bipartisanship in his 1950 book *War or Peace*. Dulles wanted to invite opposition congressmen to help design policies, not just criticize. A proposed cabinet-level foreign policy council never happened, but Dulles worked closely with Democrats.

As Cold War internationalists, Eisenhower and Dulles clashed more with isolationist Republicans than with mainstream Democrats. Republican Senators opposed Eisenhower's appointment of Charles Bohlen as ambassador to Russia, fearing he was too soft on the Soviets and too tied into the Roosevelt-Truman administrations. They tried handcuffing the president by threatening to stop paying America's dues if the United Nations admitted Communist China. After twenty years of opposing Democratic presidents, Eisenhower sighed, congressional Republicans had forgotten how to cooperate with the executive branch.

LIKE GEORGE WASHINGTON, Eisenhower entered public office anxious to preserve his reputation as an American hero. Both generals preferred staying above partisan matters, appearing virtuous, and remaining
beloved. Controlling his temper publicly, blowing off steam privately,
Eisenhower dealt with his critics generously. He acknowledged that diversity strengthened democracy. Eisenhower described his leadership style as
relying on "fair, decent, and reasonable dealing with men, a reasonable
recognition that views may diverge, a constant seeking for a high and
strong ground on which to work together." Contrary to a reputation for laziness fed by his advancing age, his many naps, and his penchant for golf,
Eisenhower spent hours wooing his congressional critics, especially fellow
Republicans. After the first year, noting Republican cooperation "despite
the headlines on Republican discord," the president rejoiced, "Persever-
ance was producing results."

Eisenhower wanted to lead America by setting the right tone rather
than necessarily crafting the right phrase or grand policies. Sensing postwar
Americans' exhaustion after two decades of depression and war, he became
a symbol of serenity and maturity. A professional soldier who insisted on
being drafted into politics, Eisenhower considered Truman's "ward-boss
strong-arm tactics" self-destructive and undignified. "I am not one of the
desk-pounding types that likes to stick out his jaw and look like he is boss-
ing the show," Eisenhower explained. Eisenhower's Washington-like, enlightened appreciation for opposing views reinforced his accommodating
instincts. He demonstrated great discipline when attacked. He refused to
joust with segregationist Southern governors, Red-baiting demagogues, or
anti–New Deal ideologues. Critics scoffed that under "Eisen-hoover," the
bland led the bland. But Eisenhower often outfoxed opponents, making
them appear petty. In retrospect, historians appreciate his deft "hidden
hand" that calmed volatile situations.

While remaining dignified, Eisenhower worked at staying popular. His
election campaigns featured cutting-edge television ads. His administration
began broadcasting press conferences, prompting reporters' grumblings that
this essential communication medium would become an artificial, scripted
show. The president privately embraced Republican Party chairman
Leonard Wood Hall's "politics is show business" philosophy while publicly
disdaining it. Eisenhower appreciated television as a consensus-generating
device, with Americans rallying around common values, a standard national narrative, and a popular president.

At his best, Eisenhower put his personal and Republican seal of approval on the Cold War consensus Truman and his team had forged. A Senate vote in 1953 of 69 to 10 for foreign aid delighted Eisenhower. "This reflects something more important than money," the president said. "It signifies an unprecedented unity that crosses party lines and promises steady purpose in the conduct of our foreign affairs." A "united America" conveyed a message of "common purpose" to "the peoples of the Soviet World."

As a leader, Eisenhower was far more the corporate CEO than an entrepreneurial Lone Ranger. He shared with many responsibility for decisions while deflecting blame toward others. This technique proved particularly effective in defusing many crises in a volatile world. In 1954, Eisenhower avoided a military mess by relying on congressional "advice" he solicited that American soldiers should not rescue French forces in Dien Bien Phu, Vietnam. A decade later, Lyndon Johnson would get pulled into Vietnam, partially because he feared being criticized for tolerating a blow to American prestige. Eisenhower's congressional cover shielded him from blame.

In 1955, Eisenhower again cleverly orchestrated congressional consultations to help stop China's shelling of Quemoy and Matsu, small strategic islands in the Straits of Taiwan. Playing a dangerous game of nuclear brinksmanship, Eisenhower nudged China into relenting, without deploying any U.S. troops. The discreet president let generals and congressmen utter the threats. "Let's keep the Reds guessing," Secretary Dulles had advised.

And in 1956, when Russian tanks rolled into Budapest, Eisenhower averted world war while focusing the world's anger on the Soviets. Eastern European democrats were disappointed to learn that Americans would not fight for their freedom. Eisenhower feared that an aggressive intervention would risk nuclear confrontation without liberating Hungary.

However, Eisenhower's elusiveness did not serve him or the country during Senator Joe McCarthy's relatively short, nasty, brutish political ascendancy. Republicans had been far more tolerant of McCarthy's ravings when he attacked the Truman administration. After Eisenhower returned the Republicans to power, McCarthy continued attacking the government, including members of his own party. Many Republicans believed that only Eisenhower could squash McCarthy. But Eisenhower refused to confront McCarthy directly, vowing, "I will not—I refuse—to get into the gutter." Eisenhower's avoidance reflected his loftiness, some moral laziness, and political shrewdness—he recognized McCarthy as a parasite who fed off all publicity, positive or negative. Eisenhower distanced himself from McCarthy and waited for the demagogic junior senator to stumble. When McCarthy miscalculated and attacked Eisenhower's beloved army in 1954, Eisenhower withheld crucial documents. Eisenhower's quiet obstruction-ism helped make McCarthy look foolish and emboldened moderate Republican senators to lead the charge against the growing national and party embarrassment.

Still, this indirect approach muffled the president's moral voice. McCarthy's Red Scare demanded bold leadership. Other moral heroes opposed McCarthy. The broadcaster Edward R. Murrow and the lawyer Joseph Welch filled the void. Murrow humiliated McCarthy with an on-air exposé, and Welch confronted the bullying senator in a congressional hearing.

In the area of civil rights, Eisenhower again tried to dodge controversy and responsibility. He saw the presidency as a unifying platform more than a bully pulpit for initiating change. Eisenhower chose not to get involved even as the South exploded with civil rights clashes. He was forced to intervene when mobs prevented nine young black students from integrating Little Rock's Central High School in 1957. Eisenhower sent in the Army's 101st Airborne Division. Eisenhower was a nationalist, not a moralist. The defiance of federal authority enraged him more than the oppression of young black students.

A career soldier, Eisenhower detested American politics' harsh burlesque. More than most, he blurred the lines between moderate policies, consensus building, nonpartisanship, and bipartisanship, bringing all these approaches together in his disdain for political shenanigans and personalities. Yet Eisenhower was realistic enough—and an experienced enough power player—to know that party identity and political grandstanding were important.

Characteristically, before the 1954 midterm elections, Eisenhower wavered among nonpartisanship, bipartisanship, and aggressive Republican partisanship. Following Franklin Roosevelt's approach, he preferred speaking broadly to "this Nation," often refusing to endorse specific Republican candidates. Displaying his era's faith in science, Eisenhower said his bipartisan policies were "arrived at through widespread study of relevant fact" and "expressed in a sound public opinion, which is of course the real power in a free system." In "our foreign policy," he said, "we must be America—we must not be parties."

Still, as a tough competitor who wanted to win, Eisenhower knew that party loyalty counted. Eisenhower did not want the Republicans to lose Congress. Divided government, with its "stagnation, frustrations, and political feuds" would yield a "cold war of partisan policy." Eisenhower feared too much structural bipartisanship would intensify the partisanship by empowering both Democrats and Republicans.

IRONICALLY, THE DEMOCRATS' 1954 midterm gains freed Eisenhower to work with the Democrats, marginalizing his Republican critics. Net Republican losses of one Senate seat and eighteen congressional seats turned both houses over to the Democrats, who would control Congress until 1994. Secretary Dulles sniffed, "I am not worried at all about the partisanship of people with whom I deal, whether they are partisan Republicans or partisan Democrats, because I don't think any of them who have stature are going to introduce partisanship into foreign policy." The administration had the "primary constitutional authority" to decide on policy, and the need to speak with "one voice." Senate Majority Leader Lyndon Johnson agreed that a "nation cannot exist in the field of foreign affairs and defense when it speaks with two voices." The Texas Democrat promised to meet the president "at least halfway—and perhaps further, if the circumstances warrant."

On paper, the president and the senator seemed destined to clash, but they established an extraordinary, unexpected partnership. The egotistical, flamboyant Senator Johnson, only forty-six years old and already majority leader, was a Franklin Roosevelt protégé in Congress during the New Deal. Seeing Eisenhower's commitment to continuity, Johnson played the compromiser, not the firebrand. It is not "the business of the opposition to oppose," Johnson said, vowing to advance programs that would serve America.

President Eisenhower, Secretary Dulles, Senator Johnson, and other Senate leaders fulfilled the president's promise of "unreserved cooperation" in "the traditionally bipartisan areas—military security and foreign relations." "Let the general good be our yardstick on every great issue of our time," Eisenhower exclaimed. In August 1955, the *New York Times* would celebrate how "Two Parties and One Foreign Policy" created a "triumph of 'the center.'"

Throughout his second term, as Eisenhower tired, Johnson thrived. Despite the general good mood and placid tone at the top, foreign policy crises erupted in Lebanon, Taiwan, Berlin, and Cuba. After the Russians launched *Sputnik* in 1957, Americans felt humiliated that the Russians had made it into space first. Johnson responded by helping to create the National Aeronautics and Space Administration (NASA) in 1958. Most notably, Johnson oversaw passage of the 1957 Civil Rights Act, defying fellow Southern Democrats to pass the bill.

Eisenhower's popularity strengthened his foreign policy. He made America's Cold War policy politically untouchable, protected by a bipartisan agreement. William S. White, the *New York Times'* shrewd observer, concluded "that when centrists coalesce in this country they not only can create and control but, equally importantly, can protect bipartisanship." With consensus politics dominating, the question was, "How far inland from 'the water's edge' must a politician be 'bipartisan.'" Many supposedly domestic issues, from the federal budget to civil liberties, affected foreign policy. Such "where will it end?" questions reflected the assumption that "the new and almost total bipartisanship seems to have a long life ahead."

Voices on the left and the right warned, however, that a bipartisan consensus could lead to a dangerous complacency. "This country will not be damaged by intelligent debate on foreign policy," the *Wall Street Journal's* frustrated editorial board insisted. "The damage can come if bipartisan advocates ever succeed in stifling the debate." While the consensus was good for Cold War containment, it would breed the conditions leading to the Vietnam debacle a decade later.

Looking back, subversive, creative, and intellectual currents were fermenting amid the apparent uniformity in the 1950s. Even before an angry oppositional culture emerged in the 1960s, a broader, more popular, more frivolous culture was muscling aside America's WASP gentility. Americans still appreciated leaders more than celebrities, ideas more than images, but their priorities were changing. In 1958 the Gallup poll asked which famous people Americans would most like to have to dinner. Only one celebrity, Will Rogers, made the top twenty, and he was seventeenth, behind Winston Churchill, Jesus, eight presidents, and two first ladies. But that same poll foreshadowed the coming celebrity-obsessed culture when it asked respondents to identify the authors of thirteen statements. Nearly three-quarters of those surveyed knew that the Lone Ranger said "Hi, Ho Silver," and nearly two-thirds knew that Mae West said "Come up and see me sometime." But barely one-third knew that Franklin Roosevelt said "The only thing we have to fear is fear itself" and only 14 percent remembered that Woodrow Wilson wanted to make the world "safe for democracy."

Eisenhower stood for balancing between the old culture and the new, between traditional politics and the modern, televised variety, and between Left and Right. In 1963, watching the extremist Barry Goldwater advance toward the Republican nomination, Eisenhower defended his legacy. The iconic ex-president proclaimed that he despised people who "go to the gutter on either the right or the left, and hurl rocks at those in the center."

America entered the 1960s with a strong, romantic, nationalist tradition of presidential leadership. National security fears reinforced the desire for presidential vigor, as did the growing sense that the country needed bold leadership on domestic issues, too. John Kennedy won the presidency promising to offer that guidance. Even in his tragically brief tenure, Kennedy would find that such muscular moderation could create its own momentum, propelling the leader and his country in unexpected but welcome directions.

7

JOHN F. KENNEDY AND CIVIL RIGHTS

Moderation and the Challenge of Change

THE LEGEND OF JOHN F. KENNEDY portrays a young, vigorous leader mobilizing Americans with the poetry of his words, the clarity of his vision, and the decency of his actions. In this tale, Dwight Eisenhower presided complacently over America's consensus culture, building on Harry Truman's bipartisanship, then John Kennedy tapped into the emotion and idealism bubbling right below the surface. Illustrating the power of presidential rhetoric in shaping American nationalism, John Kennedy's greatest lines are carved in stone and etched in our collective hearts. "Ask not what your country can do for you, ask what you can do for your country," is an alluring American aphorism that every president since has tried to outdo, but failed to top.

John Kennedy's civil rights speech of June 1963 helped build the myth. Appalled by police violence against peaceful protestors in Birmingham, Alabama, the president pointed Americans toward the path of righteous reform. Speaking partially extemporaneously and partially from a hastily written text his speechwriter, Theodore Sorensen, delivered five minutes before the red television lights flashed on, Kennedy spoke from his heart. Defining civil rights as a moral issue, he made the quest for racial equality a national crusade "as old as the Scriptures and . . . as clear as the American Constitution."

Actually, the historical facts are messier than this one-dimensional, inspiring story. Kennedy's civil rights speech was so significant because in it he shifted dramatically from his earlier, more cautious, statements. Initially, Kennedy was uninterested in civil rights' great moral challenge. By the summer of 1963 his consciousness had been raised, to use an expression that would soon become popular, and he applied the president's moral authority to secure black equality.

Kennedy's personal transformation anticipated many white Americans' eventual awakening. Kennedy's conversion demonstrates the power of positive center seeking. Moderates risk being immobilized by the status quo, never facilitating bold changes no matter how necessary. John Kennedy helped implement the most radical American initiative since slavery ended, a legal push for full African American civil rights. By leading, waking up to the issue's moral stakes, and explaining it to the nation, Kennedy helped mainstream the civil rights movement. In so doing, he helped America regain its soul. Slowly, spasmodically, America began righting the great wrongs done to the descendants of the slaves, who even in the 1960s lived in a segregated world of crude stereotypes and primitive laws.

Presidents are not kings, Martin Luther Kings, that is. The leader of such a diverse and complicated country cannot be a radical change agent. Still, John Kennedy's awakening to the civil rights challenge in 1963 demonstrated one modern president's power to adapt and lead constructively, effectively, moderately, and progressively.

LIKE ABRAHAM LINCOLN, John Kennedy grew in office, becoming more authoritative yet more sensitive while honing his reforming vision. Kennedy was not born a generational superstar, groomed for greatness and oozing it from every pore. He entered politics as a skinny, inexperienced replacement for his older brother, Joe Jr., who died in World War II. Kennedy entered the White House as an undistinguished playboy senator, more celebrated than accomplished, more showman than statesman.

Born in 1917, Kennedy graduated Harvard in 1940 and joined the navy in 1941, becoming a hero when, as he put it, "they sank my boat." In 1946 he ran successfully for Congress, and won a Senate seat six years later. The youngest man ever elected president, his formative political experiences were watching Franklin Roosevelt defeat the Great Depression and fascism.

At the same time, as one of the richest men ever elected president, his formative personal experiences prepared him to be indulgent. Family films now housed in his presidential library show a young preppie gliding on the tennis court with the grace that would woo the masses and a coddled insouciance that initially would alienate earnest Adlai Stevenson liberals. When Kennedy launched his presidential bid in 1960, Senate veterans like Lyndon Johnson dismissed this lightweight who had so many absences and so few legislative achievements. The grand dame of the Democratic Left, Eleanor Roosevelt, condemned Kennedy as soft on McCarthyism; insensitive to unions; deaf to blacks' needs; and dominated by his controversial father, Joe Kennedy, who was spending "oodles of money" to buy the presidency.

Throughout the presidential campaign, Kennedy revealed his capacity to mature. During the bitter West Virginia primary, Kennedy discovered the depth of the poverty in many regions there. Risking mockery as a rich kid learning what others already knew, Kennedy admitted to being ashamed. Subsequently, he frequently mentioned the blighted lives, lost opportunities, and primitive health care he witnessed in Appalachia.

The first president born in the twentieth century, Jack Kennedy was a post-party man, peddling his attractive personality when campaigning and governing. Kennedy landed in the Oval Office thanks to a carefully orchestrated popular surge. "A whole generation tends to 'connect' with Kennedy as one of its own," the pollster Louis Harris reported, using that generation's lingo. Kennedy's speeches, which quoted Sidney Hook, Thomas Jefferson, and Goethe, cast him as an intellectual, master of the classical education millions received in high school and college. But for all his Harvard affect and vast wealth, Kennedy was also a Boston Irish pol with an inherited chip on his shoulder for not being fully accepted in American society. Although he spoke the modern technocrat's cool, sophisticated lingo of hopes and dreams, he also spoke the political boss's slang of gains and losses, are you with me or against me? Representing the veterans who had fought under Franklin Roosevelt, Harry Truman, and General Dwight Eisenhower, Kennedy was a liberal nationalist, a Cold Warrior, and a consensus-oriented centrist.

Kennedy was particularly formidable because he was a celebrity politician. The modern conversation with voters required a mastery of television and image making. Kennedy's many secrets—about his poor health, his compulsive adulteries, his father's influence—made him a master performer.

What a genteel mother considered "poise," detractors would call "deception" and supporters would call "great P.R." The first televised presidential debate, with Vice President Richard Nixon, watched by an estimated 70 million people, proved to be the turning point in the 1960 general election. Kennedy's image and presence proved more impressive and influential than his words and his policies, a lesson he took to heart.

The entertainer Frank Sinatra's preinaugural gala celebrated new links between Hollywood and Washington. With a father who produced movies and dozens of "industry" drinking buddies and girlfriends, Jack Kennedy had long frolicked in Tinseltown. Surrounded by Hollywood stars, President Kennedy made the White House appear glitzy, not frumpy, alluring as well as impressive. This president fused two central streams in American culture: he made power glamorous.

The decline of the studio system and rise of television increased the spotlight on actors, who built their own brand names. American popular culture was becoming more integrated, with television, advertising, radio, movies, and glossy magazines feeding off each other. In America's emerging celebrity culture, fame was its own justification. And it all made Kennedy's star quality more potent.

For Kennedy, television was a magical machine, extending his reach into American homes. The great national touchstone, television presented a static, suburban, homogenizing, and narcotizing collective image. In the early days, live theatrical presentations by thoughtful playwrights such as Paddy Chayefsky, and the carryovers from radio such as *Amos 'n' Andy*, gave the medium some bite. By 1960, American TV land was a world of happy families and happy endings. The leading shows when Kennedy ran for president were all-American Westerns such as *Gunsmoke* and *Bonanza* and reassuring family comedies such as *My Three Sons* and a defanged *Dennis the Menace*. John, Jackie, and their young family generated the same warm, familiar feelings as did the Anderson family of *Father Knows Best* or the Nelson family of *The Adventures of Ozzie and Harriet*.

Since the 1930s, the family patriarch, Joseph P. Kennedy, had positioned his family for American success. Now the Kennedys' fame bubbled over, elevating them from political figures to popular icons. Every corner of American popular culture offered proof of their popularity—the "Jackie look" sweeping the fashion world, the Kennedy comic books, board games, phonograph records, paper dolls, coloring books, salt shakers, and playing cards.

The American people's romance with the Kennedys went beyond the usual inaugural honeymoon. Television personalized the presidency, bringing the White House into every American household. Kennedy granted reporters—and television cameras—unprecedented access. Both CBS and NBC produced up-close looks at the new president. By the second broadcast, one Gallup Poll found that 73 percent of those surveyed approved of the president, just months after he barely won the election. When CBS *Evening News* expanded from fifteen minutes a night to half an hour on Monday, September 2, 1963, it featured an extended interview starring two of America's most beloved TV personalities: Walter Cronkite and John F. Kennedy.

Millions felt they knew Kennedy, despite never having met him. "Your son is even more inspirational than we thought he could be," the style arbiter Letitia Baldridge told Joseph P. Kennedy shortly after the inauguration; "your daughter-in-law is fabulous." After watching yet another television special detailing his glamorous lifestyle and beautiful family, the president confessed, "We couldn't survive without TV."

Overall, the new president seemed more concerned with remaining popular than transforming America. Former Secretary of State Dean Acheson complained to Harry Truman about Kennedy's preoccupation with image. "It makes one look at oneself instead of at the problem," Acheson wrote. "How will I look fielding this hot line drive to short stop? This is a good way to miss the ball altogether." As he faced tough opponents like Soviet Premier Nikita Khrushchev or tried to mediate between business leaders and striking workers, loyal Southern Democrats and angry black activists, John Kennedy would learn that image making might be key to winning the White House, but he needed substance to succeed as president.

DESPITE REPORTERS' CODDLING, John Kennedy's on-the-job training was brutal. The fear of nuclear destruction haunted him and his advisers. At home, deep racial, class, and regional divisions threatened America's social fabric and the Democratic Party. Kennedy's mandate for leadership was fragile; slight shifts of voters in Illinois and Texas would have elected Nixon—and some speculated that the winning votes were cast by dead people counted in Mayor Richard Daley's Chicago and Vice President Lyndon Johnson's Austin. Moreover, twice in his first six months at work, the Pulitzer Prize–winning author of *Profiles in Courage* seemed to be modeling for a profile in cowardice and confusion.

An unproven president promising vigorous leadership risked becoming addicted to action for its own sake. The fear of appearing anemic propelled Kennedy to put into action an Eisenhower administration plan to invade Cuba. Since the 1959 revolution, when Fidel Castro declared himself and his country Communist, the Soviets had established a beachhead off Florida's coast. Many American policymakers and national security officials became obsessed with Castro and Cuba.

This fixation led to Kennedy's first major fiasco, a botched invasion of Cuba weeks into his presidency. Fourteen hundred Cuban exiles volunteered to liberate their homeland, while obscuring America's role in training, equipping, and directing them. Brigade 2506's landing at the Bay of Pigs failed on April 17, 1961, partially because the president, lulled by months of mass adulation, was too concerned with his own image and unwilling to take a strong stand diplomatically.

As Cuban forces overwhelmed the exiles, military and intelligence experts begged the commander in chief to dispatch Navy jets and destroyers. "No," Kennedy insisted, "I don't want the U.S. to get involved in this." "Hell, Mr. President," Admiral Arleigh Burke, the naval chief of staff responded, "We are involved."

The Bay of Pigs confirmed Republican fears—and Soviet speculation— that Kennedy was immature, arrogant, and impulsive. This debacle could have derailed the fledgling presidency. Fortunately, this veteran image-builder knew how to respond. Privately, Kennedy blamed others: Dwight Eisenhower for first approving the operation, the CIA and Joint Chiefs of Staff for advancing a foolish plan, and his staff for not stopping him.

Yet publicly the president apologized to the American people. At his next press conference he barred questions about Cuba, but was ready when a reporter predictably asked about the Bay of Pigs. "There's an old saying that victory has a hundred fathers and defeat is an orphan," the president said, coining the phrase. "I am the responsible officer of this government." Government by epigram worked. Admirers would remember this debacle "as one of his most courageous moments." When polls showed that public support for their humble commander had skyrocketed to 82 percent approval, Kennedy learned yet again about the power of appearances: "Jesus, it's just like Eisenhower. The worse I do, the more popular I get."

The Bay of Pigs encouraged the crude Soviet Premier Nikita Khrushchev to bully the inexperienced American when they met in Vienna six weeks later. Kennedy dominated the public appearances in June

This July 26, 1961, Bill Mauldin cartoon captures John Kennedy's frustration and initial sense of impotence, as he sinks into quicksand with the bullying Soviet leader Nikita Khrushchev, who threatens, "I'll bury you." (Library of Congress)

1961, charming the Europeans. But in the private sessions, the lumbering Russian peasant with ham-sized fists humiliated the handsome, lithe American millionaire. Khrushchev portrayed Soviet Communism as a liberating force for the world, opposing America's imperialism and colonialism. Kennedy sputtered defensively. "He treated me like a little boy," the president confessed. "I think I know why he treated me like this," Kennedy indiscreetly told *New York Times* reporter James Reston. "He thinks because of the Bay of Pigs that I'm inexperienced. Probably thinks I'm stupid, Maybe most important, he thinks that I had no guts."

The Bay of Pigs and the tongue-lashing in Vienna taught Kennedy to be more cautious militarily and more aggressive diplomatically. He learned to doubt the experts, trust his instincts, and never underestimate the enemy.

Kennedy found his footing over the summer when Khrushchev authorized building the Berlin Wall. The wall would prevent East Germans from fleeing Communist East Berlin to freedom in the West. Kennedy responded with appropriately indignant rhetoric, backed up by more troops and more funds to defend West Berlin. The president proclaimed that "an attack" on West Berlin "will be regarded as an attack upon us all."

Kennedy is often remembered as a liberal crusader, a younger, more vigorous, FDR. Initially he acted more like Eisenhower, a consensus politician using his popularity to fight the Cold War. Domestically, Kennedy's agenda remained benign and fuzzy. He dithered on civil rights for over two years. He frequently hedged on controversial matters but offered sweeping lyrical proclamations on apple pie questions. In a July 1961 press conference, one reporter asked about the Freedom Riders, the black and white students integrating Greyhound buses throughout the South. Racists had been harassing the students, sometimes violently. The president avoided the civil rights question, dodged the moral issue, and ignored the unfolding national drama. Instead, his dry legalistic analysis affirmed the importance of facilitating interstate commerce. One month later, a reporter asked about funding the Peace Corps. Playing the nationalist preacher rather than the slippery pol, the president eloquently described the enlightening impact young Americans could have by teaching English to Third World students.

Almost despite himself, Kennedy's feel-good freedom talk revitalized liberalism. He built on Theodore Roosevelt's popular nationalism, Franklin Roosevelt's expansion of the presidency in the national imagination, and the Truman-Eisenhower national security imperative. Kennedy's patriotic calls for optimism, idealism, and self-sacrifice resonated more widely than the president intended. "Negroes are getting ideas they didn't have before," Kennedy's one black adviser, Louis Martin, reported in 1962, impressed by the Freedom Riders and other initiatives. "Where are they getting them?" Kennedy wondered. "From you!" Martin replied. "You're lifting the horizons of Negroes."

Kennedy knew that fame was fleeting and talk was cheap. His political caution was self-protective and reflected his minimal electoral mandate. Kennedy's cautious policymaking protected his celebrity status. It also earned him political capital that gave him the political cover to sing his democratic song—and ultimately start fulfilling it.

BY OCTOBER 1962 Kennedy realized that by leading from the center, he could achieve greatness. During the tense days of the Cuban Missile Crisis John Kennedy functioned as a cool statesman, disproving the modern caricature of him as a testosterone-crazed warmonger. Kennedy viewed the Soviet missile base in Cuba as a personal insult from Nikita Khrushchev. "He can't do that to me!" the president exclaimed on October 16, as the crisis began. Nevertheless, Kennedy remained calm.

Surviving the Bay of Pigs fiasco, managing the Berlin crisis, and living under the shadow of nuclear confrontation toughened Kennedy. His experiences also made him more amenable to compromise. During the Cuban Missile Crisis in October 1962, he first sought alternatives to military confrontation. Kennedy's top advisers recommended raids "to take out the missile sites," and speculated about Florida's vulnerability to conventional bombing from the Soviet weapons in Cuba. It was not easy for President Kennedy to emerge as the moderating force. He knew he could not retreat. With Khrushchev poised to exploit any sign of weakness, moderation appeared as risky as military action.

Kennedy's strategy cleverly threaded the needle through a small, risky opening. Quarantining Cuba—imposing a blockade—rather than attacking provided an assertive but limited response. It affirmed American military strength without bloodshed. Kennedy knew he could resort to more aggressive military options if necessary, but once he authorized an attack he could not turn back. Given the high stakes and great risks, choosing this strategy may have been one of the most momentous—and shrewd— presidential decisions ever made.

Kennedy's restraint worked. Nikita Khrushchev blinked. The Soviet premier respected the blockade and removed the missiles. The quarantine fulfilled Kennedy's promise to act against the missiles without inflaming the crisis. A secret deal with Khrushchev to remove "some of our Turkey missiles" implied reciprocity. But the Turkish missiles were unimportant strategically, and the secrecy gave Kennedy the public victory.

Although the crisis was genuine, it cracked the shell of immunity that often shielded Cold War presidents from criticism. Truman, Eisenhower, and Kennedy enjoyed unusual latitude in making foreign policy. But many Republicans believed Kennedy had not earned such respect. The Missile Crisis erupted three weeks before the 1962 midterm elections, in which the administration hoped to defy tradition and maintain strength in Congress.

Most Americans rallied around the president. Still, Kennedy's harshest Republican critics, such as Representative Thomas B. Curtis of Missouri, dismissed the crisis as "contrived for election purposes." Kennedy faced skeptics in his own party, too. When he briefed twenty bipartisan congressional leaders, just before addressing the American people about the crisis, the most bellicose senators demanding that he invade Cuba were Democrats.

By 1962 "bipartisanship" had become a weapon both parties wielded against their adversaries. Kennedy was less adept at insulating foreign policy from partisan debate than Harry Truman or Dwight Eisenhower had been. Kennedy bore some responsibility for the intensifying debate. He had narrowly squeaked into the presidency after blasting Eisenhower's foreign policy during the campaign. Kennedy extended an olive branch by appointing Eisenhower's Undersecretary of State, C. Douglas Dillon, as secretary of the treasury, but Republicans remained bitter.

Belying his reputation for nonpartisanship, former President Eisenhower attacked Kennedy's foreign and domestic policies from the start. Kennedy's failure to brief the Republicans before the Bay of Pigs irked Eisenhower. He insisted that bipartisanship only worked with consultation "before, not after, the hour of decision."

Ideologues on both the left and the right were criticizing Kennedy's entire approach to foreign policy, not merely a particular presidential response. On the right, some isolationists still muttered about avoiding all foreign imbroglios. Many more critics excoriated Kennedy's foreign policy for responding too feebly to the Soviet threat. On the left, intellectuals and students rejected the Cold War's fundamental assumptions. One month after Kennedy's election, Harper's Magazine featured the radical sociologist C. Wright Mills on the cover, publicizing his polemic against the Cold War and for Fidel Castro's revolution, called "Listen, Yankee." The article—and similarly titled book—denounced American foreign policy in ways that were shocking then and trendy now: blaming America for many tensions worldwide, chiding Americans for their woeful and self-destructive ignorance regarding the world, and romanticizing Third World revolutionaries as noble alternatives to clumsy, arrogant Americans.

Many of Mills's disciples helped draft the Port Huron Statement in June 1962, blasting American foreign policy for its Cold War belligerence and the military-industrial complex for perverting American society. "We are people of this generation, bred in at least modest comfort, housed now in universities, looking uncomfortably to the world we inherit," the momentous manifesto began, paying homage to the Constitution. Pinpointing modern America's two defining sins as racism and nuclear proliferation, the ambitious activists launched their sweeping "effort in understanding and changing the conditions of humanity in the late twentieth century."

Despite these rumblings, the quiescent status quo held—and continued to dominate. With the 1962 midterm elections looming, the New York Times editorialized against attacking the administration's foreign policy during the campaign. "Foreign policy must be debated," Republican Congressman Melvin Laird responded. Laird mischievously quoted Senator John F. Kennedy, who in 1960 had quoted "Mr. Republican" Senator Robert Taft to justify criticizing President Eisenhower. Taft had warned, "If you permit appeals to unity to bring an end to criticism, we endanger not only the constitutional liberties of our country, but even its future existence." The New York Times columnist Arthur Krock agreed, saying democracies needed vigorous but responsible debates to improve. Krock recalled that Senator Vandenberg himself had criticized the Truman administration occasionally and had complained that Truman made bipartisanship a one-way street. "They never bring us in before the take-offs," Vandenberg muttered, "just after the crash landings."

The Cuban Missile Crisis did not decide the midterm elections. Democrats lost four congressional seats and Republicans gained two. The Democratic majority held. Kennedy's major congressional challenge remained the Southern Democrats, who were increasingly furious with his solidifying civil rights stance. The tensions with Southern Democrats intensified as Kennedy matured. He was realizing that he could not ignore American racism any longer.

For all his savoir faire and media posturing, Kennedy had not cut the expected profile in courage. Wags sneered that Kennedy talked like the British World War II icon Winston Churchill but acted like the infamous prewar appeaser Neville Chamberlain. As a committed Cold Warrior, President Kennedy had concentrated on foreign affairs, telling his buddy Charles Bartlett, "As far as I'm concerned, 90 percent of the domestic problems are in the hands of [Special Assistant Theodore Sorensen's assistant] Mike Feldman. . . . If Mike Feldman's a crook, we're all in jail." Ironically, the experience of the Cuban Missile Crisis sensitized Kennedy to challenges much closer to home.

THE CUBAN MISSILE CRISIS changed John Kennedy from an eloquent figurehead who broadened Americans' horizons with idealistic rhetoric into an activist leader. He began to challenge his fellow citizens to realize their highest ideals, especially regarding the Declaration of Independence's celebrated affirmation that "All men are created equal." In the spring and summer of 1963, the Kennedy presidential reality began catching up with the Kennedy rhetoric; he finally emerged as the transformational leader he had long sounded like. He sought a more comprehensive war on poverty. He proposed a more genuine peace-seeking dialogue with the Soviet Union, during a speech at American University. And he finally tackled the civil rights question directly and courageously.

Although many now remember the civil rights movement as a clear-cut case of good versus evil—partially thanks to Kennedy's rhetoric—he himself had long been stymied by the competing interests at play. His own Democratic Party was torn between the New Deal liberal coalition and the entrenched Southern segregationists, who dominated the Senate through seniority privileges. Kennedy also sensed many Northern voters' ambivalence about civil rights. Televised images of Southern sheriffs hosing down black protestors and unleashing attack dogs dismayed Northerners and cried out for a solution. Still, few Northerners would open their schools and neighborhoods to true integration. One of America's great strengths, its constitutional conservatism, in this case caused unacceptable paralysis rather than providing welcome stability.

Yet as Kennedy's attitudes changed, he perceived that changing public opinions were shifting the political dynamics. A series of events made civil rights a burning issue in the 1960s, thanks to longstanding trends that had already started transforming American society. Throughout America, capitalism's creative destruction and anonymous market forces undermined traditional patterns and redistributed power, for better and worse. The New South business revolution, the great black migration during and after World War I, blacks' entry into the burgeoning union movement, and the rise of consumerist mass prosperity undermined "Jim Crow" segregation laws. The new American economy sought mass markets and skilled laborers, regardless of race.

Politically, red, white, and blue patriotism was defeating white versus black racism. Franklin D. Roosevelt's New Deal taught America's leaders to appeal to all "forgotten Americans." The surge of black enrollment into the once-racist Democratic Party, and the NAACP strategy of demanding equality through the courts, invalidated America's rigid system of racial exclusion. Proud of having defeated Nazism and committed to confronting communism, many Americans wondered how to fight oppression worldwide effectively when oppression festered at home. Clever activists, especially Martin Luther King Jr., embraced the consensus and challenged Americans to fight for "Negro liberty" too.

By the 1950s, and thanks to leaders like Dr. King, African Americans were not just relying on the courts, the Congress, or the presidency to grant them rights; they were taking their fight to the streets. In September 1957, when Dwight Eisenhower dispatched troops and federalized the National Guard to escort nine black children into Little Rock Central High School, many embarrassed Americans realized the situation had to change. The Cold War consensus helped propel the civil rights movement forward— even as the movement's progress was undermining that very consensus.

Senator Kennedy had supported civil rights dutifully, not passionately. His core constituents in Massachusetts rarely pressured him to tackle the issue, and he feared alienating powerful Southerners as he yearned for national office. "Somehow, some warmth has to be added to this image of intellectual liberalism," one black campaign adviser, Marjorie Lawson, insisted. Blacks have to feel from a candidate "not only that he understands, but that he cares about human dignity." Black voters sought a national gesture to demonstrate that concern.

During the presidential campaign Kennedy showed that he had the potential to be that kind of humane leader. He acted instinctively and decently when on October 19, 1960, a minor traffic violation sent Dr. King to a rural jail in Georgia. Robert Kennedy worked behind the scenes to free King. John Kennedy called Mrs. King to reassure her. Martin Luther King Sr., a Baptist minister, was so touched by the Kennedys' assistance that he vowed to drop a suitcase of votes in Kennedy's lap, despite his being a Catholic. When asked about "Daddy" King's religious prejudices, Kennedy, aware of his own father's sins, grinned. "Well," he said, "we all have fathers, don't we?"

As president, Kennedy fought racial inequality tentatively. He appointed forty blacks to prominent positions and five to federal judgeships. His brother, Attorney General Robert Kennedy, invigorated the Justice Department's Civil Rights Division, viewing equal education and voting rights as keys to black advancement. Still, Kennedy did not confront the Southern senators blocking major civil rights legislation.

Kennedy's passivity continued an unfortunate presidential tradition. Most presidents after the Civil War tolerated racism, deferring to America's strong traditions of localism, constitutionalism, and laissez faire. Franklin Roosevelt failed to champion antilynching legislation because he wanted to keep Southerners supporting the New Deal. Threats of embarrassing protests during the debate about entering World War II forced Roosevelt to integrate munitions plants by Executive Order. Similarly, during the 1948 convention Harry Truman offered a platitudinous platform plank on civil rights. Truman acted boldly only when pushed by liberals, and Southern "Dixiecrats" bolted. The result, Executive Order 9981, integrated the federal civil service and the armed forces.

Martin Luther King Jr. urged Kennedy to provide "vigorous" leadership and pass "meaningful laws." King advocated using Executive Orders as Roosevelt and Truman had done, and setting a moral example. The preacher also urged the president to set an example by boycotting any segregated activity. "The President is the embodiment of the democratic personality of the nation," King argued. "His own personal conduct influences and educates."

Kennedy preferred dodging conflict. When an African diplomat driving on Route 40 between Washington and New York was refused any service, even a glass of water, at a rest stop, the international denunciations embarrassed Kennedy. "Tell them to fly," Kennedy barked to the State Department protocol officer.

Similarly, when Kennedy and King first met after the election, the president sounded sympathetic but withheld resources. "If we go into a long fight in Congress, it will bottleneck everything else and still get no bill," the president feared. "He's got the understanding and he's got the political skill," King told Kennedy's aide, Harris Wofford, about the president, "but the moral passion is missing."

The civil rights movement continued to challenge the administration. A new generation of black and white activists cooperated. During the Freedom Rides, which began May 15, 1961, Kennedy first complained that these black and white radicals riding Greyhound buses together embarrassed him and America as he prepared to visit Canada. "Can't you get your goddamned friends off those buses?" he asked Wofford, one of his emissaries to liberals. "Tell them to call it off! Stop them!" As shocking at that sounds to the modern ear, polls showed that 64 percent of Americans surveyed condemned the rides, with only 24 percent approving them.

Kennedy had yet to see civil rights as a larger moral issue that would trump his concerns for serenity at home and smooth relations abroad. Days later, the issue became personal. In Montgomery, Alabama, a Justice Department aide the Kennedy brothers had sent South, John Seigenthaler, tried to stop angry Southerners beating two young female Freedom Riders. Stepping out of his car, the bespectacled bureaucrat identified himself as a federal agent. He was clubbed from behind and left bleeding on the pavement. The Kennedy brothers were furious. Like Eisenhower, they responded most viscerally to the assault on federal authority. Nevertheless, two months later the president gave his legalistic, clinical response to reporters about interstate commerce and Freedom Riders.

Beyond political or moral concerns, Kennedy wondered how much the president could do in America's federal system. Kennedy did not know whom he could dispatch when the local police failed to protect blacks or civil rights workers. Lacking faith that J. Edgar Hoover's FBI would help, fearing that deploying federal troops would evoke memories of the Civil War, Kennedy was stuck.

The middle path that Deputy Attorney General Byron White suggested appealed to Kennedy's approach. White proposed organizing federal officials already working in law enforcement to control immigration, firearms, tobacco, and liquor, as U.S. marshals. With that impressive-sounding title, these poorly trained deputies, many of whom had never fired a gun, would be sent into some of the era's most explosive situations.

To his frustration, Kennedy had to react based on others' initiatives, frequently depending on the kindness of hostile Southern governors. When in 1962 a black veteran, James Meredith, tried to register at the all-white University of Mississippi at Oxford, Governor Ross Barnett objected. Robert Kennedy called the governor, reminding him that Mississippi was bound by the Constitution. Governor Barnett disagreed. "Are you getting out of the Union?" the Attorney General asked. "It looks like . . . we don't belong to it," the governor answered, as if the Civil War were ongoing.

Five hundred thirty-eight federal marshals, some hastily deputized, arrived in Ole Miss on September 30, 1962. A mob shouting "2–4–1–3, we hate Kennedy" threw bottles, bricks, buckshot, and acid at the marshals. Handcuffed by the president's order to rely on tear gas, not guns, 160 marshals were wounded. The president sent in five thousand army troops, who again were ordered not to fire, but to intimidate. Watching these assaults on the nation's authority, President Kennedy realized he had to act.

In jail at that time for an act of civil disobedience, Martin Luther King wrote his "Letter from a Birmingham Jail," diagnosing John Kennedy's too polite paralysis. In seeking progress, King did not fear the Ku Klux Klansman, but the white moderate, "who is more devoted to 'order' than to justice; who prefers a negative peace which is the absence of tension to a positive peace which is the presence of justice."

Finally, President Kennedy mobilized. His handling of the Cuban Missile Crisis made him feel more secure in his power and ready to be bold yet temperate. The cumulative impact of the Southern outrages made him feel angry and motivated. The ever-present nuclear threat made him think more clearly about America's future and his own legacy. Kennedy was not the first white leader to stand tall on civil rights, but he was not the last, either.

Kennedy in June 1963 was finding his moral voice even as his advisers were worrying about his prospects for reelection in 1964. Preparations for a trip to the critical state of Texas for the fall of 1963 had begun, and reflected the administration's growing concerns. Still, Kennedy decided to address the issue of equality for all citizens on television in June 1963.

Most of Kennedy's advisers, except his brother Bobby, tried to stop him. They feared his initiatives would fail and undermine his standing. But Kennedy persisted. "There comes a time when a man has to take a stand and history will record that he has to meet these tough situations and ultimately make a decision," Kennedy told Secretary of Commerce Luther Hodges. In confronting civil rights as a moral issue, Kennedy demanded "equal rights and equal opportunities" for all Americans. He vowed to introduce a sweeping bill to Congress within the week "to make a commitment it has not fully made in this century to the proposition that race has no place in American life or law."

Even after this turning point, the process would be difficult. The Democratic Party lost its foothold among Southern whites during the civil rights battles—and has yet to recover. Shortly after Kennedy's speech, racists murdered Mississippi's NAACP leader, Medgar Evers, in front of his wife and children.

In making this most controversial move, Kennedy tried to appear as moderate as possible. His speech emphasized the promise of freedom for all Americans and the need to treat everyone in the country equally and fairly. Kennedy spoke more about Americans and their common needs than about blacks or whites. He demanded congressional legislation to open all public facilities to all Americans, regardless of their race. Kennedy did not

On June 11, 1963, John Kennedy addressed the nation on civil rights and began to show how a muscular moderate could help tame and implement radical
reforms. (John F. Kennedy Presidential Library)

lambaste the Southern governors, the segregationists, or even the Ku Klux
Klansmen. He sought a bipartisan coalition. He met with former President
Eisenhower as well as congressional leaders from both parties and all re-
gions. He asked for a forward-looking national perspective on this problem.

Kennedy knew the risks he was taking. "He always felt that maybe this
was going to be his political swan song," Bobby Kennedy later recalled.
When his mass transit and farm bills stalled in Congress, the president admitted, "Civil Rights did it."

In taking a stand as a muscular moderate on civil rights, Kennedy showed a
noble willingness to spend political capital. He used his widespread popularity

to change the course of the debate and push the nation forward. The move
was risky, but it could have enhanced his stature. It certainly boosted his historical standing.

Tragically, John Kennedy's assassination on November 22, 1963, deprived him of a chance to follow through on this new vision. The murder's
meaninglessness troubled his widow. "If it had at least been for his civil
rights stand," Jackie Kennedy mourned. Failing that, she helped make his
death a monument to American idealism and self-confidence by labeling
Kennedy's all-too-brief White House moment "Camelot."

For all the vicissitudes of his too-brief tenure, John Kennedy was lucky
to govern a country that still largely shared a broad political consensus. Although his rhetoric and style departed from the Eisenhower years, his policies were more similar than different. Both Eisenhower and Kennedy
enjoyed consistently high popularity ratings. Both benefited from the political and cultural climate. At the movies, Americans still watched newsreels
with heroic soundtracks and wry asides. These newscasts epitomized the
mid-century American culture in which patriotism invigorated traditional
gentility. Eisenhower and Kennedy were both patriotic heroes who
emerged as larger-than-life presidents.

In this new, proud, prosperous America, in this political world of bipartisan, Cold War heroes, Americans trusted their leaders and themselves.
Building the president up was an act of patriotism during a new kind of war.
The Cold War's lifestyle war brought image making to the forefront at a
time when other presidential weapons like party loyalty were being dulled.
Kennedy cherished his popularity and did not seem destined to be a revolutionary. But the civil rights agitation had stirred him up, just as he was feeling more confident in office. Suddenly, in 1963 he was set to try building a
new consensus, seeking common ground on a wrenching, divisive issue.
That he began by seeking broad support demonstrated his vision, his political ideals. That he had begun to realize how difficult it would be to keep
the nation together revealed his insight and America's rocky road ahead.

Kennedy's new approach to governing ended abruptly with his assassination. Ironically, the trauma of his death would guarantee passage of the
sweeping civil rights legislation he envisioned. But even the aura of the
martyred president would not be enough to keep together the already splintering country, the already imploding consensus. These would be among
the unhappy lessons Kennedy's successor, Lyndon Johnson, would learn,
most painfully.

8

THE CONSENSUS COLLAPSES

Lyndon Johnson and the Limits of Moderation

IN NOVEMBER 1963, Americans united to mourn John Kennedy, their fallen president. The cult of Camelot capped a decade of growing public admiration for the presidency. Fed by Cold War patriotism, postwar domesticity, a liberal New Deal nationalism, a bipartisan foreign policy, and the particular affection many Americans had for both "Ike" and "JFK," an aura of reverence enveloped the presidency. The Kennedy eulogies suggested that to succeed, a president needed a winning smile, a beautiful wife, a charming family, flashes of wit, flights of oratory, ease in globetrotting, and the occasional flourish in managing a crisis. The late president's popularity suited America's emerging celebrity-obsessed popular culture and long-standing search for national heroes. But that popularity was fragile, rooted in the new quicksand of journalistic approval rather than on more traditional foundations of party loyalty. And Kennedy's celebrity status obscured serious divisions over the ambitious policy agenda he belatedly had begun to advance, along with a broader discontent rising among some of America's most privileged citizens.

President Lyndon B. Johnson initially benefited from the popular veneration for the presidency, reinforced by the mass mourning. He enjoyed high public approval ratings, great legislative successes, and a landslide election victory in 1964. But even at his most popular, Johnson never bathed in the popular affection that Kennedy, Eisenhower, or Johnson's mentor Franklin Roosevelt had enjoyed. And Johnson's mismanagement of the Vietnam War not only ruined his presidency, it helped destroy the Cold War consensus and aura of reverence that Harry Truman, Dwight Eisenhower, and John Kennedy had built.

Lyndon Johnson was a master legislator. A Democratic loyalist who worked closely with the Republican Dwight Eisenhower, Johnson built his career on "Concession, Patience, Maneuver." As Senate majority leader, Johnson demonstrated a genius for careful compromises. Yet his personality was impulsive and intimidating; he often bullied fellow senators into the consensus he sought. As president, the spotlight shining on Johnson's personality made him look terrible. The constructive bullying that worked in the Senate chamber appeared buffoonish or dictatorial when viewed in the White House via television. At the same time, Johnson's addiction to ambiguity and secrecy, which served him so well as a legislator, eroded his presidential credibility.

It is easy to blame the collapse of the American consensus on Lyndon Johnson. His lies about the Vietnam War were so blatant, his behavior often so loutish, that it seems he single-handedly polluted the American political atmosphere. But neither Lyndon Johnson nor the Vietnam War destroyed the consensus. Cracks in the consensus had emerged even under Eisenhower.

The 1950s had witnessed epidemics of juvenile delinquency, intellectual alienation, spreading anxiety, and disquieting change. Sarah Lawrence College's former president, Harold Taylor, noted the range of terms used to describe 1950s youth, from "silent," "conformist," "soft," and "apathetic" to "beat" and "delinquent." These were also James Dean's "rebels without a cause." Writing in January 1961, before the tumult of the mid-1960s, Taylor warned that many young people were already rejecting the Eisenhower era's "public-relations culture, its policy of drift, its cultivation of affluence, and its political rhetoric." The frustration fed edgy movements in folk music, rock, and jazz, Allen Ginsburg's poetry and Norman Mailer's fiction. These rebels rejected the era's uniformity, a homogeneity particularly striking compared to today's social, cultural, and political diversity. The upheavals of the 1950s anticipated the rebellions of the 1960s.

Every war in American history has produced dissent. The protests against the Vietnam War, however, were more popular, intense, and potent.

The youth rebellion that targeted the Vietnam War was a result of the collapsing consensus, not its cause. Similarly, Lyndon Johnson's incompetent leadership did not create the problems, but rather made matters worse.

WHILE JACKIE KENNEDY mourned the meaninglessness of her husband's murder in November 1963, his successor sought to inject meaning into the death. "Everything I had ever learned in history books taught me that martyrs have to die for causes," Johnson later recalled. "That was my job. I had to take the dead man's program and turn it into a martyr's cause."

Lyndon Johnson harnessed the emotions surrounding John Kennedy's death to advance a liberal agenda. He rammed through civil rights legislation as the centerpiece of the Great Society, his grand attempt to outdo Franklin Roosevelt's New Deal, Harry Truman's Fair Deal, and John Kennedy's New Frontier. Johnson remained haunted by Kennedy's ghost, unsure whether his achievements were appreciated for themselves or perceived as Camelot's dividends. The uncertainty fed his insecurity, his monumental egoism, and a growing anger.

During the first few weeks of his administration, Johnson emphasized "continuity" and "consensus." A creature of Capitol Hill, Johnson was also a son of the Texas hill country who saw how government programs transformed rural life. Johnson wanted to continue Franklin Roosevelt's unifying mission of using government to help forgotten Americans. By 1960, the domestic equivalent of the Cold War foreign policy consensus, liberal nationalism, was generating ambitious governmental programs to build the country and alleviate misery. Both Republican and Democratic presidents implemented big nation-building projects. The federal highway system, federal housing loans, the GI bill, and other, similar ventures facilitated the prosperity of America's middle class while creating a new political center.

Lyndon Johnson's burst of domestic legislation in 1964 and 1965 surpassed the New Deal. Johnson muscled through an ambitious array of laws that transformed the way the government helped the poor, the sick, the old, and the homeless. He introduced these changes without relying on the justification of a national emergency and initially with minimal rancor. Considering Americans' traditional suspicions of big government, the mandate Johnson forged for expanding the federal government was revolutionary, albeit fleeting.

Seeking to remain above the fray publicly even while micromanaging legislative strategy privately, Johnson played the patient, pastoral consensus builder. He frequently quoted the Prophet Isaiah: "Come now, and let us reason together." Initially he ran the presidency like a majority leader, his aide Elizabeth Carpenter observed: "It's the way of trying to bring about a meeting of minds on close votes . . . striving for the impossible, settling for the possible. But deliver. Deliver!"

Both a master accommodator and a secretive showman, Johnson had been reconciling competing forces all his life. A tall, hulking, bulldog of a man, he lacked his late predecessor's grace and good looks. Raised on the Texas frontier by a schoolmarm mother and a hard-drinking father, Johnson internalized the genteel Victorian ethic emphasizing formalistic public behavior. The contradiction between his true personality and his public persona ultimately eroded his standing.

Initially, the public rallied around Johnson's patriotic platitudes as a welcome balm after Kennedy's murder. Johnson believed "there is always a national answer to each national problem." "Reasonable men" could forge a common ground, led by the president, who must foster a "fundamental unity of interest, purpose and belief" in the nation. This task was "do-able"—a favorite Johnson expression—because "the farmer in Iowa, the fisherman in Massachusetts, the worker in Seattle, the rancher in Texas have the same hopes and harbor the same fears." The new president united George Washington's enlightened rationalism with a Lincolnian pragmatism and an affirmative nationalism that the two Roosevelts had shaped.

Johnson moved quickly upon taking office. The election was less than a year away. Johnson's first State of the Union address, in 1964, laid the foundations for the Great Society, his plan to end poverty and ignorance in America. He soon won passage of a tax budget and the first of what would be forty bills advancing his "war on poverty."

Lyndon Johnson would not relax until he had improved the lives of almost two hundred million Americans as dramatically as the bringing of electricity to Johnson City had transformed his constituents' lives in the 1930s. "I wanted power to use it," he said. In the spring of 1964, while skinny-dipping in the White House pool, Johnson ordered his speechwriter, Richard Goodwin, and his assistant, Bill Moyers, "to put together a Johnson program, and don't worry about whether it's too radical or if Congress is ready for it. That's my job." Be "imaginative and not bound by timid, preconceived notions," he ordered his cabinet.

Defying most of his advisers, Johnson advanced Kennedy's comprehensive civil rights bill in 1964. Johnson's bill guaranteed equal opportunity in employment while outlawing discrimination in restaurants, motels, and other public accommodations. This bold step proved that seeking consensus entailed "positive action," not accepting the lowest common denominator. "Mr. President," one adviser begged before Johnson's speech advocating the bill, "you should not lay the prestige of the Presidency on the line." Johnson retorted, "What's it for if it's not to be laid on the line?"

Viewing things nationally as a president, rather than regionally as a Texas senator, Johnson believed that progress on civil rights was a moral imperative and a national necessity. The country needed to solve the race problem to progress on other issues; the South needed to solve the race problem to be accepted as part of a modern union. "Dick, you've got to get out of my way. I'm going to run over you," Johnson warned his friend, the segregationist Georgia Senator Richard Russell, shortly after becoming president. "I don't intend to cavil or compromise." Political calculations also reinforced Johnson's seemingly altruistic pursuit of the bill. He needed to give liberals a "civil rights bill that was even stronger than the one they'd have gotten if Kennedy had lived. Without this, I'd be dead before I could even begin."

Southern Democrats and conservative Republicans alike vowed to kill the bill. Johnson first muscled the legislation through the House by threatening to bypass the Rules Committee. To stay relevant, the Committee then approved the bill, 11 to 4. The Senate was not so accommodating. Seeking bipartisan support, the president implored Republican Minority Leader Everett Dirksen to end the unprecedented three-month Senate filibuster of the bill. Johnson badgered his liberal Democratic ally, Senator Hubert Humphrey, to deliver the Senate. Johnson worked the phones and approved at least one Western water project to entice some wavering senators. Still, as the filibuster persisted and Dirksen resisted, the president told staffers dejectedly, "I just don't think a white Southerner is a man to unite this nation in this hour." Dirksen eventually succumbed to Johnson's relentless lobbying. The landmark Civil Rights Act passed in June 1964.

Johnson won the legislative battle but lost the national consensus. White Southerners were outraged and did not hesitate to attack him. Stung though not surprised by his fellow Southerners' venom, Johnson predicted that his actions had delivered the Democratic South to the Republicans for the next twenty years. He was half right: Forty years later the Democrats have not yet regained their footing among whites in the Old Confederacy.

President Lyndon Johnson signing the Civil Rights Act in 1964. He took great satisfaction in fulfilling John Kennedy's vision, and even outdoing his mentor, Franklin Roosevelt in forging a Great Society for America's middle class, not just the poor and oppressed. (Library of Congress)

Within months of taking office, Lyndon Johnson had to campaign to win the presidency in his own right. Wrapping himself in Kennedy's mantle, he nevertheless resented the Kennedy legacy for obscuring his own identity. Although Lyndon Johnson tried to star in the 1964 campaign, the defining personalities were the late President Kennedy and the new threat from the right, Barry Goldwater.

Arizona Senator Barry Goldwater made Lyndon Johnson appear calm and rational. Johnson and his running mate, Hubert Humphrey, campaigned as moderates with bipartisan support, treating the Republican nominee as a political outlaw. Senator Barry Goldwater's 1960 manifesto, "The Conscience of a Conservative," had sold 3.5 million copies. Goldwater rejected status quo opinions, fearing that Americans were too soft on communism and too hard on themselves. Rejecting what he dismissed as appeasement-oriented, reactive, "me too" Republicanism that was constantly kowtowing to modern liberalism, Goldwater vowed to resurrect Republican conservatism. Goldwater's unapologetic acceptance speech at the

1964 Republican National Convention in San Francisco inspired conservatives and perversely delighted Democrats as he thundered, "Extremism in the defense of liberty is no vice, and . . . moderation in the pursuit of justice is no virtue."

Conservatives cheered Goldwater's clarity and courage. The *Wall Street Journal*, tired of the "hoary 'politics stops at the water's edge' line," editorialized that contentious campaigns educate about important issues and can force essential changes. The *Journal* complained that addiction to consensus prevented necessary change, smothered debate, and reduced the Republicans in opposition to being "the handmaidens of the Democrats," echoing the liberal status quo.

Americans had not faced such a clear choice in decades. Democrats blasted Goldwater's "drastic departure" from what Hubert Humphrey called "the great highway of bipartisanship." Secretary of State Dean Rusk detailed the many bipartisan initiatives since the 1940s that had been designed to contain communism. Rusk concluded, "how foolish we would be to depart from the tested ways and bipartisan spirit which have served so well our security and the cause of freedom."

Apparently the voters agreed with the Democrats. Lyndon Johnson's historic 44-state, 486-electoral vote sweep in 1964 thrilled him. "Millions upon millions of people, each one marking my name on their ballot, each one wanting me as their President," Johnson recalled. "For the first time in all my life I truly felt loved by the American people." The landslide fed Johnson's ego, legitimized his presidency, and increased his political power. The Democrats gained two seats in the Senate and thirty-seven in the House, making the election a "mandate for unity," the president claimed.

Yet for all his strutting, Johnson understood that he had been seated as a guest at his own coronation. He had, in effect, won John Kennedy's second term by defeating an easily caricatured, ineffectual opponent. Moreover, although he derided Goldwater as the warmongering candidate who would escalate conflict in Vietnam, Lyndon Johnson was preparing for a massive escalation in Indochina.

THE 1964 ELECTION granted Lyndon Johnson extraordinary power. The presidency had become ever mightier over the previous thirty years. The Democratic margins of 68 to 32 in the Senate and 295 to 140 in the House gave Johnson the strongest congressional majority since Franklin Roosevelt's second term in office began in 1937.

Such presidential power was transitory and had to be deployed quickly. "I worked like hell to become President, and I'm not going to throw it away," he told his aides. "So I want you guys to get off your asses and do everything possible to get everything in my program passed as soon as possible, before the aura and the halo that surround me disappear." Alas, as Franklin Roosevelt had done in 1937 with the court packing, Lyndon Johnson soon overstepped. In his zeal to do good, Johnson made two bad mistakes. More master legislator than public educator, he proved better at passing his Great Society plans than explaining or implementing them. And to protect the Great Society and his administration from political fallout, he concealed the extent and cost of America's growing entanglement in Vietnam.

The Great Society escalated Johnson's war against poverty and for civil rights into a full-scale assault on injustice and social ugliness. Eventually, staffers counted 207 laws as "landmark" legislative achievements. Under Johnson, the federal budget topped $100 billion for the first time. Aid to the poor nearly doubled, health programs tripled, and education programs quadrupled. The permanent civil service expanded from 1 million strong when Eisenhower retired in 1961 to 1.3 million federal workers eight years later.

Tragically, the Great Society failed to provide a great solution to America's ills. As Johnson led America to respond to the racial crisis, blacks' long-smoldering anger ignited. Johnson could not forge a consensus to prevent the violence or reconcile the country's growing extremes. In March 1965, police violence against protestors in Selma, Alabama, on "Bloody Sunday" embarrassed many Americans watching on television and enraged civil rights activists, who lost faith in their more moderate leaders. Addressing a joint session of Congress, Johnson compared blacks fighting for civil rights with America's revolutionaries at Lexington in 1775. He promised "we shall overcome." In absorbing this once marginal protest slogan, Johnson attempted to mainstream the civil rights movement just as it was becoming radicalized.

On August 6, 1965, amid his major Great Society legislative blitz, Johnson signed the Voting Rights Act to expand voter registration. Five days later, the Los Angeles black ghetto, Watts, exploded. Tensions between police and civilians, a 30 percent adult unemployment rate, and the mingling of some hope amid so much hopelessness proved too volatile. Thirty-four people died, 856 suffered injuries, and more than 3,000 rioters were arrested. Property damage reached $35 million.

The political damage was incalculable. The resulting unstable mix of black anger and white indignation would cripple liberalism. Riots had already erupted in New York City, Rochester, and Philadelphia during the summer of 1964. Over the next three summers, Cleveland, Chicago, Detroit, Newark, and Jacksonville exploded in violence.

The Watts riots devastated America's new liberal-in-chief. The president "just wouldn't accept it," Johnson's aide, Joseph Califano, recalled. "He refused to look at the cables from Los Angeles. . . . He refused to take calls from the generals who were requesting government planes to fly in the National Guard." Johnson continued to resist facing unpleasant realities as the nation sank into the Vietnam quagmire.

That same summer, Johnson's attempts to fight communism also faltered, as he launched the ground war in Vietnam. Acting on their belief in the domino theory, which held that if one nation in Southeast Asia fell to communism, the rest would surely follow, Presidents Eisenhower and Kennedy had sent military advisers into the region after the French left in the 1950s. Republican and Democratic experts alike warned that keeping Vietnam from going communist was essential to preserving America's world credibility.

Remembering how the "who lost China" charge had derailed Harry Truman, Johnson feared the Right would use any perceived weakness abroad to stop his visionary revolution at home. Johnson vowed, "I am not going to lose Vietnam. I am not going to be the President who saw Southeast Asia go the way China went." Johnson ordered his aides, "Don't go to bed at night until you have asked yourself, 'Have I done everything I could to further the American effort to assist South Vietnam?'"

In August 1964, Johnson announced that North Vietnamese torpedo boats had attacked American destroyers in the Gulf of Tonkin. A congressional resolution was passed authorizing the president "to take all necessary measures" to protect American forces. Undaunted, the Communist guerrillas spearheading the National Front for the Liberation of South Vietnam, the Viet Cong, intensified their attacks.

Years earlier, frustrated by the Eisenhower era's smothering bipartisanship and instinctive interventionism, the *Wall Street Journal* had warned, "One of these days in one of these places we are going to get badly burned, and so senselessly." As predicted, America became increasingly entangled, with minimal national debate. Johnson ignored skeptical experts and failed to prepare the public for the necessary sacrifices. As early as 1965 advisers were warning that the situation was grave and that America risked "disastrous defeat" in the region, in the words of a memo written by McGeorge Bundy and Robert McNamara that year.

Fearing congressional demands for withdrawal or cutbacks in his Great Society legislation to fund the war, Johnson often escalated America's troop levels secretly. Polls showed broad support for the war initially, but Johnson never invited Americans or Congress to endorse the war effort properly. He never fully explained the commitment required to win the war or the rationale for putting American troops in Vietnam in the first place. When the American public needed a convincing explanation, Lyndon Johnson chose to soft-pedal the issue. In December 1964, after winning election as a peacemaker over Barry Goldwater, Johnson directed his aides to obscure his plans to escalate the war. "I consider it a matter of the highest importance, that the substance of this position should not become public except as I specifically direct," Johnson ordered as he intensified the war efforts.

American involvement in Vietnam war quickly grew from thousands of advisers to hundreds of thousands of troops. By 1968, 500,000 Americans troops were fighting an undeclared war, with mounting casualties. The bloody, chaotic combat brought the war home to a generation precisely when many members of that generation were growing restive. Many baby boomers were already questioning authority and the status quo. That stance primed them to lash out against Vietnam, and against the government that was entangling them in this horror. The Vietnam War's harsh, absurd conditions radicalized some baby boomers. But all wars are harsh and absurd. Their fathers' war, World War II, had been particularly brutal.

Intellectuals were also ready to pounce—and were surprised to see their words resonate and shape policy. Even before the Vietnam protests, before Lyndon Johnson became president, the trio Peter, Paul and Mary had hit the pop charts singing Bob Dylan's protest anthem "Blowin' in the Wind." The University of Michigan hosted the first antiwar "teach in" in 1965. "We Are Deluding Ourselves in Vietnam," Professor Hans J. Morgenthau warned in April 1965. "Misconceptions" were leading policy makers down a "blind alley." By 1967, a major debate was raging in the nation, fueled by college students' fear of being drafted and their growing rebelliousness.

The antiwar protests popularized and intensified yet also redirected the growing movement of political and cultural dissent. Seeking personal meaning amid affluence and asserting their unprecedented freedoms culturally, socially, and sexually, some—although certainly not all—baby boomers protested not only the war but also the state of society. America's anonymity, wealth, leisure, and freedom were dissolving authority, hierarchy, community—and conformity. A colorful, contradictory movement resulted. The antiwar movement generated headlines while seeking an immediate political result rather than a more lasting revolution. It is not clear whether the antiwar movement was most influential politically in ending the Vietnam conflict or electing Richard Nixon President in 1968. Socially and culturally, the revolution would go mainstream by the 1970s and continue transforming and unnerving America for the next half century, normalizing novelties ranging from jeans, granola, and T-shirts to premarital sex, divorce, and a disregard for traditional class distinctions.

Johnson took the antiwar criticism personally, demonizing critics as fools and traitors. During one temper tantrum in 1965, Johnson bellowed, "They all just follow the communist line—liberals, intellectuals, communists. . . . I can't trust anybody anymore. . . . I'm going to get rid of everybody who doesn't agree with my policies." Of course, retreating into his White House bunker further alienated his critics.

FOR THIRTY YEARS, presidents had been using the media to foster consensus. Franklin Roosevelt used his fireside chats to develop a national conversation about important issues, positioning the president in the center of the discussion about difficult problems. Now the media hammered away at America's common assumptions, at traditional establishment figures, and most especially, at President Lyndon Johnson.

An all-purpose, media-generated skepticism shifted the terms of the equation to the advantage of the press. Reporters discovered that protesters made good television; constructive leaders did not. The rise of television was doubly costly to Johnson. Print reporters, feeling competitive pressure from television and feeling liberated themselves from traditional journalistic restraints, became more aggressive, probing, and analytical. And the cameras were cruel to the president, making him appear stiff and insecure. He hid behind notes or a teleprompter, preventing viewers from seeing him in what his assistant, Jack Valenti, called "the manner in which he is most engaging and most effective: being himself."

By undermining the president and other politicians, reporters became the stars of the national conversation. By the end of the Johnson administration, Americans had more faith in the CBS News anchor, Walter Cronkite, than in the president of the United States. Within a decade reporters like Dan

Rather and Bob Woodward would emerge as highly paid, instantly recognizable celebrities.

Reporters' growing hostility and the White House's increasing defensiveness sparked a war for the American public's hearts and minds. Johnson and his aides combated what Jack Valenti called "the contagion of anti-Johnson virus." President Johnson crudely described critical columnists as "whores. Anytime an editor wants to screw 'em, they'll get down on the floor and do it for three dollars."

Johnson suffered from the backlash triggered by Kennedy's "news management," especially during the Cuban crises. Cozy Washington relationships became less important than professional procedures and technical facilities provided so that journalists could meet their deadlines. Johnson's vulgarity and melodramatics bred contempt among reporters. Johnson revealed himself to the press, trusting reporters' discretion, as he always had. But journalists were growing reluctant to shield the powerful.

By 1965, reporters were calling the chasm between Johnson's tall tales and the truth "Lyndon Johnson's Credibility Gap." One popular joke asked, "How do you know when Lyndon Johnson is telling the truth? When he pulls his ear lobe, scratches his chin, he's telling the truth. When he begins to move his lips, you know he's lying." Johnson threw himself at reporters more intensely, driving them around his ranch, bullying them, confiding in them. The more he gave them "the treatment," the more they gave him the business, reducing his standing with Americans.

Johnson's aides wavered between advising the president to speak to the American people directly and warning that good public relations was about strategy, not substance. Nobly emphasizing their mutual "responsibilities to the American people," Johnson and his men said that the president should "grant the Press access to the facts" and the press should "report the facts accurately." Actually, the president became more imperious and manipulative. He sometimes withheld information, sometimes leaked it, and ordered White House switchboard operators to record all outside calls to staffers, trying to catch staffers talking to reporters. Reporters usually presented information along with their own interpretations; objectivity was often praised but rarely attained.

Despite the administration's desperate search for a "counter-program for communicating," Johnson and his aides refused to give the citizens what they most craved: straight talk about the war. Johnson's secrecy, yearning for approval, and growing fury at his critics prevented him from acknowledging any mistakes. The result fragmented the body politic. The administration was making "an ass of itself by not admitting much earlier what it knew perfectly well, that some of the bombs were missing their targets," the *Economist* editorialized in January 1967. Referring to Johnson, the magazine concluded, "It is not what he does, it's the way he does it."

Johnson and his aides initially believed they were more powerful than reporters. "[W]hether the press is friendly or unfriendly . . . has little to do with the political life of the country," White House press aide George Reedy boasted to Johnson in December 1963. But after a short time in the White House, the staff agreed with Special Assistant to the President Robert Kintner that "Television establishes the images of political figures in America, fortunately or unfortunately." Kintner, who previously had been president of both ABC and NBC, said the president was a "real star" and had to be treated accordingly. "Images do not spring full blown," Jack Valenti preached to the president. "They are created like any other product of mind and imagination."

White House aides repeatedly ignored the objective conditions in Vietnam and worried more about the president's image. They complained that "television in particular is stimulating a national mob psychology working to the disadvantage of the President." White House memoranda piled up speculating about how to show "a strong and compassionate President involved in the hopes of people and their dreams and thereby diminishing some public concern about Vietnam," as one February 1965 memorandum from Jack Valenti read. But finding "a good picture possibility" was not the answer. Johnson's unpopularity stemmed from "ugly problem[s]," including the growing urban crisis, rising inflation, spreading student revolt, and, especially, the escalating war in Vietnam.

These crises, coming on the heels of the promises of the Great Society, disillusioned millions. A poll in September 1967 showed that 54 percent of those surveyed viewed Johnson less favorably than they had in 1964. Prominent pundits such as Murray Kempton doubted that the Johnson administration had "any impulse that is not vulgar or any judgment that is not trivial."

In fairness, Secretary of Defense Robert McNamara noted, the American public demanded victory in Vietnam, as did the foreign policy establishment. At one November 1967 meeting, the Washington "wise man" Clark Clifford admitted that all wars were unpopular, but insisted this mission was the noble path to pursue. Uncertainty, Clifford warned, risked making

America look weak. With such advice being reinforced by the generals' optimistic field reports, McNamara wondered, "how could President Johnson be
expected to break out of his mind-set and confront the uncomfortable truths
and unpalatable choices?"

Gradually, the president's paranoid, abusive behavior had many insiders
doubting his judgment, and even his sanity. Johnson was a bully. He often
humiliated new aides, dominating subordinates to guarantee their fealty.
Johnson blamed communists for the criticism about the war and refused to
appease critics. "The enemy is using my own people as dupes," Johnson exclaimed, when diplomats suggested halting the bombing in Vietnam. After
Arkansas's intellectual Democratic senator, William Fulbright, criticized
the war, Johnson froze out "Senator Half-bright." Like a substitute teacher
losing control, Johnson issued increasingly violent threats the more he encountered resistance. "I'll destroy you and every one of your dove friends in
six months," he barked, referring to Fulbright and other antiwar senators.

As the antiwar movement, swayed by the civil rights and sexual revolutions, decided that the personal is political, Lyndon Johnson made politics
extremely personal. Once, after Robert Kennedy, now a New York senator,
advocated a bombing halt, Johnson berated Kennedy with such ferocity
that Kennedy snapped, "I don't have to take that from you." Kennedy
walked away, questioning Johnson's stability: "If he exploded like that with
me, how could he ever negotiate with Hanoi?" The Johnson loyalist Arthur
Goldberg recalled that once when reporters pressed the president to explain why America was in Vietnam, "LBJ unzipped his fly, drew out his substantial organ, and declared, 'This is why!'" Johnson ran the White House
like a European court, playing favorites and hoarding information. Only
decades later would Secretary of Defense Robert McNamara and other sen-
ior officials learn that Johnson had suppressed pessimistic assessments or
CIA proposals for withdrawal.

The Vietnam mess dissolved the traditional proprieties. Protesters said
niceties were annoying impediments when trying to stop "genocide."
Demonstrating a moral confusion, they burned the American flag and
waved the Viet Cong flag. Secretary McNamara reported being mobbed,
spat on, and cursed in public with cries of "Baby Burner!"

The antiwar movement targeted Lyndon Johnson; he and his presidency
proved an easy target. But the New Left's assault on traditional American
institutions was part of a broader cultural and political story. "Our whole
life is a defiance of Amerika," the newspaper of the radical Students for a

Paul Michael Szep's cartoon of the "Three Spectres" haunting Lyndon Johnson illustrates how Johnson's dream of creating a Great Society for all Americans turned into the ongoing nightmare of managing the increasingly unpopular Vietnam War. (Library of Congress)

Democratic Society faction, the Weathermen, would say in 1969, "It's moving in the streets, digging sounds, smoking dope . . . fighting pigs." By 1970, three-quarters of students polled would advocate fundamental changes in the American system. This generation of students would go beyond Johnson and the Vietnam War to trigger revolutions in race relations, gender attitudes, intellectual life, political tactics, and the media.

The beleaguered president finally announced his retirement on March 31, 1968, after declaring a bombing halt "to de-escalate" the Vietnam conflict. The master politician hoped the linkage would make him appear statesmanlike. But by then he was too ensnared in his own deceits and delusions. He had vowed not to stop the bombing as recently as March 16, and he authorized more bombing just twenty-four hours after declaring the halt. Johnson was self-pitying and unapologetic, saying, "I was born the way I am, I can't do anything about it."

Traumas punctuated the rest of his administration: Martin Luther King's assassination in April, Robert F. Kennedy's murder in June, the chaotic Democratic National Convention in August, Hubert Humphrey's loss in November. Johnson left for Texas one of the most despised presidents ever.

IN THE HOUSE, and especially in the Senate, Lyndon Johnson had put his most distasteful qualities to good use. His in-your-face lobbying was the mark of an insecure, untrustworthy boor, part bootlicker, part tyrant. It worked in Capitol Hill's clubby chaos, but these traits worked for a politician, not a president.

Johnson's pollsters, misled by the numbers, declared that only "3 to 5%" disliked the president "solely on personality." They suggested a "job oriented" communications strategy. If Eisenhower had "the Father Image" and JFK was "Prince Charming," Lyndon Johnson could be "The Professional." This focus on accomplishments only perpetuated Johnson's delusions and made him introduce more legislation while still failing to charm the American public. Successful statesmanship requires more than listing achievements; effective leaders have to cast a spell.

Lyndon Johnson's personality helps explain why he failed to bewitch Americans with his particular brand of magic. His flamboyant personality tics made him awkward when trying to woo voters. Persistent psychological patterns help solve the great mystery of the Johnson presidency: How could the same man nurture the Great Society lifeline and the Vietnam bloodbath? Johnson's emotional emptiness fed his grandiosity. He knew the true character of Cold War America's have-your-cake-and-eat-it-too political culture. Americans dreamed of spreading prosperity and freedom throughout the world cost-free, risk-free. Fearing rejection, shackled by consensus, refusing to warn Americans that they needed to sacrifice, Johnson doomed his own efforts.

Unlike Franklin Roosevelt, who so carefully nudged the nation toward war and succeeded in gaining their support, Johnson surreptitiously plunged into war and failed to win the country's approval. He soft-pedaled the costs of both the Great Society and the Vietnam conflict. As the public soured on the war, Johnson refused to budge. In avoiding debate, escalating the U.S. presence secretly, and lying, Johnson demonstrated a lack of faith in the people, breeding a culture of distrust.

Rallying against Johnson, the student movement became more aggressive. Citizens in general became more restive. It became harder for the president to lead. Johnson's grating, stubborn personality exacerbated a bad situation.

Clashes between policemen and protesters were not daily occurrences, but local skirmishes became nationally televised events and therefore seemed more widespread. Cries of "pigs," "fascists," and "cowards" filled the streets and echoed nationwide on television. The radicals of the New Left deemed themselves rebels, rejecting the "overdeveloped society" of big government, big business, and big universities. They attacked poverty, racial injustice, and the war in Vietnam, viewing the urban riots and assassinations of the 1960s as proof that America was a sick, ungovernable society.

During the Vietnam conflict, victory seemed as dependent on the home front as the battlefront. Every night millions watched the bloody images broadcast into their homes via television. The Viet Cong tried to sour the American public on the war effort by humiliating American prisoners of war, wooing antiwar dissenters, and appearing absolutely unflappable. Initially, the demands of national security and appeals to party unity inhibited debate among both Republicans and Democrats. Helping to bury the two-decade, on-again, off-again truce regarding divisive foreign policy debates, Kennedy's former speechwriter, Ted Sorensen, insisted in March 1968, "We cannot tell a nation that bases its very existence on public consent that the most divisive and far-reaching issue of our times is outside the political arena."

Johnson's failures of leadership, the Vietnam quagmire, and the social movements of the 1960s shattered the postwar consensus. Faith in any kind of "common climate of American opinion" evaporated, especially among America's elite and most influential opinion makers. Clark Clifford recalled the traumatic violence of the summer of 1968, quoting William Butler Yeats: "Things fall apart, the centre cannot hold; Mere anarchy is loosed upon the world. . . . The best lack all conviction, while the worst, Are full of passionate intensity."

Individual personality flaws, bad policy choices, and an inflamed political context continued to undermine the American presidency. After Johnson, Presidents Richard Nixon, Gerald Ford, and Jimmy Carter tried to maintain the broad outlines of the bipartisan approach to the Cold War and the welfare state, but failed because of their own mixes of stubbornness, bad judgment, and bad luck. Despite these failures, in the late 1980s the consensus strategy would be partially vindicated by the relatively peaceful implosion of the Soviet Union. Still, the backlash against consensus intensified.

9

Learning from Losers

Where Richard Nixon and Jimmy Carter Went Wrong

THE TWO PRESIDENTS WHO DOMINATED the 1970s fed America's crisis of confidence. The failed presidencies of Richard Nixon and Jimmy Carter demonstrate that moderate policies do not guarantee success. Effective leaders must inspire confidence, dispel anxieties, solve problems, and build a sense of democratic community, not just steer a path between extremes.

On July 4, 1976, millions celebrated America's bicentennial by converging on lower Manhattan. Sixteen tall ships and hundreds of smaller boats from around the world floated past the Statue of Liberty to mark the Declaration of Independence's 200th anniversary. But even as President Gerald Ford urged Americans on CBS-TV's final *Bicentennial Minute* to keep the Spirit of '76 alive, and authorities rejoiced that media predictions of mass street crimes against the revelers had not come about, Americans were edgy. Crime was soaring, along with inflation, unemployment, the divorce rate, drug use, and cynicism. One year before, President Ford had refused to bail out New York City as it neared bankruptcy, prompting the *Daily News* headline: FORD TO CITY: DROP DEAD.

Manhattan symbolized America the ungovernable, unmanageable, and unlivable. Muggers lurked in the shadows. Middle-class taxpayers felt squeezed. The acrid body odor of the homeless fouled once majestic sites like the Forty-Second Street Library. Garbage overflowed on city streets. Dog droppings were scattered like minefields across the sidewalks.

One president after another in the 1970s proved unable to cope with the challenges facing the nation. Richard Nixon's resignation was the final blow in a wave of disillusioning disasters, including the bombing of Cambodia, the Kent State massacre, the Arab oil embargo, and the great inflation. President Ford, mocked as "His Accidency," was an affable but ineffectual replacement for Nixon. Ford alienated many by abruptly pardoning Nixon and then could not tame the galloping stagflation, inflation combined with high unemployment. Within months of the bicentennial celebration, Ford would lose the presidency to Jimmy Carter. Carter then spent his tenure futilely advising Americans to accept a world of limited resources, power, and horizons as Iranians kidnapped American diplomats, the Soviets invaded Afghanistan, and Americans sat in their cars in endless gas lines watching prices soar.

Significantly, both Nixon and Carter failed despite their centrism. Both were brainy politicians who preferred drafting laws to crafting coalitions. In fairness, both faced a demoralized citizenry humbled by daunting problems. Still, each contributed significantly to his respective failure. In modern America's media-centered democracy, those who fail to woo, fail to lead. As Nixon explained to his domestic affairs adviser, John Ehrlichman, "Great ideas that are conceived and not sold are like babies that are stillborn."

Although liberals despised Nixon, he governed from the center. His diplomatic breakthroughs to Communist China and Soviet Russia were so unexpected that "Nixon to China" has become shorthand for being able to act moderate because one's extremist bona fides are so solid. Domestically, Nixon actually expanded Lyndon Johnson's Great Society. In 1973, a Republican Party list of more than fifty Nixon administration accomplishments read like the Lyndon Johnson big government wish list. Nixon created the Environmental Protection Agency, an office of child development, and the Cabinet Committee on Opportunities for Spanish-Speaking People. The number of needy children receiving free or low-cost school lunches jumped from 2,864,624 in 1968 to 8,845,846 in 1973, and food stamp recipients soared from 2.9 million in January 1969 to 12.4 million in June 1973.

Just as Nixon the Republican moved left, toward the center, Jimmy Carter the Democrat veered right. Jimmy Carter initiated many of what would become Ronald Reagan's defining programs. Carter deregulated the airlines, the railroads, trucking, oil, and banking. His zero-based budgeting launched the era of budget consciousness. And his defense buildup in 1979 and 1980 predated the Reagan boost. Before their hatred of Reagan made them nostalgic for Carter, Democrats despised Carter's centrism. Some activists labeled Carter the most conservative Democrat since Grover Cleveland.

Not all politicians who aim for the center find it. Richard Nixon's policies were centrist, but his politics were immoderate. For all of Nixon's clever positioning, his kill-or-be-killed approach to politics proved self-destructive. As for Carter, he proved that the sum of the modern president's program is greater than its individual parts. Carter's discouraging speeches hurt him and his country. Craving a new, affirmative consensus, Americans resented Carter's defeatist message, laced with his impotent pessimism.

RICHARD NIXON entered the White House in 1969, after America's traumatic year of assassinations, riots, and war. The new president promised to heal the nation, end the war, calm the students, and restore American pride. He knew his legacy hinged on ending the Vietnam War honorably and calming the student rebellion. He also dreamed about realigning electoral coalitions to make Republicans the voice of America's Silent Majority.

Nixon won the presidency in 1968 campaigning as the "New Nixon," a warmer, less partisan incarnation than the pit bull he had been in the 1950s. Born to a lower middle-class family in Southern California in 1913, Nixon completed college and law school before serving in the Pacific during World War II. He ran for Congress in 1946, serving in the House with another freshman, John Kennedy. Congressman Nixon became famous as an ardent anticommunist and a political scrapper. Elected to the Senate in 1950, in 1952 Nixon became Dwight Eisenhower's running mate, representing the GI Joe generation and conservative Republicans. In 1960 he narrowly lost the presidency to Kennedy.

A tightly wound spring of negative energy, with a brooding intelligence, dark features, and darting eyes, Nixon often felt slighted by rich "Harvards" like the Kennedys. His relentless ambition and sleazy campaigning tactics during his California campaigns earned him the nickname "Tricky Dick." Convinced he had been robbed of victory in 1960 by massive voter fraud involving long-dead voters somehow casting ballots in Illinois and Texas, Nixon entered the White House competing with Kennedy's ghost, hoping finally to best his rival by becoming a consequential and popular president.

Years of searing partisan combat, followed by anguished political exile, made Nixon pragmatic. He would mollify the overwhelmingly Democratic Congress on domestic issues to make his mark abroad. The sixties revolution was reaching Middle America. Even as the cultural consensus that governed America dissolved, a new political consensus was forming. Many Great Society goals were becoming popularly accepted. Sounding remarkably liberal, Nixon vowed to deliver "clean air, clean water, open spaces, . . . a welfare reform program that will provide a floor under the income of every family with children in America—a new approach to government, reform of education, reform of health." Even more surprising, Nixon betrayed three decades of Republican attacks against the liberal economist John Maynard Keynes's theory of deficit finance by declaring himself a Keynesian. ABC's interviewer Howard K. Smith blurted out, "That's a little like a Christian crusader saying, 'all things considered, I think Mohammed was right.'"

A political weather vane, Nixon adapted Johnson's Great Society ideas and added an occasional Republican twist. He reassured conservatives that he still valued "individual responsibility and individual dignity," using code words that conveyed disdain for New Deal collectivist welfare-statism. He preferred revenue sharing through tax breaks and payouts to elaborate welfare bureaucracies. But his pragmatism, concern with foreign policy, and acknowledgment of Democratic congressional power yielded liberal results. Spending on social programs under Nixon soared from $55 billion, constituting 28 percent of the budget, to $132 billion, or 40 percent of the budget. The *Federal Register* listing of governmental regulations, which grew 19 percent under Johnson, grew 121 percent under Nixon, as the government became more enmeshed in enforcing civil rights; regulating the environment; and distributing basic health, education, and welfare services.

Conservatives accused Nixon of betraying them and his own ideals. They appealed to Nixon's tough guy self-image and his anger against the establishment for rejecting him. One young White House zealot, Pat Buchanan, claimed Nixon's "ad hoc government" alienated everyone: "Neither liberal nor conservative, neither fish nor fowl, the Nixon Administration . . . is a hybrid, whose zigging and zagging has succeeded in winning the enthusiasm and loyalty of neither left nor right, but the suspicion and distrust of both." A manager who enjoyed watching his subordinates duke issues out, Nixon directed his chief aide, H. R. Haldeman, to "be sure" two leading pragmatists, Chief Domestic Advisor John Ehrlichman and Treasury Secretary John Connally, read Buchanan's "brilliant analysis."

Nixon's inconsistency confirmed the hated "Tricky Dick" label. His moderation appeared to be insincere; his tactics unduly aggressive. Nixon's attempt to embrace sixties liberalism failed to convince Democrats or reporters, who were emerging as modern politics' great arbiters, of his sincerity. "We obviously aren't getting any credit on the environmental initiatives we have undertaken," the president glumly reported in 1970.

Even Nixon's historic forays to Russia and China stirred skepticism. The two unprecedented trips to the Communist superpowers occurred in 1972, as the White House was gearing up for reelection. The initiatives reflected Nixon's pragmatism. His annual *Foreign Policy Reports* to Congress laid the groundwork for these breakthroughs. He advocated "improved practical relations" with the Chinese, and a "realistic" approach. When President Nixon first met Chairman Mao, the two bantered about which world leaders were leftist, and which rightist. "I think the most important thing to note is that in America, at least at this time, those on the right can do what those on the left can only talk about," Nixon boasted. Unfortunately, Nixon's political partisanship and personal vindictiveness eclipsed his pragmatism and creativity.

THE VIETNAM WAR brought out the worst in Richard Nixon, just as it had brought out the worst in Lyndon Johnson. Nixon and his aides considered the war and student rebellion "the greatest national crisis since the Civil War." The president's fierce reaction to critics showed that he was more a street fighter than a statesman.

"A President must come through as very strong, bold and even ruthless when the problems of the country are involved," Nixon told H. R. Haldeman. With "TR, Wilson and FDR" as his yardsticks, "RN," as he fancied himself, craved recognition as a "strong tough man in the crunch." Forgetting the "New Nixon," President Nixon sought national "reconciliation" by crushing all his opponents: the Viet Cong, the students, and the "liberal media."

By Nixon's day, even as a new, left-leaning consensus advocated civil rights and women's liberation, consensus politics was in disrepute. "Consensus Politics? Not on your life," the political scientist James MacGregor Burns cried in the *New York Times* in 1972. Critics charged that consensus suppressed needed debate and democracies thrived on disagreement.

The break between J. William Fulbright, the Democratic chairman of the Senate Foreign Relations Committee, and Lyndon Johnson, the Democratic president, over Vietnam ended an era of bipartisan cooperation between presidents and leading senators. Senators were tired of a bipartisanship used only to bully congressional dissenters into silence. Moreover, in the mass media age, the celebrity presidency, White House centralization, and the elaborate national security apparatus marginalized senators. President Nixon's media-savvy National Security Adviser Henry Kissinger eclipsed the secretary of state, let alone mere legislators.

Nixon and his administration believed the American masses shared their disdain for the national media's liberalism and cynicism. Their ideological bias worsened the already frequently testy relations between reporters and the president. Nixon believed reporters would always pursue "a story which will be harmful to the Administration." He warned his aides, when reporters approach "always . . . be on guard." Nixon and his aides spent an inordinate amount of time grumbling about press bias, freezing out critical reporters, and scheming to get better coverage.

Nixon's addiction to presidential image-making resulted in an obsessively self-conscious administration. He and his cronies scrutinized how the press reported presidential actions, constantly second-guessing their own strategies. Some aides urged the president to be less partisan, more "judicial," to build national unity. Their appeals played on Nixon's yearning to be accepted, even by the reporters and intellectuals he loathed.

His combative relationship with an increasingly critical press hurt Nixon and the country. The adversary culture assailing "the establishment" spawned the new journalism. Reporters focused on peeling away the artifice, portraying subjects' inner lives, capturing a mood. Dazzling virtuosos like Thomas Wolfe and Norman Mailer blazed the trail. Even as Nixon resisted such analysis, his self-destructive, self-aggrandizing pathologies fascinated reporters and justified their probes.

Nixon was perennially self-pitying, bemoaning the unfair press coverage. Haldeman and the others agreed, saying that Nixon endured an "unprecedented barrage of attacks." In June 1970 America invaded Cambodia to combat Communist Viet Cong guerrilla attacks on South Vietnam via Cambodia. Haldeman listed the various catchphrases reporters used in "tearing down the presidency," including "the 'crisis of leadership,' the 'desperate gamble,' the 'complete isolation of the President,' the 'failure of confidence,' 'the credibility gap.'" In response, staffers endlessly assessed Nixon's *"style and leadership,"* wondering how to *"accentuate his concept* of the Presidency . . . and how to best stage what he does," as one aide, Dwight Chapin, told Haldeman. All this stylistic choreography sidestepped the central problem. The government had denied bombing Cambodia, even lying to its own computers by feeding in false information to cover the Air Force's tracks. Admitting this subterfuge made the war even more unpopular.

Like Lyndon Johnson, Nixon became obsessed with the question of how "to really convey the true image of a President to the nation." Nixon recognized that he could bypass reporters, reaching the people directly via television. He pressed Haldeman: "We should only do things that help on the PR impact." By controlling access and staging events that the press had to cover, Nixon's men hogtied reporters. Articulating the credo of a new age, in which almost two-thirds of Americans relied on television for news, Haldeman declared, "We only care about . . . our television coverage."

Nixon talked about appearing warm but remained stiff and snide. As the president's men wondered "how to humanize the president's image" they also generated lists of enemies. The administration was brisk and businesslike, which, Nixon noted, "from the standpoint of those qualities that appeal to most Americans means nothing less than zilch."

Nixon failed to connect the dots between his brusque politicking and his unpopularity. "He has a better grasp of Africa's over-all economic problems than any other American politician," a foreign dignitary observed, "but he doesn't understand Africans." The journalist Theodore White once asked Nixon "how he could bear campaigning, shaking hands all day, smiling. . . ." Interrupting, Nixon finished White's thought, "and all the while you're smiling you want to kick them in the shins."

The criticism exacerbated Nixon's historic insecurities, sensitivity to slights, and craving for public affection. In June 1971, the *New York Times* published the *Pentagon Papers*, the government's secret history of America's involvement in Vietnam. The Defense Department documents revealed more Democratic missteps than Republican ones, but the president resented the brazenness of the leaker, Daniel Ellsberg, and the press. Anxious

Richard Nixon wanted to be the kind of warm, charming, presidential healer this photograph depicts, showing him throwing out the first ball on opening day April 7, 1969, before the New York Yankees played the Washington Senators. (Library of Congress)

to plug future leaks, the White House formed a "plumbers unit," an in-house counterintelligence operation. The bunker mentality led Nixon's men to fancy themselves above the law. They justified any abuses by pointing to the hostile forces around them. This combination of paranoia and zeal triggered the petty crimes, evasions, and obstructions of justice that snowballed into the Watergate scandal.

INITIALLY, WATERGATE failed to stop Nixon. He felt vindicated by his landslide reelection against Senator George McGovern in 1972. A week after the second inaugural, on January 27, 1973, Nixon officially ended America's involvement in the Vietnam War. "We shall answer to God, to history, and to our conscience for the way in which we use these years," the president intoned in his inaugural address. But the daily reports about Watergate crimes quickly dispelled the high hopes the inauguration and the Vietnam peace treaty had generated. By springtime, a special Senate subcommittee had begun preparing for a summer's worth of televised hearings. By the summer of 1973, the pattern for the next twelve months was set. Each new revelation triggered denunciations, denials, evasions, and justifications. Making matters worse, the drip of revelations coincided with a dip in the economy. Nixon became withdrawn and furious.

One aide, Alexander Butterfield, had offhandedly mentioned a taping system during the Senate Watergate hearings. "Never before in the history of the Presidency have records that are so private been made so public," Nixon said when he reluctantly released 1,300 pages of transcripts of those tapes in April 1974. The many "expletives" deleted from the text and the presidential scheming shocked Americans. "We have lost our moral compass," Nixon's good friend, Reverend Billy Graham, mourned after reading the transcripts. The tapes justified the new journalism's invasive, investigative aggressiveness and tarnished the presidency.

Sometimes, Nixon governed effectively, negotiating with the Soviets and Chinese or brokering a cease-fire between Arabs and Israelis. At other moments, he became weepy, sloppy, and self-pitying. Washingtonians gossiped about a drunken president who might start a war to save his skin.

As impeachment proceedings in the House of Representatives accelerated, Republicans abandoned their president. Chief of Staff Alexander Haig asked Nixon's physician to deny him all sleeping pills or tranquilizers. Secretary of Defense James Schlesinger instructed all military commanders to disregard White House orders lacking his countersignature. "I had seen enough so that I was not going to run risks with the future of the United States," Schlesinger later explained.

On July 24, 1974, the Supreme Court unanimously decreed that all the tapes prosecutors demanded had to be released. The "smoking gun tape" of June 23, 1972, recorded Nixon plotting with Haldeman about using the CIA to block investigators. When only seven senators still opposed an impeachment conviction, Nixon resigned.

The fall of Richard Nixon was the fault of Richard Nixon. His personality flaws destroyed his presidency. His Watergate-induced resignation was not inevitable. Had Nixon never recorded the tapes—or destroyed them before they were subpoenaed—his presidency might have survived.

Showing more wisdom at the end of his political career than he had done during it, Nixon bid staffers farewell with generous advice. He said, "never be petty; always remember others may hate you, but those who hate you don't win unless you hate them, and then you destroy yourself."

The stories of Richard Nixon and Lyndon Johnson were tragic. At their best, these smart, passionate, experienced politicians had the potential to be great presidents. But the combative conditions of the time brought out the worst in each of them, destroying their careers, weakening their office and the country. These two not only alienated the majority of Americans in the center, their failures made Americans doubt that their country had a viable center.

NIXON'S SUCCESSOR, Gerald R. Ford, was a creature of Congress. A genial Midwesterner, Ford arrived in Congress in 1949 and served as House Minority Leader for eight years. When leading his party, Ford reserved the Republicans' right to challenge the Democratic incumbents when necessary, and to cooperate when possible. As president, he faced a steep inflation rate and a traumatized country. Ford called a joint bipartisan conference on inflation in September, 1974 to unite the executive and legislative branches against "a common enemy." Completing the historical circle, demonstrating that the question of bipartisanship was tactical, Democratic National Chairman Robert S. Strauss echoed the Republicans' Johnson-era caution, saying of President Ford, "We will support him when we think he is right, and we will oppose him when we think he is wrong."

Like Nixon, Ford failed to understand that tactical moderation had to go hand in hand with substantive centrism. Ford's classiest, most statesmanlike, and most nation-building move, his blanket pardon of Richard Nixon, backfired because he made it unilaterally. Ford sprang the pardon on the nation, the Congress, and most of his advisers, without laying the proper foundation. The New York Times condemned this "profoundly unwise, divisive and unjust act" that immediately destroyed the new president's "credibility as a man of judgment, candor and competence." Ford's pardon, and the huge Democratic gains in the 1974 midterm elections, frayed relations up and down Pennsylvania Avenue while boosting Democratic self-confidence. Despite Ford's call for a "time to heal," his short tenure was tense and trying for the nation.

IN 1976 JIMMY CARTER parlayed one term as Georgia governor into the presidency. He positioned himself as a centrist, healing leader for a demoralized country. Carter's question, "Why not the best," suggested that the stumbling presidents of the 1960s and 1970s had been second-raters. His vow, "I'll never lie to you," repudiated the deceptions of Vietnam and Watergate. Carter was a man for all voters: modern yet traditional; a progressive thinker from conservative small-town America; a good ole' Southern boy, who charmed Northerners by quoting Bob Dylan and Dylan Thomas.

The Watergate scandal made an obscure outsider seem appealing. Carter announced his candidacy in December 1974, shortly after Richard Nixon resigned. Carter's "Peanut Brigade" of family members and old friends appeared authentic and amateurish, the antidote to Nixon and his gang of slick professionals. Carter narrowly unseated President Gerald Ford, without securing a policy mandate or defining an ideological focus.

Carter's populist moderation often seemed like toadying. Running on personality, as Carter endorsed welfare reform or tax reform, conservatives assumed he was conservative; as he railed against Vietnam and Watergate while endorsing civil rights and universal health care, liberals assumed he was liberal. This ambiguity proved infuriating once Carter began governing. Carter delivered too literally on his promise of a modest approach. Reporters, who had fostered this campaign of personality and humility in 1976, quickly turned on Carter after his inauguration in 1977. The down-to-earth charms from the campaign trail of handling his own luggage and keeping his own counsel seemed inappropriate in the still-imperial White House covered by an increasingly imperious press.

The transition from small town Georgia politics to superpower Washington governance brought out Carter's odd combination of naiveté and arrogance. He approached the complicated decisions facing him in the Oval Office as the "A" student he had always been rather than as the master politician and national leader America needed. Buried in policy analyses and position papers, he sought just the right answer on the budget, deregulation, or military spending, contemplating rather than acting.

Carter's responses to problems were inadequate. He thought that by talking about honesty, efficiency, humility, and human rights he could improve the world. He tried solving the energy crisis with a 113-point plan. He disliked the big-picture governing and sweeping rhetoric essential for presidential leadership. Carter's media adviser, Gerald Rafshoon, told him,

Jimmy Carter's informality, such as carrying his own luggage as he campaigned on "Peanut One" in 1976, surrendered valuable leadership weapons in the presidential arsenal and made it harder to hold the already-splintering center together. (Library of Congress)

"When you're a preacher, you're great. When you're an engineer you put me to sleep, you put yourself to sleep."

Amateurishly, Carter abandoned valuable traditions that boosted the president's glamour and power. The president and his wife, Rosalynn Carter, disdained the Washington social scene and renounced many imperial trappings, such as playing "Hail to the Chief" when he entered a state dinner. Carter's speechwriter, James Fallows, tried teaching his boss to woo reporters, "the real audience," the "professional opinion brokers who set the tone for how we are perceived by the millions who watch television and read the newspapers and magazines." Richard Nixon had understood the new media universe he had to dominate but could not get beyond his hatred of reporters. Jimmy Carter also came to town fighting reporters and remained hostile. Carter's successor, Ronald Reagan, would respect media power, work it, and thrive.

As president, Jimmy Carter vacillated between pandering and inspiring, playing the populist and being progressive. As a result, he would appear to be too demagogic and too principled, too sensitive to polls yet enslaved by his own agenda. Once, when meeting with AFL-CIO leaders who had supported him enthusiastically in 1976, Carter began walking out before the union representatives spoke. Their formidable leader, George Meany, asked the president to stay and listen. Meany explained that although they shared Carter's goal of fighting inflation, they disagreed with him about lowering wages. When Meany finished, Carter walked out of the room anyway, saying, "If you can't support me I'd rather not talk."

Other times, Carter seemed too eager to please both at home and abroad. His style particularly infuriated conservatives, who were gaining political strength. His accommodating foreign policy of befriending the Soviets and signing away the Panama Canal so enraged Republicans that they stopped pretending to be bipartisan. In May 1978, all thirty-eight Republican senators protested the Carter administration's "15 short months of incoherence, inconsistency and ineptitude." The senators complained, "our foreign policy and national security objectives are confused and we are being challenged around the globe by Soviet arrogance."

In February 1979 Senate Minority Leader Howard Baker Jr. eulogized Republicans' moribund commitment to bipartisanship, saying that Senator Arthur Vandenberg "was right in his time, but I think we're right in our time." Reporters asked Republican National Chairman Bill Brock if he feared voters would object to making foreign policy a partisan issue. Brock insisted, "I think people are sufficiently concerned with the obvious failing and the incompetence of the Administration in foreign policy to accept our stand."

THE FOREIGN POLICY CRISIS reflected a deeper existential crisis. During the 1960s the revolution of young people taking drugs, defying society, listening to rock music, and wearing long hair remained marginal; in the 1970s the counterculture went mainstream. Institutions and attitudes shaken in the 1960s shattered in the 1970s. Cultural bombshells such as *The Godfather, The Exorcist, Fear of Flying,* and *Gravity's Rainbow* combined with the political and economic traumas of Watergate, Vietnam, the energy crisis, and stagflation to undermine traditional faith in the family, the church, and the government. Marijuana use among high school seniors peaked in 1978.

The pace of cultural and social change, once relatively stately, became accelerated, even manic. The floodgates of the sexual revolution, the backlash against authority, and the culture of questioning had burst open. The

black and white moral crusade to desegregate the South hit complicated
questions about integrating schools, neighborhoods, and offices that threatened traditional boundaries between private and public domains, North
and South. As the personal became political, feminism and the sexual revolution revised Americans' most intimate life-scripts, often pitting wives
against husbands, children against parents.

Amid all the leisure and liberation, all the questing and ESTing, many
Americans felt unmoored. Families were imploding, communities were ex-
ploding, and the nation seemed adrift. Freed of tradition, overindulged by
materialism, their most infantile cravings overstimulated by advertising,
Americans often withdrew from communal concerns into quests for inner
peace or a hedonistic pursuit of the perfect body.

Politically, this focus on the self risked making American democracy ungovernable. If John Kennedy's grand "ask what you can do for your country"
liberal nationalism represented the cumulative inspiration of the two Roosevelts, Harry Truman, and Dwight Eisenhower, the cumulative dysfunction of
Johnson, Nixon, Ford, and Carter shaped the 1970s' special interest selfishness. A "Black Power" or "Woman Power" or "Polish Power" sensibility arose,
asserting particular racial, gender, or ethnic demands. Johnson's Great Society
seemed bogged down in bureaucracy, generating taxes and regulations, not social justice. Nixon's belligerence injected "us versus them" toxins into the national bloodstream; Carter's pessimistic impotence demoralized voters.

This new assertive individualism and subgroup solidarity often trumped
traditional nationalism. By 1980, a new phrase, "Not in my back yard"
(NIMBY), represented American citizens' response to building landfills,
prisons, and sometimes even schools or factories near their homes. "This is
the great danger America faces," Congresswoman Barbara Jordan warned at
the 1976 Democratic national convention, "that we will cease to be one
nation and become instead a collection of interest groups; city against sub-
urb, region against region, individual against individual."

Valuing the "I" not the "us," Americans demanded their rights but often
ignored their responsibilities. Power shifted from the presidency, the most
nationalist of branches, with one individual embodying the nation seeking
the common good, to the Supreme Court, where judicial activists consecrated individual rights. Consigning controversies to abrupt, all-or-nothing
courts frequently exacerbated conflicts, as *Roe v. Wade*'s revolutionary le-
galization of abortion in all fifty states in 1973 illustrated. Center-seeking

presidents traditionally tried laying groundwork, building coalitions, com-promising, setting scenes, and crafting a communal narrative. Americans might have responded to a president who subsumed all these transforma-tions under a broader national enterprise, perhaps updating the Four Free-doms in seventies-speak. Instead, the courts frequently short circuited the political process.

American intellectuals in particular seemed lost. Despite decades of Soviet oppression, many American elites still trusted Marxism to secure communal justice. Many New Left radicals who landed in the universities and corners of the media world after the 1960s hopelessly romanticized the Cuban revolution, Vietnam, and the Third World. These "tenured radicals"—in Roger Kimball's biting phrase—continued the old Left's tendency to rail against liberal democratic imperfections while tolerating what the French intellectual Raymond Aron called "the worst crimes as long as they are committed in the names of the proper doctrines."

The intellectual and cultural crisis in confidence fed the political malaise. Americans lost faith in their leaders' competence and responsive-ness. One survey in 1959 had estimated that 85 percent of Americans took great national pride in their political institutions. By 1973, 66 percent of those polled were "dissatisfied" with government. Moreover, despite sun-shine laws to make bureaucracies more accountable and a more consumer-oriented, user-friendly government, the percentage of people who believed that what they thought "doesn't count much anymore," jumped from 37 percent in 1966 to 61 percent in 1973. Clint Eastwood's *Dirty Harry* movies and Telly Savalas's *Kojak* television show celebrated renegade urban cow-boys fighting social chaos and the sniveling bureaucrats who supervised them. The Bicentennial-year hit movie, *Network*, had Americans opening their windows and shouting, "I'M MAD AS HELL AND I'M NOT GO-ING TO TAKE IT ANYMORE."

The great inflation of the 1970s also reflected a loss of confidence. The almighty dollar's power eroded as wholesale prices jumped 14 percent from 1973 to 1974 alone, giving a 1967 dollar only about 68 cents' worth of buy-ing power. Jimmy Carter's "misery index" from 1976, the combination of inflation and unemployment, nearly doubled in four years, from 12.5 to over 20. As the inflation rate, the unemployment rate, the prime interest rate, and the divorce rate all soared, a specter of failure haunted American society, slowly strangling Carter's presidency.

America faced hard choices as the 1970s ended. Busing students across town lacked the moral clarity of outlawing segregation; the conflict over abortion complicated the push for women's rights. But Martin Luther King Jr. had taught how to make expanding civil rights about building a better America, using the language of Christianity, the Declaration of Independence, and Cold War patriotism. Americans needed another effective leader to lead them away from their selfish interests, back toward common, centrist goals. They needed to feel confident enough to acknowledge their neighbors' needs, to perceive happiness, stability, and liberty as collective accomplishments and communal adventures, not personal assets or selfish journeys.

UNFORTUNATELY, Jimmy Carter failed to offer such leadership. He squandered goodwill and power with his amateurism, arrogance, and half-measures. He seemed unable to whip inflation, manage the energy crisis, balance the budget, tame the media, or master foreign affairs.

Mr. "Why Not the Best" soon embodied American defeatism at its worst. When Carter called the push for energy independence the moral equivalent of war, comedians reduced Carter's roar to the acronym MEOW. When he tried to manage special interest groups, he alienated them while spurring press complaints that he indulged them. Honest to a fault, in a *Sixty Minutes* interview with Dan Rather, the president of the United States gave himself only "a B" in leadership, "a B minus" in foreign policy, and a "C" in domestic policy.

Carter championed human rights to exorcise the demons of Vietnam and restore America's foreign policy luster. Yet his administration stumbled repeatedly overseas. Anti-American forces overran Nicaragua and Iran. The Soviets inserted themselves in the Horn of Africa, Central America, and the Middle East. Europeans, especially Germany's Helmut Schmidt, criticized America for being too soft. "Liberal idealism need not be identical with masochism, and need not be incompatible with the defeat of freedom and the national interest," Professor Jeanne Kirkpatrick exclaimed in 1979. By June 1979 Carter, with a record low of 33 percent approval, was less popular than either Lyndon Johnson or Gerald Ford had been at their respective lowest points. Increasingly, both Washington insiders and academic experts questioned the viability of American democracy and the presidency.

Many Americans also found Carter too critical of America and of himself. This discomfort culminated in July 1979, when Carter reassessed his administration at Camp David for ten days. "I feel I have lost control of the government and the leadership of the people," he admitted at one session. The longer he retreated, the more publicly he processed his thoughts, the weaker he looked.

Carter discussed his retreat in a televised speech analyzing America's "crisis of confidence" as reflected in Americans' search for individual meaning and loss of national purpose. He detailed the materialism, cynicism, pessimism, skepticism, apathy, alienation, and defeatism threatening America's social and political fabric. Carter's speech was searing, thoughtful, and self-critical. It was also ill-advised and self-destructive. Americans did not want a president preaching a gospel of doubt and negativity.

It was thus a weakened president in November 1979 who faced the crisis that ruined his presidency. Iranian fundamentalists violated the American embassy's sanctity to kidnap diplomats and Marine guards. The media's daily tally of how long the crisis continued, combined with Carter's refusal to conduct normal business until the hostages were freed, amplified the Islamic radicals' impact. The hostage crisis lingered for 444 days, until Carter left office.

Most Americans demanded a military response immediately, but Carter initially trusted diplomacy. In his futile search for solutions, Carter became as rigid as Nixon and Johnson had been during Vietnam. The president in crisis seemed at once unsteady and too stubborn, too willing to negotiate with the Iranians and too unwilling to consider alternative proposals for a solution. After months of dithering, he finally attempted a military rescue, which failed. When Secretary of State Cyrus Vance then resigned on principle, Carter was brittle and ungracious.

Six weeks after the hostage crisis began, the Soviets invaded Afghanistan. Feeling betrayed after his overtures toward Moscow, Carter overreacted. Like an out of step dancer, Carter skipped softly when a hard kick was needed, and hit hard when a soft-touch might have worked better. Henry Kissinger sighed that the Carter administration "has managed the extraordinary feat of having, at one and the same time, the worst relations with our allies, the worst relations with our adversaries, and the most serious upheavals in the developing world since the end of the Second World War." Carter went into his 1980 reelection campaign with the

Soviets ensconced in Afghanistan, the hostages lingering in Iran, and little hope for an end to either crisis.

LYNDON JOHNSON, Richard Nixon, and Jimmy Carter each faced storms of overseas upheaval, domestic turmoil, and political backlash, exacerbated by presidential clumsiness. Stabs at centrism could not compensate for the bigger failures, for Johnson's incompetence in Vietnam, Nixon's nastiness toward his enemies, or Carter's impotence and gloominess. None of the three succeeded in communicating a larger vision of America and its purpose. Johnson and Nixon, in particular, discovered that Americans love winning wars, but hate fighting them. Historically, presidents have endured particularly harsh criticism during wartime. When wars succeeded, the denunciations were mostly forgotten; when wars failed, the condemnations continued. Carter suffered as America experienced an unprecedented foreign humiliation in Iran. That these external hits took place at a time of general social confusion intensified the sense of national crisis.

These presidential failures offer the political twist on Leo Tolstoy's opening line of *Anna Karenina*, "Happy families are all alike; every unhappy family is unhappy in its own way." Successful presidents appear moderate because their triumphs often forcefully redefine the center, while each failing president misses the center in his own particular way. The journalist Carl M. Cannon notes that "posterity rewards success." The Nixon and Carter presidencies demonstrated the need for muscular moderation on a grand scale, not stabs at centrism writ small.

By the end of Jimmy Carter's presidency, the accumulated political train wrecks over two decades had shaken Americans. Many experts agreed with Carter, suggesting that Americans prepare for an age of limitations. Politicians and academics doubted that the American presidency, as defined by the Founders and developed over two centuries, could master this unnerving new world. And some not only assumed that the country lacked a viable center, they insisted that this chaotic, diverse country never had one. One bicentennial anthology featured leading thinkers contemplating sobering topics such as "The Democratic Distemper" and "The End of American Exceptionalism." Surprisingly, the man who would reaffirm Americans' faith in progress, their country, the presidency, and the center was an aging former Hollywood actor, dismissed by Carter as both a dunce and a fanatic.

10

RONALD REAGAN'S
MODERATE REVOLUTION

Resurrecting the Center

IN MID-MARCH 1981, six weeks into his tenure, America's new president visited New York City. It was a bold move, considering that Ronald Reagan's conservatism could have earned him a hostile reception in America's liberal and Democratic capital. When the president arrived in Manhattan, throngs lined the streets, cheering. The next night, he attended the Broadway hit *Sugar Babies*. After the final curtain, Mickey Rooney, Reagan's Hollywood buddy and the star of the show, asked everyone to remain seated until the president and First Lady Nancy Reagan left. As the Reagans exited, the audience spontaneously sang "America the Beautiful." Marveling at his warm reception and the coast-to-coast excitement when the first space shuttle, *Columbia*, launched in April, Reagan concluded, "Americans are hungering to feel proud & patriotic again."

Attributing this surge of patriotism to the American people was both sincere and shrewd. Reagan enjoyed making his greatest successes appear populist, spontaneous. Sharing credit with Americans vindicated their broader wisdom in choosing him and following him. Ronald Reagan worked hard to restore Americans' faith in their nation and themselves. He saw himself as standing tall against the prevailing American culture of cyn-icism, selfishness, and self-doubt.

Reagan understood American political culture's fragility following the 1960s and 1970s. When pressed, therefore, he usually chose popularity over principle, compromise over conscience. An odd ideologue, he tempered a rigid worldview with flexibility and pragmatism. A great salesman, this wheeler-dealer evangelist could settle for the proverbial half a loaf and sell it as a revolution in bread making.

By 1980, the bipartisan consensus had not just collapsed; most opinion leaders characterized America's past and present as combative and chaotic. America the beautiful now appeared to be America the racially, ethnically, religiously, and economically fragmented. Reporters, entertainers, advertis-ers, and even many politicians heaped scorn on most authority figures and traditional institutions. America's leaders treated America as ungovernable and thus risked making it so.

America's popular culture and political culture had become adversarial. The baby boomer sensibility reigned. Popular culture in the 1950s had perpet-uated the status quo. The new cultural sensibility celebrated the idiosyncratic, the alternative, the controversial, the crude, the extreme. A healthy political culture emphasizes forces binding a country together; America's headline-driven politics and culture emphasized conflicts pulling the country apart.

The great American disconnect resulted. In the past, most Americans had endured rough, unstable, hardscrabble, hand-to-mouth living conditions; by 1980 most enjoyed safe, comfortable, conventional, cradle-to-grave prosper-ity. Yet despite all the comforts, America's national culture and politics pre-sented wild kaleidoscopes accentuating the negative and the divisive.

The three two-term presidents after 1980 tried to steady themselves in postmodern America's increasingly choppy seas. Ronald Reagan, Bill Clin-ton, and George W. Bush each rode particular popular waves toward the great American center, perched on a particular fragment of the political culture. Reagan stood as a patriotic hero, restoring mainstream America's confidence. Clinton stood as the baby boomers' values-man, cautiously tri-angulating amid apparent peace and prosperity. George W. Bush stood as the courageous cowboy, riding the wave of fear and fury generated by Sep-tember 11, 2001, to reelection in November 2004.

At their strongest, all three presidents articulated a welcoming national narrative that transcended party identity. But Reagan, Clinton, and Bush had distinctive leadership styles. Reagan defined a meaningful and muscular middle. Although he frustrated conservatives by being too compromising, he enacted some substantive changes that enraged liberals. Tax cuts, deregulation, a retreat from assuming that government could solve every problem, and a more assertive foreign policy reoriented America. That Reagan succeeded in packaging his policies in patriotic, Rooseveltian, dulcet tones despite the growing cynicism about America's national mission makes his achievement all the more impressive.

Each of the three presidents also struggled with a dilemma linked to centrism. Ronald Reagan tried leading a revolution from the center; his ideology repudiated the Great Society status quo, but his temperament, leadership techniques, and patriotism tethered him to mainstream public opinion. There "is an *opportunity here for base-broadening*," Reagan's aide Richard Darman advised in 1982, "if we can keep 'conservatives' from being upset while showing the President as 'balanced,' i.e., principled but willing to be reasonably flexible." A revolution through the back door, or down the center aisle, resulted.

Bill Clinton's dilemma concerned the substance of his centrism. He rarely put much meat into his moderation, failing to use his popularity and American prosperity to solve big problems. George W. Bush seemed least interested in the center. Although Bush united the public after September 11, he and his aides cared more about securing the minimum coalition necessary to accomplish their mission than remaining popular. Bush's house intellectual, Peter Wehner, explained that "many of our greatest and most successful leaders were polarizing and divisive figures in their day. Indeed, transformational, consequential figures—men and women who are agents of important change–are *almost always* polarizing."

Of the three presidents, Reagan's luck lasted longest. The surprising thaw in Soviet–American relations overshadowed the 1987 stock market crash, the Iran-Contra scandal, and assorted presidential gaffes. Reagan's happy ending vindicated the bipartisan consensus Harry Truman choreographed and Dwight Eisenhower consecrated. Modern America's most successful politicians, especially Presidents Reagan, Clinton, and Bush, understood that Americans still spoke a common language and wanted to hear a unifying voice. At their best, these leaders continued George Washington's quest for that broad middle, inviting citizens from both sides of the aisle, from all corners of this vast land, to open their hearts and minds and embrace a grand American vision that is neither solely red nor blue, but is red, white, and blue.

AS A MAN WHO rooted his identity in the old-fashioned, idyllic Midwest he spent his entire adult life fleeing, Ronald Reagan found 1980s America strange and unnerving. Reagan had last felt culturally at home in the strait-laced 1950s. In the ensuing decades, a surge of freedom liberated Americans from small-town America's rigid script, for better and worse. The starchy, buttoned-down, black and white, all-for-one-and-one-for-all world of the fifties had become a chaotic, casual, creative, colorful, individualistic cavalcade. The presidency, once seemingly unassailable and increasingly imperial, had become embattled. The failures of Lyndon Johnson, Richard Nixon, Gerald Ford, and Jimmy Carter sowed doubts that any president could lead effectively. Operating amid such low expectations, Reagan appeared particularly successful as a president as he restored Americans' faith in their country and government.

Ronald Reagan sought to renew the American center by pushing it to the right, back where he believed it belonged. Born in small-town Illinois in 1911, the tall, broad-shouldered Midwesterner went on to spend three decades as a Hollywood actor. There, he romanticized and realized the American dream. He then spent nearly two decades as a conservative California politician fighting the sixties' culture wars while experiencing upheavals within his own family. Although he came to embody American traditionalism, he was the first divorced president ever, plagued by rebellious children. As adults, they continued acting out against him and his second wife, Nancy. Originally a New Deal Democrat, Reagan believed his party had become the party of high taxes, red tape, and communist appeasement. He often quipped, "I never left the Democratic party, the Democratic party left me."

America's traditionally cranky conservatism was reeling from Franklin Roosevelt's exuberant assault on Hooverism, the generalized disgust with Senator Joe McCarthy's demagoguery, and Lyndon Johnson's caricature of Barry Goldwater conservatives in 1964 as trigger-happy reactionaries. Conservatives learned that they needed a lighter touch and pragmatic leaders. Reagan was self-confident and relentlessly, infectiously, happy. His "smiley face" conservatism reassured Americans that they could solve the problems they faced. A conservative crusader with a pragmatic governing record, Reagan was an amiable ideologue, an accommodating extremist. His conservative ideology grounded his identity, disproving those who dismissed him as an empty suit. His warmth and patriotism softened his ideology, charming millions even when they disagreed with him. Most Americans laughed as he jibed, "Republicans believe every day is the Fourth of July, but the Democrats believe every day is April 15" (tax day).

Even as liberalism surged and millions "liberated" themselves from many "hang-ups" in the 1970s, conservatism found new strength ideologically and institutionally. From California to Massachusetts, conservatives organized grassroots rebellions against high taxes and burdensome bureaucracies. Grudgingly accepting desegregation and even basic equal rights for women, conservatives rejected 1930s big government, 1960s morality, and 1970s détente.

Just as Reagan occasionally played the clueless actor to appear less political, he often tempered his right-wing rhetoric with centrist policies. Jousting with student radicals, he said hippies look like Tarzan, walk like Jane, and smell like Cheetah. Yet Reagan understood politics as the art of the possible, sweetened by lofty dreams of the improbable. Governing California from 1967 through 1975, he refused to "jump off the cliff with the flag flying if you can't get everything you want." He recalled, "If I found when I was governor that I could not get 100 percent of what I asked for, I took 80 percent." Governor Reagan's moderate abortion and welfare policies belied his fiery rhetoric. "You want a principled man, which Reagan is," the economist Milton Friedman said. "But he is not a rigidly principled man, which you don't want."

The shorthand of the 1980 presidential campaign obscured Reagan's pragmatism. During the Republican primary, he played the right-wing macho man to his main opponent, the establishment Republican George H. W. Bush. President Jimmy Carter hinged his reelection hopes on painting Reagan as a dangerous extremist. This strategy reflected Carter's weakness as he stumbled into the campaign in a country facing double-digit inflation and outrageous interest rates, Americans still held hostage in Iran, and the Soviet Army occupying Afghanistan. Reagan's strategy downplayed his conservative ideology, excoriating Carter for doubting America's future, crippling America's economy, and undermining national pride.

Ronald Reagan appealed to mainstream Americans as the candidate of 1950s nationalism. He believed the country that framed the Constitution, settled the West, freed the slaves, industrialized the continent, and crushed the Nazis could handle the 1980s. Appealing across the partisan aisle, he spent much of the general campaign delivering glittering generalities about

American greatness while his advisers tried to obscure his prickly pro-
nouncements romanticizing the Vietnam War and dismissing the dangers
of car pollution.

The contradictions of the campaign would be the paradoxes of his presidency. "Let Reagan be Reagan," his conservative allies would plead, yearning for Reagan the right-winger. Yet in balancing, in contradicting, in
talking "right" while staying in the center, in slinging sentiment to cloak
substance, Reagan was being Reagan.

Reagan's new populism did not speak to the dispossessed, but to those
with possessions to lose. The New Deal and the post–World War II boom
created history's first mass middle-class society. Building on the seventies'
tax revolts, sixties-fed anxieties, and fifties nostalgia, Reagan wooed the
"Silent Majority," urban ethnics and first-generation suburbanites who felt
the Great Society neglected and overtaxed them. He also tapped into Cold
War fears of Soviet expansion. "We Republicans have to show people we're
not the party of big business and the country-club set," Reagan proclaimed.
"We're the party of Main Street, the small town, the city neighborhood;
the shopkeeper, the farmer, the cop on the beat, the blue-collar and the
white-collar worker."

Many liberals were terrified. The cartoonist Jeff MacNelly pictured Ku
Klux Klansmen with a torch, writing out two letters "RR" in flames. "I just
don't understand how any woman, black or white could vote for Reagan,"
one female social worker said. "He wants to take us out of the work force,
he's against the ERA [Equal Rights Amendment, and] abortion.... He'd
put us back on the plantation." White males fed up with high taxes and social upheaval provided the base for the winning coalition. Reagan united
Midwestern Protestant evangelicals with Northeastern Catholics, rock-
ribbed Republican Chamber of Commerce businessmen with overburdened
"Reagan Democrat" union men, neoconservative intellectuals with macho
military and Western types.

Judging the 1980 election by Reagan's 50.7 percent share of the popular
vote, and factoring in his "high negatives" in post-election polls, Reagan
barely won an "ABC" ("Anybody But Carter") election. Reagan, however,
conjured up a broad mandate from the electoral college landslide of 489 to
49. Reporters, prodded by Reagan's people, began discussing Reagan's
"mandate." The splashy $20 million inauguration launched the Reagan
revolution confidently and colorfully.

RONALD REAGAN was in fact a committed conservative, promising a conservative counterrevolution. The myth that Reagan had a mandate grew because Reagan explained America's many problems neatly and coherently. Reaganism blamed liberalism for the disorder and despair, the inflation and recession, urban chaos at home and humiliation abroad. Reagan promised to relieve Americans' tax burden, restrain inflation, reduce crime, revive prosperity, rejuvenate the cities, restore morality, revamp the military, and rekindle pride in the nation. In his first inaugural speech Reagan urged "We the People" to "dream heroic dreams." In reaffirming faith in America, Reagan burned his brand on America's revival as Americans rediscovered faith in themselves.

Reagan viewed solving the nation's economic crisis as the first act in his conservative revolutionary drama. His "supply side" gospel of Reaganomics proposed cutting taxes and simplifying government to lower inflation and spur economic growth. If there was a Reagan revolution, it occurred during the administration's first seven months, from late January 1981 until that August. Reagan spearheaded a decades-long national obsession about budget cuts and tax cuts. The president proposed regulatory rollbacks, a changed monetary policy, eighty-three major program cuts totaling $41.4 billion for fiscal year 1982, and tax cuts for individuals averaging 10 percent a year over three years.

Yet despite feeling politically strong and ideologically vindicated by defeating Carter, Reagan governed moderately. He packed his cabinet with moderate millionaires, not conservative activists. Both the Departments of Energy and Education, bureaucracies that President Carter had created and candidate Reagan had targeted, survived. Reagan's ideological point man, the thirty-four-year-old Director of the Office of Management and Budget David Stockman, would grow increasingly frustrated as cabinet secretaries protected their bureaucratic turfs by opposing budget cuts. Just as Franklin Roosevelt the master showman told two speechwriters fighting over contradictory policies to "weave the two together," Ronald Reagan settled arguments between clashing aides by smiling and saying, "Okay, you fellas work it out."

Championing a laissez-faire doctrine, David Stockman did not think "people are entitled to any services." Reading the political situation accurately, Reagan accepted the government's responsibility to the "truly needy." Reagan protected seven basic social programs, including Social Security and

Medicare, which served 80 million people and consumed approximately 60 percent of federal expenditures, costing $210 billion annually. Legitimizing "entitlements" to preserve the "social safety net" acknowledged the American consensus supporting the welfare state. Embracing the status quo infuriated conservatives and limited the revolution but kept Reagan popular. Ultimately, Reagan chipped away at the budget with a toothpick, not a sledge hammer.

Reagan read the polls carefully, understanding his limited mandate. Shrewdly, he played to the center, trusting that his iconic status with conservatives and the specters of Jimmy Carter and Ted Kennedy would mollify the Right. When a reporter asked what the White House offered conservatives, one aide snorted, "symbolism."

Reagan cared less about budget cuts and more about tax cuts, defense increases, and deregulation. A big picture patriot, Reagan believed in compromising, having learned how to negotiate by confronting the gruff studio head Jack Warner. He compromised on his tax and budget cuts' timing, scope, and duration. Reagan understood that even if the numbers were more modest than he hoped, he won by securing any budget and tax cuts, especially both together.

Stockman and his comrades concluded that Reagan was too kind and too consensus driven. Stockman wanted to cut corporate goodies, not just social welfare programs. His revolution needed an "iron chancellor," not an amiable former actor. David Stockman also discovered that America's "Madisonian" government of checks and balances fragmented power and resisted radical shifts. Addicted to the welfare state status quo, Americans were unwilling to go cold turkey. Lacking a Republican majority in Congress, Reagan could not turn America abruptly to the right.

Instead, Reagan adjusted the country's navigating coordinates, tweaking accepted ideas. America's ship of state tacked right a few degrees. This midcourse correction's impact emerged years later, even as the New Deal welfare state survived. Reagan sensitized Americans to the dangers of deficits while generating obscene budget deficits. Nevertheless, his legacy of attacks on budget overruns, high taxes, and big government outlasted both the Reagan deficits and any lingering embarrassment about his hypocrisy.

Reagan's centrism angered his core supporters. He did little to advance the conservatives' "abc" social agenda fighting abortion, busing, and crime. Under Reagan's watch, many of the reforms of the 1960s were mainstreamed. Most conservatives believed "that your 1980 conservative agenda and promises have not been matched by your presidential performance," the conservative activist Richard Viguerie warned Reagan in October 1983. Many supporters now saw him "as just another politician bending to the pressures from the Washington crowd."

Reagan's limited challenge to the status quo nevertheless encountered great resistance. Democrats claimed that the Republicans neglected the poor, favored the rich, and starved needy children. Reagan and his aides particularly resented these charges. Reagan boasted, "We are providing 95 million meals a day—that is 1/7th of all the meals in this country; providing medical care for 47 million Americans and subsidized housing for more than 10 million." In one meeting of Reagan's Legislative Strategy Group in 1983, key officials charged with shepherding Reaganomics through Congress debated: "How do we sustain: bipartisan spirit (or quest therefore); positive association with interest in fairness; [and] movement toward a practical program of deficit reduction/economic recovery?"

As Reagan navigated between his vision and political realities, Americans distinguished between the man and his movement. Most Americans disliked Reagan's program, but liked his "amiable, friendly, and easy-going personality," as one pollster reported. Americans also liked Reagan's assertive, sentimental, patriotic leadership style. Democratic House Speaker Tip O'Neill fumed that if a legislator complained that budget cuts hurt the elderly, Reagan replied, "You don't think I would do anything to hurt the aged of America, do you?" If a congressional member said, "I am concerned about education," Reagan answered, "You don't think I am going to destroy the educational system of America, do you?"

On Capitol Hill, with the economy still listing, inflation still growing, the president pushing ahead, and many voters cheering the return of affirmative White House leadership, many Democrats rushed to ride the popular wave. Southern Conservative "boll weevils" had cooperated with the Republicans for years. Now even Tip O'Neill admitted that "the formulas of the past are no longer adequate" and searched for "new approaches to improving our economy."

O'Neill would insist that the congressional year's true headline was the Republicans' remarkable unanimity. Despite Reagan's willingness to compromise, he was a tough competitor. Reaganite public relations hid steel spines behind soft smiles, Southern belle style. Once the bargaining ended, Reagan and his aides demanded loyalty. They punished wandering Republicans and pressured wavering Democrats.

Reagan could not sell his most sweeping proposals to the nation. Just as Republicans often minimized government's important achievements to focus welfare system abuses, headlines portrayed the needy recipients who would suffer. The president's 59 percent approval rating after one month in office was lower than most other modern presidents' rating after two months. By spending political capital to advance his program, Reagan risked his personal popularity.

A master salesman who believed in his product, Reagan took to the stump to sell his budget package. Reagan was championing his program when a deranged gunman shot him on March 30, 1981, outside the Washington Hilton. In escaping death, Reagan morphed from a partisan ideologue into an American legend. Tossing off witticisms that minimized his brush with death, he epitomized 1940s Hollywood insouciance. When a nurse held his hand, he joshed, "Does Nancy know about us?" When the surgeon approached, Reagan quipped, "I hope you're a Republican." This prompted the physician's classy response, "Today, Mr. President, we're all Republicans."

Reagan's personal trauma reaped political rewards. He became the people's president, the man Americans loved to like. His poll ratings jumped. Americans' patriotic spirit soared. Opposition to his programs folded, temporarily. Reaganism, however, was derailed.

Reagan's subsequent legislative victories obscured the fact that he had sold Americans on Reagan, not Reaganomics. On May 8, the Democratic-controlled House of Representatives passed Reagan's budget by sixty votes. The Reagan revolution's first round reduced the personal income tax rate by almost one-quarter and dropped the capital gains tax from 28 to 20 percent, reducing taxes by $162 billion. The rollback was smaller than Reagan wanted but much larger than Democrats had anticipated.

Days later, Reagan overstepped—and learned his limits. He approved an initiative limiting Social Security's early retirement plans. The Senate unanimously repudiated any proposal threatening the "well-being of all retired Americans." Reagan learned that Social Security was American politics' third rail, electrified and deadly to the touch, as in the New York City subway system. Thereafter, he farmed out Social Security issues to a bipartisan commission.

By the summer of 1981, the Reagan revolution had peaked. Once again Reagan applied his governing formula, securing a flashy victory on the economic front while sacrificing his social agenda. Reagan signed bills cutting taxes and shrinking the budget by $35.2 billion, yet boosted defense spending. Meanwhile, in July Reagan nominated the moderate conservative Sandra Day O'Connor as America's first female Supreme Court Justice, pragmatically playing to the center on social issues.

Reagan had calculated correctly. Conservatives had nowhere to go. Most Americans cheered his bravado while finding his compromises calming. In August, Reagan fired striking air traffic controllers en masse. His resolve earned the business community's trust worldwide. Federal Reserve Board Chairman Paul Volcker called this move against the controllers' PATCO union Reagan's "most important single action" against inflation because it demonstrated governmental discipline in labor relations and other matters.

Still, despite his rapid success, Reagan had reached his limits. In September the Democrats counterattacked. They emphasized the "fairness" issue, claiming that Reaganomics unfairly hurt the poor. Reagan's legislative triumphs now allowed his rivals to append his name to the growing recession, as Reagan's economic medicine took its time to begin curing America. Much of the next seven and a quarter years would be spent scrambling on the scrimmage line Reagan and his men had reached so quickly.

ESPECIALLY AFTER STARTING his administration so successfully, Ronald Reagan preferred big-picture governing, laced liberally with compromise, to hand-to-hand combat for the conservative cause. Ronald Reagan was a preacher, dominating Theodore Roosevelt's bully pulpit. Relying on staffers who combined insider savvy honed during the Nixon and Ford administrations with the brashness of "movement" outsiders, Reagan mastered the new politics of sound bites and photo ops, spin doctors and handlers. Reagan's image making united Americans behind broad, if undefined, ideas rather than specific, partisan policies.

In an era of spin control, the fear of negative headlines tempered Reagan's revolutionary ethos. Every morning, staffers planned the "line of the day," hoping to shape the coverage. When Democrats or reporters highlighted something embarrassing, aides scrambled to squelch the story. Usually, the fear of controversy kept the administration within the national consensus.

Reagan intuitively understood modern leadership as salesmanship. Staffers used the president's appealing personality to stabilize their volatile legislative coalition. "If you can write a nation's stories, you needn't worry about who makes its laws," said George Gerbner, the communications scholar.

Information Age Americans immersed in popular culture were bombarded with plotlines. Reagan excelled as storyteller in chief, reconstituting America's communal narrative so he could get credit for resurrecting the center and bringing on "Morning in America." "The American electorate seeks from its national leadership this sense of shared values, this reaffirmation of traditional American beliefs," Reagan declared in 1983. "They do not want a President who's a broker of parochial concerns; they do . . . want a definition of national purpose, a vision of the future."

Reagan pitched to a nation wired to respond to a master salesman's cultural and political mass appeal. For all the apparent information diversity that cable, computers, and VCRs delivered, the growing penetration of media hardware, along with the growing concentration of media content providers, focused America's national conversation. A pack mentality yielded remarkably similar headlines from seemingly diverse sources, day after day. During the 1980s, a wave of mergers searching for "synergy" would weave newspapers, television stations, Hollywood studios, and music companies in an ever more concentrated and conformist web.

Always eyeing the center, Reagan often compromised on core principles, although he resisted admitting it. In 1982, Reagan acted responsibly by agreeing to "revenue enhancements," what taxpayers and IRS agents called tax hikes. The Tax Equity and Fiscal Responsibility Act of 1982 limited the galloping deficits. That July, forty-two conservatives claimed the tax hike undermined Reagan's "original economic recovery plan and reneges on his pledge not to balance the budget on the backs of the American taxpayer."

Contrary to his reputation for being a hands-off leader, Reagan worked hard to sell the sell-out to Congress. He appealed to legislators' "spirit of bipartisanship and compromise." His briefing papers suggested, "Acknowledge the concern about big deficits," saying, "I don't like increased taxes—even $20 billion—or defense cuts any more than you all do. No compromise is perfect–but a compromise is required if the House is going to pass an acceptable budget." When lobbying, Reagan dared not call his tax increases "revenue enhancements." He insisted, "I will not raise taxes just to pay for more spending programs." Republicans, grumbling, remained loyal.

Despite massive federal deficits hitting 5 percent of the Gross Domestic Product in 1986, the great inflation ended. And after a sharp, short recession, the economic miracle of the 1980s and 1990s began. Many economists attributed the low inflation rate to Federal Reserve Chairman Paul Volcker's tight monetary policy. A Carter appointee, Volcker graciously shared credit with Reagan, saluting him for his PATCO leadership and for not interfering with the Federal Reserve's occasional deflationary belt-tightening. Here, Reagan's instincts and ideology meshed. Reagan believed the supply side doctrine that inflation could be controlled by adjusting the money supply, and he deferred to Volcker as the money supply manager.

The lure of the center neutralized Reagan's conservative sting. Reagan further frustrated conservatives by floating to reelection in 1984, minimizing policy details, partisan appeals, and visits to contested congressional districts. Ideologues demanded a substantive campaign, but the president decided to mimic Franklin Roosevelt and be presidential. The pragmatists' winning recipe was more apple pie than red meat: "Crime, Education, Economics—Unity," Reagan's Chief of Staff James Baker said. When interviewers asked about planned, deficit-reducing program cuts, Reagan replied, "I'm not going to discuss things like that and what we may do in a second term." Reagan said he "never mentioned" his welfare reform plans during his California reelection campaign: "I didn't want to politicize it."

The 1984 campaign trumpeted "God, patriotism and Reagan," ABC's correspondent Sam Donaldson sneered. This upbeat campaign of balloon drops and slogans threw symbols at substance. If blacks and women feared Reagan's program, Reagan's commercials featured happy blacks and women prospering in Reagan's America. A heartwarming, tear-jerking "Morning in America" ad celebrated America's renaissance with a country twang.

Reagan's growing centrism may have made him underestimate his political power and undersell his program. Peace and prosperity guaranteed Reagan's landslide more than arresting images or stirring rhetoric. Reagan could have pushed harder for more of a mandate to further his political revolution. But such historical hindsight misses the intensity of the opposition Reagan endured, especially in the media. The drubbing Reagan gave Walter Mondale was only obvious in retrospect; many early polls predicted a Democratic victory.

In 1984, Reagan once again preferred broad approval and less controversy to ideological purity. Judging by the political resistance that grew during his second term and Reagan's effectiveness in resurrecting an American center, his calculations were correct. Big picture pragmatic governance was more fitting than playing to the base or advancing a principled revolution.

This 1984 campaign poster broadcasts Ronald Reagan's vow
during his "Morning in America" reelection campaign—and
throughout his presidency—to bring America back, showing
the power of patriotism in uniting and inspiring this large, diverse nation. (Library of Congress)

RONALD REAGAN'S surprising instinct for moderation yielded its greatest
rewards in the arena where zealotry seemed most dangerous: relations with
the Soviet Union. Reagan built his national reputation and political base
crusading against communism, linking his anticommunism with his fears of
big government. The communist infiltration in Hollywood helped propel
Reagan into politics. Throughout the 1970s, as Republican Presidents
Richard Nixon and Gerald Ford negotiated with the Soviets, Ronald Reagan was the leading hard-liner. When Reagan entered the White House,

the *Bulletin of Atomic Scientists* moved the iconic doomsday clock on its front cover closer to midnight, fearing growing tensions with the Soviets.

Reagan's anticommunism was out of step with the ethos of the 1960s and 1970s. Well into the 1980s, a strong Marxist streak shaped American liberalism, American intellectual life, and the still-vital American labor movement. Many American elites believed that only some form of socialism or communism could mass-produce social justice. Simultaneously, and paradoxically, the hope for a kinder, gentler communism mingled with fear of nuclear war if Americans criticized Soviet and Chinese human rights abuses too aggressively. By the 1980s, many intellectuals, having lost confidence in America's foreign policy, viewed the Cold War as an American power grab.

Just as Reagan the tax cutter "enhanced revenue," Reagan the anticommunist sweet-talked the Soviets. Actually, Reagan had a pacifist streak that tempered his militancy. Reagan's mother's Disciples of Christ theology instilled within him a hatred of war that matured into skepticism about stockpiling nuclear weapons to preserve peace.

Reagan believed God saved him from assassination in March 1981 to make peace. While recovering, Reagan wrote directly to Soviet leader Leonid Brezhnev. However, Reagan's attempt to forge a personal connection fizzled. The Soviet leader was too infirm to negotiate seriously or participate in summits, as would be Brezhnev's two successors over the next four years. The letter revealed that Reagan hated communism "as a form of insanity" but sought peace between the peoples. By branding the Soviet Union the "evil empire" in 1983 and rebuilding America's military, Reagan sought to defeat seventies' defeatism and resurrect fifties' moral clarity. Intellectuals mocked Reagan for doubting the nuclear stalemate doctrine and for remaining imprisoned in Cold War assumptions. Henry Steele Commager, a leading American historian, pronounced Reagan's evil empire oration "the worst presidential speech in American history."

Characteristically, Reagan swaggered publicly while acting moderately. In September 1983, the Soviets downed Korean Air Line Flight 007, killing 269 civilians. Reagan lamented the loss of life but allowed the Soviets an opportunity to try to make amends. To conservatives' frustration, Reagan did not avenge these deaths.

Nevertheless, Reagan's muscular rhetoric and assertive patriotism captured the popular imagination. Movies such as *Red Dawn*, Sylvester Stallone's

Rambo: First Blood Part II, and Arnold Schwarzenegger's *Commando* reflected Cold War desires for super-sheriffs to defend America against criminals at home and communists abroad. Reagan fed this pop patriotism by saluting these celluloid warriors. In 1985, after Arab terrorists hijacked a TWA jet, Reagan joked, "Boy, I'm glad I saw Rambo last night. Now I know what to do next time."

Alas, especially in dealing with Middle Eastern terrorism, Reagan's rhetorical grandstanding magnified his impotence. The further a foreign policy issue was from the Soviets and communism, the less sure-footed Reagan was. He was particularly flat-footed in Middle Eastern matters. In October 1983, when Hezbollah-backed terrorists in Lebanon murdered 241 Marines with a truck bomb, Reagan dithered. The violence achieved its goal: the Americans left. After sneering that in Lebanon "Tip O'Neill may want us to surrender, but I don't," in February 1984 Reagan ordered a phased "redeployment"—not a withdrawal, of course—of 1,400 Marines from Beirut to Navy ships offshore. Reagan's flaccid response to this massacre—and a series of kidnappings in Lebanon—telegraphed a message of American weakness to the world. Decades later, it became clear that timidity and hesitancy emboldened the mass murderers of September 11, 2001, and other Islamist terrorists.

Fortunately, Reagan responded effectively when a Soviet leader finally was ready to negotiate. Both Mikhail Gorbachev and Ronald Reagan started the process that ended the Cold War. Both leaders jointly nurtured their budding personal relationship. Ronald Reagan proved surprisingly nimble. He could be tough, refusing to concede on the Strategic Defense Initiative antimissile defense system during the October 1986 Reykjavik summit and eloquently chiding Gorbachev during a 1987 visit to Berlin to "tear down this wall." But during the same Iceland meeting Reagan entertained sweeping proposals to eliminate all nuclear weapons. Shortly after the Berlin bombast, Reagan signed the sweeping Intermediate-Range Nuclear Forces Treaty, eliminating whole classes of nuclear missiles.

Conservatives feared Reagan was going soft on them. Charlton Heston urged his old friend to "resist the temptations of a Yalta waltz with the Soviet bear." Reagan replied, "I'm willing to dance but intend to lead." Administration officials insisted that Ronald Reagan hadn't changed, "the Soviets have changed."

Ronald Reagan's unexpected pragmatism with the Soviets redeemed his presidency even as scandals haunted his second term. In 1986 the

Republicans lost control of the Senate. In 1987, the Iran-Contra scandal stymied the administration, the stock market crashed, and the restive Senate rejected Reagan's Supreme Court nominee, Robert Bork. By 1988, the president appeared tired, sometimes addled, and was often mocked, especially after former Chief of Staff Donald Regan revealed that an astrologer influenced the president's scheduling. Yet the patriotic mood continued, the economic boom survived the crash, and Reagan the Cold Warrior emerged as the peacemaker.

The Soviet Union's transformation gave Reagan's administration—and the forty-year Cold War era—a happy ending. Historians still debate whether Soviet domestic rot, Mikhail Gorbachev's personality, the American defense buildup, or Reagan's individual vision felled the Soviet Union. But to the American public, this victory immortalized Reagan.

America's Cold War victory was a decades-long bipartisan achievement. The win vindicated America's post–World War II foreign policy and reconstituted the American center after the dispiriting sixties and seventies. The Soviet Union's collapse abruptly ended the decades-long love of Marxism that had transfixed the American Left. With the nearly century-long debate between capitalism and communism settled in favor of free enterprise, it became easier to find a broad, inclusive center of gravity to give American society political ballast.

"LET US RESOLVE that we the people will build an American opportunity society in which all of us—white and black, rich and poor, young and old—will go forward together arm in arm," Reagan purred in his second inaugural speech. At his best, the three Ps Reagan presided over—patriotism, peace, and prosperity—helped him forge a center confident in America as a land of opportunity. True, Reagan was lucky. He became president as Americans were emerging from the despair of Vietnam and Watergate, the economic boom was ready to launch, and Soviet society was imploding. But Reagan's muscular moderation improved the country's mood, facilitated the economic recovery, and smoothed the process toward a triumphal peace with the Soviets.

Reagan's centrist appeals were glorious, poetic distractions from the important, occasionally messy prose of governance. By lifting the national mood often, no matter what was happening, Reagan's paeans pegged opponents' utterances as irresponsible diversions. In 1987, after the Iran-Contra scandal revealed illegal arms shipments to Nicaragua, Reagan and his aides tried to revive the presidency with Reaganesque patriotic fluff. "We must opportunistically create events where the President exhibits his diverse qualities: leadership, compassion, identity with real people and real emotions and on behalf of the country," one staffer, William Henkel, urged. We need to "find heroes," Henkel said, noting that "Springtime means baseball, families, patriotism, parades, festival, feel-good wishes." Ronald Reagan's reimmersion in those "symbols, values, and memories" saved him so he could negotiate with Gorbachev.

Had Ronald Reagan been the rigid saber-rattler his opponents claimed he was, relations with the Soviets would not have unfolded so smoothly. The formidable Anatoly Dobrinin, the veteran Soviet ambassador to the United States, acknowledged that Reagan's surprising suppleness sustained Gorbachev's domestic and international reforms. "If Reagan had stuck to his hard-line policies in 1985 and 1986," Dobrynin said, "Gorbachev would have been accused by the rest of the Politburo of giving everything away to a fellow who does not want to negotiate. We would have been forced to tighten our belts and spend even more on defense." Reagan's greatness— along with Gorbachev's—proved the unfashionable notion that individuals shape history and vindicated his moderate, flexible, peace-through-strength approach.

Reagan's supply side economics produced huge deficits, cut social programs while preserving corporate handouts, and collectively shifted the tax burden from the wealthy to those in the middle class and working classes. Yet the economy boomed so much under Reagan that most Americans benefited individually. The inflation rate dropped, with only a short recession resulting. Interest rates leveled out, and Americans enjoyed a sustained two-decade run of prosperity. In assessing the many ingredients that tamed inflation and made America's fiscal pie grow, most economists credit Reagan's modified tax cuts and synchronization with Paul Volcker's Federal Reserve Board policies.

Always the Franklin Roosevelt pragmatist seeking that muscular middle, Ronald Reagan dismissed talk of the "Reagan revolution." In his farewell address, Reagan labeled his era the "great rediscovery, a rediscovery of our values and our common sense." Reagan's incremental centrism facilitated the Reagan reconciliation, where the sixties met the eighties. Just as Dwight Eisenhower ratified the New Deal by not undoing Franklin Roosevelt's handiwork, Reagan's America integrated many of the sixties' and seventies' ideological, cultural, social, and stylistic transformations into the mainstream.

Unfortunately, the eighties' libertarianism and materialism became socially toxic when combined with the sixties' anti-authoritarianism and antitraditionalism. The resulting indulgence addicion fueled the lurking social, moral, and communal crises. Reagan could conjure up patriotic national feelings, but his vision remained more individual than communal, ultimately advancing today's extravagances over yesterday's values.

Reagan's America resumed Americans' historic celebration of themselves without resolving the collective doubts raised during the 1960s and 1970s. Modern American consumerism triggered both a giddy pursuit of happiness and a gloomy sense of dislocation and perennial dissatisfaction. The mass, middle-class society distributed consumer creature comforts on an unprecedented scale. By the 1980s, telephones, televisions, and even air conditioners were ubiquitous and treated as necessities; new luxuries, including calculators, microwaves, VCRs, personal computers, and food processors, were now modernizing most American households, even those considered poor.

For all the available comforts, consumer culture was surprisingly corrosive and unsettling. Although owning many things, many Americans lacked deep moorings. Money served as a social solvent while lubricating arrivistes' climb to the top of society. A hard-driving, high-earning, big-spending nation pushed the enlightenment legacies of emancipation and individualism to their logical—and often illogical—extremes. Urbanization, individuation, automation, media penetration, mobility, prosperity, consumerism, and the rights revolution developed over decades. The resulting "radical individualism," the sociologist Robert Bellah explained, created a largely "negative" process of "giving birth to oneself" by "breaking free from family, community, and inherited ideas." A nation of disconnected searchers, divorced from traditional "sources of authority, duty and moral example," hoped to "find themselves" somehow—and feared they might not.

Greater national wealth did not produce happier children or adults. As American leisure culture became a carnival of sensual delights, even as more Americans rejoined the communal patriotic celebration, this addiction to pleasure often brought individual and mass misery. With six-year-olds averaging two hours of television watching daily, researchers linked children's excessive TV exposure to growing youth violence and crime, mass vulgarity, and an attention deficit disorder epidemic afflicting one in ten youngsters by the start of the new millennium. By 2004, experts estimated that "20 percent of all adolescents suffer from serious emotional or behavioral problems." Similarly, America's therapeutic society was plagued by depression, anxiety, anorexia, and other mental health ailments. Millions sought counseling; took drugs, both legal and illegal; or simply wallowed. By 1999, even the tough TV mobster Tony Soprano would see a psychiatrist and take antidepressants.

For all his moralizing rhetoric, Ronald Reagan's guilt-free prosperity launched an era of ostentation and indulgence. Americans' pursuit of happiness would frequently degenerate into an obsessive pursuit of pleasure. Consumption risked becoming compulsive, not just conspicuous. The super-sizing of America ensnared rich and poor alike in a relentless competition. The average single-family home size mushroomed, from 983 square feet in 1950, to 1,500 square feet in 1970, to 2,329 square feet by 2003. Americans would be spending $3 billion a year on closets alone, with wealthy patrons spending over $100,000 each to customize storage spaces.

As what people perceived to be their "needs" escalated, idealism, altruism, and nationalism waned; selfishness and materialism triumphed. Most Americans had enough money to overspend on some things. And it cost nothing to be envious or money-hungry. In 1967, as baby boomer idealism peaked, 40 percent of college freshmen in one poll most valued being rich and 80 percent sought a meaningful philosophy of life. Twenty years later, 80 percent desired wealth and only 40 percent valued seeking meaning. A different survey found that three of four twelve-year-olds wanted "to be rich."

Still, when Mr. Reagan came to town, Americans happily buried the 1970s, trying to forget the traumas of Watergate, Vietnam, the energy crisis, stagflation—that knockout punch of high inflation and high unemployment combined—and the Iranian hostage crisis. Few Americans in the 1970s would have predicted the great eighties bull market, America's patriotic revival, the end of the Cold War, or the Soviet Union's retreat. By the end of the 1980s, many Americans felt restored, and Ronald Reagan had ushered in many of these successes.

And yet the restoration was incomplete, the new consensus fragile. The Reagan boom coexisted with poverty, racism, crime, family breakdown, urban deterioration, national self-doubt, and epidemics of individual psychic distress. Americans remained insecure. And despite Reagan's homage to national unity, millions felt marginalized.

In seeking the American center, Ronald Reagan also intensified the idealistic and nationalistic forces that would make the center thrive. Reagan's newly restored consensus was like Oriole Park at Camden Yards, one of many urban redevelopment projects hatched in the 1980s. This newly constructed "classic" baseball field mixed an old-fashioned historic feel with the latest luxuries. The combination made Yuppies feel simultaneously virtuous and coddled. Similarly, most Americans celebrated the restored center, finding comfort in the revived sense of national purpose and progress. But this renewed consensus, like Camden Yards, also felt forced, glitzy, artificial, and impermanent, lacking the original's depth, solidity, and seeming unanimity. Baltimore's new stadium could not solve or even paper over the serious urban blight lurking so close to the revelers. The Reaganite consensus, like Camden Yards, would only be fully tested once launched in the 1990s.

11

BILL CLINTON AND
THE PERILS OF TRIANGULATION

The Need to be Muscular as Well as Moderate

ON THE SURFACE, BILL CLINTON should be this book's hero. Intelligent, idealistic, magnetic, Clinton was a political virtuoso. At his best, Clinton combined Ronald Reagan's showmanship, Harry Truman's righteousness, Richard Nixon's shrewdness, Lyndon Johnson's ambition, and John Kennedy's populist braininess. Clinton was also a centrist. The "change I seek and the change that we all must seek isn't liberal or conservative," he proclaimed. "It's different and it's both." Such flexibility, explained ever so charismatically, charmed the American people.

Yet despite his talents and moderation, Bill Clinton foundered as president. His insubstantial achievements offer a cautionary tale about centrism's seductions, about the dangers of crowd pleasing rather than principled, muscular moderation. Clinton lacked the essential ingredient that Abraham Lincoln and the two Roosevelts had, or that John F. Kennedy discovered: a bottom line, a sense that some core issues demanded firmness, not compromise, something beyond remaining in office.

Clinton's indulgent egotism—in many ways characteristic of his generation—undermined his quest for greatness. Presidents who love to be loved too much fail to accomplish much. "The character flaw Bill

Clinton's enemies have fixed upon—promiscuity—is a defining characteristic of his *public* life as well," the political columnist Joe Klein wrote in
1994. Republican Newt Gingrich acknowledged Clinton's concerns "about
race, international trade, and the U.S. position in the world—but he has
no consistency in fighting for anything."

Clinton's presidency was a dizzying time of abrupt policy shifts and stormy
controversies. He thought big and talked big, but ultimately governed small.
His broad prescriptions produced minor cures and left a record dotted with
sweeping promises but limited results. He wanted to be his generation's John F.
Kennedy, renewing America with vigorous, idealistic leadership; he ended by
being remembered as a president whose reach too often exceeded his grasp.

Clinton's uncanny ear for the American zeitgeist saved him from many perils and has made him a popular ex-president. But as president, Clinton was too
mired in the center and anxious for Americans' approval. Abraham Lincoln,
Theodore Roosevelt, and Franklin Roosevelt sought the popular center to
move America forward. All three occasionally adjusted their own stands
to broaden their support, but each risked popularity to defend core principles
when meeting pressing challenges. Although Clinton could be as inspiring as
Lincoln or the Roosevelts, he failed in policy making. Clinton's don't-rock-
the-boat governance proved that moderation can lead to mediocrity if the
president lacks the backbone to push his agenda and his constituents.

A Reaganized Democrat who tried to Reaganize his party, Clinton
should have been the Republicans' favorite Democrat. He balanced the
budget, reformed welfare, and defied special interest groups. At the same
time, America enjoyed apparent peace and prosperity during his terms.
Rather than branding his administration with a big government vision as
previous Democratic presidents had done—the New Deal, the New Frontier, the Great Society—Clinton delivered the Reaganesque verdict: "The
era of big government is over." Yet he still disgusted many opponents.
Conservatives labeled America's president a "queer-mongering, whore-
hopping adulterer; a baby-killing, dope-tolerating, lying, two-faced, trea-
sonous activist."

Critics attacked Clinton so intensely because, as the first president produced by the sex, drugs, and rock'n'roll sixties, he embodied many of the
cultural fears haunting millions of Americans, even as they enjoyed the
nineties' boom. With more and more traditional guardrails removed each
year, American culture was veering dangerously off track. Many Americans feared that sensationalist reporters and voyeuristic reality shows,

crude rappers, and ecstatic ravers, were leading society in a mad dash to the bottom. This apparent uninhibited hedonism fed a verbally violent political culture that Clinton, an iconic baby boomer, would master sometimes and suffer from frequently.

Clinton's greatest presidential achievements were his own survival and enduring popularity despite his shortcomings and self-inflicted wounds. He failed to reform the health care system or transform race relations. The Clinton economic boom proved no more equitable than the Republican boom. America's larger structural, political, and cultural quandaries remained unresolved. Clinton's cloud of benign policy "Band-Aids" hid his more serious failures. He usually avoided political risk, hoarding his popularity, except in 1998, when he fought to remain in power amid the Monica Lewinsky scandal. Clinton's sheer tenacity then demonstrated the potential he had to transform the presidency. He possessed the political skill but lacked the personal determination.

Clinton could have been a great president, a model moderate. Instead, history will remember him as a stunted president of unfulfilled potential. Jim Hightower, the Texas Democrat and populist sage, judged Clintonian centrism in his 1997 book *There's Nothing in the Middle of the Road but Yellow Stripes and Dead Armadillos*. Clinton's spineless centrism gave moderation a bad name.

BILL CLINTON was a center seeker by temperament, not just ideology. He recalled being a "peacemaker" growing up in Arkansas: "I hated conflicts. It was a source of great pain in my childhood." Born in 1946 into a complicated, colorful Southern family, Clinton learned how to charm away problems while at the same time developing vast appetites that revealed a deep personal neediness. Raised by a narcissistic mother and an alcoholic stepfather in Hope, Arkansas, Bill protected his younger brother Roger and his own fragile psyche by smoothing over tensions. Schoolmates remember young Bill as a happy child perpetually attempting to ingratiate himself; no one knew his home life was volatile.

Typically, Clinton tried splitting the difference when facing his generation's defining act, the Vietnam draft. Many of his high school buddies served in the army; some died. Most of his friends from Georgetown University (class of 1968) and fellow Rhodes scholars secured deferments. Clinton's Oxford University roommate Frank Aller was so despondent about resisting the draft that he committed suicide. Bill Clinton worked the system, trying to charm his way into the safe ROTC, until it became clear he would not be drafted. Writing to his recruiter, a young Clinton admitted his motivation: "to maintain my political viability within the system."

Clinton's strategy worked. He attended Yale Law School from 1970 to 1973, where he met the woman he would marry in 1975, Hillary Rodham. Going home to Arkansas, he rocketed to the top of state politics. In 1979, the thirty-two-year-old Clinton became America's youngest governor. Running Arkansas for twelve of the next fourteen years, Clinton built his national reputation as a moderate Southern Democrat, intent on pulling the party back to the center.

Leading a conservative Old Confederacy state while continuing to work the yuppie Rhodes and Yale networks, Clinton was uniquely positioned to help Democrats meet Ronald Reagan's challenge. Lyndon Johnson's Great Society bureaucracy, the Supreme Court's rights revolution, the New Left student movement, Jimmy Carter's self-critical seventies, the rise of identity politics, and the presidential primaries' polarizing impact had soured Democrats on the American consensus. Too many Democrats now envisioned a fragmented America, a multicultural mosaic emphasizing each interest group's uniqueness rather than the people's cumulative power and similarities once assembled. Clinton nevertheless rejected Reaganism as too greedy and selfish. To win in Arkansas, and the rest of the country, Clinton needed to make the liberal commitment to social justice appear populist, popular, and patriotic again.

After Ronald Reagan's landslide reelection in 1984, Clinton and other mostly Southern, moderate Democrats helped launch the centrist, populist Democratic Leadership Council. The DLC propelled Clinton into the national spotlight and gave his presidential pursuit its rationale. Clinton learned from Reagan to focus on the big picture and tap into Americans' patriotic idealism. Rejecting Washington's "tired" partisanship, Clinton vowed "to break through all the either/or debates that dominated national public discourse." Clinton understood that, after Reagan, Democrats would have to endorse budgetary discipline, limited taxation, restrained bureaucracies, a more assertive foreign policy, and a beefed-up defense. A proud nationalism in the tradition of Theodore and Franklin Roosevelt would neutralize modern selfishness. "We recognize that we are a community," Clinton told the DLC in 1991. "We are all in this together, and we are going up or down together."

Three intellectual and political traditions shaped Bill Clinton: populism, progressivism, and pragmatism. A Southern Baptist, he channeled the sweaty, generous, intimate populism of William Jennings Bryan and Lyndon Johnson, delivering the goods to the people—peppered with positive, tub-thumping, uplifting rhetoric. A child of the 1960s, he embraced the rights-oriented progressive agenda championing civil rights, feminism, environmentalism, and a redistribution of wealth and power. A rational, ambitious Ivy Leaguer, his pragmatic faith in the American dream trusted creative, not radical, experimentation to perfect society, while he and his peers pursued individual glory and gold.

Synthesizing these diverse traditions, Clinton believed that the "conservative" and "liberal" political labels presented false choices and also threatened his political future. He and his allies despised conservatism but feared being labeled as liberals. Reagan—and many a Southern demagogue—had demonized liberalism so effectively that Clinton preferred a more fluid and centrist "Third Way" politics without the ideological labels or baggage.

Clinton stewed as Massachusetts Governor Michael Dukakis failed to capture the popular center during the 1988 presidential campaign. Republicans branded Dukakis a wooly, elitist, tax-and-spend liberal. Bill and Hillary Clinton, idealistic congressional staffers like George Stephanopoulos, and hardened consultants like James Carville brooded. They dreamed of running a hard-hitting but lightfooted campaign in 1992, refusing to get boxed into corners while counterpunching fast, hard, and often.

This will to win launched Bill Clinton toward the voter-rich center in 1992 while nevertheless encouraging an anything-goes strategy that occasionally mocked his campaign's pious postures. As a New Democrat, Clinton crafted a centrist message seeking a "New American Majority." But this New Democrat was also a tough Democrat. Clinton's consultants attacked and counterattacked from an Arkansas political bunker that Hillary Clinton christened the War Room.

Mastering the presidential campaign's theatrics, Bill Clinton often demonstrated his centrism with symbolic gestures. He distanced himself from Democratic business-as-usual by flying home during the primaries to oversee the execution of Ricky Ray Rector, a retarded African American with an IQ of 70, who had killed a police officer during a robbery. Just before the Democratic Convention, Clinton burnished his credentials as a steely centrist at one of the Reverend Jesse Jackson's Rainbow Coalition events. The night before Clinton spoke, Sister Souljah had addressed the

Coalition. Sister Souljah was a rap singer who had rationalized the recent Los Angeles riots, saying, "If Black people kill Black people every day, why not have a week and kill white people?" Clinton labeled the rapper a racist. Clinton's condemnation embarrassed Jackson, his host, but impressed reporters. He looked courageous confronting African American extremism before an African American audience.

Observers debated whether Clinton was a muscular moderate, redefining the Democratic center, or an unprincipled panderer. Many "Reagan Democrats" returned to the Democratic Party after he proclaimed, "We offer our people a new choice based on old values . . . . The choice we offer is not conservative or liberal. In many ways, it is not even Republican or Democratic. It is different. It is new." Others scoffed. "Doonesbury" readers voted that the icon representing Clinton in Garry Trudeau's cartoon should be a waffle.

The 1992 campaign was brutal. Allegations that Clinton had dodged the draft, betrayed his wife, and benefited illegally from their Whitewater investment property clouded his campaign. Clinton's surprise victory over the incumbent George H. W. Bush vindicated his centrist strategy while reinforcing his sense of destiny. With a third-party candidate, Ross Perot, siphoning off 18 percent of the popular vote, Clinton received only 43 percent of the popular vote but an impressive electoral college margin.

Clinton tapped into surprising amounts of enthusiasm. He attracted moderate Reagan Democrats back to the party. His tenacity impressed Democratic partisans. And he thrilled many Democratic idealists with his charm and vision. Millions flocked to the polls enthusiastically for the first time in their voting lives. They believed the "Man from Hope" was the baby boom generation's John Kennedy, reaffirming faith in themselves and their democratic experiment.

IT IS DIFFICULT to shift overnight from wooing to governing, from the campaign trail's sweeping promises to the Oval Office's nuanced policy papers. Bill Clinton's inexperience made him particularly prone to pandering. Even before inauguration day, Clinton's compulsive need to crowd-please hurt him. On Veterans' Day, November 11, 1992, just days after the election, NBC's Andrea Mitchell asked the president-elect how he would handle military opposition if he kept his campaign promise to allow openly gay soldiers. Intoxicated by victory, speaking too candidly about his progressive views, and sincerely thanking a key constituency, Clinton said he was ready to welcome

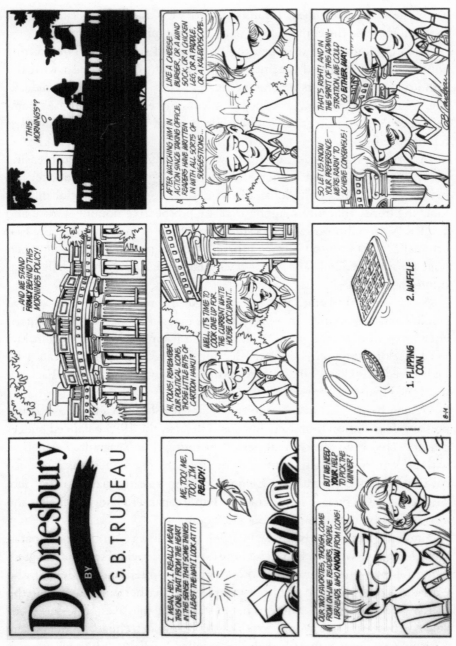

Garry Trudeau's cartoon of August 14, 1994, showed that even many Democrats were fed up with Bill Clinton's triangulating: Readers voted that Clinton should be depicted in the Doonesbury strip as a waffle, rather than a flipped coin. In the third panel, an invisible man represents President George H. W. Bush, and a feather represents Vice President Dan Quayle. DOONESBURY ©1994 G. B. Trudeau. Reprinted with permission of UNIVERSAL PRESS SYNDICATE. All rights reserved.

gay soldiers. He proclaimed "I think there are ways that we can deal with this that will increase the comfort level of a lot of the military folks here."

This rookie mistake upstaged the presidential transition. The ensuing controversy highlighted the incoming president's culture clash with the military and stirred fears among moderates about Clinton's closet radicalism. Clinton's subsequent backpedaling culminated in the military's cumbersome "don't ask, don't tell" policy. His idealistic supporters and gay allies felt betrayed.

In forming his cabinet, Clinton was similarly torn between pleasing every Democratic constituency and offering big picture governance. His search for a cabinet that "looks like America" triggered a special interest lobbying frenzy that often emphasized the prospective nominees' race and gender. When Clinton's stated desire to appoint a woman to one of the four original cabinet positions turned into a desperate, prolonged search for a female attorney general, *The New Republic* lamented "the cultural balkanization of our politics."

As his amateurish mistakes accumulated, the new president resembled an old Democrat. Nineteen weeks after the inauguration, with his inexperienced staff dizzy from journalists' hits, Clinton hired a Washington insider as counselor to the president. In selecting David Gergen, a moderate who had served Presidents Nixon, Ford, and Reagan, Clinton steered back toward the bipartisan center.

Gergen helped Clinton secure two major legislative victories, with impressive cooperation from Republicans. The first, the 1993 balanced budget bill, reflected the political realities of operating in a Reaganized America, with a Democratic twist. Clinton wooed Wall Street by demonstrating fiscal responsibility. He satisfied Democrats by increasing taxes on the rich. The result was a budget surplus rather than Reagan-era budget deficits, and a continuation of the 1980s' economic boom.

Similarly, in passing NAFTA in 1993, Clinton was nimble and bipartisan. George H. W. Bush had signed the North American Free Trade Agreement to loosen the commercial flow among the United States, Mexico, and Canada. The American public was generally apathetic about it, but the heavily Democratic labor unions hated it, fearing massive job losses. Concerned that America would export jobs to import cheap products, the African-American activist Jesse Jackson called NAFTA, "Shafta."

Cooperating with his nemesis, Republican Congressman Newt Gingrich, Clinton arm-twisted skeptical Democrats to broker a deal. He secured more concessions from Mexican trade negotiators to satisfy reluctant Democratic legislators. And he courted the American people. When Gerald Ford, Jimmy Carter, and George H. W. Bush appeared at the White House for the signing of the Israeli–Palestinian Oslo Accords on September 13, 1993, Clinton recruited the three ex-presidents for a bipartisan, pro-NAFTA press conference the next day. Somehow Clinton's note cards for the conference were mixed up. Unfazed, the president spoke spontaneously and eloquently. "Now I understand why he's inside looking out and I'm outside looking in," former President Bush marveled, (anticipating a friendship that would become a rare symbol of bipartisanship a decade later, after the 2004 tsunami). Clinton's rickety coalition for NAFTA of 234 supporters to 200 opponents rested on 132 Republicans. Gergen praised Clinton's work passing NAFTA as a "textbook case in presidential leadership."

By contrast, Clinton failed to enact his first term's centerpiece legislation, health care reform, largely because he missed the center. By 1993 Democratic politicians had convinced Republican politicians that the health care system was broken. "America's ready for health-care reform and so are we," South Carolina's Republican Governor, Carroll Campbell, declared in an official response to a Clinton speech, as Republicans scrambled to offer their own reform plans.

Such an ambitious reform could only pass through a divided Congress with just the right combination of bipartisan goodwill and political fear. Clinton and his wife, Hillary Rodham Clinton, squandered their chance. In what David Gergen and many others deemed a payoff for squelching 1992's rumors of Bill's adultery, the First Lady chaired this health-reform effort. Rather than developing a plan jointly with Congress, Mrs. Clinton prescribed a 1,354-page big government program unsuited to the small-government era that Ronald Reagan had pioneered.

Hillary Clinton refused to compromise. She urged her husband to wave a pen in his 1994 State of the Union address, promising to veto "legislation that does not guarantee every American private health insurance that can never be taken away." The First Lady bashed critical doctors, pharmaceutical companies, insurance executives, and conservatives. Mrs. Clinton mocked those who "drive down highways paid for by government funds" and "love the defense department" but object "when it comes to . . . trying to be a compassionate and caring nation."

The Clintons' operatic marital dynamics kept the president tied to Hillary's rigid strategy even as the health care initiative fizzled. The Clintons further alienated Congress by bypassing the usual procedures and slipping this major reform into a budget bill in 1993–1994. Strangely, President Clinton did not lobby as intensely or as nimbly as he had for the balanced budget and NAFTA. The bill lingered in congressional committee; neither the Senate nor the House even voted on it. Bill Clinton's failure to deliver any kind of health care reform symbolized a broader failure to fight as effectively for policies and principles as he later would for political survival, in 1998.

IN FAIRNESS, throughout 1993 waves of controversy distracted the president. Bombarded by increasingly aggressive reporters, the Clinton fall from grace was dizzying. Traditional journalists and ever-proliferating Web sites mocked the president's pricey haircuts and the First Lady's hairstyle revolutions, her fanatic liberalism and his empty centrism. Six months after joining the administration, one of Hillary Clinton's best friends, Vince Foster, killed himself, complaining that in Washington, "ruining people is considered sport." The Clintons spent their first White House Christmas hosting friends and relatives while fending off humiliating revelations, repeatedly washed through America's 24/7 news cycle, about President Clinton's adulteries while governor and Mrs. Clinton's profanity-laced responses.

The baby boomer culture was cannibalizing one of its own. The Clintons had embodied and helped shape the adversary culture, the sexual revolution, the questioning of authority; these forces now undermined them. The shift in media coverage of presidents, which began with Theodore Roosevelt and intensified with Franklin Roosevelt dominating the news, turned destructive. Vowing that they would not be the patsies their predecessors had been, when John Kennedy cheated or Richard Nixon schemed, journalists were more critical and less inhibited. Reporters had described the presidential candidates in 1960 favorably 75 percent of the time; reporters in 1992 offered favorable coverage only 40 percent of the time. The jokes about Jack Kennedy's accent and Jackie's pearls had been benign; the jokes about Bill's libido and Hillary's alleged lesbianism were nasty.

In the 1940s and 1950s, reporters had aggrandized leaders and built a common culture, even at the risk of hypocrisy; by the 1990s, journalists denigrated politicians and fragmented American national identity. The rise of the penny press in the mid-1800s had created a large, diverse mass market for supposedly objective news. Individuals with different political affiliations encountered the same, frequently unifying, news narrative. Radio and then television accelerated this process of building national identity through a common national media experience. Throughout the tumultuous 1960s and 1970s, Americans trusted CBS's "Uncle Walter" Cronkite and other network stalwarts. The big three networks—CBS, NBC, ABC—broadcast similar, seemingly objective, news shows, which attracted nearly 90 percent of the television news audience.

The media revolutions that moved beyond the three-network universe aggrandized and diminished the presidency. The CNN cable revolution brought 24/7 news. The talk radio revolution filled the airwaves with harsh, opinionated, often explicit chatter. The Internet revolution opened a world of unfiltered discussions and unsubstantiated rumors. As the focal point of these all-consuming media, the first presidential rock star, Bill Clinton, endured unprecedented attention and abuse. His jogging habits, addiction to McDonald's, underwear preferences, and sexual history became public fodder, along with an obsessive dissection of his marriage.

In the 1990s advocacy journalism, postmodern cynicism, and the Internet's overcrowded marketplace of media voices ended the era of journalistic objectivity. Fewer newspapers and television stations tried being dispassionate. Ronald Reagan's rise to power had brought to the fore conservatives' critique of what they called the "liberal media." Since the 1980s, many studies had demonstrated that most leading reporters were liberal in their voting records, attitudes, and lifestyles. Some studies claimed these common perspectives led reporters to highlight certain stories and dismiss others. Viewing Republicans as plutocrats and Democrats as underdogs, journalists were more likely to write about rich Republicans bankrolling conservatives than about equally wealthy Democrats bankrolling liberals.

Liberals denied that the mainstream media favored their views, pointing to the harsh coverage the Clintons endured. Reporters were cynical and supercritical, not liberal, *Newsweek's* Steven Waldman insisted. Americans seemed to be reverting to the pre-penny-press nineteenth century, when partisans expressed warring political identities—and reinforced their worldviews—by reading explicitly partisan papers and only believing those statements that undermined their opponents.

The talk radio host Rush Limbaugh led the conservative charge against the "dominant media elites" for treating Mr. and Mrs. America like "bumbling idiots." Nationally syndicated in 1988, Limbaugh's show reached 20 million people via 665 stations by 1996. Mimicked by dozens of other "shock jocks," feeding off the Clintons' antics, Limbaugh became a political and cultural force. In 1994, Clinton blasted Limbaugh's daily tirades, his "unremitting drumbeat of negativism and cynicism." Speaking live to KMOX radio, Clinton fumed, "After I get off the radio with you today, Rush Limbaugh will have three hours to say whatever he wants, and I won't have any opportunity to respond, and there's no truth detector." Clinton's tantrum made Limbaugh "the leader of the opposition," *National Review* snickered.

Clinton also faced a newly hostile Washington. The conservatives cultivated an institutional thicket of think tanks, policy journals, political clubs, publishers, lobbying firms, law firms, PR firms, government relations departments within major corporations, and broadcast outlets. Paralleling the New Deal brain trusters and the New Frontier Ivy Leaguers who arrived in Washington and never left, the Reagan revolution had created permanent colonies of Beltway Reaganauts. Their careers would be spent revolving between government and the sometimes-private and sometimes-nonprofit, but always conservative, sector.

Many of the Clintons' toughest critics entered politics as Reaganites. Ann Coulter was a lawyer who first clerked for a judge Reagan had appointed. She transitioned from public service to caustic political commentary in the mid-1990s. Her first book, *High Crimes and Misdemeanors: The Case Against Bill Clinton* (1998), called for Clinton's impeachment. Kenneth Starr first came to Washington from California to work in the Reagan Justice Department in 1981. He would prosecute Clinton as independent counsel during the Monica Lewinsky scandal in 1998.

Under persistent pressure, the Clinton administration became the angriest administration since Richard Nixon's. Fury clouded Clinton's judgment during the health care debacle, when managing the Whitewater real estate scandal, and when handling reporters in general. Rather than building on their generational and cultural ties with the Washington press corps, the Clintons frequently froze out the press. Rather than presiding over an era of good feelings, Clinton found himself buffeted by an increasingly nasty political culture.

Ronald Reagan had chuckled when pegged as a "good time Charlie"; it softened his reputation as an ideologue. Bill Clinton resented the barbs aimed at his addiction to poll-driven popularity, not principles. In 1993, when a *Rolling Stone* reporter asked what he would "stand up for and die for," the president exploded. If "you convince" readers "I don't have any convictions, that's fine, but it's a damn lie," Clinton snapped, without specifying any principles. Targeting the press for not giving him "one damn bit of credit," he claimed, "I have fought more damn battles here for more things than any President in the last twenty years." Richard Nixon, Lyndon Johnson, and Jimmy Carter learned that fighting the press was the wrong way to defeat it. It took years for Bill Clinton to learn that lesson and try to master the new media universe he inhabited.

BY 1994 Clinton's centrist presidency was in shambles. Americans appeared increasingly cranky, polarized, adrift, and insecure. Clinton watched helplessly as the health care reform died in committee, souring Democratic prospects for the 1994 midterm elections. Newt Gingrich offered a Reaganite "Contract with America," nationalizing the 435 House and 35 Senate races. This strategy gave reporters and Republicans an opening to portray Clinton paradoxically as both a fickle, incompetent incumbent and a "tax and spend" liberal.

In November 1994, Republicans seized power in the House of Representatives for the first time since Dwight Eisenhower's presidency forty years earlier. Thirty-four House incumbents, all Democrats, lost their seats. Clinton insisted to reporters at a press conference that "the president is relevant here," repeating the word "relevant" four times in one excruciating rant.

Various factors shaped the election. Many House Democrats were arrogant, complacent, and corrupt. Still, White House moderates and Clinton's DLC allies blamed Clinton's reversion to old Democrat, big government policies for the defeats.

Clinton endured this criticism masterfully. He apologized to a DLC meeting, saying that he had learned his lesson, that the struggling middle class, "folks the Democratic Party ought to be championing," felt abandoned. Republicans "had a two-word message: 'less government.' Our message took an hour to recite," Clinton later admitted.

Bill Clinton rediscovered the center by turning to a quirky controversial political adviser, Dick Morris. To avoid media ridicule for using a consultant who advised Republicans too, Clinton secretly consulted Morris by telephone, code-naming him "Charlie." Morris advocated "bite size" initiatives, speaking "the new language of opportunity-responsibility" that could succeed rather than big government "class-warfare" programs that would fail. He challenged Clinton to redefine the presidency "by compromise, reconciliation, values, and healing—skills at which this president was awfully good." The president needed to "take a middle course," to "tri-angulate, create a third position, not just in between the old positions of the two parties but above them as well."

With the Machiavellian Morris whispering sweet poll numbers in his ear, Clinton tacked right. Morris poll-tested policy stances, tactical moves, even the Clintons' summer vacation plans. During the 1995 budget show-down, Clinton rejected Gingrich's tax-cutting demands while appropriat-ing the traditional Republican mantra demanding a balanced budget. This strategic resolve and philosophical fluidity reflected Morris's influence.

Clinton searched for the right phrasing. America's "common ground" seemed too vague. Labeling Republicans "extreme" sounded too divisive. Gradually, Clinton mentioned "values" when speaking about everything from the budget to Bosnia, even as Republicans mocked his terrible values role modeling.

Although the epitome of baby boomer irresponsibility to conservatives, Bill Clinton and his wife Hillary represented their generation's return to tradition, too. By becoming parents, and often by enduring the fallout of their self-indulgence, many elite baby boomers had rediscovered traditional strictures against divorce, adultery, and drug use. More broadly, many wor-ried about a values crisis in America.

Many Americans—and legions of experts—feared their children were being poisoned in a "socially toxic environment." A sugary diet of televi-sion, video games, junk food, and mall visits perverted the soul. Too many parents, too busy indulging themselves, feared saying "no." Television and the Internet made ever-younger children savvy consumers, targeted ever more aggressively by marketers. Typically children watched an estimated 40,000 commercials annually. Most ten-year-olds could identify 300 to 400 product brands. More and more thoughtful Americans recoiled at the loss of community, the bottomless pit of greed, the soul-scarring selfishness of society. Politically, special interest agendas, politicians' perennial fund-raising, perpetually cynical headlines, and aggressive identity politics threatened the communal sense of nationalism.

Trying to allay these anxieties, Clinton mastered his new role as accommodator-in-chief. He offered a laundry list of reforms on the cheap: raising the minimum wage, tweaking health insurance, and increasing scholarships and job training. The president advocated paternalistic, small-scale policy initiatives to improve middle-class Americans' quality of life. For the first time since the 1960s, a Democratic president challenged the

Republican dominance of moral issues. He denounced teenage smoking, proposed the V-chip parental control on television, and championed school uniforms.

Hoping for reelection, in his 1996 State of the Union address Clinton channeled Ronald Reagan, declaring, "The era of big government is over." "This is not much fun," one staffer grumbled as Clinton approved Republican budget cuts eviscerating Democratic programs. "This is not what most of us came here to do."

Clinton's mysterious moderating shift divided and demoralized his White House staff. Most of his aides advocated a more liberal, confrontational approach. These advisers hated Reaganomics and preferred echoing Harry Truman's 1948 partisan attack on the "Do Nothing" Republican Congress. Capitol Hill liberals were apoplectic. When Clinton "triangulates," complained Nebraska Senator Bob Kerrey, "he strangulates the Democrats in Congress."

Nevertheless, the strategy worked. Clinton's approval rating steadied at 60 percent. Clinton as the "good father" became especially popular with "soccer moms," suburban women fearing America's moral and economic decline. This virtuous pose was risky for a man whose libido launched a thousand late-night TV jokes. In August 1996, listing "the top ten things overheard" at the president's fiftieth birthday party, the comedian David Letterman delivered the unnervingly prescient line: "Young lady, how'd you like to come out to the limo and help me solve my mid-life crisis?" Americans compartmentalized, responding to Clinton's centrism while forgiving their president's trespasses. When pollsters asked respondents to name the best aspect of Bill Clinton's character, the most frequent response was that he had no character.

Invigorated by his popularity, Clinton squelched internal White House debate about his compromises. In 1996, during his reelection campaign, he signed a Republican bill allowing states not to recognize gay marriages that other states sanctioned. This legislation betrayed the Democrats' nationalist orientation and human rights commitments as well as their gay constituency. If "there are people here who don't like it," Clinton snapped, "well, I've created seven and a half million new jobs and maybe it's time for them to go out and take some of them."

Throughout the spring and summer of 1996, Clinton struggled with welfare reform. Recalling candidate Clinton's 1992 promise to end welfare "as we know it," Republicans fashioned a "workfare" bill putting recipients to work. Hillary Clinton's comrades at the Children's Defense Fund claimed the bill would impoverish a million children. The president vetoed the first two versions, but the Republicans returned with a third, more palatable, bill. With Morris screaming "if he vetoes, he'll lose," Hillary Clinton withdrew from the debate.

Compromise came more easily to Bill Clinton. "What good will you do if you lose?" Morris insisted, sounding the Clintonites' characteristic "the ends justify the means" trumpet blast. Secure in the belief that he was amassing power to do good, Clinton asked Morris, "You think I'll carry Congress if I sign the bill?" He then ended welfare as three decades of Americans had known it.

Clinton easily beat the 1996 Republican presidential nominee, Senator Robert Dole, becoming the first two-term Democratic president since Franklin D. Roosevelt. Dole was no match for Clinton's agility—or the Democrats' aggressive operation. The Kansas senator appeared old-fashioned and rigid. Exit polls showed Clinton making gains since 1992 with liberal Republicans, liberal independents, and moderate independents, whereas Dole appeared to be a captive of the Far Right without Reagan's light touch.

Clinton's turnaround in two years was impressive. Still, he did not even win 50 percent of the popular vote, and only carried four of the eleven Southern states. Despite all the grandstanding, a broad national consensus— and a Democratic Congress—remained out of his reach.

MANY DEMOCRATS' high hopes from 1992, and his own towering ambitions, made Bill Clinton's actual presidency ultimately disappointing. Despite his scaled-down policies, Clinton still wanted to be a consequential president. He regretted that no major war or economic upheaval would allow him to prove his greatness. Instead, Clinton looked to Theodore Roosevelt's peaceful but momentous presidency, promising to help Americans transition to a brave new world. In his second inaugural address, Clinton again triangulated between liberalism and Reaganism, declaring, "Government is not the problem, and government is not the solution. We—the American people—we are the solution."

Clinton resented reporters' and many liberals' criticisms that his initiatives were mere baby steps. In April 1995, he marked the fiftieth anniversary of Franklin Roosevelt's death by matching Roosevelt's historical footprint as a Democratic leader with his own. Roosevelt's biographer, the famous historian Arthur M. Schlesinger Jr., retorted, "FDR loved a good fight; Clinton seems by temperament an accommodator. Accommodation has its uses but it can too easily become appeasement."

The insulted president wrote to Schlesinger: "Those who fought me tooth and nail the last two years know well that I believed in and relished the battles." Clinton then hosted Schlesinger and other old Roosevelt and Kennedy hands at a White House lunch. Charmed but still skeptical, Schlesinger noted, "we all felt that if he acts the way he talked, things would improve—but still wonder about the 'if.'" Clinton desperately wanted to be a consequential president. He packed his Oval Office hideaway with monumental presidential biographies. But he could not resist cheap and easy victories, especially as the stock market soared and foreign troubles seemed unimportant to the president, reporters, and most Americans.

Moreover, despite all Clinton's center seeking, many Republicans found him and his wife unbearable. Clinton's potential to hijack their agenda terrified them. But beyond the power calculus, the media sensationalism, the conservative fiefdoms, and the fraying Capitol Hill relations, the hatred ran deeper. Attitudes about sexual discipline alienated Clinton's baby boomer elite from their rivals. Clinton's shape-shifting, combined with his moral sloppiness, renewed the intensity of America's sex wars, which since the 1960s had Americans debating their most private actions in very public ways.

With Republicans in the House perpetually furious at him, Clinton feared gridlock, the ailment overshadowing his epoch of divided government and small-scale solutions to huge problems. In his second inaugural speech, rejecting "the politics of petty bickering and extreme partisanship," Clinton invited Democrats and Republicans "to be repairers of the breach," warning, "nothing big ever came from being small." Clinton wanted to lead a civic renaissance, to return to civility, renew democracy, and restore the national soul. He positioned the president as moral arbiter and preacher, not simply head of government and head of state. This was an ambitious—and necessary—approach in an increasingly cynical country, with too many valuable people abandoning politics and those who participated turning nasty.

Clinton decided to focus his second term on America's race problem. As a white Southerner popular among African Americans, Bill Clinton was uniquely positioned to lead boldly. In his first term, when honoring Martin Luther King Jr. in Memphis, Clinton challenged African Americans to lead crusades within black communities against black crime, poverty, and irresponsibility. On July 14, 1997, in San Diego, Clinton unveiled a blue ribbon commission to explore modern race relations as part of the "President's Initiative on Race."

Rather than blaming white racism, the commission addressed the subversive threat of "racialism." The commission report claimed that too many minority groups emphasized their divergences from the nation, ignoring Americans' common ground. A new consensus had to build community while celebrating diversity. Government could only do so much; "racial reconciliation" would come from individual initiatives, especially honest dialogues nurturing national unity with a multicultural sensibility.

Nothing in Clinton's record suggested he would take the risks necessary to push the American conversation about race far enough to accomplish anything. Unfortunately, his personal peccadilloes made the issue moot. By January 1998, Clinton was battling the Monica Lewinsky scandal with the grit and ingenuity that his health care crusade and racial reconciliation agenda needed. Unlike his grandiose reforms, he survived. As the nation gossiped about the president's dalliance with a twenty-something intern, Clinton lost his moral voice. Staffers scoured the 1998 State of the Union address to avoid any references to values or anything else that might trigger snickering. As the *Washington Post*'s John Harris observed, "It's a little awkward to play the preacher when the congregation is talking about your 'genetic material.'"

Clinton's misbehavior came at a very awkward time for him, politically and historically. Republicans were angry and powerful, galvanized by the backlash against the baby boomers' counterculture, which Clinton's values-talk had also acknowledged. Reporters were cynical and powerful, energized by the search for the next Watergate and able to cycle through stories faster and with fewer restraints than ever before. Many citizens, although skeptical about the powerful, were fascinated by the sordid details yet forgiving because of a general assumption that all leaders sinned.

Rather than lifting America's horizons, as he had promised in January 1997, Clinton survived by lowering the country's expectations of its leaders. His "everybody does it defense" situated Clinton in a parade of presidential adulterers, establishing a lowest common denominator morality. Civilization is a tissue of ties, a fragile web of constraints enveloping humans and elevating them to live together, work together, love together, and dream together. Clinton's defense resonated because modern popular culture frequently defied those restraints on behavior, reducing Americans to their crudest selves. Hip-hop and rap dazzled black and white kids with songs like "Big Pimpin'," (1999) wherein the rapper Jay-Z, spewing profanity, treated scantily clad women on a yacht like money-sucking receptacles. Against this cultural context, Clinton's awkward fumblings were child's play. Whereas George Washington had defined himself and his fellow Americans by their high-minded fealty to cultural constraints, Bill Clinton saved his job by defining himself and his fellow Americans by their submission to base impulses.

A master of political jujitsu, Clinton deflected the Republican attack, mobilizing Democrats while demonizing the Republicans as dour, intrusive, puritans. Playing hardball, he muscled allies to override their consciences for the sake of party loyalty. After defending her husband on the *Today* show in January 1998, Hillary Clinton crowed, "I guess that will teach them to f—k with us." During the midterm elections of November 1998, Democrats fought an aggressive, partisan campaign. They even surprised themselves by gaining five seats in the House and not losing any Senate seats. This election marked only the second time since the Civil War that an incumbent president's party had gained congressional seats in a midterm election.

Nevertheless, the Democratic triumphs could not prevent Clinton's impeachment in the House of Representatives in December 1998 for perjury and obstruction of justice. On February 12, 1999, Senate Republicans failed to get the two-thirds vote they needed to convict and remove the president, but half the Senate voted to convict on the obstruction charge. The impeachment showed how much Republicans hated the president and how poorly Clinton managed congressional relations, a critical area for any president.

The scandal revealed American politicians, reporters, and lawyers at their tawdriest, awash in cynicism, sensationalism, dishonesty, and partisanship. Rather than convincing Americans to rely on each other, Clinton convinced many that they could only trust their fellow partisans. Rather than demonstrating the center's transforming potential, Clinton made moderation look mushy. "In a democracy, the challenge of leadership is not to find the path of least political risk," George H. W. Bush's budget guru Richard Darman wrote of Clinton. "Society can find that on its own." The Clinton scandal bruised the nation's psyche and roughened the nation's soul, questioning many of the illusions that propped up the president as America's model man.

IT IS NOW CLEAR that as Clinton fiddled, worrying about his political fate, Osama bin Laden and his Islamist terrorists plotted to make American cities burn. Clinton's failure to subdue or kill bin Laden before September 11 is part of a bipartisan march of folly. Jimmy Carter's impotence during the Iranian hostage crisis and the Reagan-era flight from Lebanon after Hezbollah murdered 241 Marines telegraphed American weakness to Islamist terrorists long before bin Laden declared war on America.

Other presidents' myopia and the public's somnolence do not justify Bill Clinton's failure to foresee the threat. Leaders, especially those aspiring to mythic status, must anticipate dangers, not peddle excuses. Osama bin Laden issued his anti-American fatwa declaring war in 1998. Al Qaeda bombed two American embassies in Africa in 1998 and a Navy destroyer in Yemen in 2000 on Bill Clinton's watch. Clinton has admitted, "I tried and I failed to get bin Laden. I regret it. But I did try. And I did everything I thought I responsibly could." The relevant question here is not, "Did Bill Clinton fail?" but "Did his centrism cause the failure?"

Al Qaeda's growing impudence and violence over a decade illustrates the dangers of following public opinion rather than leading it. Illusions of a post–Cold War era promising peace and prosperity lulled citizens and reporters, pollsters and politicians. The National Commission on Terrorist Attacks Upon the United States noted in 2004 that no American polling organization bothered surveying Americans about terrorism in the year and a half before 9/11. The 2000 presidential campaign ignored bin Laden and terrorism as issues. Two of Clinton's National Security Council experts, Daniel Benjamin and Steve Simon, lamented in 2002, "too many missed opportunities, too many missed clues, and too much systemic blindness," which imprisoned America in "an old paradigm for thinking about terrorism."

The end of the Cold War, combined with baby boomer skepticism about government institutions, shaped the pre–9/11 conventional wisdom discounting the importance of the CIA, the FBI, and national security concerns. In April 1999 the *New York Times* doubted terrorism charges against bin Laden, running a headline: U.S. HARD PUT TO FIND PROOF BIN LADEN DIRECTED ATTACKS. The 9/11 Commission report concluded that under Clinton—and his successor George W. Bush—"The U.S. government took the threat seriously, but not in the sense of mustering anything like the kind of effort that would be gathered to confront an enemy of the first, second or even third rank."

Both presidents bear responsibility for the government's halfhearted actions. Clinton had found political redemption by being cautious, not courageous, thinking small, not big. He was no Franklin Roosevelt, perceiving the Nazi threat before most Americans did; he was no Harry Truman or Ronald Reagan, understanding how to contain the cancer of Soviet communism. Moreover, Clinton was distracted when the terrorist threat appeared strongest. Al Qaeda's August 7, 1998, assaults against America's embassies in Kenya and Tanzania coincided with the height of the Lewinsky psychodrama, when the president of the United States testified before the independent counsel and publicly confessed committing adultery. The terrorists bombed the USS *Cole* on October 12, 2000, just weeks before Americans elected Clinton's successor.

Despite these distractions, Clinton's limited maneuverability reflected his malleability, not his political fallibility. Clinton and his national security aides insisted that during the August 1998 crises the president ordered everyone "to do the right thing," regardless of politics. And Clinton authorized missile strikes against bin Laden. But the actions were limited, only symbolic. The missile strikes mostly amounted to one attack on a factory possibly connected to bin Laden's operation and one mistimed missile strike on an Al Qaeda camp. Other opportunities vanished, or were not developed. Bureaucratic prudence trumped operational daring.

To declare all-out war on Al Qaeda—and on the terrorists' Taliban hosts—would have been justified after Osama bin Laden declared war against the United States and the West, let alone after the actual attacks. Subsequent reports showed that Clinton and other world leaders had satellite maps of the terrorist training camps in Afghanistan. But such an action would have required a steely determination to lead the public where it did not yet realize it needed to go and to defy an international community lulled by the status quo. Reflecting public opinion at the time, there was more public outrage, and more concerted international action, when the Taliban defaced an ancient stone Buddha than when these renegade leaders of Afghanistan hosted terrorists who killed Americans and other innocents.

Clinton insists that he remained concerned about targeting Al Qaeda and conveyed that urgency to his successor. When questioned about this, President George W. Bush vaguely remembered a mention, but recalled Clinton's greater emphasis on North Korea and the Israeli–Palestinian peace process. The Bush administration did not take the Clinton administration's warnings seriously enough. Unfortunately, tensions between the arriving Republicans and the departing Democrats precluded a Cold War–style bipartisan cooperation.

When CIA Director George Tenet heard about the World Trade Center attack while breakfasting on the morning of September 11, 2001, he immediately wondered if it had "anything to do with this guy taking pilot training," meaning Zacaria Moussaoui, the "twentieth hijacker." A Clinton holdover, Tenet claims he appreciated how dangerous Osama bin Laden was, but could not mobilize either of his bosses, Bill Clinton or George Bush.

Conservative ideologues root Clinton's inability to respond to Al Qaeda effectively in his 1960s-style skepticism about the defense establishment. There was a culture clash between the crew-cut, buttoned-down national security types and the question authority, let-it-all-hang-out Clintonites. Yet although George W. Bush and his people were more culturally in sync with the military, they were no more vigilant before 9/11. The failure to appreciate the threat ran deeper than culture clashes in the White House. Leaders refused to push the American public and the international community where both needed to be to understand and fight the Islamist terrorist threat clearly.

America's ineffectual response to the bin Laden threat epitomizes the limits of Clinton's leadership. Clinton frequently was smart enough to grasp the challenges of terrorism, racism, and other issues. He was farseeing enough to generate creative solutions. But his self-inflicted political wounds, addiction to high favorability ratings, and unwillingness to defy conventional wisdom prevented him from solving America's knottiest problems. Clinton never figured out how to win public approval by confronting sacred cows and shaping public opinion. That the historical, political, and popular conditions of the 1990s did not encourage such bold leadership is only a partial excuse. Real leaders change conditions, especially in response to real threats.

CLINTON ENDED his presidency with tremendous potential unfulfilled. His failures to risk, to lead, and to challenge were as debilitating as his lack of personal discipline. Democratic leaders must be responsive to the people, but they cannot be slaves to public opinion or conventional wisdom. Offering moderation with no muscle, Clinton perfected a spineless centrism, a poll-driven posture whose addiction to popularity diminished the presidency's transformational potential. In a pallid but fitting tribute to Bill Clinton's leadership, the 2000 campaign to succeed him lacked passion. Both George W. Bush and Al Gore learned from Bill Clinton to blur distinctions, to cross wires.

Clinton triangulated and postured, fighting powerful cultural and social forces with political Band-Aids. Thus, America's failing, dysfunctional schools were "cured" by championing school uniforms; the health care crisis, with 20 million uninsured, prompted a patients' bill of rights; and America's moral degeneration, stoked by family breakdown, inspired the V-chip. This approach abhorred big government solutions with gargantuan, ponderous bureaucracies clumsily trying to tackle a social problem, but the cascade of micro-responses would keep government as big and active and intrusive as ever. This approach also suited reporters, who pursued stories about V-chips and school uniforms, interviewing kids and experts, showing where these specific, vivid programs worked and how they came up short.

This feel-good politics, this have-your-cake-and-eat-it-too leadership, applied cheap, kitschy cosmetics to cover up complex problems. All the president's talk about values distracted Americans from important conversations and actions about the spreading cultural pathologies and serious international threats. A new day of "Big Government Lite" seemed to be dawning, thanks to the compelling, conflicted, seductive celebrity-in-chief. Fixing the schools, encouraging good parenting, and improving the moral climate are more educational concerns than presidential agenda items; the commander-in-chief is not running the local school board. To the extent that these issues do become national, they require more sweeping responses.

Statesmanship entails hard choices. Unfortunately, American politics in the Clinton era valued the quick emotional fix over the enduring but difficult solution. George W. Bush's subsequent tumultuous reign would make many Americans nostalgic for the seemingly simpler days of Bill Clinton. But American democracy is no better served by an illusionist than by a pugilist. Neither model is what the people should want—or what the country desperately needs.

12

GEORGE W. BUSH

Imprisoned by Conviction?

BILL CLINTON DEMONSTRATED the perils of moderation without muscle. His successor, George W. Bush, illustrated the dangers of muscle without moderation. Bush is a conviction politician. His critics find him far too imprisoned by these convictions, which they abhor. "You may not agree with me, but you know where I stand," Bush often said, defiantly.

Americans believe they want a principled politician for president. The defining American political legend of George Washington confessing to chopping down the cherry tree immortalizes his stubborn integrity. Consecrating Abraham Lincoln as a martyr for the antislavery cause celebrates his principled rigidity, not his political agility. Hollywood's heroic politicians stand on principle, be they Jimmy Stewart filibustering the Senate in 1939's *Mr. Smith Goes to Washington* or President Josiah "Jed" Bartlet on NBC's *The West Wing* charming viewers with his righteousness.

Although moderation without conviction is futile, conviction without moderation can be dangerous, damaging the body politic. Popular politics requires compromise; democracy needs a broad, inviting center with maximum public investment. Conviction politicians risk being imprisoned by ideology, handcuffed to the world they wish to see rather than adjusting to the world that is.

George W. Bush's administration foundered repeatedly on the shoals of his rigidity. Sticking to his partisan principles yielded public approval ratings of 26 percent. Bill Clinton was a first-class apologizer, charming the world as he bit his lip and repented for cavorting with Monica Lewinsky or not stopping the Rwanda genocide. By contrast, Bush was famously inflexible, uncurious, and unapologetic. Even when it would have been politically expedient to do so, he acknowledged no doubts and reconsidered no decisions. Bush failed to improvise effectively amid domestic disaster in New Orleans and the overseas war in Iraq. His policies and politics alienated millions, further polarizing the American public.

Great leadership requires good judgment. Shrewd leaders know that if they are half-a-step ahead of their constituents, and are headed in the right direction, they will be perceived as geniuses; if they are three giant steps ahead they are scorned as fools. Moreover, success earns credibility and followers' indulgence, whereas failure is not forgiven. The Iraq war's growing body count and confusion undermined Bush's popular standing, highlighting his failure to forge a deep consensus for action before launching the war.

Although America's continuing war in Iraq makes it premature to pronounce Bush's war policy a success or failure, by 2008 the domestic political fallout from his my-way-or-the-highway governing style could be assessed. Bush frittered away the broad support he received after the September 11, 2001, terrorist attacks. He won reelection in 2004 by mobilizing true believers. He consistently shunned doubters, let alone critics.

Especially given the mess in Iraq, Bush's ends did not justify his means. Like Richard Nixon, George W. Bush depleted too much of the good faith oxygen a democratic ecosystem needs. His contentious second term demonstrated that democracies need leaders seeking broad support, especially for controversial policies.

GEORGE W. BUSH ran for president in 2000 as a moderate who worried conservatives. The fifty-four-year-old's thin political resumé included losing a congressional race and helping his father in the White House before catapulting to two terms as Texas governor. Bush vowed to focus on domestic policy. As a Texan, his interest beyond America's borders seemed limited to Mexico. He advised extreme caution when contemplating involvement overseas. "When America uses force in the world," Bush proclaimed at the 2000 Republican Convention, "the cause must be just, the goal must be clear, and the victory must be overwhelming."

Calling himself a "compassionate conservative," Bush vowed to reconcile conservatism with modern America's commitment to social justice and equal opportunity. He and his rival, Al Gore, played to the center during the 2000 presidential campaign. Bush the Republican supported affirmative action, a patient's bill of rights, and distributing all kinds of government goodies. Vice President Al Gore, the Democrat, supported the death penalty, morality crusades to curb Hollywood, and tax cuts. America's reigning ideology now combined 1960s-style middle-class welfarism with 1980s-style moralism, tempered by 1960s-style cultural liberalism and 1980s-style fiscal conservatism.

The relatively calm election campaign ended in an ugly political storm, the extended electoral deadlock. Gore won nearly 51 million popular votes; Bush won nearly 50.5 million. Both needed Florida's 25 electoral votes for an electoral college majority. Bush's margin of 500 votes out of 5.8 million cast in Florida triggered an automatic recount and weeks of strife.

After the Supreme Court pronounced Bush the winner in a five to four vote, Bush promised to "change the tone in Washington, D.C." Repudiating the caricature of America the fractious, and unconsciously echoing George Washington, the president-elect proclaimed, "Together, guided by a spirit of common sense, common courtesy and common goals, we can unite and inspire the American citizens." In a sign of the Constitution's enduring power, most Americans accepted Bush as the legitimate president.

Considering that Bush lost the popular vote by more than half a million ballots, many expected him to exhibit cautious, centrist leadership. Some pundits assumed he would appoint Democrats to prominent cabinet posts, as Abraham Lincoln, Franklin Roosevelt, and John F. Kennedy had done. But acting as if he had a clear mandate from the people, Bush forged a mandate for himself.

No matter how "compassionate" Bush had appeared during the campaign, he emphasized "conservatism" while governing. Bush believed that his father, President George H. W. Bush, had missed winning a second term by failing to articulate that "vision thing" and alienating conservatives. Reading Ronald Reagan's record through the prisms of his father's failure and his own Texas-sized persona, George W. Bush decided that Reagan had won reelection by sticking to his principles. In fact, Reagan had succeeded by having a vision but knowing how to bargain, where to yield, and when to declare victory after compromising.

Bush also defined himself as a strong leader, in contrast to Bill Clinton and Al Gore. The new president acknowledged his predecessor's "talents." But, Bush asked, "in the end, to what end? So much promise, to no great purpose." Mocking the contemplative Gore as cowardly, Bush disdained moderation as "the politics of the roadblock, the philosophy of the stop sign." Bush had roused the Republican convention with repeated cries, "They had their chance. They have not led. We will."

Inspired by this false idea of how the popular and successful Reagan had operated, the new president governed as a conservative activist. But conservatives' persistent complaints throughout the 1980s testified to Reagan's actual centrism. Most conservatives' delight with Bush suggested how ideological and polarizing he would be.

Learning from Franklin Roosevelt and Reagan to start strong, Bush began with tax cut legislation, a popular gambit in a Reaganized America. He proposed a $1.6 trillion tax cut over ten years. The Democrats' $1.2 trillion counterproposal conceded the victory to the president. As with Reagan's economic proposals in 1981, the debate centered on how much, not why.

Unlike Reagan, George W. Bush advanced the conservative social agenda along with the libertarian economic vision. While cutting taxes and constructing a more conservative cabinet, Bush proposed eliminating estate taxes, what conservatives called the "death tax." Bush's "Faith-based Initiative" mobilized churches to tackle social problems—and terrified liberals by blurring the line between church and state. He rejected the Kyoto protocols to reduce greenhouse gas emissions, fearing that they would unfairly burden America's economy—and terrified environmentalists that he would poison the planet. He spoke about the "sanctity of life"—and terrified pro-choice advocates that he would outlaw abortion.

Bush brought a crisp, corporate feel to the White House, demanding discipline, punctuality, clean living, and clean language. But if the West Wing felt like a Boy Scout convention, filled with earnest, sober, well-dressed white-bread types, the president himself remained a frat boy. Bush's mischievous streak, his promiscuous dubbing of colleagues with nicknames, his lopsided grin, and his loping walk telegraphed a mix of aristocratic entitlement and devil-may-care insouciance that infuriated most Democrats.

Bush's chief strategist, Karl Rove, reinforced Bush's instinct to veer right. Anticipating the 2004 elections, the political consultant, often touted as Bush's "brain," targeted three to four million culturally conservative evangelicals who had stayed home and not voted in 2000. Rove was a history buff lacking the humanities student's math-phobia. His arithmetical mind, hardened by partisan warfare, sought the winning margin, no matter how narrow. One Democratic senator proposed minor changes to make Bush's tax cuts less favorable to the wealthy and more palatable to the majority of the Senate. The senator promised that with those changes, "I guarantee you'll get seventy votes out of the Senate." Rove replied, "We don't want seventy votes. We want fifty-one." The senator, who was from a red state, voted for the bill anyway. But resentment lingered, and such anecdotes circulated in Washington.

Bush critics attributed to Rove supposedly unprecedented power, as if consultants had not manipulated public opinion for decades. The president deputized Rove to do his political dirty work. Like Reagan, Bush did not mind being "misunderestimated," as the Yale College and Harvard Business School graduate once said. But as Rove's legend grew, Bush bristled. By 2004, First Lady Laura Bush would snap that Rove was "very happy to have his role overstated."

Americans—and reporters—like affirmative leadership. Initially, Bush's rectitude and certitude contrasted nicely with Bill Clinton's personal and political sloppiness. Reporters were surprisingly kind to him. In 2000, an inexperienced, untested son of a president had surprised even many Republicans with the millions of dollars he raised and millions of votes he won so easily. At the time, George W. Bush often had a deer-in-the-headlights look when the cameras rolled. His words would float around, unmoored to conventional rules of diction and sometimes flying in the face of facts or logic. Aides cringed, shocked at the contrast between their relaxed and resolute boss and the unappealing facsimile they saw on TV. Ensconced in the White House, day by day Bush worked on his image until he appeared more presidential, even on television.

Bush's first one hundred days in office boosted his popularity. "The doubts about Bush's legitimacy are gone now; even his most zealous Democratic critics in Congress acknowledge that," the Los Angeles Times reported. Princeton University's presidential expert, Fred Greenstein, marveled that if Bush continued being so effective, historians would pronounce him "a Reagan without the rhetoric," or a Dwight Eisenhower who surpassed low popular expectations.

The initial surge of support was illusory. Seeking minimal majorities, riling the base, ignoring opponents' rising fury, and refusing to admit mistakes, Bush inevitably overreached. Even as reporters were editing their profiles on Bush's surprising start, he was losing his grip on Congress. Bush's domestic push faltered after he enacted the tax cuts, paralleling the Reagan revolution's success then slowdown in 1981.

Bush's governing approach was too muscular, given his political frailties. House Republicans lost two seats in the 2000 congressional elections, reducing their majority. Senate Republicans lost four seats, leaving the upper chamber evenly split. Vice President Dick Cheney's tie-breaking vote gave Republicans control there. In May 2001, when Senate Republicans agreed to cut $305 billion in education funds, Vermont Senator James Jeffords deserted the party his ancestors helped found in the 1850s. Bush aides underestimated the power of one patrician senator with a safe seat in a state that prized independence. They tried bullying him, including removing him from the guest list for a White House reception honoring a Vermonter as teacher of the year. Jeffords charged the president with abandoning "moderation, tolerance, fiscal responsibility."

Characteristically, Bush dismissed the criticism. Jeffords graciously waited to defect until the tax cuts had passed. The Republicans then lost the Senate majority. The loss embarrassed the president and limited Republicans' ability to muscle through legislation. "I think the president is going to have to come back to the center, where he campaigned, and away from the right, where he governed," the moderate Democratic vice presidential nominee and Connecticut Senator, Joseph I. Lieberman, observed.

During the summer of 2001, the economy soured. The unemployment rate rose. The budget deficit soared, because Bush increased funds for education, Medicare, and other social needs despite cutting taxes. Democrats predicted Bush would break a campaign promise by balancing the budget with the Social Security surplus. The president's month-long vacation in August 2001 at his Crawford, Texas, ranch reminded reporters of Ronald Reagan's lazy days at his California ranch. Little did anyone realize just how negligent this lassitude would appear soon after Bush returned to the White House.

ON SEPTEMBER 11, 2001, when terrorists murdered nearly three thousand Americans, America's post–Cold War sense of security crumbled. But the tragedy reintroduced an intimacy, a shared vulnerability, to the country. The rescuers' nobility, the victims' biographies, etched into the country's collective soul, helped reaffirm and redefine America's national identity. A great leader could have built on the tragedy to forge a new, constructive American consensus.

On September 14, 2001, after the most devastating terrorist attack in American history, George W. Bush reassured the nation—at least initially—with his warm embrace of the rescue workers at the World Trade Center and his seemingly clear vision. (The White House/Getty Images)

Initially, the president seemed as unnerved as everyone else in the country. Bush steadied himself quickly and admirably. His poignant visit to the World Trade Center ruins, when he draped his arm over a rescue worker's shoulder while addressing others through a megaphone, telegraphed a humanity, a physicality, that reassured Americans. "Great harm has been done to us," Bush told Congress. "And in our grief and anger we have found our mission and our moment." Bush was describing his people and his presidency.

Within days, his headstrong, optimistic, cowboy patriotism made Bush seem the right man for the job. His Texas swagger reassured most Americans at a time when dithering would have been demoralizing. His restrained statesmanship probably saved Arab Americans from acts of mass revenge. Bush boasted to Karl Rove, "My job is not to worry about the political consequences, and I don't," even as he peeked at polls. Politically, Bush had no worries: his popularity rating soon rose to 90 percent.

Clear-eyed and sure-footed, Bush pursued the Islamist terrorists. By mid-December 2001, the military had disrupted Al Qaeda and deposed Afghanistan's Taliban leaders. The Treasury choked off the flow of money to the terrorists, one of many initiatives Bush, and before him Clinton, should have implemented long before September 11. America's invasion of Afghanistan was justified, effective, and courageous, despite warnings about the Soviet Union's failure in Afghanistan in the 1980s. Impatient, pessimistic reporters pronounced America caught in a "quagmire," just days before the Taliban leaders fled.

With America reeling, looking for leadership, Bush became a bipartisan hero, albeit momentarily. Even his toughest opponents acknowledged his surprising strengths. In late October, after the Afghanistan invasion, fourteen of fifteen Al Gore supporters the *New York Times* interviewed contrasted Gore's tendency to "micromanage" and get mired in complexity with Bush's clarity of thought, action, and expression. In January 2002, the *Los Angeles Times* proclaimed, BUSH RECORD LAUDED BY FORMER CLINTON AIDES, as Democrats praised Bush's "dream team" of Colin Powell, Donald Rumsfeld, Condoleezza Rice, and Dick Cheney. "The Bush administration has done a very good job up to now in Afghanistan," Bill Clinton's Secretary of State, Madeline Albright, acknowledged.

The president had found America's center, not via Clintonesque triangulation but through bold leadership. As 2002 began, George W. Bush appeared popular and effective, earning praise for his "realism," the foreign policy establishment's highest compliment. His initial success in Afghanistan was impressive. Bush pulled off the paradox epitomized by his 2002 State of the Union introduction: "Our nation is at war, our economy is in recession and the civilized world faces unprecedented dangers. Yet the state of our union has never been stronger." "I couldn't tell if the speech was given by a Republican or a Democrat. It was a very centrist speech," an impressed Diane Feinstein, California's often partisan Democratic senator, gushed.

Domestically, the president's State of the Union address celebrated a major bipartisan achievement, the No Child Left Behind Act. This "cornerstone" of Bush's compassionate conservatism created national benchmarks for student progress. Bush governed within the same post–Great Society "Third Way" consensus that forced Ronald Reagan to maintain the welfare state and stopped Bill Clinton from expanding it. The president hailed an unlikely ally, saying, "some of the folks in Crawford Coffee Shop will be amazed to hear me say that I like Ted Kennedy." But, he chuckled, "If you have a legislative battle, you want him on your side, you don't want him against you." Bush preached, "It is more important to focus on our children than political parties in the country." In November 2003, a similar bipartisan spirit enabled Congress to pass the Medicare modernization bill.

That year Bush launched his most impressive bipartisanship achievement, the President's Emergency Plan for AIDS Relief, known as Pepfar. Within five years, Congress had allocated more than $19 billion to help those suffering from AIDS worldwide. More than 1.4 million people received lifesaving drugs, up from 50,000 before the initiative began, and more than 6.7 million people received other forms of care.

The 2002 congressional midterm elections solidified Bush's power. Incumbents' parties only gained seats at midterm three times in the twentieth century. In 2002, the Republicans gained eight House seats and two Senate seats, retaking the upper chamber.

George Bush seemed to have found the American center, but he had not constructed it. His muscular leadership formula worked initially because results like toppling the Taliban and sending Al Qaeda operatives scurrying into caves vindicated it. But Bush did not realize how much of his support was on loan, contingent on continuing success. He failed to create enough insulation in case of failure. Meanwhile, his steamroller style began alienating his newfound Democratic allies.

GEORGE BUSH'S aggressive strategy was a high-wire act with no safety net. When Franklin Roosevelt led America during World War II, "Dr. New Deal's" perceived successes firmed up "Dr. Win the War's" political standing. Even so, Roosevelt cultivated public opinion, understanding from Abraham Lincoln's experiences the challenge of keeping a democracy on a war footing long enough to win. George Bush lacked Roosevelt's record, as well as his political sensitivity.

Bush did not seem to understand where Americans stood, and did not seem to care. His foreign policy constantly risked implosion, buckling under the weight of his brawny rhetoric. Targeting Al Qaeda and its host regime was the easy part of America's war on terrorism. Still, even in Afghanistan, fighting dragged on, as America became mired in what candidate Bush had derided as "nation building" when Bill Clinton did it in Haiti, Somalia, and the Balkans. Osama bin Laden and too many of his henchmen remained alive. Bush did not confront the Saudis, who bankrolled and rationalized the terrorism. His posturing against the Syrians and the Iranians often seemed ineffectual. It was not clear how effective his efforts to uproot the homegrown Islamist terrorist network were. At the same time, civil libertarians began cataloguing governmental infringements of privacy and civil liberty, which generated indignant headlines and undermined America's moral standing in the world.

Bush's greatest achievement was a negative one. Every quiet month signified a grand accomplishment, defying post–9/11 predictions of a terrorist epidemic against America. But it was difficult to prove why no repeat attacks had occurred by 2008, and more difficult to turn the absence of a tragedy into real political capital.

Bush failed to build a new American consensus based on the national solidarity resulting from 9/11. Continuing the Reagan-Clinton commitment to "happy talk," Bush wooed Americans with more tax cuts rather than challenging them to make sacrifices. Many Americans reconsidered their values after September 11. There had to be more to life than working and shopping. There had to be more to combating terrorism than returning to the malls and paying lower taxes. Franklin D. Roosevelt understood the importance of an active home front. Theodore Roosevelt, John Kennedy, and Ronald Reagan appreciated the power of inspiring national visions. Bush's elusive hopes about exporting democracy to the Middle East failed to rouse Americans, especially as violence escalated in Iraq and Gaza despite democratic elections.

The corporate scandals that hit in late 2001 and 2002 compounded Bush's failure to forge a new altruism. Since the 1990s or even earlier, the brigands of Enron, the gluttons of Tyco, had been living lavishly by ransacking their own companies, robbing their own stockholders. In November 2001, the value of Enron stock plummeted from $90 per share to practically nothing, as a massive shell game unraveled. A few months later, the Tyco conglomerate's leading executives were accused—and eventually convicted—of stealing $150 million from company coffers.

The high-tech economy sent economic indicators soaring while leaving too many people behind. The postwar manufacturing-based economy had spread wealth more equitably. Within corporations, pressure to survive demanded cost-cutting and corner-cutting, which fueled mass layoffs and widespread cheating.

A culture of expendability fed a culture of expedience, with many looking out for themselves rather than the corporate or common good.

Increasingly workers earned only a fraction of what their CEOs did. The terrorism issue protected Bush from the scandals' political fallout, but the diminished social capital and national goodwill further darkened the national mood.

George Bush's failure to forge a broad, lasting base of support during his first two years in office hobbled his efforts to justify the invasion of Iraq to the American people in 2003. Going to war, or not, is the most profound choice a president can make. The decisions before September 11 by both Bill Clinton and George W. Bush not to pursue Al Qaeda more aggressively were as fateful as many a presidential directive to begin combat.

Democracies demand a thoughtful, thorough decision-making process before launching a war. This became especially true in post-Vietnam America. Empowered by the media, skeptical of authority, and traumatized by the futile sacrifices in Indochina, Americans were more critical of military moves and demanded quick results.

Bush Junior ignored his father's example, and he paid the price. President George H. W. Bush's worldwide consultations, culminating in the 1991 Persian Gulf War, were excruciating, but secured international and national backing for a force to push Iraq out of Kuwait. Bill Clinton waited for years—and sustained much criticism for his dithering—before launching the 1999 NATO bombing campaign to dislodge Serbian troops from Kosovo. George W. Bush lacked his father's diplomatic deftness or his predecessor's patience. The younger Bush seemed too eager to take on Iraq to nurture the necessary alliances at home and abroad.

With no new consensus beyond agreement that America's professional military should hunt terrorists, building a consensus for a war that did not seem absolutely necessary was difficult. September 11 made officials more fearful of the damage rogue regimes could cause. In his 2002 State of the Union address, Bush labeled Iraq, Iran, and North Korea "an axis of evil," threatening world peace. Officials asserted a new "right of preventive, or peremptory, self-defense." Bush and his team targeted Iraq first because Americans already viewed Saddam Hussein as dangerous. Saddam's Iraq had attacked both Iran and Kuwait. Saddam struggled against the United States following the Gulf War. The Clinton administration had passed bipartisan legislation demanding regime change in Iraq. And Saddam had spent two decades seeking nuclear, chemical, and biological weapons. "We don't want the smoking gun to be a mushroom cloud," National Security Adviser Condoleezza Rice warned on CNN.

Bush shrewdly requested a congressional resolution authorizing a war in Iraq. "In the wake of September 11, who among us can say with any certainty to anybody that the weapons might not be used against our troops or against allies in the region?" asked Senator John Kerry, the Massachusetts Democrat. Guarding her husband's legacy, her national security credentials, and her standing as a moderate, Senator Hillary Clinton of New York called Bush's strategy "a continuation of, frankly, a bipartisan policy." She explained that Americans had to "recognize . . . we are in a new set of circumstances" demanding new "plans and strategies." Even some opponents of the war assumed Saddam Hussein had weapons of mass destruction and warned he would use them if attacked.

Amid the debate, it became clear that September 11 had changed America's president. While leading America into war, George Bush found a voice and a vision. Though no Winston Churchill, he looked squarely into the camera, speaking in crisp, clear sentences. He now concentrated on foreign policy. This leader whose mandate seemed so fragile, who seemed destined to be a caretaker president, was gambling his presidency, his nation's security, and the world's stability, on a "trust me" war, an invasion whose legitimacy rested on the faith Americans have in their president.

Distancing himself from his father, Bush continued to rely on a romanticized image of Ronald Reagan to define his presidency. Bush imagined Reagan as more headstrong than he actually had been. Reagan "didn't say, 'Well, Mr. Gorbachev, would you take the top three bricks off the wall?'" Bush said in a May 2002 interview about Reagan's legacy. "He said, tear it all down." Actually, although Reagan's rhetoric was sweeping, his actions were more circumspect. Reagan did not knock down the Berlin Wall, and he negotiated with Gorbachev for two years before making his dramatic pronouncement.

The debate about going to war, publicly and in Congress, was stunningly superficial. The "peaceniks" mocked Bush's IQ; a Canadian official called Bush a "moron." Antiwar protesters labeled "Bushitler" as the villain and Saddam as the victim.

In response, the administration offered definitive interpretations of murky evidence suggesting that Saddam possessed possible weapons of mass destruction or was tied to Al Qaeda. Bureaucratic trench warfare resulted in distorted intelligence assessments that sold the war rather than assessing the war's rationale. Prowar advocates often overstated Iraqis' willingness to embrace Western-style democracy.

To convince a skeptical public and reluctant allies and to counter the many experts warning against getting bogged down in Iraq, the administration dispatched its most credible spokesman, Secretary of State Colin Powell, to the UN Security Council in February 2003. Powell was a legendary African American soldier, whose ascent to power reflected America' great progress and his own formidable bureaucratic skills. A *Washington Post* editorial deemed the evidence Powell presented of weapons development, Al Qaeda collaboration, and Iraqi attempts to evade weapons' inspections, "irrefutable." Even so, before the invasion in March 2003, American support for the war—contingent on UN approval—hovered at 60 percent.

Rarely in this age of poll-driven politics had an American leader defied so much of the conventional wisdom, dismissing so many experts so boldly and calmly. Bush did not falter during the tense build-up to the war. He also did not adjust, learn, mollify, or compromise. Even Franklin Roosevelt in 1940 and 1941 was less bold than Bush was in 2003. Roosevelt eased Americans toward entering World War II through half-steps such as the Lend-Lease program, and only achieved clarity after Pearl Harbor, when the Japanese attacked.

Americans were not prepared for the Bush doctrine of preemption, with its necessary ambiguities. Powell warned that the more Iraq appeared to be a war of choice, the less patience Americans would have for it. Powell believed in deploying America's military only with clear, limited objectives, no alternatives, and an overwhelming force all but guaranteeing victory. Many Bush staffers dismissed the Powell doctrine as too hesitant and unprincipled. Powell's post-Vietnam insight recognized that in an age of instant media, presidents lack the luxury of time during a war.

The American mission in Iraq confirmed the prescience of the Powell doctrine, becoming a cautionary tale against outdistancing the American mainstream, especially during wartime. Iraq's slide into sectarian chaos, with Americans caught in the middle, brought the Bush presidency to the brink of failure. Justifying the war based on eliminating weapons of mass destruction (WMD) that remain undiscovered—or may never have existed—kept Americans debating the premise behind the war. Secretary of Defense Donald Rumsfeld's insistence on a lean, agile army rather than an overwhelming force further strained the country's patience. Numerous international protests emboldened the war's critics at home, who feared for America's international credibility and worried about America's soul after the Abu Ghraib torture scandal of 2003 was uncovered in 2004. Bush himself, however, seemed unfazed by the rancorous criticism or the growing debacle.

GEORGE W. BUSH launched the Iraq war in March 2003, a year and a half before Americans would be asked to decide whether to reelect him. From one perspective, Bush's move into Iraq was heroic, historic. Had stability followed after America overthrew Saddam Hussein, historians would hail Bush as courageous, visionary. But in a democracy, the riskier the step, the faster and clearer the success must be. Bush gambled on that kind of clean success guaranteeing his reelection. The growing chaos in the Persian Gulf throughout 2004 made Bush's reelection effort much harder than he or Karl Rove expected.

The Iraq war came to define Bush's presidency, and exemplified his stubbornness. Bush would run for reelection and be judged by history based on the war's outcome. With Iraq growing as an albatross around his neck, and in keeping with his now well-defined political persona, Bush shifted from his big tent, compassionate conservatism in 2000 to run an unapologetic, red-meat campaign seeking to mobilize his core red-state supporters.

The Bush campaign built on the popular political paradigm, the red state, blue state dichotomy. In the 1990s, network television electoral maps began charting states that voted Republican in red and states going Democratic in blue. The paradigm became familiar during the Bush–Gore post-election purgatory in 2000. The red–blue dichotomy offered a shorthand overstating a growing political polarization. Strategists and journalists pitted urban, cosmopolitan, secular, liberal regions voting Democratic against rural, provincial, religious, conservative areas voting Republican.

Considering how involved the Iraq mission proved to be, Americans demonstrated remarkable patience. The 9/11 trauma kept many Americans loyal to the president and the war effort. Throughout the 2004 campaign, many antiwar critics were frustrated by their failure to convince millions to abandon the president. Mainstream Democrats themselves were cautious. "I don't think any United States senator is going to abandon our troops and recklessly leave Iraq to whatever follows as a result of simply cutting and running," Senator John Kerry said in September 2003. A year later, as the Democratic presidential nominee, Kerry honorably refused to renounce his initial support for the war. Instead, Kerry attacked Bush's execution of the war.

Both conservatives and liberals claimed their opponents' attack machine dominated the airwaves. Conservatives accused the mainstream media of undermining the Bush administration; liberals complained that the mainstream media deferred to the commander-in-chief, resulting in a disastrous war and massive violations of civil liberties. Somehow, partisans rarely detected a bias in their own favor.

Bloggers hoped to revolutionize politics, to undermine the media-party monopoly, mount insurgent candidacies, and, as one progressive study dreamed, build "communities of activists and generate new political activity online." But even as new business and cultural models emerged on the more collaborative Web 2.0 of Wikipedia, YouTube, and myspace.com, the political blogosphere failed to deliver. The blogs did not reverse "fifty years of political cynicism in one glorious explosion of civic re-engagement," as the Internet guru Joe Trippi hoped. Instead, political blogs mostly served as partisan hit squads. From the left, the financier George Soros pumped $15 million into Moveon.org and other blogs to oppose Bush, whom he compared to the Nazis and the Soviets. From the right, the trial-by-blogging launched against Democratic nominee Senator John Kerry transformed his experiences on a Swift boat in Vietnam from a badge of honor into a mark of shame.

The blogs were the Internet era's shrill speakers' corners. Blogs prized short, punchy, even mean, interactions. Over 25 million Americans read blogs daily. Eighty percent of mainstream media reporters monitored them. Ironically, blogs became incubators of pungent political commentary, reinforcing the red–blue paradigm. Internet spats spilled over into the mainstream media, generating "buzz" and frequently upstaging traditional journalists. Journalists usually looked elsewhere for more politically constructive voices. However, bloggers were effective in countering the conventional wisdom and detecting frauds. Bloggers discovered veteran CBS News anchor Dan Rather's reliance on apparently forged documents in 2004 used to question George W. Bush's National Guard service. In perhaps the bloggers' breakthrough moment, Rather resigned.

Supporting a controversial and bullheaded president, Republicans also played to their base. Bush's pollster Matthew Dowd preached that the country's growing polarization minimized the number of independent swing voters, transforming the campaign into one of mobilizing believers, not persuading doubters. Tacking right, the campaign focused on "wedge issues" to motivate the Christian evangelical believers, who constituted approximately 40 percent of the Republican Party. Republicans charged that Democrats would encourage gay marriages, high taxes, mass abortions, and retreating from Iraq and Afghanistan. They painted John Kerry of Massachusetts as an effete, flip-flopping, France-loving, big government, sixties-addled, elitist city-slicker, more NASDAQ than NASCAR, more wind-surfer than churchgoer, a dissident not a patriot.

By contrast, Bush played the Texas Ranger. At the Republican National Convention, Bush declared that when it came to fighting terrorism, "you know where I stand." He recalled workers in hard hats shouting at him "Whatever it takes," when he visited the Twin Towers' ruins. The president vowed, "I will never relent in defending America, whatever it takes." Balancing self-promotion with self-deprecation, Bush did acknowledge, "Some folks look at me and see a certain swagger, which in Texas is called 'walking.'"

Bush's swagger became a campaign issue. The Democrats mocked Bush's campaign promise to be a "uniter not a divider," listing it as the first of "Bush's Broken Promises." Chuck Hagel, a Republican senator, feared the lack of bipartisan cooperation in Congress and across the country posed a greater threat to the union than terrorism.

Despite the mounting casualties and intractable problems in Iraq, during a time of violence and uncertainty many Americans preferred a muscular leader to a moderate. Bush's unapologetic, surprisingly passionate campaign earned grudging admiration, even from liberal sources. The *New York Times* described Bush as a "street-smart, intuitive politician" and "a president of consequence." The Republican assault on Kerry convinced just enough voters that it was better to stick with a tough guy type who could be too intimidating than to turn to a peacenik who could be too accommodating.

Bush's lurch rightward worked, just barely. The Dowd-Rove efforts mobilized Republicans on election day in equal numbers to Democrats, an impressive historic first considering that there were many more Democrats registered. The 2004 election was close, although not as close as 2000. Bush only attracted 3 million more votes than Kerry nationwide, out of 121 million votes cast. This time, Bush won Florida clearly. This election pivoted on securing Ohio's twenty electoral votes, which Bush won with a thin 118,000 vote margin out of 4.5 million cast.

Unlike his hero Ronald Reagan in 1984, Bush worked hard to solidify Republican congressional strength and leave the Republican Party "stronger, broader and better." Republicans gained only two House seats but four Senate seats. The electoral map of a blue Northeast and Pacific Coast and a vast red middle and South triggered waves of exaggerated discussion about a polarized America, divided into blue Democratic cosmopolitans and red Republican traditionalists.

Bush's strategy appalled Republican moderates such as his former Environmental Protection Agency Administrator Christine Todd Whitman. Conservatives risked alienating moderates by dismissing them as RINOs, Republicans In Name Only. How is it possible to govern maturely, she wondered, "when you have people that think *SpongeBob SquarePants* is a bigger threat to the future of this country than tax reform?" The president must lead all the people and reach out to the center, Whitman insisted.

Bush's commitment to be tough on terrorism had upstaged his compassionate conservatism. His independence and his zeal, combined with his imperviousness to critics and missteps in Iraq, made him now more a "divider" than a "uniter." Bush entered his second term with a Republican Senate, a Republican House, and a relatively compliant Supreme Court. But he would have to remember that his base strategy had worked only barely; his margin of victory was narrow. Faced with a growing Iraqi crisis and an increasingly restive nation, Bush needed to find the center, win big in Iraq, or risk having his second term follow in the footsteps of the Clinton and Nixon second-term disasters.

GEORGE W. BUSH damaged America's national fabric by failing to lead the country as a whole. "I've got the will of the people at my back," he said as he won reelection. "I'll reach out to everyone who shares our goals." With that kind of attitude, rather than leading Americans back from the brink of the Clinton years, Bush pushed his fellow citizens further away. His my-way-or-the-highway presidency fed fears of an ever-widening chasm in America, as his critics responded in kind.

Traditionally, the end of an election campaign begins a time of national healing. In November 2004, however, many dumbfounded Democrats concluded that anyone who had chosen George W. Bush had to be as "ignorant" or "repellent" as he was. The *New York Times* led the howl of the blue states. The *Times* published historian Garry Wills's lament calling election day, "The Day the Enlightenment Went Out." Wills claimed America's "fundamentalist zeal, . . . religious intolerance, fear of and hatred for modernity" now resembled "the Muslim world, . . . Al Qaeda, . . . Saddam

Hussein's Sunni loyalists." The columnist Maureen Dowd sneered, "W. ran a jihad in America so he can fight one in Iraq."

This Bushophobia of America's "best and brightest" produced dozens of hysterical critiques that further fouled the political atmosphere. By spring 2006, many intellectuals so applauded Kevin Phillips's anti-Bush sentiments in his best seller *American Theocracy* that they overlooked the title's inanity. Calling America a theocracy—despite its secular democratic political, economic, and entertainment systems, enjoying its array of constitutionally protected freedoms—distorted the term. The label –reinforced the trendy, false, destructive comparisons between the Bushies and the Jihadists. One year later, the journalist Joe Conason topped Phillips with his ominous best seller, *It Can Happen Here*.

America's *Crossfire* culture became increasingly shrill. Partisans whipped their followers into an Internet-fed frenzy, libeling opponents and lionizing their own in the unfiltered blogosphere's virtual echo chamber. Al Franken became a Democratic icon—and eventually a U.S. Senate candidate— with hatchet jobs packaged in book form such as *Lies and the Lying Liars Who Tell Them*. He and others declared Bush the worst president ever, a liar, a boob, a fanatic, a warmonger. Republicans proved equally harsh in demonizing Democrats, with screeds such as *Liberalism Is a Mental Disorder* by the aptly named Michael Savage. Bill O'Reilly and D'nesh D'Souza accused liberals of aiding Osama bin Laden.

Both parties agreed about the sorry state of bipartisan relations—and blamed each other. Democrats blamed President Bush, Karl Rove, Vice President Dick Cheney, the "Republican attack machine," and the Christian Right for arousing demagoguery, in a blaze of fights over abortion, gay rights, gun control, and Iraq. Democrats also blamed the administration's unilateralism with the Congress, the administration's strong-arming of the Congress by using recess appointments to seat conservative judges, and Bush's attacks on the Democrats' patriotism. Republicans blamed the Clintons, their manic consultant James Carville, and the media, which conservatives viewed as the liberal attack machine. "Perhaps if conservatives had had total control over every major means of news dissemination for a quarter century, they would have forgotten how to debate, too, and would just call liberals stupid and mean," the right-wing pundit Ann Coulter sneered.

Fox News, launched in October 1996, promised "fair and balanced" reporting to counter the perceived liberal bias. After September 11, Fox cheered America and played politics increasingly more aggressively. Reporters called

Osama bin Laden "a dirtbag," "a monster," overseeing a "web of hate." The channel's patriotic populism, colorful graphics, and assertive conservatism attracted viewers. By January 2002, Fox was "the most watched news channel," relied on by 22 percent of Americans surveyed and reaching 77 million homes during prime time, with surveys showing many self-identified centrists watching, too.

CBS News President Andrew Heyward feared "the Fox effect" would ruin America's "long-standing tradition . . . of middle-of-the-road journalism that is objective and fair." The Fox News revolution, combined with the rise of the blogosphere, catapulted millions of politically aware Americans into a self-reinforcing universe confirming preexisting prejudices. The information revolution's technologies of personalization, from the iPod to TiVo, polarized the nation further. The plethora of technologies, media outlets, and Internet sites allowed individuals to cherry-pick their information sources. Just as during the nineteenth century's dark age of partisan journalism, the American public consumed a steady partisan diet of one-sided information. Americans risked losing common references and a common language.

The unifying pool of communal heroes and villains shrank. Many Americans, uninterested in politics, lived in a virtual world, dominated by celebrity court jesters like Anna Nichole Smith and Paris Hilton. The vocal minority of politically engaged Americans increasingly lived in two, mutually exclusive, competing partisan worlds with contrasting pantheons and enemies' lists.

Both political parties had constructed competing institutional, ideological, and social universes inside the Beltway, especially on Capitol Hill. Republicans had seized congressional power in 1994, vowing to avenge decades of Democratic arrogance. Manipulative gerrymandering created safe minority districts and safe districts for many partisan Republicans and Democrats. With campaigning so expensive, incumbents' advantage in fund-raising further insulated ensconced extremists from moderating electoral pressures. The low cost of jet travel had most members commuting home for half the week, limiting the camaraderie that had led older conservatives like Orrin Hatch to befriend liberals like Ted Kennedy. And aggressive, partisan battles undermined Congress's traditional coalition building. Contrasting legislators' polarization with their constituents' center seeking, one *Washington Post* reporter, Juliet Eilperin, complained of "fight club politics" poisoning an increasingly unrepresentative House of Representatives.

These attacks found traction, and both parties' attack dogs found stardom, in an increasingly nasty culture. America's cultural vulgarities and excesses encouraged political vulgarities and excesses. Thanks to the media, the zealots often carried the day, dominating the airwaves, lobbying fiercely, intimidating opponents, and punishing those who did not back them completely. Moderate politicians often had to seek out the center, or underlying consensus, beyond the din, while risking the wrath of those most engaged with the particular flashpoint issue of the moment.

Ironically, this angry politics resulted from a culture overdosing on pleasure. America's anything goes, orgasmic popular culture overstimulated the hypothalamus, the brain's pleasure center. Psychologists explained that firing up the pleasure centers overrode "aversive" instincts, meaning fear of punishment. America's rowdy, undisciplined culture dissolved traditional inhibitions. Seventy percent of Americans believed people were ruder; public life on the street, in Congress, and on the airwaves had coarsened; and children seemed particularly untamed.

As the United States hit the 300 million population mark in October 2006, Americans were richer, freer, better fed, better educated, and better entertained than ever. Many Americans were also more spoiled, more privileged, angrier, testier, and, unhappier. Although the institutional and cultural forces polarizing the nation preceded Bush—and would outlast him—his heavy-handed political style exacerbated these tensions when Americans desperately needed a healer.

GEORGE W. BUSH'S disastrous second term confirmed many Americans' worst fears. The president's rigidity helped derail his administration. His take-no-prisoners stance with Congress on symbolic social and cultural issues enraged Democrats. The nation's mood soured. Feuding politicians immobilized the Congress. Bush's push to privatize Social Security stalled. His powerful government appeared impotent to help millions as Hurricane Katrina devastated the New Orleans basin. And Iraq descended into civil war. Amid it all, Bush remained insulated from bad news, dismissed critics, resisted change, and never admitted making mistakes. This "conviction politician" appeared imprisoned by his rhetoric and earlier decisions.

On Monday, August 29, 2005, a catastrophic hurricane slammed into New Orleans. The picturesque city's system of levees could not withstand the floodwaters that hit eighteen to twenty-five feet and that seeped through the defenses as well. A disaster of biblical proportions ensued, especially punishing to the poor, who could not flee in private cars. The reported rumors of tens of thousands of dead, massive looting, and gang rapes of refugees gathered in the New Orleans Superdome proved exaggerated. Still, America's twenty-fourth largest city, with a pre-flood population of nearly half a million, became a ghost town, with many neighborhoods abandoned.

The New Orleans disaster was not the president's fault, but he responded slowly and appeared more loyal to his incompetent subordinates than concerned about the suffering Southerners. Legally, the mayor of New Orleans and the governor of Louisiana were primarily responsible for saving their citizens. But in an era of presidential dominance, Bush was blamed for the ineffective government response to the disaster.

The indictment emphasizing "how Bush blew it" resonated because it summed up criticism of Bush in many realms. The budget cuts and shoddy repair work that had weakened the infrastructure in New Orleans impeached Bush's conservative revolution against big government. Mismanagement and cronyism made Bush's stubborn loyalty to subordinates appear foolish. Bush's glib endorsement of his incompetent Federal Emergency Management Agency director, Michael Brown, "Brownie, you're doing a heck of a job," became one of the president's most infamous lines. The days of delay as Bush continued vacationing at his ranch, mugging at photo-ops, made him look insensitive. The federal government's plodding intervention during the first days of compelling misery and constant news coverage made him appear incompetent and insulated from bad news. And the disproportionate suffering of New Orleans' poor and black citizens impugned the entire Reagan-Bush era as an uncaring reign of error.

The New Orleans disaster proved to be a turning point in Americans' attitude toward the war in Iraq. CNN's Anderson Cooper admitted that after Katrina "everything changed." The scale of the debacle within the United States lifted the veil on the problems thousands of miles away and emboldened the press to be more critical.

Bush appeared to be making the same mistakes in Iraq. He seemed unprepared for the scale of resistance there, self-destructively loyal to Secretary of Defense Donald Rumsfeld, insensitive to soldiers' suffering, resistant to the bad news coming in daily, and too rigid to respond effectively to what was happening. Moreover, Bush failed to convince Americans why it was important to remain in Iraq. The never-found WMDs undermined his credibility, and his assertion that a democratic Iraq would spark democratic revolution in the Middle East seemed far-fetched. The more things soured in Iraq, the more Bush seemed insulated from the complexities of the war on the ground.

The headlines about losing New Orleans and losing Iraq overshadowed any Bush successes. When bipartisanship prevailed in the Congress, reporters and voters barely noticed. The Bankruptcy Abuse Prevention and Consumer Protection Act of 2005, the Class Action Bill of 2005, the Pension Protection Act of 2006, and the Adam Walsh Child Protection Act and Safety Act of 2006 combined Bush's compassionate conservatism with Bill Clinton's policy Band-Aids. These half-measures ameliorated inequities, improving the system without overhauling it. As specific responses to particular economic challenges and social problems, they reflected the kind of leader Bush ran to be in 2000 but that history and his personality had prevented him from becoming.

Bush staffers resented media caricatures of their much-maligned boss. They described an engaged, intelligent, and activist president who kept debate in-house rather than on the news. Bush was unapologetic: "I'm not afraid to make decisions, and I hire good people and then listen to them." The president admitted he was "not very analytical," describing himself as "a gut player." "I know who I am. I know what I believe in," Bush said defiantly. "The good thing about democracy, if people like the decisions you make, they'll let you stay. If they don't, they'll send me back to Crawford."

Bush's political theory was more French than American. French presidents enjoyed a relative carte blanche. By contrast, the Constitution's checks and balances moderate America's leader regularly, fueling a vigorous democratic conversation back and forth between elections. The country's political vitality requires statesmen willing to lead from the center rather than partisans rushing ahead, leaving public opinion behind.

AS THE 2006 MIDTERM ELECTIONS loomed, polls showed Bush's disapproval rating hitting 60 percent. Republicans still supported him, but less enthusiastically than before. And his support among moderates and independents had dwindled. Bush refused to waver or concede error. As a result, many of the Republican candidates for the House and Senate in 2006 distanced themselves from the president, although they could not really escape his shadow or the cloud hanging over the corruption-scarred Republican Congress.

Democrats wisely shelved their ideological conflicts and aimed for the center. Congressman Rahm Emanuel, a Bill Clinton protégé, and Senator Chuck Schumer, sought electable candidates. Most Senate winners were moderate, "blue dog" Democrats tacking right. Pennsylvania's Bob Casey was pro-life and anti-gun control. Virginia's James Webb had been Ronald Reagan's undersecretary of the Navy. Missouri's Claire McCaskill defined "Being a Democrat" as "being moderate and truthful and strong."

The star of the 2006 Democratic campaign, Senator Barack Obama, embodied this centrist spirit. Obama's national debut in 2004 electrified the Democratic convention with a charismatic keynote speech urging unity. Two years later, Obama cleverly timed a book tour to coincide with the midterm campaign. This gangly, youthful looking, forty-five-year-old charmed America. Oprah Winfrey, the high priestess of American popular culture, begged him to run for president. His book, *The Audacity of Hope*, identified the "common values and common ideals that we all believe in as Americans." Obama blamed the nation's unproductive polarization on "baby boomer politics." Obama's new generation of leaders promised to heal, building a more idealistic and gentler America with these common building blocks of goodwill and shared dreams. Americans wanted leaders tilling common ground rather than sowing seeds of division.

Another leader of "baby boom" backlash, the political comedian Jon Stewart, born in 1962, attacked both political extremists and the media. Stewart became a particular hero to young Americans—and their primary source of news—by skewering Republican incompetence, Democratic impotence, and the media's passivity. Stewart said his comedy came "from feeling displaced from society because you're in the center. We're the group of fairness, common sense, and moderation." Stewart called "liberals and conservatives . . . two gangs who have intimidated rational, normal thinking beings into not having a voice on television or in the culture."

Stewart's fake news show on Comedy Central, *The Daily Show*, was more educational than inspirational. An Annenberg Center survey found *Daily Show* viewers better informed than peers who avoided late-night comedy news shows. Political scientists said Stewart's 2004 coverage increased young people's voter turnout and boosted John Kerry's candidacy. Yet surveys also showed that Stewart fans lost faith in politicians, reporters, and the system.

In the 2006 midterm elections, many voters rejected Republican legislators to punish George W. Bush for his partisanship and his failures. To a nation still reeling from the shock of September 11, traumatized by the Iraq war, seeking solutions to the Islamist threat, worried about the economy, unnerved by a coarsening culture, craving community in an increasingly multicultural nation, and frustrated with many politicians' shortsightedness, the centrist message resonated. Americans wanted unity. They yearned for some calm and clarity.

In the elections, six Republican senators lost their seats and the Democrats gained thirty House seats as they regained control of both houses of Congress. THE VITAL CENTER PREVAILS, the Democratic Leadership Council post-election press release rejoiced. "America is a pragmatic nation, not a radical one," *Newsweek's* Anna Quindlen lectured President Bush as she branded the election a blow against "overreaching" and in favor of "moderation."

Once again, President Bush seemed poised to return to the center. He fired Donald Rumsfeld after the election. He turned to a bipartisan Iraq Study Group for advice. He spoke about changing the tone in Washington. But once again, Bush veered abruptly right. After much anticipation, the president ignored the Iraq Study Group's advice, relying instead on a new wave of troops called the surge to subdue the Iraqi civil war. And he quickly found himself skirmishing with the Democrats about Attorney General Alberto Gonzales, the growing Bush-generated budget deficit, and the correct strategy for managing the Iraq war. The result, predictably, was greater political tension, lower poll ratings for Bush, and more popular and Democratic doubts about the prospects of winning in Iraq, even as the surge helped subdue violence and trigger progress.

MORE THAN MANY LEADERS, George W. Bush recognized the dangers of Islamist terrorism. Unfortunately, his go-it-alone style failed to convince Americans to remain vigilant as memories of September 11 faded. Even worse, many Democrats were so disgusted by Bush and "his" war that they lost perspective, even making the false comparison so popular in the blogosphere between America's president and America's enemies. "The villains are no longer the terrorists," New York's Democratic Congressman Jerrold Nadler claimed at a news conference protesting the neglect of 9/11 rescue workers in 2007. "The villains live in the White House." The longer the Iraq war dragged on, the more the casualties mounted, the more Democrats underestimated the threat of Islamist terror.

This tepid yet polarized response to extreme Islamism highlighted the risk of excessive partisanship in an age of terror. George W. Bush's rigidity was no more successful than Bill Clinton's inconstancy. But the vicious rhetorical attacks both of them endured raised fears among citizens and commentators that America was becoming ungovernable.

Many worried that it was unreasonable to expect moderation from politicians in such an age of excess. Examining modern American culture's media-fed, garish burlesque, it seemed all too easy to connect the dots between Washington's polarizing crankiness and consumerism's instant gratification, pop culture's anything-goes sensuality, corporate America's predatory selfishness, the blogosphere's angry posturing, and the media's headline-driven hysteria. The early twenty-first century's shoot-from-the-hip, hyper-individualistic environment would have tried the reason-based patience of George Washington and Abraham Lincoln and tested the nation-building skills of Theodore Roosevelt and Franklin Roosevelt.

Yet even in this age of the antihero, the need for great centrist leaders remains. Bill Clinton's political success as "the Good Father" and the appeal of George W. Bush's "compassionate conservatism" pitch reflected a collective yearning for a steadying hand in the White House to bring more ballast to society. After 9/11 many Americans, facing a dangerous world, craved a constructive centrism, a muscular moderation, a president unafraid to lead boldly, who could forge a new American consensus. Americans not only had to find the right leader, they had to restore faith in themselves and in their grand national project.

CONCLUSION

CENTER SEEKING IN THE TWENTY-FIRST CENTURY

Is Political Moderation
Possible in an Age of Excess?

MODERATE LEADERS are made, not born. Even millions who voted for them never expected the gawky, inexperienced Abraham Lincoln to become the graceful bard of American nationalism or the paralyzed playboy Franklin Roosevelt to redefine the American social contract and defeat fascism. One of the modern presidency's keenest students, Bill Clinton, recognized the situational dimension of statesmanship when he complained that the prosperous 1990s deprived him of a Great Depression or a great war to prove himself. Rumors have it that after 9/11 he envied his successor, George W. Bush, who now faced that kind of reputation-making, historic challenge.

Moderation and greatness are not synonymous; moderation is not the only path to successful leadership. But seeking the center has provided the best road map to American presidential success, because Americans on the whole have been a remarkably centered people. As the Founders envisioned, most Americans over the centuries have been too busy enjoying good lives, expanding liberty, and pursuing happiness to embrace extremism.

Effective moderate leadership creates a constructive democratic partnership between a flexible but anchored leader and a cooperative, even if

273

occasionally skeptical, nation. Americans need to appreciate the historical factors that shaped the nation's moderate political tradition and the factors conductive to center seeking today. America's leaders need to learn from their predecessors just how to seek that golden mean as a path to presidential success.

Amid the traumas of September 11, 2001, Americans rediscovered the common values and shared fate that make a nation great. New York, the capital of "blue" America, the symbol of secular decadence to fundamentalists, of foreign chaos to nativists, and of selfishness to radicals, became Everytown, USA. As the nation mourned, Americans rediscovered the many ties uniting them along with the many ideals rooting them and elevating them. In the immediate aftermath of 9/11, often-underappreciated firefighters, police officers, and soldiers became local heroes. The superficial celebrities of Hollywood became altruistic philanthropists, raising money for the victims. Normally invisible neighbors became close friends.

As the tears flowed, blood banks and charitable coffers overflowed; as Americans shared fears, they also forged bonds. Supposedly godless America improvised a universal but sacred ritual of lighting candles, dropping notes, and leaving flowers or mementoes at the sites of the violence or the victims' homes, fire stations, and offices. Supposedly selfish America recorded a surge of voluntarism in a country that already had one of the West's highest percentages of volunteers and per capita giving rates. Supposedly superficial America used the frequently inane vehicle of popular culture to pray together, dream together, and trigger a nationwide conversation about the meaning of life and what the future held. And all those depersonalizing, individuating technologies, from the cell phone to the personal computer, became essential, miraculous couriers, conveying final goodbyes from trapped husbands to wives, informing the doomed passengers on United Airlines 93 of their predicament so they could take control of their fate. Technology helped weave nearly 300 million Americans into a community, not of uniform opinions, but of common concerns and binding morals.

Tragically, the tensions of the Iraq war since 2003 have made many view 9/11 as a symbol of extremism, not centrism. Many mainstream Democrats criticized George W. Bush for hijacking 9/11 into a jingoistic symbol that led to the Iraq debacle, massive violations of civil liberties, and more polarization between "red" and "blue" Americans. Senator Barack Obama, running for president as the saint of centrism, stopped wearing his American flag lapel pin because he claimed the symbol occasionally obscured "true patriotism." Nevertheless, historians should remind Americans of all the good they saw in each other and did for one another when first faced with Osama bin Laden's Islamist evil.

PRESIDENTS HAVE OFTEN defied expectations, for better and worse. Quiet, shy, and cerebral, James Madison would have been voted least likely to start a major political party, especially after so eloquently warning against faction in the *Federalist Papers*. Loud, bombastic, and vain, Theodore Roosevelt would have been voted least likely to mediate labor disputes or to win a Nobel Peace Prize for arbitration skills ending the Russo–Japanese War.

Once in the Oval Office, the unexpected occurs: contingency counts. Presidents make decisions that change the course of history and their historical destinies. John F. Kennedy's decision to quarantine Cuba, not bomb it, may have saved the world. Abraham Lincoln's decision to evolve toward emancipation may have saved the Union. Who knows what might have occurred had Ronald Reagan chosen to spurn Mikhail Gorbachev rather than embrace him? And who knows what would have happened had Bill Clinton pursued Osama bin Laden more vigorously and succeeded in apprehending him, or if George W. Bush had treated Saddam Hussein more benignly?

American presidents enter into office with a strong historical tradition already luring them toward the center. The Madisonian legacy fragments power in the Constitution, forcing the chief executive to find allies in Congress, to avoid crossing the Supreme Court, and to court the American people. The Jeffersonian twist on John Locke's formula of "life, liberty, and property" added the "pursuit of happiness" to America's mission, thus consecrating individual calm over social tumult. The Hamiltonian heritage makes the government a force for nationalism. And the Washingtonian imperative emphasizes reason, tolerance, and diplomacy as essential presidential traits.

The biographical tomes crowding many presidents' bookshelves recount the tales of successful muscular moderates who preceded them. Abraham Lincoln withstood tremendous pressure from abolitionists demanding the immediate emancipation of slaves and appeasers hoping to mollify the slaveholding border states. Theodore Roosevelt used the bully pulpit to be emphatic but not fanatic, subtly distinguishing between leading vigorously and acting like a headstrong dictator. Franklin Roosevelt triggered massive but controlled social transformations, preserving fundamentals while initiating some essential changes. Harry Truman responded to a national emergency with bipartisanship and creativity, overseeing new structures fostering international cooperation amid American national restraint. Under Dwight Eisenhower, the new Cold War consensus became absorbed into American culture, reinforcing American policy on a mass level. Somewhat paradoxically, experience made John Kennedy more flexible in facing the Soviets and more principled in handling civil rights, as he learned that even moderates sometimes need to take strong stands and impose change.

None of these presidents was perfect. Some made serious mistakes. Others could be temperamental or deceitful. But all were nimble enough to improvise while solid enough to preserve their political identities. All also displayed great faith in the American people. They trusted that society functioned, they believed in American ideals, they appreciated America's ability to progress, and they banked on American unity and altruism. In short, they were nationalists, but as American nationalists, they were not just romantic and patriotic, but also idealistic, pragmatic, and optimistic.

AMERICANS AND THEIR LEADERS should realize that despite their daily addiction to media-produced bad news, modern America is full of good news. The novelist John Updike once described the magic of the mailbox, the many things that had to go right for him to send and receive his letters and manuscripts so reliably. This nation of 300 million takes for granted the daily miracles that make so many systems function so regularly, so smoothly. Daily, millions defy gravity by soaring up skyscrapers in elevators, working and living at once unattainable heights, or hurtling through the air in a metal projectile to get from one location to another in the time it used to take ancients to cross their hometowns. Americans process megabytes of information effortlessly, heat food almost instantly, view the world globally. When the rare bridge collapses or plane crashes, experts determine what went wrong, reflecting the assumption that all of these systems should always function perfectly.

More broadly, modern America's mass prosperity has democratized culture and creativity, intellectualism and idealism. Just as the Washington Beltway's red–blue clamor drowns out America's many pockets of political harmony, popular culture obscures much that is sublime, altruistic, and temperate. Never before have so many people had the leisure to pursue their interests or try to fulfill their ideals. Never before could so many people express themselves so freely.

Americans are fulfilling national ideals, living the enduring phrases from the Declaration of Independence and the Constitution. The

Founders' visions have become so familiar, so ubiquitous, that they verge on being clichés. Americans enjoy a deep commitment to human life, unprecedented amounts of liberty, and massive opportunities for the pursuit of happiness. Thomas Jefferson's five-word affirmation—that all men are created equal—has expanded impressively over time. Since 1776, the phrase has empowered African Americans, women, the poor, and immigrants, inviting them to partake ever more fully in America's cornucopia. "We the people" truly formed a "more perfect union" in establishing, as Abraham Lincoln described it, a government "of the people, by the people, for the people."

Throughout the twentieth century, ambitious presidential programs became markers charting Americans' progress. Business, labor unions, and consumers now enjoy a much squarer deal than Theodore Roosevelt ever dared imagine. Franklin Roosevelt's New Deal became old hat. And the United States evolved into a Great Society, a center of justice, equality, enlightenment, learning, and art, a polity constantly growing, usually improving. FDR's Four Freedoms—of religion and of speech, from want and from fear—have become minimal expectations rather than unattainable delusions. Millions of people around the globe yearn to join the great American experiment, and every year more than a million immigrants take their first courageous steps toward making their own particular American dreams come true.

Modern America is in fact bound together, coast to coast, by a rich web of common cultural, political, economic, and social ties. The vast interstate system's ubiquitous green and white highway signs and every all-American franchise's commercial signs impose a generic look on a land that remains dazzlingly diverse. The invisible infrared light traveling through fiber-optic cables distributing radio shows, television programs, and Internet content across the continent standardizes the American experience more than ever before. Thanksgiving unites believers and nonbelievers, natives and immigrants, blacks and whites, Christians and Jews, Hindus and Moslems, in a uniquely American celebration that retains its sanctity. A trip south to Mexico highlights the spectacular difference a cartographers' line in the nineteenth century could make. The schoolyard riposte, "It's a free country," actually has great meaning, on multiple levels. Americans remain defined—perhaps more than ever before—by common American experiences, even in an age of hyper-individualism and of "bowling alone" rather than together.

In fact, despite all the commercials stimulating self-absorption, America remains a nation of self-sacrificing joiners and selfless givers. One analysis estimated that ninety-three million Americans volunteered more than twenty billion hours in 1995. Individuals donated nearly $109 billion to charities in 2005, dwarfing the per capita giving rates of Europeans and Canadians. An alternative spring break has become increasingly popular among today's college students, as members of this supposedly narcissistic generation opt to help others in the Third World rather than having fun in the sun.

America's elaborate network of religious and secular nonprofit organizations responds creatively to modern challenges. Habitat for Humanity enlists thousands in a proactive response to homelessness, building more than 200,000 houses for a million people living in 3,000 communities worldwide. After Hurricane Katrina, a former police officer, Rev. John Raphael, minister of New Hope Baptist Church in New Orleans, helped rebuild that battered city's communal infrastructure by leading marches against crime, posting "Thou Shalt Not Kill" billboards in unsafe neighborhoods, and leading followers to shout one word, "Enough!" Such moral heroes can be found throughout America, volunteering for a better America.

America's enduring power and beauty were particularly apparent on the ugliest day in recent memory, September 11, 2001. Historians have yet to do justice to the inspirational anomalies of 9/11. We have to reconcile our critique of caddish America with the nobility of the first-responders and World Trade Center personnel, of the Pentagon rescuers, and the Flight 93 airline passengers. We have to square our laments about selfish America with the altruism of Abraham Zelmanowitz, the fifty-five-year-old Orthodox Jewish computer programmer who refused to abandon his wheelchair-bound friend, Ed Beyea, on the twenty-seventh floor, or the ten Port Authority employees who carried their handicapped co-worker, John Abruzzo, down from the sixty-ninth floor. Zelmanowitz and his friend perished; the other eleven survived. We have to temper our diatribes against American greed by contemplating the $180 million in profits the securities firm Cantor Fitzgerald has paid out to the families of its 658 employees murdered that day, or the $16 million another firm, Keefe, Bruyette & Woods, raised for scholarships for the families of its 67 lost employees, by donating the profits of every trade executed in four special days of trading. We need to reexamine our assumptions about divided red–blue America when we think about the nationwide outpouring of blood, money, and voluntarism, or the still-anonymous Hasidic Jew who pulled a Pakistani Muslim stranger, Usman Farman, out of the debris, saying, "Brother, if you don't mind, there is a cloud of glass coming at us, grab my hand, let's get the hell out of here." And we need to ponder the mysteries and morality of supposedly secular, "blue" America, as we remember the makeshift memorials that consecrated the scarred landscapes in New York, Virginia, and Pennsylvania, or as we consider the 9/11 widow and her three-year-old son, who every night after September 11 went outside into the cool night air, lit a sparkler, picked out the most brilliant star in the sky, and said good night to "Daddy."

The attacks brought out a vulnerability, an altruism, a community feeling, even in New York, reputed to be the toughest of cities. The massive recovery effort demonstrated American society at its most sensitive and most sophisticated. Volunteers flocked to help. Strangers discovered a fraternal bond. In the tragedy's aftermath, editors tended to run mini-biographies instead of statistical portraits of the victims. Rather than emphasizing the victims' particular group identities, these pictures of normal lives tragically interrupted caught Americans in the act of living, loving, working, and playing, without political tests, without moralizing. No one asked where they stood on gay marriage or abortion, no one cared about their class or color—all were mourned equally.

Democrats and Republicans must build on these strengths and commonalities to improve the country. A quarter of a century into the Reagan revolution, the country has been Reaganized. A consensus is reemerging, bringing back traditional values with a makeover. As the baby boomers age, their rediscovery during the 1990s of enduring standards has become ever more relevant, all leavened with a most welcome tolerance. The sixties teens relearned some of the lessons their elders accepted automatically, about the importance of families, the need for a moral center, and the desirability of balancing rights with responsibilities. Filtered through what the political scientist Alan Wolfe calls modern Americans' "Eleventh Commandment"—thou shalt not judge thy neighbor—liberals and conservatives can find common ground.

Tragically, both Left and Right often approach many problems myopically, polemically. Conservatives have monopolized talk about "values." Most of the Right's "culture wars" are "sex wars" opposing abortion, premarital sex, homosexuality, and women's expanded roles. Appalled, many liberals have taken an "anything goes" stance, dismissing all public debate about personal behavior or values as repressive. This liberal abdication shortchanges necessary discussions about popular culture's sexism, greed, and violence. Similarly, conservatives ignore materialism's corrosive social impact. Combatants on both sides of the great political divide need to cooperate, answering two questions: How do we foster a culture that hones our finer sensibilities rather than stimulating our basest instincts? How do we develop a communal ethic that is broad enough to be accepting, yet rigorous enough to set standards for our youth and ourselves?

Polls and anecdotal impressions find Americans improvising what Reagan's Secretary of Education, William Bennett, called "constructive hypocrisy." As opposed to the media-generated and championed "anything goes" nihilism, most Americans are not ready to jettison traditional moral strictures against abortion, homosexuality, or teenage sex. Often, many seem less concerned with the particular acts in question and more worried about undermining tradition or violating the integrity of institutions like marriage. Still, most modern Americans are too pragmatic and tolerant to shun friends or relatives who indulge in once-frowned-upon behaviors. Moreover, many make decidedly nontraditional lifestyle choices themselves. *Roe v. Wade* keeps abortion legal, with as many as 1.2 million procedures performed annually, yet even many pro-choice Democrats cheer Hillary Clinton's calls for the procedure to be "safe, legal and rare." Similarly, most Americans still disapprove of changing the definition of marriage but accept gay friends, relatives, colleagues, and leaders. And despite their own sexual histories, many worry that Hollywood's festival of promiscuity warps the American sensibility, encouraging young people to "hook up" casually without taking emotional responsibility for their actions.

Americans are equally inconsistent about money. The statistics showing that Americans work more, spend more, build larger houses, and fritter away money on consumerist spending sprees are accurate. But equally true are the polls showing Americans concerned about the impact of materialism on their kids and their country, critical of the yawning gap between what CEOs earn and what workers earn. In these yearnings to lead a better, more balanced, more ethical life lie the seeds for individual and national renewal, including a renewed commitment to the common good.

Centrists from both parties can find common ground on other, more specific issues. "Post-partisanship is not simply Republicans and Democrats each bringing their proposals to the table and working out differences," California's Republican Governor Arnold Schwarzenegger preached. It is generating ideas in common. "The left and right don't have a monopoly on conscience . . . . You can be centrist and be principled . . . . What is more principled than giving up some part of your position to advance the greater good of the people?" People from both sides of the aisle recognize that 47 million uninsured Americans need adequate health care. Realistic Americans know that 12 million illegal aliens need to be integrated into the country somehow. Humane Americans agree that 30 million poor people— with an estimated 2.2 million people living in 775 "underclass" neighborhoods breeding poverty, crime, and alienation—is too many for such a rich country. Most accept that the era of big government is not quite over and that government remains part of the solution, even as big government had become part of the problem by the 1970s.

Amid the media circus and the political fights, calls for centrism have grown louder, especially after the 2006 campaign. During the 2008 presidential contest, the middle became the place to be, as the leading candidates spurned Bush-style rigidity. On the Republican side, Senator John McCain built his national reputation by deviating from the partisan orthodoxies of President Bush and the Christian Right. This iconoclasm obscured McCain's conservative voting record and triggered the independent voters' surge of support for him in the early primaries.

On the Democratic side, the titanic nomination struggle played out as a generational clash between Senator Barack Obama, the lyrical centrist, and Senator Hillary Clinton, the savvy incrementalist. Obama, born in August 1961, struck a popular chord by repudiating the shrill partisanship of the baby-boomer-dominated Clinton–Bush era. His "Yes We Can" call for change sang a song of centrism inviting a new generation to stop fighting the battles of the 1960s and start healing America. Clinton championed a step-by-step, pragmatic approach to politics, boasting that her scars from the baby-boomer political wars made her battle-tested and ready to lead.

"I grew up in a middle-class family in the middle of America," Clinton said when launching her presidential exploratory committee in January 2007, suggesting that she was born to be balanced. Just two weeks earlier, launching his second term, Governor Schwarzenegger said voters were "hungry for a new kind of politics, a politics that looks beyond the old labels, the old ways, the old arguments." The governor wanted "to move past partisanship, past bipartisanship to post-partisanship," which he defined as "Republicans and Democrats actively giving birth to new ideas together."

Ultimately, George W. Bush represented both poles in the Republican debate over centrism. His 2000 campaign championed a more moderate, compassionate conservatism. Bush expanded on his father's "kinder, gentler" approach, with more vision and more government involvement. But by 2006 the Bush presidency represented a more rigid conservatism than Ronald Reagan's. Reagan believed in big-tent governing, doing what he could to woo all Americans with his patriotic paeans to unity. By contrast, in the biting words of Will Marshall, president of the centrist Progressive Policy Institute, George W. Bush was "much too comfortable being president of half the country."

As party grumbling mounted about Karl Rove's play to the hyperpartisan base, *New York Times* columnist David Brooks articulated a post-Bush conservative centrism. He stressed culture's role in shaping individuals; the need for strong ethics; the imperative to defeat Islamist terrorism; and his own version of "common good" Americanism, which leading liberals such as Michael Tomasky of the *American Prospect* were touting, too.

The secret may not lie with any one centrist program or another. But there is great merit in searching for that center, building a broad-based, patriotic commitment to a common good, especially at the presidential level. All or nothing approaches often yield "nothing," not "all." Presidents should be game theorists, maximizing benefits for as many as possible, rather than warriors seeking clear victories for their side—and defeats for fellow Americans. Leaders must try building bridges, forging consensus, and playing to the center not to the base; citizens, especially today, need a renewed appreciation of what binds us together as Americans and the country's many positive attributes.

America has a deeper, enduring consensus about the value of liberty, democracy, and equality, as well as the uniqueness of America's mission. If within this solid consensus the two parties quarrel over economic theories, policy details, specific leaders' personalities, or government's exact dimensions, that is natural and healthy. It is the slash and burn, all or nothing, red versus blue, my way or the highway rhetoric from both left and right in the Bush and Clinton years that has been so unnatural and unhealthy. Political parties work when they help individuals come together to solve problems; coalition building works best when people have a variety of affiliations, when people might pray together one morning and go to competing political meetings that night. Political parties become destructive when they demonize and polarize, becoming one of a series of reinforcing elements that pit half the country against the other half.

After the December 2004 tsunami killed over 200,000 people in Indonesia, President Bush appointed George H. W. Bush and Bill Clinton to spearhead America's humanitarian response. Americans contributed over $1 billion within months. Early in 2005, the two ex-presidents traveled to the region. Their government plane only had one stateroom. Bill Clinton, fifty-eight, still recovering from heart surgery, insisted that Bush, eighty, take the bedroom on the overnight flight. Clinton said he just wanted to play cards. When Bush awoke, his bitter rival from 1992 was sleeping on the floor. "We could have switched places, each getting half a night on the bed, but he deferred to me. That was a very courteous thing, very thought-ful, and that meant a great deal to me," Bush told reporters. The story shows American politics at its best, what it can and should be. But must the politicians be retired for such civility to emerge?

Although there is no crystal ball, history suggests what might work and what will fail. History teaches us that winning an election or reelection does not guarantee presidential success. Three of the four American presi-dents since 1980 have been two-term presidents. Bill Clinton and George W. Bush serve as the Scylla and Charybdis of modern presidential leader-ship, each offering an alluring but ultimately flawed model that successors should avoid. Clinton's search for the center lacked substance. By prefer-ring policy Band-Aids to serious solutions, he shortchanged his supporters, frittered away his talents, and limited his legacy. Bush stumbled by spurning the center, dissipating much of the goodwill his bold actions had generated in first responding to the 9/11 tragedy. The terrorism issue, which should have been faced in a bipartisan manner, became increasingly controversial and polarizing. Ronald Reagan, for all his flaws, ended his presidency on a high note and is now widely perceived as a success because he never forgot the great American middle or the broader all-American vision.

Despite the continuing allure of the liberal presidential superhero as a full-service model, admiring a president's tactics is not the same as endorsing his program. Ronald Reagan's moderation was not mushy or flabby—he had core non-negotiable principles defining certain cherished positions. But the combi-nation of his tactical fluidity, his light personal touch, and his broad, all-encompassing patriotic vision proved remarkably successful. Bill Clinton at his best, and George W. Bush at his best, also demonstrated these traits. How-ever, for both temperamental and ideological reasons, neither sustained them.

Liberals and conservatives, critics and fans, can recognize that Reagan's muscular moderation tapped into a broader American leadership tradition. From Abraham Lincoln's fluid "my policy is to have no policy" to Franklin D. Roosevelt's commitment to "bold persistent experimentation," the most ef-fective presidents have been pragmatists. They built large coalitions around significant issues. Moreover, they rooted their moderate ways and rhetoric in the reigning ethos of the time, be it George Washington's eighteenth-century enlightenment, Abraham Lincoln's nineteenth-century pragmatism, or both Roosevelts' twentieth-century romance- and idealism-tinged realism.

Although patriotism is a dirty word these days, all too frequently linked to xenophobia and intolerance, great moderates must be good, patriotic nationalists. Today's attacks on patriotism and nationalism ignore all the good that liberal democratic nationalism has accomplished, and the fact that nationalism remains the fundamental constitutive vehicle for modern states. Nationalism need not be narrow, defensive, or aggressive. Patriotism can in fact tap into a communal idealism, harnessing millions to accomplish great things together.

Patriotism is about the us, not just the I; nationalism is about each nation's romance with the land and myth making about the past. Mining group pride and common goals can elevate not denigrate, include not exclude. Abraham Lincoln's cautious but egalitarian nationalism helped Northerners evolve beyond their initial racism to make the fight for union a fight against black slavery. Theodore Roosevelt's romantic, affirmative patriotism helped industrializing Americans create a communal counterbalance to business power and sing a collective song of American altruism and ambition. Franklin Roosevelt's can-do, optimistic communalism reassured and mobilized Americans during the dark days of the Depression, then inspired Americans to share their four basic freedoms with the rest of the world. Similarly, John Kennedy's idealistic nationalism was Lincolnian in challenging white Americans to fulfill their moral obligations to the civil rights movement and Rooseveltian in tapping national pride to improve the world through constructive Cold War ventures like the Peace Corps.

DEMOCRACY MAY BEGIN in conversation, as the philosopher John Dewey taught, but in the modern, media-centered era, democratic leadership begins with great storytelling. Effective nationalist leadership is also successful narrative leadership. The greatest presidents often found the center by inviting their fellow citizens to join in a grand communal adventure together. If the president did not author the story, he at least put his rhetorical imprint on it. Theodore Roosevelt's bully pulpit was the vehicle for inviting "the plain people" to join him in a mission of national pride and progressive reform. In the 1930s, Franklin Roosevelt welcomed the "forgotten man"—and woman—into the quest for economic, moral, and political renewal. In the 1940s he welcomed all Americans, but most especially the GI Joes and Rosie the Riveters, to join in the task of saving the world—a tale the Cold War presidents then continued. In the 1960s,

John Kennedy swept many Americans up in a broad attempt to fix the world, only to realize in 1963 that the next truly heroic chapter had to be written at home, with blacks and whites together. And in the 1980s, Ronald Reagan renewed national pride by retelling the tale of America as "the shining city upon a hill," starring all his fellow Americans.

By contrast, many of the twentieth century's least effective presidents failed to construct a compelling, inviting narrative. Lyndon Johnson first wove most Americans into a legend of America as a Great Society as a way of healing after the assassination of JFK—fighting the Cold War, securing for blacks the civil rights they deserved, and helping poor Americans get the help they needed. But during the Vietnam War millions of Americans rejected both Johnson's tale and their own particular role in that epoch. In the 1970s, Jimmy Carter was particularly unsuccessful in convincing Americans that he had authored the correct plot. Americans were much more comfortable with Reagan's tale of America's renewed greatness than with Carter's sour story about coping in an age of limits. Finally, George W. Bush's war on terror offered a compelling story line, but it relegated most Americans to too passive a role, and Bush suffered huge defections when his "war on terror" bogged down in a lengthy and costly war in Iraq that failed to find the weapons of mass destruction so central to the war's rationale.

A broad and vital bipartisanship should be the centerpiece of this compelling national narrative. Bipartisanship cannot be a one-way street, only opened to the opposition when the president or the congressional majority needs an illusion of unity. To work, bipartisanship needs to be the result of an ongoing dialogue and serious cooperation in shaping policies.

True bipartisanship can only flourish in a climate of civility. Presidents should take responsibility for improving the civic climate in America. In 1976, Jimmy Carter hurt Gerald Ford by popularizing the "misery index," the combined rate of inflation and unemployment, to illustrate the scale of economic dislocation. Future presidents should seek to maximize a "civility index," the sum of the voter turnout rate and the percentage of people believing the country is going in the right direction. Similarly, presidents need to collectivize Ronald Reagan's classic question from 1980, "Are you better off than you were four years ago?" Muscular moderates need to start asking, "Are *we* better off as a national community, as citizens, than we were four years ago?"

For all America's sophistication, the American presidency remains a remarkably personal office, highly dependent on the presidential personality. George W. Bush's second term demonstrated the dangers of too much rigidity and the need for a certain fluidity; Clinton revealed the risks of too much fluidity. For both, their inner demons shaped their external actions. Bush's born again, recovering alcoholic persona required discipline, regularity, and deference from subordinates. Clinton's lifelong need to be loved and aversion to conflict propelled his shapeshifting.

As George Washington himself emphasized, the spirit of enlightened moderation, a culture of reasonableness, cannot only be generated by the commander in chief. Americans must take more responsibility for what we collectively are doing to our politics, our culture, our country, and ourselves. The escapist combination of partisanship, cynicism, and frivolity embodied in too much of contemporary culture invites flights from responsibility; the privileges of citizenship demand the opposite. We all must begin finding our inner moderate. We must reward those who seek the center. We must repudiate those who through vitriol, demagoguery, or mockery divide, polarize, or distract from important issues at hand to attract our entertainment dollars or score some cheap political points. We need to learn the lessons of George Washington's enlightenment, Abraham Lincoln's flexibility, Theodore Roosevelt's romantic nationalism, Franklin Roosevelt's experimentation, Harry Truman's bipartisanship, Dwight Eisenhower's consensus building, John Kennedy's principled malleability, and Ronald Reagan's muscular moderation.

Citizens in a democracy get the leadership they deserve, for better or worse. If we, collectively, revitalize the center, our presidents will become center seekers. If we demand the best of our leaders, we may just get the best leaders.

ACKNOWLEDGMENTS

As the culmination of nearly a quarter century of my learning, researching, writing, and lecturing about American history with a particular focus on the presidents, this book reflects my great debt to my teachers and my students. Time and again while writing this book I returned to ideas I had encountered in graduate school, thanks to Professors Bernard Bailyn, Alan Brinkley, and David Herbert Donald, among others who taught in the Harvard University History Department during its golden age in the 1980s. Time and again I was humbled by how much I had learned from them then, and how much more I still have to learn from them now. My students, first at Harvard and for the last eighteen years at McGill University, have been ideal partners in this intellectual journey, engaged and engaging, questioning critically but rarely cynically.

My work has been greatly informed by the extraordinary resources at the Library of Congress, the National Archives, and the various presidential libraries across the United States. I have been fortunate to benefit from multiple and sometimes lengthy stays at the Herbert Hoover Presidential Library in West Branch, Iowa; Franklin D. Roosevelt Presidential Library in Hyde Park, New York; Harry S. Truman Presidential Library in Independence, Missouri; Dwight D. Eisenhower Library in Abilene, Kansas; John F. Kennedy Presidential Library in Boston, Massachusetts; Lyndon B. Johnson Presidential Library in Austin, Texas; Richard Nixon Library in Yorba Linda, California; Richard Nixon Presidential Materials Project at the National Archives in College Park, Maryland; Gerald R.

Ford Presidential Library in Ann Arbor, Michigan; Jimmy Carter Presidential Library in Atlanta, Georgia; and Ronald Reagan Presidential Library in Simi Valley, California. This book also cites material gleaned from a rewarding visit to the Thomas P. O'Neill Papers at the John J. Burns Library, Brookline, Massachusetts. I thank all the archivists for their help. Photographs in the book appear courtesy of the John Kennedy Library, the Library of Congress, the National Archives, Getty Images, and Universal Features Syndicate, representing Garry Trudeau.

I have been blessed with crackerjack research assistants. Special thanks to Erica Fagen; Bonnie Goodman, who among many other invaluable kindnesses, including footnoting and proofreading help, has maintained my Web site (www.giltroy.com) creatively and dependably from its inception; Brett Hooton, who assisted with so much of the book's basic research thoroughly and insightfully; Edie Kaminsky; and Michelle Shain, who has helped both substantively and organizationally in so many ways. Special thanks also to the footnote brigade from the McGill University Honors Seminar of 2006–2007 (with one honorary member), who did the first round of footnoting: Kayvon Afshran; Cal Kufta; David Olson; Kristen Rohr; and Jacqueline Wilson.

McGill University continues to be a most welcoming academic home. I owe particular thanks to Principal and Vice-Chancellor Heather Munroe-Blum, Dean of Arts Christopher Manfredi, Chair of the History Department Catherine LeGrand, and the friendly and efficient departmental support staff and colleagues.

My agent, Brettne Bloom of Kneerim & Williams, has been unflaggingly supportive, extremely wise, and always helpful. I look forward to working with her on many more projects.

The individual who has helped this book the most has been my extraordinary editor, Lara Heimert, vice president and editorial director of Basic Books. Lara approaches a chapter draft as a sculptor approaches clay, adding immeasurably to its quality. I am deeply grateful to her for her keen eye, compelling vision, and deep historical insight, as well as her good humor and warmth throughout the whole process. Others who helped at Basic include the excellent copy editor Sharon DeJohn, Jeff Hardwick, Brandon Proia, the superb project editor Meredith Smith, and the enthusiastic and intelligent publicity and marketing teams.

Even with all this help, any errors of fact or opinion remain my own.

I also thank my friends and family. I am blessed with friends who feel like relatives and relatives I like as much as my friends. I remain particularly grateful to my wonderful parents and father-in-law, for their constant support in so many ways.

As one friend noted, I somehow failed to write this book *on* moderation *in* moderation. I am especially grateful to my wife and children for all the patience and indulgence during many late-night and long-day marathon writing and editing sessions. Dedicating the book to them acknowledges but cannot begin to quantify how important they are to me.

A Note on Sources

In today's postmodern information age, the state of historical scholarship is like the state of the blogosphere: creative and chaotic. On one hand, there is a welcome diversity of interpretations, methods, approaches, and opinions. Voices long squelched are now heard loudly and clearly. On the other hand, there is a disturbing lack of focus, an unnerving inability to find a common language, and a lamentable preference for the marginal, the sensational, the cynical, and the hypercritical over the mainstream, the sober, the respectful, and the constructive.

This book contradicts the conventional wisdom by arguing for the centrality of centrism in American history, valuing the moderate leader over the extremist, and appreciating nationalism as a constructive force in American history. This argument also assumes that leadership counts and that the historical narrative can help us understand how individuals shape history for better and worse. This generation of American historians has been far more effective in showing how the United States failed to live up to American standards than in explaining just how and why America has been so successful for so many millions of people over so many decades. The historiographical and methodological revolutions that began in the 1960s—paralleling and incorporating broader transformations—demolished the traditional "consensus" history that dominated the American historical profession in the 1950s. We need to pick up the pieces and construct a new consensus history that acknowledges diversity, complexity, and failure, while also explaining this country's cohesion, stability, and greatness.

As a work of synthesis, this book builds on the research and analysis in my previous books on American history. *See How They Ran: The Changing Role of the Presidential Candidate* (Cambridge, MA, 1991, 1996) assessed the history of campaigning based on over 100 manuscript collections in 15 states. *Mr. and Mrs. President: From the Trumans to the Clintons* (Lawrence, 2000), originally published as *Affairs of State: The Rise and Rejection of the Presidential Candidate* (New York, 1997), resulted from intensive research in the relevant presidential libraries and covered the eleven couples who lived in the White House from Eleanor and Franklin Roosevelt to Bill and Hillary Clinton. *Morning in America: How Ronald Reagan Invented the 1980s* (Princeton, 2005, 2007) emerged from my extended stays at the Ronald Reagan Presidential Library. *Hillary Rodham Clinton: Polarizing First Lady*, rev. ed. (Lawrence, 2006, 2008), built off the Clinton chapter in *Mr. and Mrs. President* but pivoted on an analysis of Hillary Clinton's many speeches and writings as First Lady.

Among the many broad works on the presidency and American history that proved particularly inspirational, Richard Hofstadter's *The American Political Tradition and the Men Who Made it* (New York, 1948), Arthur M. Schlesinger, Jr.'s *The Vital Center* (Boston, 1949), and Stephen Skowronek's *The Politics Presidents Make* (Cambridge, MA, 1993) stand out. An important new work about the "traditional forces of compromise, equilibrium and the vital center" in American history is Morton Keller's *America's Three Regimes: A New Political History* (New York, 2007). John T. Woolley and Gerhard Peters's The American Presidency Project (Santa Barbara: University of California, available at http://www.presidency.ucsb.edu/) is an extraordinary primary source depository, while Alan Brinkley and Davis Dyer's *The American Presidency* (Boston, 2004) portrays each president vividly. James David Barber's *The Presidential Character: Predicting Performance in the White House* (Englewood Cliffs, NJ, 1992) has been overplayed, but Barber's discussion of the "rigidification process" as a factor in presidential failure is accurate.

On nationalism, see Benedict Anderson, *Imagined Communities: Reflections on the Origin and Spread of Nationalism* (London, 1983, 2000), Ulrich Beck, *Democracy Without Enemies* (Malden, MA, 1998), and Thomas Bender, *A Nation Among Nations: America's Place in World History* (New York, 2006).

On the modern historian's obsession with America's failures, see Howard Zinn's bestselling *A People's History of the United States* (New York, 1980, 1995, 1998, 1999, 2003). Todd Gitlin's *The Twilight of Common Dreams: Why America Is Wracked by Culture Wars* (New York, 1995) discusses this phenomenon intelligently and critically.

On the inevitable scholarly debate about how much of a compromise there was at Thomas Jefferson's dinner, see Jacob E. Cooke, "The Compromise of 1790," *The William and Mary Quarterly*, 3rd Ser., Vol. 27, no. 4 (Oct., 1970), 523–545, and Norman K. Risjord, "The Compromise of 1790: New Evidence on the Dinner Table Bargain," *The William and Mary Quarterly*, 3rd Ser., Vol. 33, no. 2 (Apr., 1976), 309–314.

George Washington: A Collection (Indianapolis, 1988), available at http://oll.libertyfund.org/title/848/101874/2199324, is a terrific primary-source anthology edited by W. B. Allen.

Major Washington biographies include James Thomas Flexner's *Washington: The Indispensable Man* (Boston, 1974), Richard Norton Smith's *Patriarch: George Washington and the New American Nation* (Boston, 1993), and Joseph J. Ellis's *His Excellency: George Washington* (New York, 2004). Useful smaller studies include Edmund S. Morgan's *The Genius of George Washington* (New York, 1977) and Gordon S. Wood's *Revolutionary Characters: What Made the Founders Different* (New York, 2006). Ron Chernow's *Alexander Hamilton* (New York, 2004), Joseph Ellis's *American Sphinx: the Character of Thomas Jefferson* (New York, 1997), and the two classic views, Henry Adams, *History of the United States of America during the administrations of Thomas Jefferson* (New York, 1986), and Dumas Malone, *Jefferson and His Time*, 6 vols. (Boston, 1948–1981), broadened the story.

For the Jacksonian era, I was lucky to write after the publication of Sean Wilentz's impressive *The Rise of American Democracy: Jefferson to Lincoln* (New York, 2005), Michael Holt's *The Rise and Fall of the American Whig Party* (New York, 1999), and the long-awaited second volume of William W. Freehling's *The Road to Disunion, Volume II: Secessionists Triumphant 1854–1861* (New York, 2007). His first volume was *Secessionists at Bay, 1776–1854* (New York, 1990). Jean Baker's *Affairs of Party: The Political Culture of Northern Democrats in the Mid-Nineteenth Century* (New York, 1998) is also an indispensable guide to the period's political culture.

Illuminating views of Jackson include Arthur M. Schlesinger, Jr.'s *The Age of Jackson* (Boston, 1945) and Robert V. Remini's *The Life of Andrew Jackson* (New York, 1988). Ted Widmer's *Martin Van Buren* (New York, 2005) is very insightful.

For the pre-Civil War, James M. McPherson's *Battle Cry of Freedom: The Civil War Era* (New York, 1988) is the best recent overview. David M. Potter's *The Impending Crisis, 1848–1861* (New York, 1976) has a compelling account of the Compromise of 1850, as does Merrill Peterson's *The Great Triumvirate* (New York, 1987). Clement Eaton's *The Freedom-of-Thought Struggle in the Old South*, rev. ed. (New York, 1964) offers a classic look at the Confederacy. Recent, insightful, laudatory biographies of Northern radicals include David S. Reynolds, *John Brown, Abolitionist: The Man Who Killed Slavery, Sparked the Civil War, and Seeded Civil Rights* (New York, 2005) and Henry Mayer, *All on Fire: William Lloyd Garrison and the Abolition of Slavery* (New York, 1998). On the Causes of the Civil War, see also Kenneth M. Stampp, *The Causes of the Civil War: Revised Edition* (New York: 1992) and Arthur M. Schlesinger Jr., "The Causes of the Civil War: A Note on Historical Sentimentalism," *Partisan Review* XVI (1949): 969–81.

The Collected Works of Abraham Lincoln, 8 vols., ed. Roy P. Basler, capture Lincoln's voice. My views on Lincoln's "policy to have no policy" have been most shaped by David Herbert Donald's majestic *Lincoln* (New York, 1995) and his elegant essays emphasizing Lincoln as a working politician in *Lincoln Reconsidered* (New York, 1956). On Lincoln and his difficult allies, see Doris Kearns Goodwin, *Team of Rivals: The Political Genius of Abraham*

Lincoln (New York, 2005); Allen C. Guelzo, "Lincoln and the Abolitionists," *The Wilson Quarterly* 24: 4 (Autumn 2000): 58–70; and T. Harry Williams, *Lincoln and the Radicals* (Madison, 1965).

In addition to the vivid *The Letters of Theodore Roosevelt*, 8 vols., ed. Elting E. Morison (Cambridge, 1951–1954), Theodore Roosevelt's *Autobiography* (New York: Da Capo Press, 1985, c1913) offers Roosevelt's views on many controversies. Archibald Willingham Butt, *The Letters of Archie Butt, Personal Aide to President Roosevelt* (New York, 1924) and the Whitelaw Reid Family Papers in the Library of Congress help fill in the context. John Morton Blum first developed the idea of Roosevelt as more effective in setting precedents than implementing thorough reforms in his *Republican Roosevelt* (Cambridge, 1954). More recent studies include Lewis L. Gould's valuable *The Presidency of Theodore Roosevelt* (Lawrence, 1991), H. W. Brands' lyrical *T. R.: The Last Romantic* (New York, 1997), Edmund Morris's comprehensive *Theodore Rex* (New York, 2001), and Aida D. Donald's evocative *Lion in the White House: A Life of Theodore Roosevelt* (New York, 2007). Among the vast literature on progressivism, two books that were particularly influential were Richard Hofstadter's *The Age of Reform* (New York, 1955) and Michael McGerr's *A Fierce Discontent: The Rise and Fall of the Progressive Movement in America, 1870–1920* (New York, 2003).

The many works of Arthur Schlesinger and William Leuchtenburg on Franklin D. Roosevelt still stand out, along with James MacGregor Burns's two volume biography *Roosevelt: The Lion and the Fox* (New York, 1956) and *Soldier of Freedom* (New York, 1970). An excellent, more recent look at Roosevelt in the world context is Alonzo L. Hamby, *For the Survival of Democracy: Franklin Roosevelt and the World Crisis of the 1930s* (New York, 2004), while a focused popular study is Jonathan Alter's *The Defining Moment: FDR's Hundred Days and the Triumph of Hope* (New York, 2006). On foreign policy, see the definitive Robert Dallek, *Franklin D. Roosevelt and American Foreign Policy* (New York, 1979); on liberalism and domestic policy see Alan Brinkley's authoritative *The End of Reform: New Deal Liberalism in Recession and War (New York, 1995) and Voices of Protest: Huey Long, Father Coughlin, and the Great Depression (New York, 1982)*. On radicalism, see Harvey Klehr, *The Heyday of American Communism: The Depression Decade* (New York, 1984), and on labor and consumerism, see Lizabeth Cohen, *Making a New Deal: Industrial Workers in Chicago, 1919–1939* (Cambridge, 1990). A stimulating contrarian view of the New Deal is Amity Shlaes's *The Forgotten Man* (New York, 2007). Two influential sources on FDR's leadership before World War II remain Robert Divine's *Roosevelt and World War II* (Baltimore, 1969) and *Reluctant Belligerent* (New York, 1965).

For post-war America, see James Patterson's *Grand Expectations: The United States 1945–1974* (New York, 1996), and his equally extraordinary sequel, *Restless Giant: The*

United States from Watergate to Bush v. Gore (New York, 2007). See also John Lewis Gaddis, The Cold War: A New History (New York, 2005).

On Truman, the papers at the Truman library are extremely helpful, including Clark Clifford's visionary strategy memos for the 1948 campaign. Also see the various editions collecting Truman's letters and diaries, especially Robert H. Ferrell's Dear Bess (New York, 1983) and Off the Record (New York, 1980). The best biography is Alonzo L. Hamby's Man of the People: A Life of Harry S. Truman (New York, 1995). See also Robert J. Donovan, Conflict and Crisis: The Presidency of Harry S. Truman 1945–1948 (New York, 1977); Arthur Vandenberg, Private Papers of Senator Vandenberg (Boston, 1952); and Dean Acheson, Present at the Creation: My Years in the State Department (New York, 1969).

On Cold War culture, see Andrew J. Falk, "Reading Between the Lines: Negotiating National Identity on American Television, 1945–1960," Diplomatic History 28:2 (April 2004): 197–225; Richard Polenberg, One Nation Divisible: Class, Race, and Ethnicity in the United States Since 1938 (New York, 1991); Alan Ehrenhalt, The Lost City: Discovering the Forgotten Virtues of Community in the Chicago of the 1950s (New York, 1995); and Stephen J. Whitfield, The Culture of the Cold War (Baltimore, 1996).

Eisenhower's moderation becomes clear from reading his correspondence in the Eisenhower Library, especially his exchanges with the conservative Edgar Newton Eisenhower and the moderate Milton Eisenhower. On Eisenhower, also see his memoirs: Dwight D. Eisenhower, Mandate for Change (Garden City, NY, 1963), Chester J. Pach, Jr. and Elmo Richardson, The Presidency of Dwight Eisenhower, rev. ed. (Lawrence: University Press of Kansas, 1991), and most important, Fred I. Greenstein, The Hidden-Hand Presidency: Eisenhower as Leader (New York, 1982).

In his compelling essay on Kennedy in Private Lives/Public Consequences (Cambridge, 2005), William H. Chafe roots Kennedy's Civil Rights speech in the lessons he learned from the Cuban Missile crisis. Richard Reeves vividly recreates Kennedy's presidency in President Kennedy: Profile of Power (New York, 1993). See also Arthur M. Schlesinger, Jr., A Thousand Days (Boston, 1965), Ernest R. May and Phillip D. Zelikow, The Kennedy Tapes: Inside the White House During the Cuban Missile Crisis (Cambridge, 1997), and Robert Dallek, An Unfinished Life: John Kennedy 1917–1963 (Boston, 2003).

Lyndon Johnson's Handwriting File is particularly revealing. The memoranda from Robert Kintner, Bill Moyers, George Reedy, and Jack Valenti in the Office of the President File, Special Files, and the Confidential File illustrate modern media strategy being hatched. Robert Dallek's Flawed Giant: Lyndon Johnson and His Times, 1961–1973 (New York, 1998) is even better than his Kennedy book and defines "Liberal Nationalism." Lyndon Baines Johnson, The Vantage Point: Perspectives of the Presidency, 1963–1969 (New York, 1971) is mostly polite with occasional flashes. Among many Vietnam books, Robert McNamara's In Retrospect: The Tragedy and Lessons of Vietnam (New York, 1995) best captures the fragile relationships between the president and his aides, the administration and its critics, the Johnson presidency and the truth. On the sixties, see, for example, Maurice Isserman and Michael Kazin, *America Divided: The Civil War of the 1960s* (Oxford, 2004).

Richard Nixon's marginalia in the President's Handwriting File catch Nixon in all his moods and masks. *From: The President: Richard Nixon's Secret Files*, ed. Bruce Oudes (New York, 1989) is a revealing collection of memoranda, while *The Haldeman Diaries* (New York, 1994) captures Nixon in the act of being himself. Richard Milhous Nixon, *RN: The Memoirs of Richard Nixon*, 2 vols. (New York, 1978) offer Nixon's self-justifying view of the world. For secondary sources on Nixon, see David Greenberg, *Nixon's Shadow: The History of an Image* (New York, 2003) and Stephen E. Ambrose, *Nixon*, vol. 2, *The Triumph of a Politician, 1962–1972* (New York, 1989). On Watergate, see Stanley Kutler, *Wars of Watergate* (New York, 1990).

Jimmy Carter's Handwriting File in the Carter Library is also revealing; his memoir *Keeping Faith* (Toronto, 1982) is disappointing and stiff. On the 1970s, see David Frum, *How We Got Here* (Toronto, 2000), Bruce Schulman, *The Seventies* (New York, 2001), and Philip Jenkins, *Decade of Nightmares: The End of the Sixties and the Making of Eighties America* (New York, 2006).

Ronald Reagan emerges as a more agile thinker and political player in Kiron K. Skinner, Annelise Anderson, and Martin Anderson, eds., *Reagan, In His Own Hand* (New York, 2001), *Reagan: A Life in Letters* (New York, 2003), and *The Reagan Diaries*, ed. Douglas Brinkley, 8–9, 13 (New York, 2007). For a contrasting opinion, see David A. Stockman, *The Triumph of Politics: How the Reagan Revolution Failed* (New York, 1986). On individualism in the 1980s, see Robert N. Bellah et al., *Habits of the Heart: Individualism and Commitment in American Life* (Berkeley, 1985).

James MacGregor Burns and Georgia Jones Sorenson critique Clinton's triangulation in *Dead Center: Clinton-Gore Leadership and the Perils of Moderation* (New York, 1999). Bill Clinton, *My Life* (New York, 2004) is stately and tedious, John F. Harris, *The Survivor: Bill Clinton in the White House* (New York, 2005) is riveting. David Gergen's *Eyewitness to Power: The Essence of Leadership: Nixon to Clinton* (New York, 2000) offers insider's perspective on the health care debacle; Theda Skocpol's *Boomerang* (New York, 1997) offers a more institutional analysis. Dick Morris's *Behind the Oval Office: Winning the Presidency in the Nineties* (New York, 1997) captures the complex relationship between Clinton and his political guru. George Stephanopoulos's *All Too Human: A Political Education* (Boston, 1999) charts a Clintonite's lost idealism.

On the failure to respond to Al Qaeda, see the *Final Report of the National Commission on Terrorist Attacks Upon the United States* (Washington, DC, 2004); Daniel Benjamin and Steve Simon, *The Age of Sacred Terror: Radical Islam's War Against America* (New York,

2002); and Richard A. Clarke's unnerving, depressing *Against All Enemies: Inside America's War on Terror* (New York, 2004).

On the Bush administration, the White House website http://www.whitehouse.gov/ features his speeches and public statements. Of Bob Woodward's insider accounts, see especially *Bush at War* (New York, 2002) and *State of Denial* (New York, 2006). Perhaps the best book yet on Bush is Robert Draper's *Dead Certain* (New York, 2007).

On contemporary American values, see Alan Wolfe, *One Nation After All* (New York, 1998); Stephen L. Carter, *Civility* (New York, 1998); Robert D. Putnam, *Bowling Alone* (New York, 2000); Sam Roberts, *Who We Are Now* (New York, 2004); Barbara Ehrenreich, *Bait and Switch: The (Futile) Pursuit of the American Dream* (New York, 2005); and David Callahan, *The Moral Center: How We Can Reclaim Our Country from Die-Hard Extremists, Rogue Corporations, Hollywood Hacks, and Pretend Patriots* (Orlando, 2006).

On media, see Paul Starr, *The Creation of the Media* (New York, 2004) and Mark Halperin and John Harris, *The Way to Win* (New York, 2007).

On American unity and partisanship, see Arthur M. Schlesinger, Jr., *The Disuniting of America* (New York, 1991, 1992). *Culture War?: The Myth of a Polarized America* (New York, 2005) by Morris P. Fiorina with Samuel J. Abrams and Jeremy C. Pope is essential reading about what unites America. Jacob S. Hacker and Paul Pierson's *Off Center* (New Haven, 2005, 2006) is tendentious. Juliet Eilperin's *Fight Club Politics: How Partisanship Is Poisoning the House of Representatives* (Lanham, MD, 2006) captures some of the structural elements involved. Both Ronald Brownstein's *The Second Civil War: How Extreme Partisanship Has Paralyzed Washington and Polarized America* (New York, 2007) and Cass Sunstein's *Republic.com 2.0* (Princeton, 2007) make powerful pleas for unity rooted in shrewd analyses of how partisanship has spread.

One of the most compelling recent arguments for a centrist foreign policy is Peter Beinart's *The Good Fight: Why Liberals—and Only Liberals—Can Win the War on Terror and Make America Great Again* (New York, 2006), while an intelligent argument focused more on domestic policy is Ted Halstead and Michael Lind's *The Radical Center: The Future of American Politics* (New York, 2001). See also Michael Tomasky, "Party in Search of a Notion," *American Prospect*, April 18, 2006.

NOTES

As a work of synthesis, this book rests on the tremendous body of work American historians have generated exploring and explaining America's past. This book shows that I do not always agree with my fellow historians, but I always learn from them. Nearly every sentence in the book could be footnoted, contradicted, and to use one favorite term of modern historians, contextualized. But just as when we lecture, we historians occasionally have to plunge ahead, marking broader trajectories without saluting or engaging the many smart, insightful people who have blazed our intellectual trails. For that reason, to limit the footnotes, I mostly cite direct quotations. Wherever possible, I tried to cite an easily accessible source, and I did not cite the most famous presidential statements that can be found easily from information already provided in the text.

Instead of numbered footnotes, each citation is keyed to the first two or three words in the quotation or relevant phrase and the page number on which the material appears.

All the Web citations were accessed on February 10, 2008.

INTRODUCTION:
PRESIDENTS AS MUSCULAR MODERATES

2   "fixed insolent ...": Henry Lee, quoted in James Madison, *The Writings of James Madison*, vol. 6, ed. Gaillard Hunt (New York, 1900), available at http://oll.libertyfund.org/title/1941/124382/2487696.

2   "In general ...": Thomas Jefferson, The Works of Thomas Jefferson, Federal Edition, vol. 6 (New York and London, 1904–1905), available at http://oll.libertyfund.org/title/803/86764/1992065.

2 "men of sound …": Thomas Jefferson, "Memorandum on the Compromise of 1790," in *Liberty and Order: The First American Party Struggle*, ed. Lance Banning (Indianapolis, 2004), available at http://oll.libertyfund.org/title/875/63852/1329738.

2 "spirit of …" through "individual advantages …": George Washington, *George Washington: A Collection*, ed. W. B. Allen (Indianapolis, 1988).

3 "sensible men": George Washington to Patrick Henry, January 15, 1799, in Allen, *George Washington*, 662.

3 "enjoying peace…": George Washington to Anne Cesare, Chevalier la Luzerne, August 10, 1790, in John C. Fitzpatrick, ed., *The Writings of George Washington from the Original Manuscript Sources, 1745–1799*, vol. 31 (Washington, 1931–1944), 84.

4 "There is something …" and "a political climate …": "What Sen. Joseph Lieberman Said," *WorldTribune.com*, April 22, 2007, http://www.worldtribune.com/worldtribune/07/front2454213.136805556.html.

4 "If you agree …": quoted in Joe Klein, *Politics Lost: How American Democracy Was Trivialized by People Who Think You're Stupid* (New York, 2006), frontispiece.

5 "the violence …": James Madison, "The Federalist Papers, no. 10," in *The American Republic: Primary Sources*, ed. Bruce Frohnen (Indianapolis, 2002), available at http://oll.libertyfund.org/title/669/68070/1655180.

6 "particularly rotten apple": Ulrich Beck, *Democracy Without Enemies* (Malden, MA, 1998), 107.

6 parochialism …: Thomas Bender, *A Nation Among Nations: America's Place in World History* (New York, 2006), 6.

6 "postnational": See Tony Judt, *Postwar: A History of Europe Since 1945* (New York, 2005), 693–694; David W. Noble, *Death of a Nation: American Culture and the End of Exceptionalism* (Minneapolis: University of Minnesota Press, 2002); Stephen Shapiro, "Reconfiguring American Studies?: The Paradoxes of Postnationalism," *The 49th Parallel, An Interdisciplinary E-Journal of North American Studies*, available at http://www.49thparallel.bham.ac.uk/back/issue8/shapiro.htm 2007.

9 "goodly fabric": Allen, *George Washington*, 579.

11 "Soldiering is …": "Camp Life: Civil War Collections," *Gettysburg National Military Park*, available at http://www.nps.gov/history/museum/exhibits/gettex/index.htm.

11 "a sort of bird …": William Safire, *Safire's New Political Dictionary* (New York, 1993), 471–472.

11 "bad and immoral men …": John Stuart Mill, *On Liberty* (London, 1859; reprint, New York, 2005), 66.

12 "must know how …": Socrates, in Plato, *The Republic*, Chapter XXXIII (1994–2000), available at http://classics.mit.edu/Plato/republic.11.x.html.

14 "What's the matter…": Thomas Frank, *What's the Matter with Kansas: How Conservatives Won the Heart of America* (New York, 2000).

14 academic debunkers: Howard Zinn, *A People's History of The United States* (New York, 1980, 1995, 1998, 1999, 2003); Todd Gitlin, *The Twilight of Common Dreams: Why America Is Wracked by Culture Wars* (New York, 195), 7–36.

14 insecurities: Susan Jeffords, *Hardbodies: Hollywood Masculinity in the Reagan Era* (New Brunswick, N.J. 1994).

14 antislavery zealotry …: See David S. Reynolds, *John Brown, Abolitionist: The Man Who Killed Slavery, Sparked the Civil War, and Seeded Civil Rights* (New York, 2005) and Henry Mayer, *All on Fire: William Lloyd Garrison and the Abolition of Slavery* (New York, 1998).

14   "creative extremists": Martin Luther King Jr., *Why We Can't Wait* (New York, 1964; reprint, New York, 2000), 77.

15   "We Shall ...": Malcolm X with Alex Haley, *The Autobiography of Malcolm X* (New York, 1965), 286.

17   "softest pillow": Sean Wilentz, *The Rise of American Democracy: Jefferson to Lincoln* (New York, 2005), 72.

CHAPTER 1:
WASHINGTON'S WAY

19   "reticence and ...": "Washington the Warrior: The Man," *The History Channel Website*, http://www.history.com/exhibits/washington/theman.html.

20   "If I could not ...": Joseph J. Ellis, *His Excellency: George Washington* (New York, 2004), 216.

20   virtuous, self-sacrificing ...: See Edmund Sears Morgan, *The Genius of George Washington* (New York, 1977), 20; Gordon S. Wood, *Revolutionary Characters: What Made the Founders Different* (New York, 2006), 16.

21   perceived moral authority ...: See Ellis, *His Excellency*, 12, 68–69.

21   A brilliant politician ...: See Richard Norton Smith, *Patriarch: George Washington and the New American Nation* (Boston, 1993), xix.

21   "Be easy ...": Smith, *Patriarch*, xix–xx.

21   "My dear General ...": Morgan, *Genius of Washington*, 5–6.

21   The revolutionary generation ...: See Forrest McDonald, *The Presidency of George Washington* (Lawrence, 1974), 15.

22   "mark for Suspicion ...": George Washington, "Speech to the Officers of the Army, March 15, 1783," in *George Washington: A Collection*, ed. W.B. Allen, 217 (Indianapolis, 1988).

22   "I have not only ...": See Ellis, *His Excellency*, 144.

22   "anonymous summons ..." through "in the name ...": Washington, "Speech to the Officers of the Army," in Allen, *George Washington*, 217, 219, 220.

22   "the greatest man ...": Garry Wills, *Cincinnatus: George Washington and the Enlightenment* (Garden City, 1984), 13. See also Ellis, *His Excellency*, 139.

23   cool pragmatist made ...: See Ellis, *His Excellency*, 139–146.

23   "pacific and friendly ...:" George Washington, "Circular to the States," from "Head Quarters, Newburgh, June 14, 1783." in Allen, *George Washington*, 242.

24   Even the act ...: See Ellis, *His Excellency*, 184–197.

24   "no local prejudices ...": George Washington, "The First Inaugural Speech, April 30, 1789," in Allen, *George Washington*, 461–462.

25   "a government of ..." and "by *prudence* ...": Allen, *George Washington*, 537.

25   "Gentlemen ...": George Washington to Ezekiel Price et al., Selectmen of the Town of Boston, July 28, 1795, in *The Writings of George Washington*, ed. Worthington Chauncey Ford, vol. 13, 74 (New York, 1892).

27   "an influence ..." See McDonald, *Presidency of Washington*, 78.

27   "he would be ...": Wood, *Revolutionary Characters*, 57.

27   "gift of silence": See Ellis, *His Excellency*, 194.

27   "opposition to ...": Thomas Jefferson to The Marquis de Lafayette, April 2, 1790, in *The Works of Thomas Jefferson*, ed. Paul Leicester Ford, vol. 6, 40 (New York, 1904).

28   "It proves how ...": Thomas Jefferson to William Short, May 27, 1790, in Ford, *Works of Jefferson*, vol. 6, 58.

29   "mutual forbearance ..." : George Washington to David Stuart, March 28, 1790, in Allen, *George Washington*, 540.

29   "assimilate ..." through "reconcile ...": George Washington to David Stuart, June 15, 1790, in Allen, *George Washington*, 542.

29   "both sides ..." Washington to Stuart, June 15, 1790, in Allen, *George Washington*, 542.

29   Hamilton rejected ...: See Ellis, *His Excellency*, 205–206.

30   "against the baneful ...": James Thomas Flexner, *Washington: The Indispensable Man* (Boston, 1974), 241.

30   "daily pitted ...": Ron Chernow, *Alexander Hamilton* (New York, 2004), 390.

30   "calculated to make ...": Flexner, *Washington*, 323.

30   "the powers ..." and "the temper ...": Flexner, *Washington*, 248.

31   "infamous Papers ..." and "the peace ...": John Tebbel and Sarah Miles Watts, *The Press and the Presidency: From George Washington to Ronald Reagan* (New York, 1985), 12.

31   "painful": Flexner, *Washington*, 266.

31   "speculative ..." and "more charity ...": George Washington to the Secretary of State, August 23, 1792, in Allen, *George Washington*, 578.

31   "if, instead ..." through "Without them ...": Washington to Secretary of State, August 23, 1792, in Allen, *George Washington*, 578–579. Emphasis in original.

31   "[T]his regret ..." through "fatal consequences ...": George Washington to the Secretary of the Treasury, August 26, 1792, in Allen, *George Washington*, 580–581. Emphasis in original.

32   "North & South ..." and "if they have ...": Ellis, *His Excellency*, 220.

32   "we are *all* ...": Flexner, *Washington*, 262. Emphasis in original.

32   "womanish attachment ...": Darren Staloff, *Hamilton, Adams, Jefferson: The Politics of Enlightenment and the American Founding* (New York, 2005), 103.

33   "public character ..." and "those intemperate ...": George Washington to Governor Henry Lee, August 26, 1794, in Allen, *George Washington*, 596.

33   "party man": George Washington to Thomas Jefferson, July 6, 1796, in Allen, *George Washington*, 641.

33   "*Men, not Principles*": George Washington to Governor Jonathan Trumbull, August 30, 1799, in Allen, *George Washington*, 666. Emphasis in original.

33   "sensible men ..." and "a rallying point ...": George Washington to Patrick Henry, January 15, 1799, in Allen, *George Washington*, 662.

33   "the restless ...": Washington to Trumbull, August 30, 1799, in Allen, *George Washington*, 665.

33   "in your opinion ...": Flexner, *Washington*, 299.

33   "prophecy ...": Chernow, *Alexander Hamilton*, 454.

34   "to learn from ...": George Washington to Alexander Hamilton, July 3, 1795, in Allen, *George Washington*, 609–610.

35   burning effigies ...: Ellis, *His Excellency*, 227.

35   "a just and ...": George Washington to Alexander Hamilton, October 29, 1795, in Allen, *George Washington*, 615.

35   "national character ..." and "exaggerated and ...": Washington to Jefferson, July 6, 1796, in Allen, *George Washington*, 641.

35   "infamous scribblers": George Washington to Alexander Hamilton, June 26, 1796, in Allen, *George Washington*, 639.

36   "the best actor …": Wood, *Revolutionary Characters*, 53.

36   "Rather than it …": Thomas Jefferson to William Short, January 3, 1793, in Ford, *Works of Jefferson*, vol. 7, 203.

36   "the most disinterested …": Quoted in David H. Fischer, "The Myth of the Essex Junto," *The William and Mary Quarterly* 3rd Ser., 21 (April 1964): 223.

37   "difference of opinion …" and "We are all …": Sean Wilentz, *The Rise of American Democracy: Jefferson to Lincoln* (New York: Norton, 2005), 97.

37   "all the good …": Thomas Jefferson, Inaugural Address, 4 March 1801, in Ford, *Works of Jefferson*, vol. 9, 196, 200.

CHAPTER 2:
COMPROMISERS, ZEALOTS, AND CIPHERS

39   "if a dissolution …": Sean Wilentz, *The Rise of American Democracy: Jefferson to Lincoln* (New York, 2005), 224.

40   "generation of …" through "unwise and unworthy …": Thomas Jefferson to John Holmes Monticello, April 22, 1820, in "The Letters of Thomas Jefferson: 1743–1826: 'A Fire Bell in the Night,'" *From Revolution to Reconstruction … and What Happened Afterwards*, available at http://odur.let.rug.nl/~usa/P/tj3/writings/brf/jefl260.htm.

41   "I consider …": Wilentz, *Rise of Democracy*, 296.

42   "The bank …": Andrew Burstein, *The Passions of Andrew Jackson* (New York, 2003), 200.

42   "ardor of …": Robert V. Remini, *The Life of Andrew Jackson* (New York, 1988), 168.

42   "moderation …": Wilentz, *Rise of Democracy*, 379.

42   "the *United Colonies* …" and "forms a *government* …": Wilentz, *Rise of Democracy*, 381. Emphasis in original.

43   "No my friend …": Quoted in Wilentz, *Rise of Democracy*, 383.

43   "I have had …": Quoted in Wilentz, *Rise of Democracy*, 387.

44   "one great …": James Monroe, First Inaugural Address, March 4, 1817, available at http://www.yale.edu/lawweb/avalon/presiden/inaug/monroe1.htm.

44   "Cotton capitalism": Clement Eaton, *The Freedom-of-Thought Struggle in the Old South*, rev. ed. (New York, 1964), 27.

44   "a positive …": James M. McPherson, *Battle Cry of Freedom: The Civil War Era* (New York, 1988), 56.

45   "what society …": Eaton, *Freedom-of-Thought*, 27.

45   "On this subject …": Wendell Phillips Garrison, *William Lloyd Garrison, 1805–1879: The Story of His Life, Told by His Children*, vol. 1 (New York, 1885), 224–226.

45   "an unqualified …" and "abolition doctrines …": McPherson, *Battle Cry of Freedom*, 55.

45   "Death …": McPherson, *Battle Cry of Freedom*, 57.

45   "Everything has …": McPherson, *Battle Cry of Freedom*, 53.

46   "the principles …": Ted Widmer, *Martin Van Buren*, ed. Arthur M. Schlesinger (New York, 2005), 153.

46   "the Judas …": Widmer, *Martin Van Buren*, 155.

47   "Let the assassin …": Isaac Bassett, "Foote Threatens Benton," in *A Senate Memoir*, available at http://www.senate.gov/artandhistory/art/special/Bassett/tdetail.cfm?id=16.

47   "final settlement": McPherson, *Battle Cry of Freedom*, 76.

47   "I do not believe ...": Quoted in David M. Potter, *The Impending Crisis, 1848–1861* (New York, 1976), 114.

48   "we went ...": Quoted in McPherson, *Battle Cry of Freedom*, 121.

49   "Free society! ...": Muscogee *Herald*, quoted in *New York Tribune*, September 10, 1856; see Kenneth M. Stampp, *The Causes of the Civil War: Revised Edition* (New York: 1992), 210.

50   "If I can't ...": Robert S. Kelly, quoted in John Gihon, *Governor Geary's Administration in Kansas with a Complete History of The Territory until July 1857* (Philadelphia, 1857), available at http://www.kancoll.org/books/gihon/g_chap21.htm.

50   "every five ...": Wendell Philips, quoted in David Brion Davis, *Inhuman Bondage: The Rise and Fall of Slavery in the New World* (New York, 2006), 266.

50   Other abolitionists blasted ...: Henry Mayer, *All on Fire: William Lloyd Garrison and the Abolition of Slavery* (New York, 1998), 457–458.

51   "The more I ...": McPherson, *Battle Cry of Freedom*, 123.

51   "see how ...": Ralph Waldo Emerson, "The Assault Upon Mr. Sumner: Speech at a Meeting of the Citizens in the Town Hall, in Concord," May 26, 1856, in *The Works of Ralph Waldo Emerson, Fireside Edition*, vol. 11, 232 (Boston and New York, 1909).

51   "the fanatics ...": *Richmond Enquirer*, February 18, 1840, quoted in Eaton, *Freedom-of-Thought*, 213.

52   *The Interest in Slavery* ...: Eaton, *Freedom-of-Thought*, 269–270.

52   "Mr. Douglas ..." and "Mr. President ...": Robert W. Johannsen, *Stephen A. Douglas* (New York, 1973; reprint, 1997), 586.

52   "If you are ...": William E. Gienapp, "James Buchanan," in *The American Presidency*, ed. Alan Brinkley and Davis Dyer, 163 (Boston, 2004).

53   "Liberty and ...": William Herndon to Charles Sumner, December 10, 1860, in Stampp, *Causes of the Civil War*, 134.

53   "The gigantic crime ..." Quoted in *Boston Courier*, January 19, 1861, in Stampp, *The Causes of the Civil War*, 134.

53   "The unhappy fact ...": See Arthur M. Schlesinger Jr., "The Causes of the Civil War: A Note on Historical Sentimentalism," *Partisan Review* XVI (1949): 969–981.

53   historical fashions ...: See David S. Reynolds, *John Brown, Abolitionist: The Man Who Killed Slavery, Sparked the Civil War, and Seeded Civil Rights* (New York, 2005).

CHAPTER 3:
ABRAHAM LINCOLN'S MIDDLE MEASURE

57   "all the moral ...": Richard Hofstadter, *The American Political Tradition* (New York, 1989), 169.

58   "I claim not ...": David Herbert Donald, *Lincoln* (New York, 1995), 9.

59   "the perpetuation ..." through "the proud fabric ...": Abraham Lincoln, "Address Before the Young Men's Lyceum of Springfield, Illinois, January 27, 1838," in *The Collected Works of Abraham Lincoln*, ed. Roy P. Basler, vol. 1, 113. (New Brunswick, NJ, 1953).

59   his own myth's ...: Hofstadter, *American Political Tradition*, 121–123.

60   national glue ...: Abraham Lincoln, "Speech in Independence Hall," February 22, 1861, in Basler, *Collected Lincoln*, 4, 240.

60   Lincoln trusted government ...: Abraham Lincoln, "Fragment on Government, July 1, 1854[?]," in Basler, *Collected Lincoln* vol. 2, 221.

60   "duly weighed …": Abraham Lincoln, "Eulogy of Henry Clay, July 6, 1852," in *Abraham Lincoln: His Speeches and Writings*, ed. Roy Prentice Basler, 270 (New York, 2001).

60   "all appetites …": Basler, *Abraham Lincoln*, 140.

60   "Better … habituate …": Allen C. Guelzo, "Lincoln and the Abolitionists," *The Wilson Quarterly* 24, no. 4 (2000): 64.

60   "tear to tatters …": Abraham Lincoln, "Eulogy of Henry Clay, July 16, 1852," in Basler, *Abraham Lincoln*, 274.

61   He explained to …: Abraham Lincoln to William H. Herndon, February 1, 1848, in Basler, *Collected Lincoln*, vol. 1, 447.

62   "That is the best …": Benjamin P. Thomas, *Abraham Lincoln* (New York, 1952), 165.

63   Southern philosopher …: Donald, *Lincoln*, 190–191.

63   "I do not believe …": H. Ford Douglas quoted in Guelzo, "Lincoln and the Abolitionists," 60.

63   "I am for …:" John T. Morse Jr., *Abraham Lincoln*, Vol. II (Boston, 1899, reprint, Charleston, 2007), 188.

63   "The man who is …:" Abraham Lincoln, "Eulogy of Henry Clay, July 6, 1852," in *Abraham Lincoln*, Basler, 270.

63   "My name …": "Abraham Lincoln to Samuel Galloway, March 24, 1860," *Ohio Archaeological and Historical Quarterly* 32 (1923): 116.

64   "the hardest stick …" and "We can prove …": Louis Maurer, "The Rail Candidate," *Currier & Ives* (1860), available at http://hdl.loc.gov/loc.pnp/cph.3a12815.

64   "[W]hether the …": James McPherson, *Battle Cry of Freedom: The Civil War Era* (New York, 1988), 230.

64   "any formidable …": McPherson, *Battle Cry of Freedom*, 230.

65   "no malice …": Abraham Lincoln, "Address to the New Jersey General Assembly, February 21, 1861," in Basler, *Collected Lincoln*, vol. 4, 237.

65   "there will be …": Lincoln, "Speech in Independence Hall," in Basler, *Collected Lincoln*, vol. 4, 241.

66   "[I]f you …": Francis Blair, quoted in Doris Kearns Goodwin, *Team of Rivals: The Political Genius of Abraham Lincoln* (New York, 2005), 340.

66   "must be done …": Goodwin, *Team of Rivals*, 343.

66   "balanced and ballasted": Donald, *Lincoln*, 262.

66   "compound cabinet …": William Seward, quoted in Goodwin, *Team of Rivals*, 318.

66   "We needed …": Abraham Lincoln, quoted in Goodwin, *Team of Rivals*, 319.

67   "no fixed …": Donald, *Lincoln*, 290.

67   "have forced …": Abraham Lincoln, "Speech to Congress, July 4, 1861," in Basler, *Collected Lincoln*, vol. 4, 426.

67   "afford all …": Lincoln, "Speech to Congress," in Basler, *Collected Lincoln*, vol. 4, 439, 438.

67   "If both factions …" and ""A limb …": Abraham Lincoln to John M. Schofield, May 27, 1863, in Basler, *Collected Lincoln*, vol. 6, 234.

68   "A more ridiculous …": Donald, *Lincoln*, 342. Emphasis in original.

68   When generals …: Donald, *Lincoln*, 314–315, 363.

68   "*official* duty …" and "radical and …": Donald, *Lincoln*, 342.

68   "would I not …": Abraham Lincoln to Salmon P. Chase, September 2, 1863, in Basler, *Collected Lincoln*, vol. 6, 429.

69   "We shall need ...": Francis Fisher Browne, *The Every-day Life of Abraham Lincoln* (New York and St. Louis, 1886), available at http://www.gutenberg.org/etext/14004.

69   "essential for the ...": Gideon Welles, *The Diary of Gideon Welles* (Boston, 1911), vol. 1, 70; vol. 4, 69, n.2.

69   "until the eagle ...": Goodwin, *Team of Rivals*, 468.

71   "a contest of ...": *Chicago Times*, September 23, 1862, in Mark M. Krug, "The Republican Party and the Emancipation Proclamation," The Journal of Negro History 48 (April 1963): 108.

72   president pragmatically focused ...: T. Harry Williams, *Lincoln and the Radicals* (Madison, 1965), xiii.

72   "If he does not ...": *New York Tribune*, June 13, 1862, 1.

72   "a practical question ...": Donald, *Lincoln*, 452.

72   "plowed round ...": Donald, *Lincoln*, 454.

72   "pestilent ...": Lincoln to Schofield, in Basler, *Collected Lincoln*, vol. 6, 234.

72   "I could wish ...": Abraham Lincoln to Charles D. Drake and Others, October 5, 1863, in Basler, *Collected Lincoln*, vol. 6, 504.

72   "conservative ...": *Harper's Weekly*, August 29, 1863.

72   "The great thing ...": Donald, *Lincoln*, 501.

73   "masterly inactivity": *New York Times*, November 12, 1860, 4.

73   "criminal vacillation": Williams, *Lincoln and the Radicals*, 186.

73   "baptism of blood": Williams, *Lincoln and the Radicals*, 171.

73   "silly ...": Williams, *Lincoln and the Radicals*, 302.

73   "a godsend to the country": George W. Julian, *Political Recollections, 1840–1872* (Chicago, 1883), 255.

74   "Jesus Christ ..." and "most conspicuous virtue ...": William Hayes Ward, *Abraham Lincoln Tributes from his Associates* (New York, 1895), 130.

74   good man whose genius ...: Joseph J. Ellis, *His Excellency: George Washington* (New York, 2004), 271.

74   "a profound ...": Goodwin, *Team of Rivals*, 596.

CHAPTER 4:
THEODORE ROOSEVELT'S DEMOCRATIC TWO-STEP

75   "We are too old ...": John Hay to Whitelaw Reid, July 22, 1902, Whitelaw Reid Family Papers, Part I, Box I (Washington, DC: Library of Congress).

75   "you are one of ...": Aida D. Donald, *Lion in the White House: A Life of Theodore Roosevelt* (New York, 2007), 183.

75   Amid crises ...: H. W. Brands, *T.R.: The Last Romantic* (New York, 1997), 488.

76   "statesmen of ...": Brands, *T.R.*, 440.

76   "any taint ...": Brands, *T.R.*, 488.

78   "the safe man ...": James B. Bryce, *The American Commonwealth*, vol. I (London, 1888; reprint, Indianapolis, 1995), 69–75.

78   "growing powers ..." through "king can do ...": Henry Litchfield West, "The Growing Powers of the President," *The Forum* 31 (March 1901): 23–24.

78   "steward of ..." and "I did not ...": Theodore Roosevelt, *Theodore Roosevelt, An Autobiography*, new introduction by Elting Morison, (New York: Da Capo Press, 1985, c1913), 372.

79   "States-rights fetich ..." Roosevelt, *Autobiography*, 366.

79   "Americans first ...": Edmund Morris, *Theodore Rex* (New York, 2001), 147.

83   "riot of ...": Roosevelt, *Autobiography*, 437.

83   "remained archaic ...": Roosevelt, *Autobiography*, 438.

83   "whether the ...": Roosevelt, *Autobiography*, 440.

83   "as long as ...": Roosevelt, *Autobiography*, 479–480.

83   "threatened by ...": Roosevelt, *Autobiography*, 480.

83   "If it wasn't ...": Frederick S. Wood, *Roosevelt as We Knew Him* (New York, 1927), 109.

84   "to do was ...": Roosevelt, *Autobiography*, 483.

84   "[n]ational calamity ...": Roosevelt, *Autobiography*, 485.

84   "What about ...": Morris, *Theodore Rex*, 165.

84   During this crisis he reread ...: Theodore Roosevelt to Robert Bacon, in Brands, *T.R.*, 458.

85   "a pretty ...": Morris, *Theodore Rex*, 227.

85   "epithet ...": Roosevelt, *Autobiography*, 497–498.

85   "I am genuinely ...": Morris, *Theodore Rex*, 151.

85   "the Presidential office ...": Theodore Roosevelt to George Otto Trevelyan, May 28, 1904, in *The Letters of Theodore Roosevelt*, ed. Elting E. Morison, 806–807 (Cambridge, 1954).

86   "a big rival ...": Robert H. Wiebe, "The House of Morgan and the Executive, 1905–1913," *The American Historical Review* 65, 1 (October 1959): 49.

86   "Northern Securities ...": Roosevelt, *Autobiography*, 445.

87   "or with any one ..." through "the public ...": Roosevelt, *Autobiography*, 450–451.

87   "psychology of ...": Morris, *Theodore Rex*, 220.

87   "When do I ...": Lewis L. Gould, *The Presidency of Theodore Roosevelt* (Lawrence, 1991), 153.

88   "the greatest ...": J. J. Dickinson, "Theodore Roosevelt: Press-Agent, and What His Newspaper 'Cuckoos' Have Done for Him," *Harper's Weekly*, September 28, 1907, 1410.

88   "Platitudes and ...": Morris, *Theodore Rex*, 222.

88   Roosevelt's charm ...: Dickinson, "Theodore Roosevelt," 1410.

88   Any cuckoos who ...: Gould, *Presidency of Theodore Roosevelt*, 154.

88   "corrupt[ed] the press ...": Oswald Garrison Villard, *Fighting Years* (New York, 1939), 277.

89   "I had to ...": William Loeb to George Bruce Cortelyou, August 11, 1904, 1–2, George B. Cortelyou Papers, Library of Congress, Washington, DC.

89   Teddy bear ...: Morris, *Theodore Rex*, 173–174.

89   "YOU yourself ...": *New York World*, July 30, 1904, 23.

89   *World* wondered whether ...: *New York World*, August 23, 1904, 27–28.

89   "Executive Usurpation": *The Campaign Text Book of the Democratic Party of the United States, 1904* (New York, 1904), 17, 51.

89   "he does things ...": *Official Proceedings of the Thirteenth Republican National Convention* (Minneapolis, 1904), 149.

89   "Our country is ...": *Official Proceedings*, 153.

90   "flesh-and-blood ...": Henry Litchfield West, "The President and the Campaign," *The Forum* 40 (November 1908): 414–415.

90   "a limited ...": Archibald Willingham Butt, *The Letters of Archie Butt, Personal Aide to President Roosevelt* (New York, 1924), 108.

CHAPTER 5:
FRANKLIN D. ROOSEVELT AND THE NEW DEAL

93   "I'm so fond ...": Ted Morgan, *FDR: A Biography* (New York, 1985), 61.
94   "Americans first ...": Edmund Morris, *Theodore Rex* (New York, 2001), 147
95   dined on boiled dandelions ...: Malcolm X with Alex Haley, *The Autobiography of Malcolm X* (New York, 1965), 14.
95   "state of mind ...": *New York Times*, February 10, 1932, 19.
96   "the overthrow ...": Manifesto quoted in Arthur M. Schlesinger Jr., *The Age of Roosevelt: The Crisis of the Old Order, 1919–1933* (Boston, 1957), 436.
96   unions organized ...: See Harvey Klehr, *The Heyday of American Communism: The Depression Decade* (New York, 1984), 44–47.
97   "We are entering ...": *New York Times*, September 11, 1932, 19.
97   "violent social ...": Schlesinger, *Age of Roosevelt: Crisis*, 418.
97   "Mr. President ...": Jonathan Alter, *The Defining Moment: FDR's Hundred Days and the Triumph of Hope* (New York, 2006), 6.
98   "What is needed ...": *New York Times*, May 23, 1932, 2.
99   "chameleon on plaid": William E. Leuchtenburg, *The FDR Years: On Roosevelt and His Legacy* (New York, 1995), 2.
99   "the same philosophy ...": Schlesinger, *Age of Roosevelt: Crisis*, 437.
99   "if he goes ...": Schlesinger, *Age of Roosevelt: Crisis*, 416.
99   "When I talk ...": *Time*, January 23, 1933, 12.
99   "If we can't ...": Raymond Moley, *After Seven Years* (New York, 1939), 11.
100   "We had forgotten ...": Moley, *After Seven Years*, 148–150.
100   "I've just had ...": Arthur M. Schlesinger Jr., *The Age of Roosevelt: The Coming of the New Deal* (Boston, 1959), 5.
101   "the most likeable ...": Klehr, *Heyday of American Communism*, 282.
101   "Hoover sent ...": Schlesinger, *Age of Roosevelt: Coming*, 15.
101   "Rules are not ...": Franklin D. Roosevelt, *The Public Papers and Addresses of Franklin D. Roosevelt*, vol. 4 (New York, 1938), 343.
102   Roosevelt recognized the benefit ...: David Brody, *Workers in Industrial America* (New York, 1980), 146.
102   forces walked away ...: See Ellis W. Hawley, *The New Deal and the Problem of Monopoly* (Princeton, 1966), 24–25.
102   "horse-and-buggy ...": James MacGregor Burns, *Roosevelt: The Lion and the Fox* (New York, 1956), 223.
103   "has been an awful...": Frances Perkins, *The Roosevelt I Knew* (New York, 1946), 252.
104   "common table ...": Roosevelt, *Public Papers*, vol. 2, 300–302.
104   William Randolph Hearst began ...: William Randolph Hearst, quoted in Alonzo L. Hamby, *For the Survival of Democracy: Franklin Roosevelt and the World Crisis of the 1930s* (New York, 2004), 300.
104   "Anybody who ...": Hawley, *New Deal and Monopoly*, 157.
104   "carrying out more ...": Leuchtenburg, *The FDR Years*, 2.
104   "piecemeal" approach ...: John Dewey, quoted in Hamby, *For the Survival of Democracy*, 269.
105   "cradle to grave": Schlesinger, *Age of Roosevelt: Coming*, 311.

105   "wanted a social security system …": Rexford Tugwell Diary, March 24, 1935, quoted in Joseph Lash, *Dealers and Dreamers* (New York, 1988), 245.

105   "a cornerstone …": Lash, *Dealers and Dreamers*, 254.

106   "ultimate socialistic …": Schlesinger, *Age of Roosevelt: Coming*, 311.

106   "We put those …": Irving Bernstein, *A Caring Society* (Boston, 1985), 50.

106   "weave the two …": Roosevelt, *Public Papers*, vol. 3, 10.

106   "I never thought …": T. H. Watkins, *Righteous Pilgrim: The Life and Times of Harold L. Ickes 1874–1952* (New York, 1990), 401.

107   "Everybody demanded …": Franklin D. Roosevelt, quoted in William E. Leuchtenberg, *Franklin D. Roosevelt and the New Deal* (New York, 1963), 114.

107   "Well, it is …": Perkins, *The Roosevelt I Knew*, 322.

108   "ancient truths …": Roosevelt, *Public Papers*, vol. 2, 12; Roosevelt, *Public Papers*, vol. 5, 232–233.

109   Roosevelt joked …: Franklin D. Roosevelt, *Public Papers* vol. 5, 383–391.

109   Herbert Hoover was still …: Leuchtenburg, *The FDR Years*, 137.

109   "Better the occasional …": Roosevelt, *Public Papers*, vol. 5, 232–236.

109   "unjust, unworkable …": Alfred M. Landon Speech, September 26, 1936, Milwaukee, quoted in Larry DeWitt, "John G. Winant: First Chairman of the Social Security Board," Special Studies #6, Social Security Administration, http://www.ssa.gov/history/mywinantarticle.html.

110   Breckinridge Long observed: Leuchtenburg, *The FDR Years*, 141.

110   "President of all …": Roosevelt, "Address Announcing the Second New Deal," October 31, 1936, available http://www.fdrlibrary.marist.edu/od2ndst.html.

110   "For box office …": Leuchtenburg, *The FDR Years*, 13.

110   "our American tradition …": Roosevelt, *Public Papers*, vol. 5, 570–571; Franklin D. Roosevelt, *The Roosevelt Reader: Selected Speeches, Messages, Press Conferences, and Letters of Franklin D. Roosevelt*, ed. Basil Rauch (New York, 1957), 168.

110   "the basic idea …": Roosevelt, *Public Papers*, 2: 299.

110   "calm argument …": Franklin D. Roosevelt, *Public Papers and Addresses of Franklin D. Roosevelt*, 1938 vol. (New York, 1941), 400.

111   "Nine Old Men …": Roosevelt, *Public Papers and Addresses*, 1937 vol., 125–133.

111   "reactionary …": Burton K. Wheeler, quoted in *New York Times*, August 12, 1939, 3.

111   "the court to …": *New York Times*, February 6, 1937, 1.

111   "usurpation …": *New York Times*, February 14, 1932, 70.

111   compared the battle …: *New York Times*, July 23, 1937, 2.

112   "The attitude …": Fireside Chat, June 24, 1938, http://www.fdrlibrary.marist.edu/062438.html.

114   "This nation will remain …": "Preface to War," *Time*, September 11, 1939.

114   Some polls estimated …: Robert Dallek, *Franklin D. Roosevelt and American Foreign Policy* (New York, 1979), 201.

115   A three-day national radio …: Dallek, *Roosevelt and Foreign Policy*, 200.

115   "worthy of the …": Wayne S. Cole, *Senator Gerald P. Nye and American Foreign Relations* (Minneapolis, 1962), 169.

115   "History is filled …": Franklin D. Roosevelt, "Statement on Neutrality Legislation," August 31, 1935, in John T. Woolley and Gerhard Peters, *The American Presidency Project* (Santa Barbara: University of California, 1999–2008) available at http://www.presidency.ucsb.edu/ws/?pid=14927.

116   "the peoples of the Americas ...": Franklin D. Roosevelt, "Annual Address to Congress," in *Franklin D. Roosevelt and Foreign Affairs*, vol. 3, ed. Edgar B. Nixon, (Boston, 1969), 153–154 .

116   "running from ...": Roosevelt, *Public Papers and Addresses*, 1940 vol., 230–233, 237.

116   "illusion that we ...": Roosevelt, *Public Papers and Addresses*, 1940 vol., 231, 238–240; Franklin D. Roosevelt, *Nothing to Fear: The Selected Addresses of Franklin Delano Roosevelt* (Boston, 1946), 279.

117   "Never before ...": Franklin D. Roosevelt, "Fireside Chat," December 29, 1940, in Woolley and Peters, *The American Presidency Project* (Santa Barbara: University of California, 1999–2008), available at http://www.presidency.ucsb.edu/ws/?pid=15917.

117   "Peace Now": *Harvard Crimson*, February 5, 1940, http://www.thecrimson.com/article .aspx?ref=186716.

117   servicemen in Mississippi ...: "God Help George Marshall," *Time*, August 18, 1941, http://www.time.com/time/magazine/article/0,9171,850093,00.html.

117   "I am waiting ...": Franklin D. Roosevelt, quoted in James Macgregor Burns, *Roosevelt: The Soldier of Freedom* (New York, 1970), 90–91.

117   "to look over your ...": Samuel I. Rosenman, *Working with Roosevelt* (New York, 1952), 71, 167.

118   "Well, I hope ...": Henry Stimson, quoted in Burns, *Roosevelt*, 92.

118   "switch" in student ...: "Switch," *Time*, October 13, 1941, http://www.time.com/time/ magazine/article/0,9171,766251,00.html.

118   "asked for a declaration ...": Dallek, *Roosevelt and Foreign Policy*, 289.

121   "Mr. Roosevelt did not ...": Norman Thomas, "Is the New Deal Socialism?" in *The American Left: Radical Political Thought in the Twentieth Century*, ed. Loren Baritz, 264 (New York, 1971).

121   "A radical is ...": Roosevelt, *Public Papers and Addresses of Franklin D. Roosevelt*, 1939 vol., 556.

Chapter 6:
Truman, Eisenhower, and America's Bipartisan Consensus

125   "Is there anything ...": David McCullough, *Truman* (New York, 1992), 325.

127   "social economic ...": Henry Wallace, quoted in *New York Times*, September 14, 1946, 4.

127   Vandenberg hailed ...: See Alonzo L. Hamby, *Man of the People: A Life of Harry S. Truman* (New York, 1995), 295.

127   "politics stops at ...": Arthur Vandenberg, *Private Papers of Senator Vandenberg* (Boston, 1952), 552–553.

127   "a united nation ...": Harry S. Truman, Address Before a Joint Session of the Congress, April 16, 1945, available at http://www.trumanlibrary.org/ww2/stofunio.htm.

127   "every one of ...": W. Averill Harriman and Elie Abel, *Special Envoy to Churchill and Stalin, 1941–1946* (New York, 1975), 444.

128   "police governments ...": Winston Churchill, "The Sinews of Peace," Westminster College, Fulton, Missouri, March 5, 1946, available at http://www.hpol.org/churchill/.

128   "22 percent ...": Hamby, *Man of the People*, 348.

128   "What happens abroad ...": Nancy E. Bernhard, "Clearer Than Truth: Public Affairs Television and the State Department's Domestic Information Campaigns, 1947–1952," *Diplomatic History* 21 (Fall 1997): 564.

128   By August 1946, 60 percent ...: Sean J. Savage, *Truman and the Democratic Party* (Lexington: University of Kentucky, 1997), 98.

128   "To Err ...": Robert J. Donovan, *Conflict and Crisis: The Presidency of Harry S Truman 1945–1948* (New York, 1977), 230, 229.

129   "others of another ...": Harry S. Truman, Press Conference, November 11, 1946, in Woolley and Peters, *The American Presidency Project* (Santa Barbara: University of California, 1999–2008), available at http://www.presidency.ucsb.edu/ws/?pid=14927.

129   "We are met ..." and "Like apples ...": Dean Acheson, *Present at the Creation: My Years in the State Department* (New York, 1969), 219.

129   "only one way ...": Arthur H. Vandenberg, quoted in James Patterson, *Grand Expectations: The United States 1945–1974* (New York, 1996), 128.

129   It must be the policy ...: Harry S. Truman, Address Before a Joint Session of Congress, March 12, 1947, available at http://www.yale.edu/lawweb/avalon/trudoc.htm.

130   "perhaps the greatest ...": Harry S. Truman, *Public Papers of the Presidents of the United States, 1948* (U.S. G.P.O., 1961–1966), 203.

131   "150 million ...": CBS, "Person to Person," May 27, 1955, Audiovisual Archives, Harry S. Truman Library, Independence, Missouri.

132   "vote-getting picture ...": Clark Clifford to Harry S. Truman, November 19, 1947, 7, 25, 29, and "Campaign Material, 1948," both Political Files, Clark Clifford Papers, Harry S. Truman Library.

132   "the special interest ...": Truman, *Public Papers, 1948*, 593.

132   "the welfare of ...": Truman Press Conference, November 11, 1946.

132   "achieved by men ...": Harry S. Truman, "Address in St. Paul," October 13, 1948, in Woolley and Peters, The American Presidency Project (Santa Barbara: University of California, 1999–2008), available at http://www.presidency.ucsb.edu/ws/?pid=13046.

134   "a true bipartisan ...": Harry S. Truman, *Public Papers, 1950*, 259.

134   "the wiser heads ...": Harry S. Truman, *Public Papers, 1952–1953*, 344, 637.

134   "Mr. and Mrs....": Andrew J. Falk, "Reading Between the Lines: Negotiating National Identity on American Television, 1945–1960," *Diplomatic History* 28 (April 2004): 208, 210.

135   22 million immigrants ...: Richard Polenberg, *One Nation Divisible: Class, Race, and Ethnicity in the United States Since 1938* (New York, 1991), 10 and chapter 1.

136   "vital...": Arthur M. Schlesinger, Jr., *The Vital Center* (Boston, 1949); Daniel Boorstin, *The Genius of American Politics* (Chicago, 1953); Daniel Bell, *The End of Ideology—On the Exhaustion of Political Ideas in the Fifties* (Glencoe, New York, 1960).

136   "No man ...": Karal Ann Marling, *As Seen on TV: The Visual Culture of Everyday Life in the 1950s* (Cambridge, 1994), 253.

136   A stable "fortress" ...: Alan Ehrenhalt, *The Lost City: Discovering the Forgotten Virtues of Community in the Chicago of the 1950s* (New York, 1995).

136   The resulting political culture ...: Stephen J. Whitfield, *The Culture of the Cold War* (Baltimore, 1996), 33.

136   Television, especially ...: Falk, "Reading Between the Lines," 200.

137   "convert" their ...: Falk, "Reading Between the Lines," 210.

138   "It should be ...": Mort Sahl, quoted in Whitfield, *Culture of the Cold War*, 21.

138   "he is a golfer": Whitfield, *Culture of the Cold War*, 54.

138   "attempted to abolish ...": Dwight D. Eisenhower to Edgar Newton Eisenhower, November 8, 1954, in *The Papers of Dwight David Eisenhower*, vol. 15, ed. Louis Galambos and Daun Van Ee, doc. 1147. Available from the Dwight D. Eisenhower

Memorial Commission, http://www.eisenhowermemorial.org/presidential-papers/
first-term/documents/1147.cfm.

139 WHEN FOREIGN POLICY …: *New York Times*, April 3, 1950, 1.
139 "under the concepts …": Dwight D. Eisenhower, *Public Papers of the Presidents of the
United States: Dwight D. Eisenhower, 1953* (Washington: W.S. G.P.O., 1959–1961), 1,
13.
139 After twenty …: Dwight D. Eisenhower, *Mandate for Change* (New York, 1963), 192.
140 "fair, decent …": Eisenhower, *Mandate for Change*, 193.
140 "despite the headlines …": Eisenhower, *Mandate for Change*, 218.
140 "ward-boss …": Patterson, *Grand Expectations*, 272–273.
140 "Eisen-hoover" …: Patterson, *Grand Expectations*, 240, 275.
140 "politics is show . .": Stewart Alsop, "Barnum of the GOP," *Saturday Evening Post*,
May 26, 1956, 27, 119.
141 "This reflects …": Eisenhower, *Public Papers, 1953*, 550–551, 553, 557.
141 "Let's keep the Reds …": Chester J. Pach Jr. and Elmo Richardson, *The Presidency of
Dwight Eisenhower*, rev. ed. (Lawrence: University Press of Kansas, 1991), 99. Pach
and Richardson are more skeptical regarding Eisenhower's effectiveness in this crisis.
141 "I will not …": Dwight D. Eisenhower, quoted in Fred I. Greenstein, *The Hidden-
Hand Presidency: Eisenhower as Leader* (New York, 1982), 169.
142 "arrived at through …": Eisenhower, *Public Papers, 1954*, 425.
143 "our foreign policy …": Eisenhower, *Public Papers, 1954*, 999.
143 "stagnation, frustrations …": *New York Times*, October 29, 1954, 16.
143 Eisenhower feared …: Eisenhower, *Public Papers, 1954*, 984.
143 "I am not worried …": *New York Times*, November 8, 1958, 1.
143 "nation cannot exist …": *New York Times*, November 8, 1958, 1.
143 "the business of …": "LBJ: The Theme Is Unity, Achievement," *Democratic Digest*
(August 1960): 7.
143 "unreserved …" to "Let the general …": Eisenhower, *Public Papers, 1955*, 15.
144 "two parties …" through "How far inland …": *New York Times*, August 7, 1955, 34.
144 "This country will …": *Wall Street Journal*, April 29, 1960, 8.
144 In 1958, the Gallup poll …: George H. Gallup, *The Gallup Polls*, 3 vols. (New York,
1972), vol. 2, 1569.
145 "go to the gutter …": "How They're Running, " *Time*, October 25, 1963, http://www
.time.com/time/magazine/article/0,9171,830482,00.html.

Chapter 7:
John F. Kennedy and Civil Rights

149 "oodles of money": Robert Dallek, *An Unfinished Life: John Kennedy 1917–1963*
(Boston, 2003), 232–234.
149 "A whole generation …": Louis Harris, "Prospects for the 1960 Presidential Election
in the State of Kentucky," March 4, 1959, Box 815, Senate Files, Pre-Presidential Papers, John F. Kennedy Papers, John F. Kennedy Presidential Library, Boston, MA.
149 Kennedy's speeches, which …: "Address by Senator Kennedy of Massachusetts, June
14, 1956," *Congressional Record*, June 22, 1956, 10800.
150 new links between …: Ronald Brownstein, *Power and the Glitter: The Hollywood-
Washington Connection* (New York, 1990), 144–145, 155.
150 to popular icons …: *Chicago Daily News*, October 3, 1963, 14.

151   "Your son is ...": Letitia Baldrige to Joseph P. Kennedy, January 24, 1961, Box 700, White House Social Files, John F. Kennedy Library.

151   "We couldn't survive ...": Thomas C. Reeves, A *Question of Character* (New York, 1991), 250.

151   "It makes one look ...": Dean Acheson to Harry S. Truman, July 18, 1961, in David McCullough, *Truman* (New York, 1992), 980.

152   "No.... I don't want ...": Richard Reeves, *President Kennedy: Profile of Power* (New York, 1993), 93.

152   "There's an old saying ...": Arthur M. Schlesinger Jr., A *Thousand Days: John F. Kennedy in the White House* (Boston, 1965), 289–290.

152   "as one of ...": Kenneth P. O'Donnell and David E. Powers, *Johnny, We Hardly Knew Ye: Memories of John Fitzgerald Kennedy* (Boston, 1972), 270.

152   "Jesus, it's just like ...": Schlesinger, A *Thousand Days*, 292.

153   "He treated me ...": Reeves, *President Kennedy*, 172.

154   "an attack" on ...: Reeves, *President Kennedy*, 201.

154   "Negroes are getting ...": Reeves, *President Kennedy*, 357.

155   "He can't do ...": Thomas G. Paterson, *Kennedy's Quest for Victory* (New York, 1989), 142.

155   "to take out ...": Ernest R. May and Phillip D. Zelikow, *The Kennedy Tapes: Inside the White House During the Cuban Missile Crisis* (Cambridge, 1997), 70, 88.

155   "some of our ...": Paterson, *Kennedy's Quest*, 147.

156   "contrived for election purposes": Thomas G. Paterson and William J. Brophy, "October Missiles and November Elections: The Cuban Missile Crisis and American Politics, 1962," *Journal of American History* 73, no. 1(1986): 87.

156   "before, not after ...": *Wall Street Journal*, June 2, 1961, 3; *New York Times*, October, 29, 1961, E9.

156   "Listen, Yankee": C. Wright Mills, *Listen, Yankee: The Revolution in Cuba* (New York, 1960).

156   "We are people ...": "Port Huron Statement, 1962," *Students for a Democratic Society Document Library*, http://www.studentsforademocraticsociety.org/documents/port _huron.html.

157   "Foreign policy must ...": *New York Times*, June 30, 1962, 18.

157   "They never bring us ...": *New York Times*, September 7, 1962, 28.

157   "As far as I'm concerned ...": Charles Bartlett Oral History, John F. Kennedy Library, 160.

158   he finally emerged ...: William H. Chafe, *Private Lives/Public Consequences* (Cambridge, 2005), 131.

159   "Somehow, some warmth ..." and "not only that ...": Chafe, *Private Lives/Public Consequences*, 131.

159   "Well, we all have fathers ...": Schlesinger, A *Thousand Days*, 29.

160   "The President is the ...": Martin Luther King Jr., "Equality Now," *The Nation*, February 4, 1961, 5.

160   "Tell them to fly": Michael O'Brien, *John F. Kennedy: A Biography* (New York, 2005), 595.

160   "If we go into ...": O'Brien, *Kennedy*, 596.

160   "He's got the ...": O'Brien, *Kennedy*, 597.

160   "Can't you get ...": Dallek, *Unfinished Life*, 384.

160   polls showed that ...: Dallek, *Unfinished Life*, 384.

161   The middle path …: Reeves, *President Kennedy*, 127.
162   "There comes a time …": Dallek, *Unfinished Life*, 605.
163   "He always felt …": Dallek, *Unfinished Life*, 604–605.
164   "If it had at least …": C. David Heymann, *A Woman Named Jackie* (New York: 1989), 409.

CHAPTER 8:
THE CONSENSUS COLLAPSES

166   "Concession, Patience, …": Lyndon B. Johnson, undated notes, desk P38, Box 1, Handwriting File, Special Files, Lyndon B. Johnson Presidential Library, Austin, TX.
166   "silent …": *New York Times*, January 29, 1961, SM5.
167   "Everything I had …": Doris Kearns, *Lyndon Johnson and the American Dream* (New York, 1976), 185.
167   "continuity": Robert Dallek, *Flawed Giant: Lyndon Johnson and His Times, 1961–1973* (New York, 1998), 6.
168   "Come now, …": William Safire, *Safire's New Political Dictionary* (New York, 1993), 137.
168   "It's the way of …": Elizabeth Carpenter Oral History, Lyndon B. Johnson Library.
168   "there is always …": *New York Times*, March 7, 1965, 26.
168   "I wanted power …": Richard N. Goodwin, *Remembering America: A Voice from the Sixties* (Boston, 1988), 271.
168   "imaginative and not …": Lyndon Baines Johnson, *The Vantage Point: Perspectives of the Presidency, 1963–1969* (New York, 1971), 327.
169   "Mr. President …": Johnson, *Vantage Point*, 28, 38.
169   "Dick, you've …": Dallek, *Flawed Giant*, 112.
169   "civil rights bill that …": Lyndon Johnson, quoted in James T. Patterson, *Grand Expectations: The United States, 1945–1974* (New York, 1996), 543.
169   "I just don't think …": Johnson, *Vantage Point*, 95, 97.
170   "me too" Republicanism: *New York Times*, June 28, 1964, SM7.
171   "hoary 'politics stops …": *Wall Street Journal*, July 6, 1964, 8.
171   "the handmaidens of …": *Wall Street Journal*, July 20, 1964, 6.
171   "drastic departure": *New York Times*, October 6, 1964, 29.
171   "how foolish we …": *New York Times*, August 30, 1964, 68.
171   "Millions upon millions …": Lyndon Johnson, quoted in Kearns, *Lyndon Johnson and the American Dream*, 209.
171   "mandate for unity": Eric F. Goldman, *Tragedy of Lyndon Johnson* (New York, 1969), 256.
172   "I worked like …": Goldman, *Tragedy of Johnson*, 259.
172   "landmark": Johnson, *Vantage Point*, 328.
172   Aid to the poor …: Johnson, *Vantage Point*, 343.
173   "just wouldn't accept it …": Joseph Califano, quoted in Allen J. Matusow, *The Unraveling of America: A History of Liberalism in the 1960s* (Cambridge, 1984), 196.
173   "I am not going …": Dallek, *Flawed Giant*, 99–100.
173   "One of these days …": *Wall Street Journal*, September 29, 1960, 12.
174   "disastrous defeat": McGeorge Bundy and Robert McNamara to Lyndon Johnson, January 27, 1965, quoted in Robert McNamara, *In Retrospect: The Tragedy and Lessons of Vietnam* (New York, 1995), 167.

174   "I consider it ...": John Lewis Gaddis, *The Cold War: A New History* (New York, 2005), 169.

174   "We Are Deluding ...": *New York Times*, April 18, 1965, SM25.

175   demonizing critics as ...: Leslie Carpenter Oral History, 43–45, Lyndon B. Johnson Library.

175   "They all just follow ...": Lyndon Johnson, quoted in Dallek, *Flawed Giant*, 281.

175   "the manner in ...": Jack Valenti to Lyndon Johnson and Bill Moyers, July 14, 1965, Box 11, FG White House Central Files, Lyndon B. Johnson Library.

176   "the contagion of ...": Jack Valenti to Lyndon Johnson, January 30, 1967, 1, Box 12, Office of the President File, Special Files, Lyndon B. Johnson Library.

176   "whores": Lyndon Johnson, quoted in Dallek, *Flawed Giant*, 288.

176   "How do you ...": Dallek, *Flawed Giant*, 280–281.

176   Johnson's aides wavered ...: George Reedy to Lyndon Johnson, April 14, 1964, Box 10, Office of the President File, Special Files, Lyndon B. Johnson Library; Bill Moyers to LBJ, 11 July 1965, Box 8, Office of the President File, Special Files, Lyndon B. Johnson Library.

176   "responsibilities to the ...": George Reedy to Lyndon B. Johnson, December 5–18, 1963, 1–2, Box 10, Office of the President File, Special Files, Lyndon B. Johnson Library.

176   and ordered White House ...: Dallek, *Flawed Giant*, 288.

176   "counter-program for ...": Jack Valenti to Lyndon Johnson, November 11, 1964, "November 1964," Box 4, Handwriting File, Special Files, Lyndon B. Johnson Library.

177   "an ass of ...": *Economist*, January 7, 1967.

177   "[W]hether the press ...": Reedy to Johnson, December 5–18, 1963, 3.

177   "Television establishes ...": Robert E. Kintner to Lyndon Johnson, March 2, 1967, Box 83, PR 18, Confidential File, White House Central Files, Lyndon B. Johnson Library.

177   "Images do ...": Jack Valenti to Lyndon Johnson, November 11, 1964, "November 1964," Box 4, Handwriting File, Special Files, Lyndon B. Johnson Library.

177   "television in particular ...": Douglass Cater to Lyndon Johnson, March 28, 1968, Box 28, Handwriting File, Special Files, Lyndon B. Johnson Library.

177   "a strong and ...": Jack Valenti to Lyndon Johnson, February 24, 1965, "February 1965 [3 of 3]," Box 5, Handwriting File, Special Files, Lyndon B. Johnson Library.

177   "a good picture possibility": Elizabeth Carpenter to Lyndon Johnson, December 4, 1964, Office of the President File, Special Files, Lyndon B. Johnson Library.

177   "ugly problem[s]": Valenti to Johnson and Moyers, July 14, 1965.

177   poll in September 1967 ...: Fred Panzer to Lyndon Johnson, September 18, 1967, 1, Box 82, PR 16, Confidential File, White House Central Files, Lyndon B. Johnson Library.

177   "any impulse that ...": *New York Post*, March 18, 1966, clipping in "Elizabeth Carpenter," Box 1, Office of the President File, Special Files, Lyndon B. Johnson Library.

177   demanded victory in ...: McNamara, *In Retrospect*, 309.

177   Uncertainty, ...: Clark Clifford, *Counsel to the President* (New York, 1991), 455.

178   "how could President ...": McNamara, *In Retrospect*, 309.

178   He often humiliated ...: Joseph Califano, cited in Dallek, *Flawed Giant*, 297.

178   Johnson blamed communists ...: Lyndon Johnson, cited in Dallek, *Flawed Giant*, 488.

178   "The enemy is ...": Clifford, *Counsel to the President*, 567.

178   "I'll destroy you ...": Dallek, *Flawed Giant*, 447.

178   "I don't have to ...": Arthur M. Schlesinger Jr., *Robert Kennedy and His Times* (Boston, 1978), 767–769.

178   "LBJ unzipped his ...": Arthur Goldberg quoted in Dallek, *Flawed Giant*, 491.

178 Only decades later …: McNamara, *In Retrospect*, 294.

178 Secretary McNamara reported …: McNamara, *In Retrospect*, 258.

178 "Our whole life …": Maurice Isserman and Michael Kazin, "The Failure and Success of the New Radicalism," in *The Rise and Fall of the New Deal Order, 1930–1980*, ed. Steve Fraser and Gary Gerstle, 224 (Princeton, 1989).

179 By 1970, three-quarters …: Maurice Isserman and Michael Kazin, *America Divided: The Civil War of the 1960s* (Oxford, 2004), 268.

179 "I was born …": Lyndon Johnson, quoted in James David Barber, *The Presidential Character: Predicting Performance in the White House* (Englewood Cliffs, NJ, 1992), 34.

180 only "3 to 5%" …" Fred Panzer to Lyndon Johnson, September 18, 1967, 23–24, Box 82, PR 16, Confidential File, White House Central Files, Lyndon B. Johnson Library.

181 They attacked poverty …: *Wall Street Journal*, August 31, 1967, 1.

181 "We cannot tell …": *New York Times*, March 17, 1968, SM30.

181 "Things fall apart …": Clifford, *Counsel to the President*, 567.

CHAPTER 9:
LEARNING FROM LOSERS

184 "Great ideas …": Richard Nixon to John Ehrlichman, April 8, 1972, in Bruce Oudes, *From: The President: Richard Nixon's Secret Files* (New York, 1989), 406.

184 a Republican Party list …: Republican National Committee Research Division, "Accomplishments of the Nixon Administration," November 6, 1973, in "Cabinet Wives Program, 1974: Material, 1 of 2," Box 5, Susan Porter Files, Staff Member and Office Files, Richard Nixon Presidential Materials Project, National Archives, College Park, MD.

186 "clean air …": Richard Reeves, *President Nixon: Alone in the White House* (New York, 2001), 294.

186 "That's a little like …": Stephen E. Ambrose, *Nixon: The Triumph of a Politician, 1962–1972* (New York, 1989), 404.

186 "individual responsibility …": Richard Nixon to Pat Buchanan, February 10, 1971, "Memoranda, Feb. 1971," Box 3, President's Personal Files, White House Special Files, Richard Nixon Presidential Materials Project.

186 "ad hoc government …": Patrick Buchanan to H. R. Haldeman, January 14, 1971, 10–11, Box 9, President's Handwriting, President's Office Files, Richard Nixon Presidential Materials Project.

187 "We obviously …": Richard Nixon to H. R. Haldeman, December 1, 1970, 2, Box 2, President's Handwriting, President's Office Files, Richard Nixon Presidential Materials Project.

187 "improved practical …": Richard Milhous Nixon, *RN: The Memoirs of Richard Nixon*, vol. 2 (New York, 1978), 8, 12.

187 "I think the most …": Nixon, *RN*, vol. 2, 30.

187 "the greatest national crisis …" H. R. Haldeman to Herb Klein, June 3, 1970, FG1, Box 12, Confidential Files, White House Special Files, Richard Nixon Presidential Materials Project.

187 "A President must …": Richard Nixon to H. R. Haldeman, December 11, 1970, 3, Box 229, H. R. Haldeman Files, White House Special Files, Richard Nixon Presidential Materials Project.

188 "Consensus Politics? …": *New York Times*, February 21, 1972, 27.

188   "a story which will be …": Richard Nixon to H. R. Haldeman, December 1, 1969, Box 229, H. R. Haldeman Files, White House Special Files, Richard Nixon Presidential Materials Project.

188   "unprecedented barrage….": Haldeman to Klein, June 3, 1970.

189   "*style and leadership*": Dwight Chapin to H. R. Haldeman, November 16, 1970, Box 46, White House Central Files, Confidential Files, White House Special Files, Richard Nixon Presidential Materials Project. Emphasis in original.

189   "to really convey …": Richard Nixon to H. R. Haldeman, March 1, 1971, Box 3, President's Personal Files, White House Special Files, Richard Nixon Presidential Materials Project.

189   "We should only …": H. R. Haldeman, May 16, 1971, in *The Haldeman Diaries* (New York, 1994), 287.

189   "We only care …": H. R. Haldeman to Ronald Ziegler, July 13, 1970, Box 62, White House Special Files, Staff Member and Office Files, H. R. Haldeman Files, White House Special Files, Richard Nixon Presidential Materials Project. See also, Roger E. Ailes, October 10, 1969, in Box 53, "Image Versus Reality in Political TV," 1, Box 53, H. R. Haldeman Files, White House Special Files, Richard Nixon Presidential Materials Project.

189   "how to humanize …": Dwight L. Chapin to Jeb Magruder, February 27, 1971, The President, 1971–1974, Box 49, Confidential Files, White House Central Files, White House Special Files, Richard Nixon Presidential Materials Project.

189   "from the standpoint …": Nixon to Haldeman, December 11, 1970, 2.

189   "He has a better …": Gloria Steinem, *New York Magazine*, October 28, 1968, 28.

189   "how he could bear …": Theodore H. White, *America in Search of Itself* (New York, 1982), 2.

190   "We shall answer …": Nixon, *RN*, vol. 2, 263–264.

191   "Never before in …": "President Nixon's Address to the Nation, 29 April 1974," in *The White House Transcripts*, ed. Gerald Gold, 22 (New York, 1974).

191   "We have lost …": *New York Times*, May 29, 1974, 24.

191   "I had seen enough …": Michael Schudson, *Watergate in American Memory* (New York, 1992), 12.

192   Ford reserved the …: See *New York Times*, January 31, 1965, 58.

192   "a common enemy …": Gerald R. Ford, "Remarks Opening the Conference on Inflation," September 5, 1974, in John T. Woolley and Gerhard Peters, *The American Presidency Project* (Santa Barbara: University of California, 1999–2008), available at http://www.presidency.ucsb.edu/ws/?pid=4688.

192   "We will support …": *New York Times*, September 4, 1974, 1.

192   "profoundly unwise …" *New York Times*, September 9, 1974, 34.

193   "Peanut Brigade": See Betty Pope Oral History, 16, Jimmy Carter Library, Atlanta, GA.

194   "When you're a preacher …": "Interview with Gerald Rafshoon, Miller Center Interviews," April 8, 1993, Carter Presidency Project, vol. XXI, 23, Jimmy Carter Library.

194   "the real audience": Jim Fallows to Jody Powell, December 2, 1977, Box 42, Jody Powell Files, Press Office, Jimmy Carter Library.

195   "If you can't support …": James MacGregor Burns, *Running Alone* (New York, 2006), 124.

195   "15 short months …": *New York Times*, May 5, 1978, A29.

195   "was right in …": *New York Times*, February 4, 1979, 1, 17.

196   "This is the great ...": Bruce Schulman, *The Seventies* (New York, 2001), 23–24.

197   "tenured radicals": See Roger Kimball, *Tenured Radicals, Revised: How Politics has Corrupted our Higher Education* (New York, 1990, 1991, 1998).

197   "the worst crimes...": Raymond Aron, *The Opium of the Intellectuals* (New York, 1962), ix. See also Richard J. Ellis, *The Dark Side of the Left: Illiberal Egalitarianism in America* (Lawrence, KS, 1998), Chapter 5.

197   "doesn't count much ...": Samuel Huntington, "The Democratic Distemper," in *The American Commonwealth 1976,* ed. Nathan Glazer and Irving Kristol, 17, 18 (New York, 1976).

198   Honest to a fault ...: David Frum, *How We Got Here,* (New York, 2000), 227.

198   "Liberal idealism need ...": *Commentary* (November 1979): 45.

199   "I feel I have ...": Clark Clifford, *Counsel to the President* (New York, 1991), 634, 635.

199   "has managed the extraordinary ...": Henry Kissinger, Republican National Convention, 1980, in *National Review,* August 8, 1980, http://www.nationalreview.com/flashback/flashback200409020819.asp.

200   "posterity rewards success": *Atlantic Monthly* (January/February 2007): 67.

200   anthology ...: See Huntington, "Democratic Distemper" and Daniel Bell, "The End of American Exceptionalism," in *The American Commonwealth 1976,* ed. Nathan Glazer and Irving Kristol (New York, 1976).

CHAPTER 10:
RONALD REAGAN'S MODERATE REVOLUTION

201   "Americans are hungering ...": Ronald Reagan, *The Reagan Diaries,* ed. Douglas Brinkley, 8–9, 13 (New York, 2007).

203   "is an *opportunity* ...": Richard G. Darman, April 29, 1982, Legislative Strategy Group Agenda, 1983 Budget, OA 2902, Lee Atwater Papers, Ronald Reagan Library, Simi Valley, CA. Emphasis in original.

203   "many of our greatest ...": Peter Wehner, "In Defense of Politics," October 18, 2006, Ethics and Public Policy Center Online, http://eppc.org/publications/pubID.2737/pub_detail.asp.

205   "jump off the ...": *U.S. News & World Report,* May 5, 1980, 33.

205   "You want a ...": *Fortune,* May 19, 1980, 79.

206   "We Republicans have ...": *National Review,* February 22, 1980, 217.

206   The cartoonist Jeff MacNelly ...: *U.S. News & World Report,* November 3, 1980, 33.

206   "I just don't understand ...": *Washington Post,* November 5, 1980, A23.

207   "We the People": Ronald Reagan, "Inaugural Address, January 20, 1981," in *Public Papers of the Presidents of the United States* (Washington, DC, 1982), 2.

207   The president proposed ...: "America's New Beginning: A Program for Economic Recovery," 2, February 18, 1981, OA 2991, Edwin A. Meese III Papers, Ronald Reagan Library.

207   "weave the two together": Raymond Moley, *After Seven Years* (New York, 1939), 48, 51.

207   "Okay, you fellas ...": David A. Stockman, *The Triumph of Politics: How the Reagan Revolution Failed* (New York, 1986), 109.

207   "people are entitled ...": William Safire, *Safire's New Political Dictionary* (New York, 1993), 220.

208   "symbolism": *Washington Post,* January 25, 1981, A5.

208   "iron chancellor": Stockman, *Triumph of Politics,* 11.

208   "Madisonian" government …: Stockman, *Triumph of Politics*, 9.

208   "that your 1980 conservative …": Richard A. Viguerie to Ronald Reagan, October 10, 1983, Press Release, *Conservative Digest*, Ronald Reagan Library.

209   "We are providing …": Ronald Reagan, to Betty T. Benson, Madison Alabama, March 10, 1982, 065607, Box 2, Presidential Handwriting File, Ronald Reagan Library.

209   "How do we sustain …": Legislative Strategy Group Agenda, January 27, 1983, CA 10972, Craig Fuller Papers, Ronald Reagan Library.

209   "amiable, friendly …": Patrick Caddell, *The Fire This Time: The Failure of Two-Party Politics and the Rise of the American People* (New York, 1997), 26.

209   "You don't think …": Speaker's Press Conference, May 4, 1981, 2, Press Relations, 11:1, Thomas P. O'Neill Papers, John J. Burns Library, Boston College, Brookline, MA.

209   "the formulas of …": Thomas P. O'Neill Jr., "A Deliberate Recession," November 1981, 2, Press Relations, 9:13, Thomas P. O'Neill Papers, John J. Burns Library, Boston College.

210   "well-being of …": *Washington Post*, May 21, 1981, 1.

211   "most important single …": "Summary of Discussion" with Paul Volcker, Martin Feldstein, et al., in *American Economic Policy in the 1980s*, ed. Martin Feldstein, 162 (Chicago, 1994).

211   "If you can write …": George Gerbner, quoted in Lawrence Wallack, "Drinking and Driving: Toward a Broader Understanding of the Role of Mass Media," *Journal of Public Health Policy* 5 (December 1984): 485.

212   "The American electorate …" Ronald Reagan, "Remarks at a Dinner Marking the 10th Anniversary of the Heritage Foundation, October 8, 1983," in John T. Woolley and Gerhard Peters, *The American Presidency Project* (Santa Barbara: University of California, 1999–2008), available at http://www.presidency.ucsb.edu/ws/?pid=40580.

212   "original economic recovery …": "Conservative Leaders Denounce Reagan Tax Hike," July 20, 1982, OA 6387 Elizabeth H. Dole Papers, Ronald Reagan Library.

212   "spirit of bipartisanship …": "Meeting with the Bipartisan Budget Working Group," OA 13528 Kenneth M. Duberstein, Ellen Bradley File, Ronald Reagan Library.

212   "Acknowledge the concern …": "Talking Points for Meeting with Senators Dole and Long and Representatives Rostenkowski and Conable," Tax Bill 1982, 078619, M.B. Oglesby Papers, Ronald Reagan Library.

213   "Crime, Education …": James A. Baker III, "Trip Proposals," October 25, 1984, Box 9, Series I, Memorandum File, Subseries C 1984–January 1985, James A. Baker III MSS, Ronald Reagan Library.

213   "I'm not going to …": *Washington Post*, March 12, 1984, A3.

213   "God, patriotism and Reagan": Keith Blume, *The Presidential Election Show: Campaign '84 and Beyond on the Nightly News* (South Hadley, MA, 1985), 61.

215   "as a form of insanity": Kiron K. Skinner, Annelise Anderson, and Martin Anderson, eds., *Reagan, In His Own Hand* (New York, 2001), 10–12.

215   "the worst presidential …": Mona Charen, *Useful Idiots* (Washington, DC, 2003), 11–13.

216   "Boy, I'm glad …": *Los Angeles Times*, July 1, 1985; see also Paul Slansky, *The Clothes Have No Emperor: A Chronicle of the American '80s* (New York, 1989), 133.

216   "Tip O'Neill may …": Tip O'Neill with William Novak, *Man of the House*, 364 (New York, 1987).

216   "resist the temptations …": Charlton Heston to Ronald Reagan, June 29, 1987; Ronald Reagan to Charlton Heston, July 9, 1987, 498952, Folder 294, Box 18, Presidential Handwriting File, II, Ronald Reagan Library.

216   "the Soviets have …": *New York Times*, May 29, 1988, 1.
218   "We must opportunistically …": William Henkel to Tom Griscom, March 19, 1987, 501824, FG 001, Ronald Reagan Library.
218   "If Reagan had …": Fred Greenstein, "Reagan Gorbachev and the Role of Leadership in Ending the Cold War," available at www.tompaine.come/history/1999/11/11/1.html; Fred I. Greenstein, *The Presidential Difference* (New York, 2000), 154–155.
218   most economists credit …: See, for example, John W. Sloan, *The Reagan Effect: Economics and Presidential Leadership* (Lawrence, 1999).
218   "great rediscovery, …": Ronald Reagan, "Farewell Address to the Nation, January 11, 1989," *Public Papers of the Presidents of the United States* (Washington, DC: Government Printing Office, 1991), 1720.
219   "radical individualism": Robert N. Bellah et al., *Habits of the Heart: Individualism and Commitment in American Life* (Berkeley, 1985), 82–84.
220   "20 percent …": W. Bradford Wilcox, "Children at Risk," *First Things* 140 (February 2004): 12–14. See also "Index of Social Health of the United States, 1970–2005," Institute for Innovation in Social Policy, http://iisp.vassar.edu/ish.html.
220   home size …: *U.S. News and World Report*, June 28, 2004, 60.
220   on closets …: *New York Times*, June 1, 2006.
220   40 percent of college freshmen …: *Fortune*, July 6, 1987, 26.
220   "to be rich": Martin Lindstrom quoted in the *Washington Post*, September 12, 2004.

CHAPTER 11:
BILL CLINTON AND THE PERILS OF TRIANGULATION

223   "change I seek …": James MacGregor Burns and Georgia Jones Sorenson, *Dead Center: Clinton-Gore Leadership and the Perils of Moderation* (New York, 1999), 157.
223   "The character flaw …": Joe Klein, "The Politics of Promiscuity," *Newsweek*, May 9, 1994.
224   "about race, …": Newt Gingrich, quoted in in Burns and Sorenson, *Dead Center,* 197.
224   "queer-mongering …": Jim Johnson, quoted in Joe Conason and Gene Lyons, *The Hunting of the President: The Ten-Year Campaign to Destroy Bill and Hillary Clinton* (New York, 2000), 71.
225   "There's nothing in …": Jim Hightower, *There's Nothing in the Middle of the Road But Yellow Stripes and Dead Armadillos* (New York, 1997).
225   "peacemaker …": Quoted in Burns and Sorenson, *Dead Center,* 159.
226   "to maintain my …": Bill Clinton, quoted in Lance Morrow, "The Campaign: The Long Shadow of Vietnam," *Time,* February 24, 1992.
226   "tired" partisanship … "to break through …": Bill Clinton, *My Life* (New York, 2004), 366.
226   "We recognize …": Bill Clinton, "Keynote Address to the DLC's Cleveland Convention, May 6, 1991," Democratic Leadership Council, http://www.dlc.org/ndol_ci.cfm?kaid=127&subid=173&contentid=3166.
228   "If Black people …:" David Mills, "Sister Souljah's Call to Arms," *Washington Post,* May 13, 1992, B1.
228   "We offer our …": *New York Times,* July 17, 1992.
230   "I think there….": Andrea Mitchell, "The Genesis of 'Don't Ask, Don't Tell,'
"   *The Daily Nightly Blog,* available at http://dailynightly.msnbc.com/2007/03/the_genesis_of_.html.

230   "the cultural balkanization ...": John F. Harris, *The Survivor: Bill Clinton in the White House* (New York, 2005), xxvii.

230   "Shafta": Jesse Jackson, quoted in *Trade Week in Review and Recent Publications*, August 21–27, 1993, 2, http://www.etext.org/Politics/Trade.News/Volume.2/tnb-02.154.

231   "Now I understand ...": David Gergen, *Eyewitness to Power: The Essence of Leadership: Nixon to Clinton* (New York, 2000), 282.

231   "textbook case in ...": Gergen, *Eyewitness to Power*, 285.

231   "America's ready ...": *CBS News Special Report*, September 22, 1993.

231   a payoff for squelching: See Gergen, *Eyewitness to Power*, 308.

231   "legislation that ...": *Chicago Sun-Times*, August 10, 1994, 3.

232   Strangely, President Clinton ...: See Gergen, *Eyewitness to Power*, 307.

232   Reporters had described ...: Thomas E. Patterson, *Out of Order* (New York, 1993), 20.

233   common perspectives...: Mark Halperin and John F. Harris, *The Way to Win: Taking the White House in 2008* (New York, 2006), 43–44.

233   Reporters were cynical ...: Paul Starobin, "A Generation of Vipers: Journalists and the New Cynicism," *Columbia Journalism Review* 33 (March 1995): 25–32.

233   "dominant media elites ...": Howard Kurtz, *Spin Cycle: Inside the Clinton Propaganda Machine* (New York, 1998), 231.

234   "unremitting drumbeat ...": Kurtz, *Spin Cycle*, 232.

234   Her first book, ...: Ann Coulter, *High Crimes and Misdemeanors: The Case Against Bill Clinton* (Washington, DC, 1998).

234   "stand up for ...": *Rolling Stone*, December 9, 1993.

235   "the president is ...": Bill Clinton, Presidential Press Conference on Welfare Reform, April 18, 1995, http://www.clintonpresidentialcenter.org/legacy/041895-presidential-press-conference-on-welfare-reform.htm.

235   "folks the Democratic ...": Dick Morris, *Behind the Oval Office: Winning the Presidency in the Nineties* (New York, 1997), 34.

235   "bite size": Morris, *Behind the Oval Office*, 13, 83.

235   "by compromise ...": Morris, *Behind the Oval Office*, 40.

236   "take a middle ...": Morris, *Behind the Oval Office*, 80.

236   mentioned "values": *New York Times*, December 3, 1995.

236   "socially toxic ...": James Garbarino, *Raising Children in a Socially Toxic Environment* (San Francisco, 1995).

237   "This is not ...": *Los Angeles Times*, February 11, 1996.

237   divided and demoralized ...: George Stephanopoulos, *All Too Human: A Political Education* (Boston, 1999), 344.

237   "triangulates ... he strangulates ...": *Los Angeles Times Magazine*, February 11, 1996.

237   "the top ten ...": *Late Show with David Letterman*, August 20, 1996.

237   "there are people ...": Morris, *Behind the Oval Office*, 230.

238   "if he vetoes ...": Stephanopoulos, *All Too Human*, 419.

238   "What good ...": Morris, *Behind the Oval Office*, 300.

238   "FDR loved ...": Harris, *The Survivor*, 176–177.

240   "It's a little ...": *Washington Post*, August 2, 1998, C1.

241   "I guess that ...": Carl Bernstein, *A Woman in Charge* (New York, 2007), 500.

241   "In a democracy ...": Burns and Sorenson, *Dead Center*, 289.

242   "I tried and ...": Bill Clinton, *Fox News Sunday*, September 24, 2006.

242   "too many missed ...": Daniel Benjamin and Steve Simon, *The Age of Sacred Terror: Radical Islam's War Against America* (New York, 2002), 384–385.

242   U.S. HARD PUT ...": *New York Times*, April 13, 1999.

242   The 9/11 Commission ...: *Final Report of the National Commission on Terrorist Attacks Upon the United States* (Washington, DC, 2004), 339–340.

242   "The U.S. government ...": *Final Report of National Commission*, 343.

243   "to do the right ...": *Final Report of National Commission*, 118.

243   conveyed that urgency ...: *Final Report of National Commission*, 199.

244   "anything to do with ...": Bob Woodward, *Bush at War* (New York, 2002), 5.

CHAPTER 12:
GEORGE W. BUSH

249   "change the tone ...": George W. Bush, "Victory Speech, December 13, 2000," available at http://www.cnn.com/ELECTION/2000/transcripts/121300/bush.html.

250   "in the end ...": George W. Bush, Republican National Convention, August 3, 2000, available at http://www.cnn.com/ELECTION/2000/conventions/republican/transcripts/bush.html.

251   "I guarantee ...": Barack Obama, *The Audacity of Hope: Thoughts on Reclaiming the American Dream* (New York, 2006), 130–131.

251   attributed to Rove ...: See James Moore and Wayne Slater, *The Architect: Karl Rove and the Dream of Absolute Power* (New York, 2006).

251   "very happy ...": *New York Times*, February 7, 2004.

251   "The doubts about ...": *Los Angeles Times*, April 29, 2001, A1.

251   "a Reagan without ...": *Los Angeles Times*, April 29, 2001, A1.

252   "moderation, tolerance ...": *Seattle Post-Intelligencer*, May 25, 2001.

252   "I think the ...": *Washington Post*, May 25, 2001.

253   "My job is ...": Bob Woodward, *State of Denial* (New York, 2006), 206.

254   "micromanage": *New York Times*, October 20, 2001.

254   BUSH RECORD ...": *Los Angeles Times*, January 7, 2002.

254   "realism": *Los Angeles Times*, January 7, 2002.

254   "I couldn't tell ...": Diane Feinstein, CNN, January 28, 2002.

254   "some of the folks ...": George W. Bush, University of New Hampshire, January 8, 2002, http://www.whitehouse.gov/news/releases/2002/01/20020108-2.html.

255   known as Pepfar: *New York Times*, January 5, 2008.

256   Within corporations ...: See David Callahan, *The Moral Center: How We Can Reclaim Our Country from Die-Hard Extremists, Rogue Corporations, Hollywood Hacks, and Pretend Patriots* (Orlando, 2006).

256   cost-cutting: : Barbara Ehrenreich, *Bait and Switch: The (Futile) Pursuit of the American Dream* (New York, 2005), 224.

257   "an axis of evil": Richard Haas, *New Yorker*, April 1, 2002.

257   "We don't want ...": Condoleezza Rice, *CNN Late Edition with Wolf Blitzer*, September 8, 2002, http://transcripts.cnn.com/TRANSCRIPTS/0209/08/le.00.html.

258   "In the wake ...": *New York Times*, October 10, 2002.

258   "a continuation of ...": Hillary Clinton, Fox News Network, *Hannity & Colmes*, June 20, 2002 (21:31), Transcript # 062002cb.253.

258   Even some opponents ...: Representative Donald M. Payne, Democrat of New Jersey, in *New York Times*, October 10, 2002.

258   Reagan "didn't say ...": Michael Isikoff and David Corn, *Hubris: The Inside Story of Spin, Scandal and the Selling of the Iraq War* (New York, 2006), 20.

259 "irrefutable": *Washington Post*, February 6, 2003, A36.

259 American support for the war …: *USA Today*, March 16, 2003.

260 "I don't think …": *Washington Post*, April 10, 2004, A01.

261 Both conservatives and …: See survey in *Washington Post*, January 12, 2004.

261 "communities of …": Chris Bowers and Matthew Stoller, "Emergence of the Progressive Blogosphere: A New Force in American Politics," New Politics Institute, http://www.newpolitics.net/node/87?full_report=1.

261 "fifty years of …": Joe Trippi, "The Revolution Will Not Be Televised: Introduction," *Joetrippi.com: The Revolution Will Not Be Televised*, http://www.joetrippi.com/?page_id=1379.

262 Chuck Hagel …: *Washington Post*, September 2, 2004.

262 "street-smart …": *New York Times*, September 2, 2004.

263 "stronger, broader …": *Washington Post*, November 7, 2004, A01.

263 "when you have …": "Interview: Christine Todd Whitman," PBS, *Frontline*, January 31, 2005, available http://www.pbs.org/wgbh/pages/frontline/shows/architect/interviews/whitman.html.

263 "I've got the will …": George W Bush, "President Holds Press Conference," 11:17 A.M., November 4, 2004, http://www.whitehouse.gov/news/releases/2004/11/20041104-5.html.

263 "ignorant …": *New York Times*, November 8, 2004.

263 "The Day the Enlightenment …": *New York Times*, November 4, 2004.

264 "W. ran a jihad …": *New York Times*, November 4, 2004.

264 *It Can Happen Here*: Kevin Phillips, *American Theocracy: The Peril and Politics of Radical Religion, Oil, and Borrowed Money in the 21st Century*; Joe Conason, *It Can Happen Here: Authoritarian Peril in the Age of Bush* (New York, 2007).

264 *Lies and the* …: Al Franken, *Lies and the Lying Liars Who Tell Them* (New York, 2003).

264 *Liberalism Is a* …: Michael Savage, *Liberalism Is a Mental Disorder: Savage Solutions* (Nashville, 2005).

264 "Perhaps if …": Ann Coulter, *Slander: Liberal Lies About the American Right* (New York, 2002), 2.

265 "a dirtbag": *New York Times*, December 3, 2001.

265 22 percent of …: *USA Today*, January 30, 2002; *LA Times*, November 23, 2003.

265 surveys showing …: Ken Auletta, "How Roger Ailes and FOX News Are Changing Cable News," *The New Yorker*, May 26, 2003, 58.

265 "the Fox effect …": *New York Times*, April 16, 2003.

265 "fight club politics": Juliet Eilperin, *Fight Club Politics: How Partisanship Is Poisoning the House of Representatives* (Lanham, MD, 2006), 5.

266 Psychologists explained …: Paul Rozin, "Preadaptation and the Puzzles and Properties of Pleasure," in *Well Being: The Foundations of Hedonic Psychology*, ed. Daniel Kahneman, Ed Diener, and Norbert Schwarz, 109–133 (New York, 1999).

266 Seventy percent …: Judith Warner, "Kids Gone Wild, *New York Times*, November 27, 2005.

267 "how Bush blew it": *Newsweek*, September 19, 2005, cover story.

267 "everything changed": quoted in Jonah Goldberg, *National Review Online*, September 5, 2007.

268 "I'm not afraid …": *Washington Post*, August 30, 2004.

269 "Being a democrat …": *The New Yorker*, May 29, 2006.

269 "common values …": Barack Obama, on CNN, *Larry King Live*, October 19, 2006.

269 "from feeling …": *The New Yorker*, February 11, 2002.

269 "liberals and ...": *New York Times,* April 20, 2003.

269 An Annenberg Center ...: National Annenberg Election Survey, "Daily Show Viewers Knowledgeable About Presidential Campaign, National Annenberg Election Survey Shows," Press Release, September 21, 2004.

000 Political scientists ...: For an optimistic view, see Paul R. Brewer and Xiaoxia Cao, "Candidate Appearances on Soft News Shows and Public Knowledge about Primary Campaigns," *Journal of Broadcasting and Electronic Media,* vol. 50, no. 1 (March 2006): 18–35. For a pessimistic view, see Jody Baumgartner and Jonathan S. Morris, "The Daily Show Effect: Candidate Evaluations, Efficacy, and American Youth," *American Politics Research,* vol. 34, no. 3 (2006): 341–367.

270 THE VITAL CENTER ...: Democratic Leadership Council, "Election 2006: The Vital Center Prevails," Press Release, November 14, 2006, http://www.dlc.org/ndol_ci.cfm?contentid=254100&subid=108&kaid=85.

270 "America is a ...": *Newsweek,* November 27, 2006, 80.

270 "The villains ...": *Daily News,* January 24, 2007.

Conclusion: Center Seeking in the Twenty-first Century

274 one of the West's ...: Arthur C. Brooks, *Who Really Cares* (New York, 2006), 120–122.

274 "true patriotism": *New York Times,* October 5, 2007.

277 One analysis ...: Robert D. Putnam, *Bowling Alone: The Collapse and Revival of American Community* (New York, 2000), 118.

278 Katrina, a former police ...: Bill Sasser, "The First Time I Was Back Since the Storm ... Drugs Were Everywhere," *Salon.com,* March 6, 2007, http://www.salon.com/news/feature/2007/03/06/new_orleans/index1.html.

278 "Brother, ...": Greg Botelho, "Saved by Jewish Man on 9/11, Pakistani Muslim Reaches Out," CNN.com, September 2, 2002, http://www.cnn.com/2002/US/08/30/ar911.usman.farman/index.html.

279 "Eleventh Commandment": Alan Wolfe, *One Nation, After All,* (New York, 1998), 50, 54.

280 "constructive hypocrisy": *Chicago Tribune,* October 30, 1995, 11.

280 even many pro-choice ...: Lydia Saad, "Public Opinion About Abortion—An In-Depth Review," *Gallup News Service,* January 22, 2002, available at http://www.gallup.com/poll/9904/Public-Opinion-About-Abortion-InDepth-Review.aspx.

280 definitions of marriage ...: Lydia Saad, "Americans at Odds Over Gay Rights," *Gallup News Service,* May 31, 2006, available at http://www.gallup.com/poll/23140/Americans-Odds-Over-Gay-Rights.aspx.

280 The statistics showing ...: Sam Roberts, *Who We Are Now* (New York, 2004), 13; Robert Frank, *Richistan* (New York, 2007), 40.

280 But equally true ...: Matthew Benjamin, "Americans See Widening Rich-Poor Income Gap as Cause for Alarm," *Bloomberg.com,* December 12, 2006, available at http://www.bloomberg.com/apps/news?pid=20601070&refer=politics&sid=atGy4g3gcN4I.

280 "Post-partisanship ...": Mort Kondracke, "Schwarzenegger's 'Post-Partisanship' Is Model for D.C.," *Roll Call,* March 1, 2007, available at http://www.realclearpolitics.com/articles/2007/03/schwarzeneggers_postpartisansh_1.html.

281 Humane Americans ...: On underclass, see Paul A. Jargowsky and Isabel V. Sawhill, "The Decline of the Underclass," Center on Children and Families, Brief 36, January

2006, Brookings Institution, available at http://www.brookings.edu/papers/2006/01poverty_jargowsky.aspx.

281   "I grew up ...": Hillary Rodham Clinton, quoted in "Hillary Clinton Launches White House Bid: 'I'm In,'" CNN.com, January 20, 2007.

281   "hungry for ...": *LA Times*, January 6, 2007.

281   "much too comfortable...": Ronald Brownstein, *The Second Civil War: How Extreme Partisanship Has Paralyzed Washington and Polarized America* (New York, 2007), 255.

282   "common good": *New York Times*, October 5, 2007; *New York Times*, April 27, 2006; Michael Tomasky, "Party in Search of a Notion," *American Prospect*, April 18, 2006, http://www.prospect.org/cs/articles?articleId=11424.

282   "We could have switched ...": *Newsweek*, March 14, 2005.

INDEX